DISTRIBUTED DATABASES
Principles and Systems

McGraw-Hill Computer Science Series

Ahuja: *Design and Analysis of Computer Communication Networks*
Barbacci and Siewiorek: *The Design and Analysis of Instruction Set Processors*
Cavanagh: *Digital Computer Arithmetic: Design and Implementation*
Ceri and Pelagatti: *Distributed Databases: Principles and Systems*
Donovan: *Systems Programming*
Filman and Friedman: *Coordinated Computing: Tools and Techniques for Distributed Software*
Givone: *Introduction to Switching Circuit Theory*
Goodman and Hedetniemi: *Introduction to the Design and Analysis of Algorithms*
Katzan: *Microprogramming Primer*
Keller: *A First Course in Computer Programming Using Pascal*
Kohavi: *Switching and Finite Automata Theory*
Liu: *Elements of Discrete Mathematics*
Liu: *Introduction to Combinatorial Mathematics*
MacEwen: *Introduction to Computer Systems: Using the PDP-11 and Pascal*
Madnick and Donovan: *Operating Systems*
Manna: *Mathematical Theory of Computation*
Newman and Sproull: *Principles of Interactive Computer Graphics*
Payne: *Introduction to Simulation: Programming Techniques and Methods of Analysis*
Révész: *Introduction to Formal Languages*
Rice: *Matrix Computations and Mathematical Software*
Salton and McGill: *Introduction to Modern Information Retrieval*
Shooman: *Software Engineering: Design, Reliability, and Management*
Tremblay and Bunt: *An Introduction to Computer Science: An Algorithmic Approach*
Tremblay and Bunt: *An Introduction to Computer Science: An Algorithmic Approach, Short Edition*
Tremblay and Manohar: *Discrete Mathematical Structures with Applications to Computer Science*
Tremblay and Sorenson: *An Introduction to Data Structures with Applications*
Tucker: *Programming Languages*
Wiederhold: *Database Design*
Wulf, Levin, and Harbison: *Hydra/C.mmp: An Experimental Computer System*

McGraw-Hill Series in Computer Organization and Architecture

Bell and Newell: *Computer Structures: Readings and Examples*
Gear: *Computer Organization and Programming*
Hamacher, Vranesic, and Zaky: *Computer Organization*
Hayes: *Computer Architecture and Organization*
Hayes: *Digital System Design and Microprocessors*
Hwang and Briggs: *Computer Architecture and Parallel Processing*
Kogge: *The Architecture of Pipelined Computers*
Sieworek, Bell, and Newell: *Computer Structures: Principles and Examples*
Stone: *Introduction to Computer Organization and Data Structures*
Stone and Siewiorek: *Introduction to Computer Organization and Data Structures: PDP-11 Edition*

DISTRIBUTED DATABASES
Principles and Systems

Stefano Ceri

Giuseppe Pelagatti

Politecnico di Milano

McGraw-Hill Book Company

New York   St. Louis   San Francisco   Auckland   Bogotá   Hamburg
Johannesburg   London   Madrid   Mexico   Montreal   New Delhi
Panama   Paris   São Paulo   Singapore   Sydney   Tokyo   Toronto

This book was typeset by Yasuko Kitajima of Aldine Press using the TeX document production system, and the camera-ready copy was produced on a CRS Alphatype phototypesetter with Computer Modern fonts using computer equipment of the Computer Science Department of Stanford University. The book designer and typesetting supervisor was Arthur Keller. The editors were Eric M. Munson and Jonathan Palace; the production supervisor was Joe Campanella. Halliday Lithograph Corporation was printer and binder.

DISTRIBUTED DATABASES
Principles and Systems

1234567890 HALHAL 8987654

ISBN 0-07-010829-3

Library of Congress Cataloging in Publication Data

Ceri, Stefano.
    Distributed databases.

    (McGraw-Hill computer science series)
    Bibliography: p.
    Includes index.
    1. Database Management.   2. Electronic data processing
—Distributed processing.   I. Pelagatti, Giuseppe.
II. Title.   III. Series.
QA76.9.D3C386   1984   001.64   84-770
ISBN 0-07-010829-3

Contents

Part 2 Distributed Database Systems

Preface

It is well known that during the 1970s computers were extensively used for building powerful, integrated database systems. The technology of database systems has built its theoretical foundations and has been experienced in a large number of applications. At the same time, computer networks have been extensively developed, allowing the connection of different computers and the exchange of data and other resources between them.

In recent years the availability of databases and of computer networks has given rise to a new field: distributed databases. A distributed database is, in brief, an integrated database which is built on top of a computer network rather than on a single computer. The data which constitute the database are stored at the different sites of the computer network, and the application programs which are run by the computers access data at different sites.

Completely new problems are faced for building and implementing a distributed database, and a great amount of research work has been done in order to solve them. This research work constitutes a new discipline having its own principles. In order to understand distributed databases, we must know more than the principles of traditional databases and computer networks: we must also integrate this knowledge with the study of the peculiar aspects of the new technology.

This book presents the principles of this new technology. It is intended for those who are professionally interested in having an up-to-date view of distributed data processing, including, for example, students and teachers of courses in computer science, researchers, system managers, system or application designers, analysts, and programmers. The book can be used for extending a traditional course on database systems with a treatment of distributed databases or for a specialized course on distributed databases. A preliminary version of this book has been used for a one-quarter course on distributed databases at Stanford University and for specialized one-week, full-time courses for professionals in Italy.

ORGANIZATION AND CONTENT

The book is made up of two parts, principles and systems, which are preceded by two preliminary chapters. **Chapter 1** is an overview of the characteristics and problems of distributed databases. It can be read by anybody with a general interest in data processing, without any specific background. **Chapter 2** discusses the aspects of databases and computer networks that are required in order to understand the rest of the book. Of course, Chapter 2 is not a complete tutorial of these fields; it just redefines terminology, notation, and basic concepts in order to keep the book self-contained. However, in order to fully understand problems, the reader should have some background on these subjects.

Part I, on the principles of distributed databases, comprises Chapters 3 to 10 and deals with all the technical issues of distributed databases. **Chapter 3** deals with the architecture of distributed databases from the viewpoint of the application programmer. The different levels of visibility which can be provided by a distributed database management system are defined and exemplified. This chapter is very tutorial in nature and easy to read. **Chapter 4** is on distributed database design. It deals with the issues of partitioning and allocating the data at the different sites of the computer network. This chapter is useful for the designer of a distributed database; additionally, the understanding of how and why data is distributed is a basic aspect for understanding the nature of distributed databases as a whole. This chapter is also tutorial in style.

Chapters 5 and 6 discuss the subject of efficiently accessing a distributed database (this field is often called distributed query optimization; however, we emphasize that these techniques can also be used for designing applications which are executed repetitively, not only for ad hoc queries). These two chapters are more difficult than the previous ones; they present in a synthetic but systematic way the approaches which have been developed by the research in this field. **Chapter 5** deals with transforming the database operations required by applications into semantically equivalent operations which are appropriate for accessing the distributed database. **Chapter 6** deals more specifically with optimization problems.

Chapters 7, 8, and 9 deal with transaction management, i.e., supporting the efficient, reliable, and concurrent execution of transactions. **Chapter 7** presents the basic techniques of transaction management and their integration in the design and implementation of distributed database systems. **Chapter 8** reviews the techniques for distributed concurrency control, i.e., for allowing the parallel execution of transactions at the different sites. **Chapter 9** reviews the techniques for the recovery of the distributed database from failures. Chapters 8 and 9, like Chapters 5 and 6, are more difficult and contain complete surveys.

Chapter 10, the last chapter of Part I, deals with the data administration function. This chapter is essentially an introduction to the problems of catalog management and of security in distributed databases.

Part II describes distributed database management systems. The emphasis is on the integration into specific systems of the techniques which have been presented in Part I. **Chapter 11** shows how and to what extent distributed databases are built with today's commercially available systems. **Chapter 12** describes SDD-1, a prototype distributed database management system which represented a milestone in this field. **Chapter 13** describes R*, the most important ongoing research effort in the development of distributed databases. **Chapter 14** contains an overview of the approaches followed by other homogeneous research prototypes. Finally, **Chapter 15** describes the major research prototypes in the field of heterogeneous distributed database systems, i.e., systems which integrate different local database management systems.

GUIDELINE FOR READERS

To facilitate the use of this book by different readers, the book is organized so that it can be read in different ways: as an overview, as a tutorial on the technical problems of distributed databases, and as a complete survey of the techniques which have been developed for solving these problems.

The following chart can be used to find a suitable reading sequence for different types of readers.

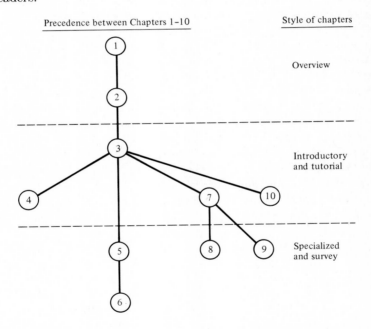

The chart shows precedences between chapters on the left and the style of each chapter on the right. The precedence tree shows, for instance, that Chapter 8 has Chapters 7, 3, 2, and 1 as precedences.

Of course, the book can be read sequentially from the beginning to the end; this is appropriate for a specific course on distributed databases. A short course, possibly complementary to traditional courses on database management, can be obtained by skipping any of the specialized chapters of Part I and any of the chapters of Part II.

Managers and professionals can also skip the more specialized chapters; for example, a reader who is only interested in an overview of distributed databases completed with an overview of existing prototypes and systems could read Chapters 1, 2, 3, 4, 7, and any one of the chapters in Part II.

ACKNOWLEDGMENTS

We wish to thank several colleagues and students who have assisted us in extending, reviewing, and correcting the manuscript: Peter Rathmann, Bob Molter, Keith Stobie, Marc Smith, Mauro Negri, and Ken Cockrell. Gio Wiederhold, Jim Larson, Alfred Spector, and Benjamin Wah have carefully reviewed this book and suggested important improvements.

Gio Wiederhold has organized a course on Distributed Databases at Stanford University which has been very useful for experiencing the usage of this manuscript as a textbook. Jim Larson has provided us with material describing existing systems which has been very useful for the second part of this book. Moreover, Section 15.3 on DDTS is the result of his cooperation. The advice and criticism of Jim Gray have greatly influenced the organization of Chapters 7, 8, and 9 on transaction management.

Laura Haas, Bruce Lindsay, and Chandrasekaren Mohan have demonstrated to us the features of the R* prototype; discussion with them has greatly increased our understanding of this system. Discussions with Jim Gray, Pete Homan, and Gerry Held have given us insight on the Tandem systems and on CICS. Discussions with Eric Neuhold have been useful for understanding the POREL system.

The "Progetto Finalizzato Informatica" of the Italian Research Council has provided a research environment in which several of the ideas of this book have been discussed and experienced at the industrial level.

Finally, we like to thank Arthur Keller and Yasuko Kitajima for the final editing of the book, and the Dipartimento di Elettronica at the Politecnico di Milano for the use of computer facilities during the preparation of the manuscript.

Stefano Ceri
Giuseppe Pelagatti

DISTRIBUTED DATABASES
Principles and Systems

Chapter 1

Distributed Databases: An Overview

In recent years, distributed databases have become an important area of information processing, and it is easy to foresee that their importance will rapidly grow. There are both organizational and technological reasons for this trend: distributed databases eliminate many of the shortcomings of centralized databases and fit more naturally in the decentralized structures of many organizations.

A typical, but rather vague, definition of a distributed database is the following: A distributed database is a collection of data which belong logically to the same system but are spread over the sites of a computer network. This definition emphasizes two equally important aspects of a distributed database:

1. **Distribution**, i.e., the fact that the data are not resident at the same site (processor), so that we can distinguish a distributed database from a single, centralized database

2. **Logical correlation**, i.e., the fact that the data have some properties which tie them together, so that we can distinguish a distributed database from a set of local databases or files which are resident at different sites of a computer network

The problem with the above definition is that both properties, distribution and logical correlation, are too vaguely defined to always discriminate between those cases which really belong to distributed databases and those which do not. In order to develop a more specific definition, let us consider a few examples.

1

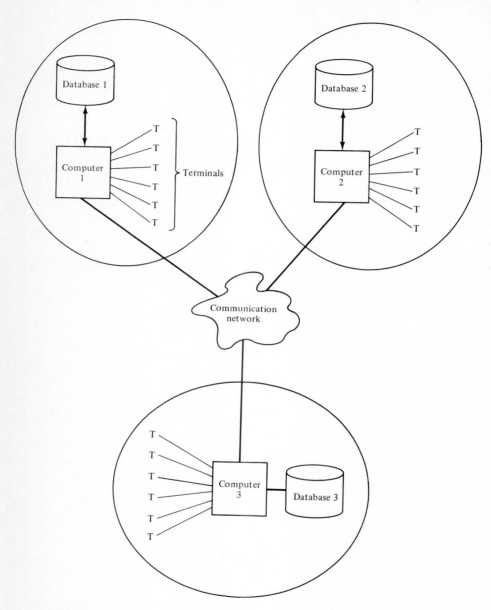

Figure 1.1 A distributed database on a geographically dispersed network.

Example 1.1

Consider a bank that has three branches at different locations. At each branch, a
computer controls the teller terminals of the branch and the account database of
that branch (Figure 1.1). Each computer with its local account database at one

branch constitutes one **site** of the distributed database; computers are connected by a communication network. During normal operations the applications which are requested from the terminals of a branch need only to access the database of that branch. These applications are completely executed by the computer of the branch where they are issued, and will therefore be called **local applications**. An example of a local application is a debit or a credit application performed on an account stored at the same branch at which the application is requested.

If we try to apply the definition of distributed databases to the situation described so far, we find that it is difficult to say whether the logical correlation property holds. Is the fact that the branches contain the information about accounts of the same bank sufficient? Should this be considered an example of a distributed database or of a set of local databases?

In order to answer these questions, let us focus on what makes dealing with a set of local databases different from dealing with the same data considered as a distributed database. From a technological viewpoint, it appears that the really important aspect is the existence of some applications which accesses data at more than one branch. These applications are called **global applications** or **distributed applications**. The existence of global applications will be considered the discriminating characteristic of distributed databases with respect to a set of local databases.

A typical global application is a transfer of funds from an account of one branch to an account of another branch. This application requires updating the databases at two different branches. Note that this application is something more than just performing two local updates at two individual branches (a debit and a credit), because it is also necessary to ensure that either both updates are performed or neither. As we shall see, ensuring this requirement for global applications is a difficult task.

In Example 1.1 the computers are at geographically different locations; however, distributed databases can be built also on local networks.

Example 1.2

Consider the same bank of the previous example, with the same applications, however with a system configuration as shown in Figure 1.2. The same processors with their databases have been moved away from the branches to a common building and are now connected with a high-bandwidth local network. The teller terminals of the branches are connected to their respective computers by telephone lines. Each processor and its database constitutes a site of the local computer network.

We see that the physical structure of the connections has changed with respect to Example 1.1; however, the characteristic aspects of the architecture have remained the same. In particular, the same computers execute the same applications accessing the same databases. An application which was local in the previous example is still local, provided that locality is not defined with respect to the geographical distribution of the computers which execute it, but with respect to the fact that only one computer with its own database is involved.

If there are global applications, it is convenient to consider this example a distributed database, because most of the features which characterized the previous example are still valid. However, the fact that the distributed database is implemented on a local network instead of a geographical network, with its much higher throughput and reliability, will in some cases change the type of solutions which are given to some problems. Let us consider an example of a system which we do not consider a distributed database in this book.

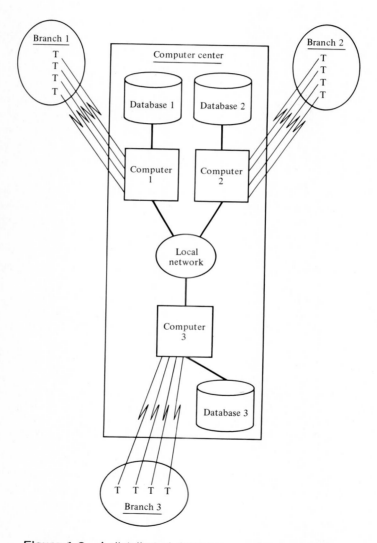

Figure 1.2 A distributed database on a local network.

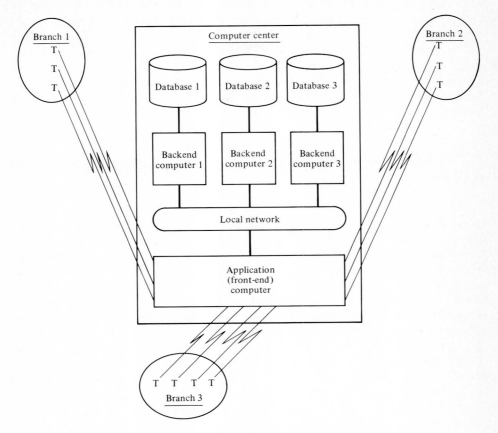

Figure 1.3 A multiprocessor system.

Example 1.3

Consider the same bank of the previous example but with the system configuration shown in Figure 1.3. The data of the different branches are distributed on three "backend" computers, which perform the database management functions. The application programs are executed by a different computer, which requests database access services from the backends when necessary.

The reason for not considering this type of system a distributed database is that, although the data is physically distributed over different processors, their distribution is not relevant from the application viewpoint. What we miss here is the existence of local applications, in the sense that the integration of the system has reached the point where no one of the computers is capable of executing an application by itself.

We can now summarize the considerations which we have obtained from the above examples in the following working definition:

A distributed database is a collection of data which are distributed over different computers of a computer network. Each site of the network has autonomous processing capability and can perform local applications. Each site also participates in the execution of at least one global application, which requires accessing data at several sites using a communication subsystem.

The most important technological problems of distributed databases derive from considering them the result of a "cooperation between autonomous sites"; this feature is emphasized by the above definition.

1.1 FEATURES OF DISTRIBUTED VERSUS CENTRALIZED DATABASES

Distributed databases are not simply distributed implementations of centralized databases, because they allow the design of systems which present different features from traditional, centralized systems. It is therefore useful to look at the typical features of traditional databases and to compare them with the corresponding features of distributed databases. The features which characterize the traditional database approach are centralized control, data independence, reduction of redundancy, complex physical structures for efficient access, integrity, recovery, concurrency control, privacy, and security.

Centralized control   The possibility of providing centralized control over the information resources of a whole enterprise or organization was considered as one of the strongest motivations for introducing databases; they were developed as the evolution of information systems in which each application had its own private files. The fundamental function of a **database administrator (DBA)** was to guarantee the safety of data; the data itself was recognized to be an important investment of the enterprise which required a centralized responsibility.

In distributed databases, the idea of centralized control is much less emphasized. This depends also on the architecture, as can be seen by considering Examples 1.1 and 1.2. Probably, Example 1.2 lends itself more to centralized control than does Example 1.1. In general, in distributed databases it is possible to identify a hierarchical control structure based on a **global database administrator**, who has the central responsibility of the whole database, and on **local database administrators**, who have the responsibility of their respective local databases. However, it must be emphasized that local database administrators may have a high degree of autonomy, up to the point that a global database administrator is completely missing and the intersite coordination is performed by the local administrators themselves. This characteristic is usually called **site autonomy**. Distributed databases may differ very much in the degree of site autonomy: from complete site autonomy without any centralized database administrator to almost completely centralized control.

Data independence   Data independence was also considered one of the main motivations for introducing the database approach. Essentially, data independence means that the actual organization of data is transparent to the application programmer. Programs are written having a "conceptual" view of the data, the so-called **conceptual schema**. The main advantage of data independence is that programs are unaffected by changes in the physical organization of data.

In distributed databases, data independence has the same importance as in traditional databases; however, a new aspect is added to the usual notion of data independence, namely, **distribution transparency**. By distribution transparency we mean that programs can be written as if the database were not distributed. Thus the correctness of programs is unaffected by the movement of data from one site to another; however, their speed of execution is affected.

Data independence was provided in traditional databases through a multilevel architecture having different descriptions of data and mappings between them; the notions of conceptual schema, storage schema, and external schema were developed for this purpose. In a similar way, distribution transparency is obtained in distributed databases by introducing new levels and schemata. In Chapter 3 the possible approaches to distribution transparency are described.

Reduction of redundancy   In traditional databases, redundancy was reduced as far as possible for two reasons: first, inconsistencies among several copies of the same logical data are automatically avoided by having only one copy, and second, storage space is saved by eliminating redundancy. Reduction of redundancy was obtained by data sharing, i.e., by allowing several applications to access the same files and records.

In distributed databases, however, there are several reasons for considering data redundancy as a desirable feature: first, the locality of applications can be increased if the data is replicated at all sites where applications need it, and second, the availability of the system can be increased, because a site failure does not stop the execution of applications at other sites if the data is replicated. In general, the same reasons against redundancy which were given for the traditional environment are still valid, and therefore the evaluation of the optimal degree of redundancy requires an evaluation of a rather complex trade-off. As a very general statement, let us say that the convenience of replicating a data item increases with the ratio of retrieval accesses versus update accesses performed by applications to it. The convenience of data replication increases because if we have several copies of an item, retrieval can be performed on any copy, while updates must be performed consistently on all copies. A more precise discussion of this problem is given in Chapter 4, when dealing with distributed database design.

Complex physical structures and efficient access   Complex accessing structures, like secondary indexes, interfile chains, and so on, are a major aspect of traditional databases. The support for these structures is the most important part of data base management systems (DBMSs). The reason for providing complex accessing structures is to obtain efficient access to the data.

In distributed databases, complex accessing structures are not the right tool for efficient access. Therefore, while efficient access is a main problem in distributed databases, physical structures are not a relevant technological issue. Efficient access to a distributed database cannot be provided by using intersite physical structures, because it is very difficult to build and maintain such structures and because it is not convenient to "navigate" at a record level in distributed databases. Let us illustrate this point by an example.

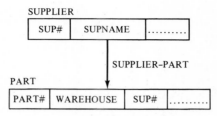

SUPPLIER

| SUP# | SUPNAME | .... |

SUPPLIER–PART

PART

| PART# | WAREHOUSE | SUP# | .... |

(*a*) A Codasyl database schema.

<u>Find</u> SUPPLIER <u>record</u> <u>with</u> SUP# = S1;
Repeat until "no more members in set"
<u>Find next</u> PART <u>record</u> <u>in</u> SUPPLIER–PART <u>set</u>;
Output PART record;

(*b*) A Codasyl–DBMS–like program for finding parts supplied by supplier S1.

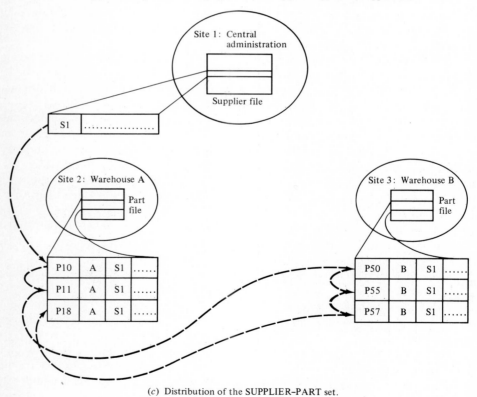

(*c*) Distribution of the SUPPLIER–PART set.

Figure 1.4 A distributed Codasyl-like database.

Example 1.4

Consider the schema of the Codasyl-like database shown in Figure 1.4a. There are two record types, SUPPLIER and PART, and one set type, SUPPLIER-PART, which connects supplier records to the parts records supplied by them. The application "find all PART records supplied by supplier S1" is coded in a Codasyl-like DML as shown in Figure 1.4b.

Let us now assume that the above database is distributed over three sites of a computer network, as shown in Figure 1.4c: the supplier file is located at site 1 (central administration), while the part file is split into two different subfiles located at two sites 2 and 3 (warehouses). Let us further suppose that we have a distributed implementation of a Codasyl system, so that we can run the same (navigational) program of Figure 1.4b on the distributed database. Suppose that the application is run from site 1. Clearly, the system would have to access a remote PART record for each iteration of the "repeat until" loop; therefore, for each access to a record not only the record itself would have to be transmitted, but also several messages would have to be exchanged.

A more efficient implementation of the same application consists of grouping, as far as possible, all remote accesses, as shown in Figure 1.5. Compare the programs in Figures 1.4b and 1.5: in the former, the clause *"find next"* requires accesses on a record-by-record basis; in the latter, the clause *"find all"* groups all accesses which are performed at the same site. The procedure shown in Figure 1.5 consists of two types of operations: the execution of programs which are local at single sites and the transmission of files between sites. A procedure like the above is called a **distributed access plan**.

1)   *At site 1*
    Send sites 2 and 3 the supplier number SN
2)   *At sites 2 and 3*
    Execute in parallel, upon receipt of the supplier number, the following program:

> *Find all* PARTS *records having*
> SUP # = SN;
> *Send result to site 1.*

3)   *At site 1*
    Merge results from sites 2 and 3;
    Output the result.

Figure 1.5   Example of access plan.

A distributed access plan can be written by the programmer or produced automatically by an optimizer. Writing a distributed access plan is similar to navigational programming in centralized databases, in the sense that the programmer specifies how the database must be accessed. However, intersite navigation should be performed at the level of groups of records, while usual one-record-at-a-time navigation can be performed for local processing at each site. Therefore, a navigational language is less appropriate than a nonprocedural, set-oriented language for building access plans.

Several problems are still to be solved in the design of an optimizer which produces automatically an access plan like the one shown in Figure 1.5. It is convenient to divide these problems into two categories: **global optimization** and

local optimization. Global optimization consists of determining which data must be accessed at which sites and which data files must consequently be transmitted between sites. The main optimization parameter for global optimization is communication cost, although the cost of accessing the local databases should also be taken into account in some cases. The relative importance of these factors depends on the ratio between communication costs and disk access costs, which depends in turn on the type of communication network.

Local optimization consists of deciding how to perform the local database accesses at each site; the problems of local optimization are typical of traditional, nondistributed databases and will not be further considered in this book.

Chapters 5 and 6 are devoted to the problem of developing global access plans for performing an application on a distributed database. The research on global optimization has produced results which are useful even if access plans are not produced automatically, because it aids in understanding how a distributed database can be efficiently accessed.

Integrity, recovery, and concurrency control In databases the issues of integrity, recovery, and concurrency control, although they refer to different problems, are strongly interrelated. To a large extent, the solution of these problems consists of providing transactions. A **transaction** is an **atomic unit** of execution; i.e., it is a sequence of operations which either are performed in entirety or are not performed at all. The "funds transfer" application, given in Example 1.1, is a global application which must be an atomic unit: either both the debit portion and the credit portion are executed or none; it is not acceptable to perform only one of them. Therefore the funds transfer application is also a global transaction.

It is clear that in distributed databases the problem of transaction atomicity has a particular flavor: how should the system behave if the "debit" site is operational and the "credit" site is not operational when the funds transfer is required? Should the transaction be aborted (undoing all operations which have been performed until the moment of site failure), or should a smart system try to execute the funds transfer correctly even if both sites are never simultaneously operational? Of course, the user would be less affected by failures if the latter approach is applied.

Clearly, atomic transactions are the means to obtain database integrity, because they assure that either all actions which transform the database from one consistent state into another are performed, or the initial consistent state is left untouched.

There are two dangerous enemies of transaction atomicity: failures and concurrency. Failures may cause the system to stop in the midst of transaction execution, thus violating the atomicity requirement. Concurrent execution of different transactions may permit one transaction to observe an inconsistent, transient state created by another transaction during its execution.

Recovery deals to a large extent with the problem of preserving transaction atomicity in the presence of failures. In distributed databases this aspect is particularly important, because some of the sites involved in transaction execution might fail, as shown in the previous example. The problem of recovery in distributed databases is dealt with in Chapter 9.

Concurrency control deals with ensuring transaction atomicity in the presence of concurrent execution of transactions. This problem can be seen as a typical synchronization problem. In distributed databases, as in all distributed systems, the synchronization problem is harder than in centralized systems. This problem will be discussed in Chapter 8.

Privacy and security In traditional databases, the database administrator, having centralized control, can ensure that only authorized access to the data is performed. Note, however, that the centralized database approach in itself, without specialized control procedures, is more vulnerable to privacy and security violations than the older approaches based on separate files.

In distributed databases, local administrators are faced essentially with the same problem as database administrators in a traditional database. However, two peculiar aspects of distributed databases are worth mentioning: first, in a distributed database with a very high degree of site autonomy, the owners of local data feel more protected because they can enforce their own protections instead of depending on a central database administrator; second, security problems are intrinsic to distributed systems in general, because communication networks can represent a weak point with respect to protection. The problems of privacy and security in distributed databases will be discussed in Chapter 10.

1.2 WHY DISTRIBUTED DATABASES?

There are several reasons why distributed databases are developed. The following is a list of the main motivations.

Organizational and economic reasons Many organizations are decentralized, and a distributed database approach fits more naturally the structure of the organization. The problems of a distributed organizational structure and of the corresponding information system are the subject of several books and papers. With the recent developments in computer technology, the economy-of-scale motivation for having large, centralized computer centers is becoming questionable. We do not further discuss this subject here; however, the organizational and economic motivations are probably the most important reason for developing distributed databases.

Interconnection of existing databases Distributed databases are the natural solution when several databases already exist in an organization and the necessity of performing global applications arises. In this case, the distributed database is created bottom-up from the preexisting local databases. This process may require a certain degree of local restructuring; however, the effort which is required by this restructuring is much less than that needed for the creation of a completely new centralized database.

Incremental growth If an organization grows by adding new, relatively autonomous organizational units (new branches, new warehouses, etc.), then the distributed database approach supports a smooth incremental growth with a minimum degree of impact on the already existing units. With a centralized approach, either the initial dimensions of the system take care of future expansion, which is difficult to foresee and expensive to implement, or the growth has a major impact not only on the new applications but also on the existing ones.

Reduced communication overhead   In a geographically distributed database like the database of Example 1.1, the fact that many applications are local clearly reduces the communication overhead with respect to a centralized database. Therefore, the maximization of the locality of applications is one of the primary objectives in distributed database design.

Performance considerations   The existence of several autonomous processors results in the increase of performance through a high degree of parallelism. This consideration can be applied to any multiprocessor system, and not only to distributed databases. For instance, the configuration of Example 1.3 also allows parallelism, but it is not considered a distributed database. However, distributed databases have the advantage in that the decomposition of data reflects application dependent criteria which maximize application locality; in this way the mutual interference between different processors is minimized. The load is shared between the different processors, and critical bottlenecks, such as the communication network itself or common services of the whole system, are avoided. This effect is a consequence of the autonomous processing capability requirement for local applications stated in the definition of distributed databases.

Reliability and availability   The distributed database approach, especially with redundant data, can be used also in order to obtain higher reliability and availability. However, obtaining this goal is not straightforward and requires the use of techniques which are still not completely understood. The autonomous processing capability of the different sites does not by itself guarantee a higher overall reliability of the system, but it ensures a **graceful degradation** property; in other words, failures in a distributed database can be more frequent than in a centralized one because of the greater number of components, but the effect of each failure is confined to those applications which use the data of the failed site, and complete system crash is rare. The techniques for building reliable distributed databases are presented in Chapter 9.

The above motivations for distributed databases are not new. Why has the development of distributed database systems just begun? There are two main reasons for this: first, the recent development of small computers, providing at a lower cost many of the capabilities which were previously provided by large mainframes, constitutes the necessary hardware support for the development of distributed information systems; second, the technology of distributed databases is based on two other technologies which have developed a sufficiently solid foundation during the seventies: computer networks technology and database technology. It is a complex task to build a distributed database on top of a computer network and a set of local database management systems at each site; it would be an infeasible effort without these building blocks.

1.3 DISTRIBUTED DATABASE MANAGEMENT SYSTEMS (DDBMSs)

A distributed database management system supports the creation and maintenance of distributed databases. In analyzing the features of DDBMSs, it is convenient to distinguish between commercially available systems and advanced research prototypes. This distinction is based on present-day state of the art. Clearly, some features which are currently experimental in advanced research prototypes will be incorporated in commercially available systems of the future. In this section, some hints are given on how hard these problems are and in which way the new features will be made commercially available; in Part II of this book we describe some of the available commercial systems (Chapter 11) and most of the research prototypes (Chapter 12–15).

Several commercially available distributed systems were developed by the vendors of centralized database management systems. They contain additional components which extend the capabilities of centralized DBMSs by supporting communication and cooperation between several instances of DBMSs which are installed at different sites of a computer network. The software components which are typically necessary for building a distributed database in this case are:

1.   The database management component (DB)
2.   The data communication component (DC)
3.   The data dictionary (DD), which is extended to represent information about the distribution of data in the network
4.   The distributed database component (DDB)

These components are connected as shown in Figure 1.6 for a two-site network.

We will use the term "distributed database management system" to refer to the above set of four components, while DDB is only the specialized distributed

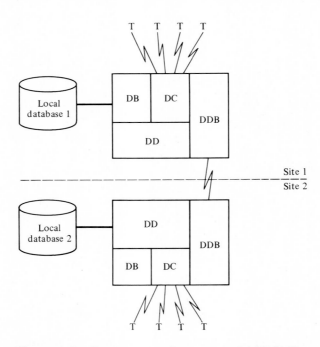

Figure 1.6   Components of a commercial DDBMS.

database component. In a similar way, we will use the term "database management system" to refer to the set of components which serve to manage a nondistributed database, i.e., the DB, DC, and DD components.

The services which are supported by the above type of systems are typically:

1. Remote database access by an application program; this feature is the most important one and is provided by all systems which have a distributed database component.

2. Some degree of distribution transparency; this feature is supported to a different extent by different systems, because there is a strong trade-off between distribution transparency and performance.

3. Support for database administration and control; this feature includes tools for monitoring the database, gathering information about database utilization, and providing a global view of data files existing at the various sites.

4. Some support for concurrency control and recovery of distributed transactions.

The access to a remote database by an application can be performed in one of two basic ways, as shown in Figure 1.7a and b. Figure 1.7a shows that the application issues a database access request which refers to remote data. This request is automatically routed by the DDBMS to the site where the data is located; then it is executed at that site, and the result is returned. In this way, the basic units which are shipped between systems are the database access primitive and the result obtained by executing this primitive. If this approach is used for remote access, distribution transparency can be implemented by providing global filenames; the primitives could then be automatically addressed to the appropriate remote sites.

Figure 1.7b shows a different approach, in which the application requires the execution of an auxiliary program at the remote site. This auxiliary program, written by the application programmer, accesses the remote database and returns the result to the requesting application.

DDBMSs provide both types of remote access, because each one of the above approaches has its own advantages and disadvantages. The solution of Figure 1.7a provides more distribution transparency while the solution of Figure 1.7b can be more efficient if many database accesses are required, because the auxiliary program can perform all the required accesses and send only the result back.

If the capability of the auxiliary program in Figure 1.7b is greater than the capability of the database access primitives of Figure 1.7a, then the second solution can be more efficient. Therefore, having powerful primitives which are capable of manipulating sets of records at a time is a very useful feature of the local DBMS in building a distributed system. However, most commercially available DBMSs are one-record-at-a-time systems, and therefore auxiliary programs are needed.

An important property of DDBMSs is whether they are **homogeneous** or **heterogeneous**. Homogeneity and heterogeneity can be considered at different levels in a distributed database: the hardware, the operating system, and the local DBMSs. However, the important distinction for us is at the level of local DBMSs, because differences at lower levels are managed by the communication software. Therefore, in the following, the term "homogeneous DDBMS" refers to a DDBMS

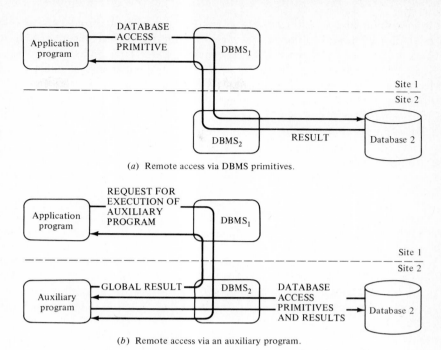

(*a*) Remote access via DBMS primitives.

(*b*) Remote access via an auxiliary program.

Figure 1.7 Types of accesses to a distributed database.

with the same DBMS at each site, even if the computers and/or the operating systems are not the same. Note that this situation is not uncommon, because the same vendor often provides the same DBMS on several computers and because software houses produce DBMSs which run on different computers of different vendors.

A heterogeneous DDBMS uses instead at least two different DBMSs. Heterogeneous DDBMSs add the problem of translating between the different data models of the different local DBMSs to the complexity of homogeneous DDBMSs. For this reason, if the development of a distributed database is performed top-down without a preexisting system, it is convenient to develop a homogeneous system. However, as it was stated in the previous section, in some cases the motivation for creating a distributed database is the necessity of integrating several preexisting databases; in this case it is required to develop a heterogenous DDBMS, capable of building a global view of the database.

Although the problems of heterogeneous DDBMSs are very hard, and therefore really heterogeneous DDBMSs exist only as research prototypes, it must be stated that commercially available systems provide some degree of support for heterogeneity. While none of these systems performs translation between different data models, which is the really hard problem, some of them support the communication between different data communication (DC) components. This type of communication was not developed especially for building distributed databases, but was developed for compatibility reasons within a centralized system. Typical examples of this situation are several DBMSs which have been produced by software houses for running on IBM computers. These DBMSs have an integrated pair of DB/DC components; however, their DC component can be substituted by IBM's standard teleprocessing monitor CICS. CICS has an intersystem communication facility (ISC) which allows the communication between programs running on different machines. Since these programs can access the local database using the local DB components, this allows implementing applications which access data from a distributed, heterogeneous database. However, it is the application programmer's responsibility to deal with the different data models. A description of CICS/ISC can be found in Chapter 11; the presentation of some of the problems of heterogeneous DDBMSs is in Chapter 15.

CONCLUSIONS

Distributed databases are important for economical, organizational and technological reasons. They can be implemented in large geographical computer networks and in small local networks. The number of applications of distributed databases will grow in the next years, as distributed database management systems will become available.

Distributed database technology extends traditional database technology in a nontrivial way. In this novel environment, several technical problems require different solutions, and several completely new issues arise.

Annotated Bibliography

Reference [1.1] surveys the main problems in the field of distributed databases and reference [1.2] surveys research efforts in this area. References [1.3] to [1.5] are books on distributed data processing systems; they deal also partially with the distributed database approach. Reference [1.6] contains the papers which were presented at a course on distributed databases. References [1.7] to [1.9] are the proceedings of three conferences which were completely devoted to distributed databases. Several papers contained in these proceedings will be referenced specifically in subsequent chapters of this book.

[1.1]   J. B. Rothnie and N. Goodman, "A Survey of Research and Development in Distributed Database Management Systems," *Proc. Third Int. Conf. on VLDB*, 1977.

[1.2]   *Database Engineering*, **5**:4, Issue Dedicated to Distributed Database Research, IEEE, 1982.

[1.3]   H. Lorin, *Aspects of Distributed Computer Systems*, Wiley, 1981.

[1.4]   G. M. Booth, *The Distributed System Environment*, McGraw-Hill, 1981.

[1.5]   O. H. Bray, *Distributed Database Management Systems*, Lexington Books, 1982.

[1.6]   *Distributed Databases—An Advanced Course,* W. Draffan and F. Poole, eds., Cambridge Univ. Press, 1980.

[1.7]   "Distributed Data Bases," *Proc. Int. Symp. on Distributed Databases,* C. Delobel and W. Litwin, eds., North-Holland, 1980.

[1.8]   "Distributed Data Bases," *Proc. Second Int. Symp. on Distributed Databases,* H. J. Schneider, ed., North-Holland, 1982.

[1.9]   "Distributed Data Sharing Systems," *Proc. Second Int. Seminar on Distributed Data Sharing Systems,* R. P. Van De Riet and W. Litwin, eds., North-Holland, 1982.

Several other journals and conference proceedings include papers on distributed databases; the most important ones are listed below (the abbreviations which will be used to reference them in the rest of this book are indicated in parentheses).

- *ACM Transactions on Database Systems (ACM-TODS)*
- *IEEE Transactions on Software Engineering (IEEE-TSE)*
- *IEEE Transactions on Computers (IEEE-TC)*
- *Proceedings of the International Conference on Very Large Databases (VLDB)*
- *Proceedings of ACM/SIGMOD Conference on the Management of Data (ACM-SIGMOD)*

Chapter 2

Review of Databases and Computer Networks

This chapter presents a brief review of some of the concepts of traditional, nondistributed databases and of computer networks, which will be used in the rest of the book. The chapter is not a complete tutorial on these subjects; only those concepts and notations which are needed in the rest of this book are defined here. The reader who has a background on databases and computer networks can skip this chapter or part of it; however, he or she should at least take a look at the notation which is used for the relational algebra in Section 2.1.1.

Section 2.1 reviews database concepts. In Section 2.1.1 we briefly present those aspects of the relational model and algebra which are used in the following chapters; we also introduce the SQL language for manipulating relational databases. Section 2.1.2 defines the terms "application," "transaction," "program," and "query," as they will be used in the rest of the book. These definitions have been included because these terms are used with different meanings in current literature, especially if one considers both research literature and the description of commercial products.

Section 2.2 presents a review of the basic concepts about computer networks; it discusses the various types of communication networks, introduces the concepts of protocols and sessions, and reviews the ISO/OSI reference architecture.

2.1 REVIEW OF DATABASES

The data model which is used in this book is the relational model. From the presentation of the first chapter, it should be clear that this model is more suitable than other models for the description of distributed database concepts. Basically, the relational model allows the use of powerful, set-oriented, associative expressions instead of the one-record-at-a-time primitives of more procedural models, like the Codasyl model. We use in this book two different data manipulation languages: **relational algebra** and **SQL**. SQL, which is an "user-friendly" language, is used in Chapter 3, dealing with the problems of writing application programs for distributed databases. Relational algebra is instead used for describing and manipulating access strategies to distributed databases.

2.1.1 The Relational Model

In relational databases, data are stored in tables, called **relations**. Each relation has a (fixed) number of columns, called **attributes**, and a (dynamic, time-varying) number of rows, called **tuples**. There is an obvious correspondence between fields of traditional file organizations and attributes of the relational model, and between records of files and tuples of relations. The number of attributes of a relation is called its **grade**; the number of tuples is called its **cardinality**.

EMPNUM	NAME	AGE	DEPTNUM
3	Jones	27	1
7	Smith	34	2
11	Bob	18	1
15	Jane	23	3
18	Mary	31	1

(a) Relation *EMP*

EMPNUM	AGE	DEPTNUM	NAME
3	27	1	Jones
7	34	2	Smith
11	18	1	Bob
15	23	3	Jane
18	31	1	Mary

(b) Relation *EMP'*

Figure 2.1   Example of relation.

Figure 2.1a shows a relation *EMP* (employee) consisting of four attributes: *EMPNUM*, *NAME*, *AGE*, and *DEPTNUM*. The relation has five tuples; for example, $\langle 3, Jones, 27, 1 \rangle$ is a tuple of the *EMP* relation. The grade of relation *EMP* is 4 and the cardinality is 5.

The relation name and the names of attributes appearing in it are called the **relation schema** of the relation; for instance,

$$EMP(EMPNUM,\ NAME,\ AGE,\ DEPTNUM)$$

is the relation schema of relation *EMP* in the above example.

The set of possible values for a given attribute is called its **domain**. Thus, for instance, *EMPNUM* takes its values from the domain of employee numbers, constituted by the positive integers, and *AGE* takes its values from the domain of ages, constituted by integers between 0 and 100. Though these two domains have some values in common, they are regarded as different domains, since the meaning given to common values is different in the two contexts; typically, it makes no sense to compare values from different domains, such as ages and employee numbers.

An important aspect of the definition of the relational model is to regard relations as **sets** of tuples; as a consequence:

1.   There cannot be two identical tuples in the same relation.
2.   There is no defined order of the tuples of a relation.

While considering relations as sets is important for deriving elegant and useful mathematical properties of relations, most relational database systems do not strictly implement relations as pure sets. Thus, in some systems replicated tuples are allowed (relations are regarded as multisets), and tuples are stored according to some internal ordering which is useful for processing.

A more formal definition of relations is based on the notion of domains; in this case, a collection of domains $D_1, D_2, \ldots, D_n$ is given a priori, and a relation of grade n over these domains is seen as any subset of the cartesian product of them. More precisely, a relation R is a set of ordered tuples $\langle d_1, d_2, \ldots, d_n \rangle$ such that d_1 belongs to D_1, d_2 belongs to $D_2, \ldots$, and d_n belongs to D_n. This definition is useful for analyzing the properties of the relational model and algebra, and this is the current definition in the research literature.

In this book, we will consider *the order of columns of a relation as immaterial*. This corresponds to considering a relation as a set of mappings from a set of attribute names to a set of values; more simply, this corresponds to disregarding the "position" of each column in a relation, as long as we can recognize columns by means of attribute names. Thus, the relation *EMP′* in Figure 2.1*b*, in which the same attributes of *EMP* appear in the order: *EMPNUM, AGE, DEPTNUM, NAME*, is exactly the same relation as that of Figure 2.1*a*.

An important property of some attributes of relations is that they are a **key** of the relation; keys are subsets of the attributes of a relation schema whose values are unique within the relation, and thus can be used to uniquely identify the tuples of the relation. Given that relations are sets of tuples, a key must exist; at least, the set of all attributes of the relation constitutes the key. The property of being a key is a *semantic* one; we do not consider an attribute as a key only because it occasionally identifies all the tuples. Thus, in the examples of Figure 2.1, *EMPNUM* is an appropriate key of *EMP* (because identification numbers of employees are unique), while *AGE* is not a key (because by simply adding more tuples, we might find two of them with the same age value). We might assume instead that identification numbers are given to employees within departments; i.e., each department has its own numeration. In this case, the appropriate key of this relation would be the pair of attributes: *EMPNUM, DEPTNUM*. Notice that a relation can have several keys; typically, one of them is selected as the **primary key**.

The **relational algebra** is a collection of operations on relations, each of which takes one or two relations as operands and produces one relation as result.

Operations of relational algebra can be composed into arbitrarily complex **expressions**; expressions allow specifying the manipulations which are required on relations in order to retrieve information from them.

Several versions of the relational algebra have appeared in the literature, which differ in the choice of operators and in the formalism used to denote them. In our book, we use operators which are similar to those of reference [2.1], though we will use a different notation. In reference [2.1], five basic operations are defined: selection, projection, cartesian product, union, and difference. These operations are complete, in the sense that they allow the same expressiveness as first-order calculus. From these operations, some other operations are derived, such as intersection, division, join, and semi-join. We follow here the same approach, but we highlight those operations which have an important application in distributed databases, such as joins and semi-joins, while we do not consider other operations, like intersection and division. The meaning of each operation is described referring to the examples of Figure 2.2.

Unary operations take only one relation as operand; they include selection and projection.

The **selection SL**$_F R$ (Figure 2.2b), where R is the operand to which the selection is applied and F is a formula which expresses a selection predicate, produces a result relation with the same relation schema as the operand relation, and containing the subset of the tuples of the operand which satisfy the predicate. The formula involves attribute names or constants as operands, arithmetic comparison operators, and logical operators. For example, given a relation schema $R(A, B, C)$, the following is a valid formula: $(A = B$ OR $A < C)$ AND NOT $A > 7$.

The **projection PJ**$_{Attr} R$ (Figure 2.2c), where $Attr$ denotes a subset of the attributes of the operand relation, produces a result having these attributes as relation schema. The tuples of the result are derived from the tuples of the operand relation by suppressing the values of attributes which do not appear in $Attr$. Moreover, replicated tuples which might result from this operation are eliminated; thus, the cardinality of the result might be less than the cardinality of the operand.

Binary operations take two relations as operands; we review union, difference, cartesian product, join, and semi-join.

The **union** R **UN** S (Figure 2.2d) is meaningful only between two relations R and S with the same relation schema; it produces a relation with the same relation schema as its operands and the union of the tuples of R and S (i.e., all tuples appearing either in R or in S or in both).

The **difference** R **DF** S (Figure 2.2e) is meaningful only between two relations R and S with the same relation schema; it produces a relation with the same relation schema as its operands and the difference between the tuples of R and S (i.e., all tuples appearing in R but not in S).

The **cartesian product** R **CP** S (Figure 2.2f) produces a relation whose relation schema includes all the attributes of R and S. If two attributes with the same name appear in R and S, they are nevertheless considered different attributes; in order to avoid ambiguity, the name of each attribute is prefixed with the name of its "original" relation. Every tuple of R is combined with every tuple of S to form one tuple of the result.

R

A	B	C
a	1	a
b	1	b
a	1	d
b	2	f

S

A	B	C
a	1	a
a	3	f

T

B	C	D
1	a	1
3	b	1
3	c	2
1	d	4
2	a	3

(a) Operand relations.

(b) Selection $\mathbf{SL}_{A=a}\ R$

A	B	C
a	1	a
a	1	d

(c) Projection $\mathbf{PJ}_{A,B}\ R$

A	B
a	1
b	1
b	2

(d) Union $R\ \mathbf{UN}\ S$

A	B	C
a	1	a
b	1	b
a	1	d
b	2	f
a	3	f

$R.A$	$R.B$	$R.C$	$S.A$	$S.B$	$S.C$
a	1	a	a	1	a
b	1	b	a	1	a
a	1	d	a	1	a
b	2	f	a	1	a
a	1	a	a	3	f
b	1	b	a	3	f
a	1	d	a	3	f
b	2	f	a	3	f

(f) Cartesian Product $R\ \mathbf{CP}\ S$

(e) Difference $R\ \mathbf{DF}\ S$

A	B	C
b	1	b
a	1	d
a	2	f

(g) Join $R\ \mathbf{JN}_{R.C=T.C}\ T$

A	$R.B$	$R.C$	$T.B$	$T.C$	D
a	1	a	1	a	1
a	1	a	2	a	3
b	1	b	3	b	1
a	1	d	1	d	4

(h) Natural join $R\ \mathbf{NJN}\ T$

A	B	C	D
a	1	a	1
a	1	d	4

(i) Semi-join $R\ \mathbf{SJ}_{R.C=T.C}\ T$

A	B	C
a	1	a
b	1	b
a	1	d

(j) Natural join $R\ \mathbf{NSJ}\ T$

A	B	C
a	1	a
a	1	d

Figure 2.2 Operations of relational algebra.

The **join** (Figure 2.2g) of two relations R and S is denoted as $R\,\mathbf{JN}_F S$, where F is a formula which specifies the join predicate. The formula of a join specification is given by conjunctions of comparisons between attributes ordinately taken from the two operands; thus, if we consider two relations $R(A, B)$ and $S(C, D)$, the following is a valid formula: $A = C$ AND $B > D$. If only equality appears in the formula, we denote the operation as an equi-join. A join is derived from selection and cartesian product as follows:

$$R\,\mathbf{JN}_F S = \mathbf{SL}_F(R\,\mathbf{CP}\,S)$$

Thus, the relation schema of the result of the join includes all the attributes of R and S, and all the tuples from R and S which satisfy the join predicate are included in the result.

The **natural join** $R\,\mathbf{NJN}\,S$ (Figure 2.2h) of two relations R and S is an equi-join in which all attributes with the same names in the two relations are compared. Since these attributes have both the same name and the same values in all the tuples of the result, one of the two attributes is omitted from the result.

The **semi-join** (Figure 2.2i) of two relations R and S is denoted as $R\,\mathbf{SJ}_F S$, where F is a formula which specifies a join predicate. A semi-join is derived from projection and join as follows:

$$R\,\mathbf{SJ}_F S = \mathbf{PJ}_{Attr(R)}(R\,\mathbf{JN}_F S)$$

where $Attr(R)$ denotes the set of all attributes of R. Thus, the result of the semi-join is a subset of the tuples of R, constituted by those tuples which give a contribution to the join of R with S.

The **natural semi-join** (Figure 2.2j) of two relations R and S, denoted $R\,\mathbf{NSJ}\,S$, is obtained by considering a semi-join with the same join predicate as in the natural join.

Finally, we introduce a synthetic notation for the n-ary union, which we will find very useful. We denote as $\mathbf{UN}(R_1, R_2, \ldots, R_n)$ the union of n relations; this is perfectly equivalent to the expression: $R_1\,\mathbf{UN}\,R_2\,\mathbf{UN}\ldots\mathbf{UN}\,R_n$, which returns the n-ary union as a result of several binary unions (since union is commutative and associative, see Chapter 5).

Relational algebra will be used in the rest of this book in order to define how the distributed database is accessed, because it describes access plans conveniently. However, relational algebra is not very "user friendly," and understanding the meaning of an algebric expression can be difficult. Therefore, when we will describe how users should program a distributed database, we will use a more user-oriented language, which can be understood more easily. We have choosen the SQL language for this purpose.

A simple statement in SQL has the following structure:

Select ⟨attribute list⟩
from ⟨relation name⟩
where ⟨predicates⟩

The interpretation of this statement is equivalent to performing a selection operation using the predicates of the "where clause" on the relation specified in the "from clause" and then projecting the result on the attributes of the "select clause." For example, if we consider the relation of Figure 2.1a, the statement:

Select *NAME, AGE*
from *EMP*
where *AGE* > 20 and *DEPTNUM* = 1

returns the following relation:

NAME	AGE
Jones	27
Mary	31

The basic statement structure can be used also for expressing queries which require a join operation in their algebraic expression; in this case more than one relation must be specified in the "from clause." For example, referring to the relations of Figure 2.2a, the SQL statement

Select *A, R.C*
from *R, T*
where *R.B* = *T.B* and *D* = 3

returns as a result the relation:

A	R.C
b	f

The execution of a statement of this type can be interpreted in the follwing way:

1. Perform the join of relation R and T using the join clause $R.B = T.B$.
2. Perform a selection with predicate $D = 3$ on the result of the join operation.
3. Project the result on attributes A and $R.C$.

The above presentation covers a small subset of the features of the SQL language; however, it is sufficient for understanding most of the examples of this book. Some additional features will be introduced when needed. For a complete presentation of the SQL language, see reference [2.6].

2.1.2 Database Applications, Programs, and Transactions

In this subsection we define the meaning of the following terms: "application," "transaction," "program," and "query." As it is always the case when one tries to clarify the meaning of a term, the definitions which are given here cannot correspond to all the possible usual meanings. However, we have tried to maintain the correspondence with the usual terminology as closely as possible.

Application An **application** is a sequence of operations which can be requested by an end-user (not a programmer!) with a single activation request. An application can be **online**, in which case it is requested by the user at a terminal and requires a response in a short time to the same user; or it can be a **batch** application, in which case it is typically requested by an operator. Each application has an associated **application code**, which is used to request its execution.

Online applications can be classified as **simple applications** or **conversational applications**, depending on the type of interaction which they perform with the end-user. Simple applications receive one input message and produce one output message (note that both messages can be a whole screen of data); conversational applications exchange several messages with the user. A **read-only application** is an application which reads data from the database without performing any updates.

Transaction   A **transaction** is an atomic unit of database access, which is either completely executed or not executed at all. The notion of transaction is therefore related to the problems of recovery and concurrency control, because atomicity must be preserved both in case of failures and in case of concurrent execution. Note that very often a transaction and an application coincide; i.e., an elementary function which is required by the user is also an atomic unit of database access. For this reason the term "transaction" is often used instead of "application." However, with the above definition the following relationship exists between transactions and applications: an application may consist of zero (if atomicity of database access is not required), one (if application and transaction coincide), or several transactions (if the atomic units of database update are smaller than the function which is performed with only one request), but a transaction belongs to only one application (otherwise it would be clearly impossible to guarantee atomicity).

Program   A **program** is the definition of a computation, including the database access. A program is also considered as a unit having its own address space which communicates with other programs only through messages and synchronization primitives.

Query   A **query** is an expression in a suitable language which defines a portion of the data contained in the database. A query can therefore be used to define the semantics of an application, or it can be used to define the function which is performed by a program which accesses the database.

If a system supports a **query interface**, the end-user can write a query and request its execution. The system automatically generates the programs which implement a read-only application, having the semantics specified by the query, and the application is executed.

Notice that in this book we use the term "application" to denote a function requested by the user, the term "query" to denote a database request, and the term "program" to denote the implementation of the application in a programming language.

2.2 REVIEW OF COMPUTER NETWORKS

The model of a computer network which we will consider in this book is shown in Figure 2.3; computers which are capable of performing autonomous work are connected by a **communication network**. The computers are called **hosts** in the literature on computer networks; we will normally use the word **site** to denote

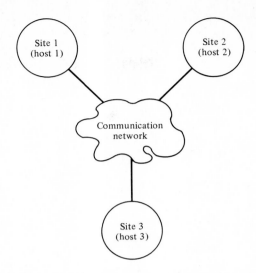

Figure 2.3   A model of a computer network.

in fact a host computer. The communication network is itself constituted of communication links of various kinds (telephone lines, coaxial cables, satellite links, etc.) and often includes several computers. These computers, which are dedicated to the communication function, are not hosts and will never be considered explicitly in this book. They are simply useful for implementing the communication network.

The basic facility which is provided by the communication network is the following: *a process running at any site can send a message to a process running at any other site of the network.*

Note that this basic facility is independent of the actual structure of the communication network; any two sites of the network can communicate.

The parameters which characterize the above basic function and will be considered in the rest of this book are:

1. The **delay** with which the message is delivered at its destination; when the utilization of the network is low, the delay depends essentially on the performance characteristics of the components which constitute the network and can be therefore assumed as statically known. However, if the network is heavily used, then the delay becomes longer, due to the waiting which is imposed on a message when other messages have to be transmitted before it; in this case, a queuing analysis is required in order to evaluate the delay.

2. The **cost** of transmitting the message. We will assume in this book that there is a fixed cost associated with each message plus an additional cost which is proportional to the length of the message.

3. The **reliability** of the network, which is essentially the probability that the message is correctly delivered at its destination. An analysis of the types of failures which may occur in the communication network is done in Chapter 7, which deals with transaction management.

In many applications it is necessary that a process at one site send the same message to processes at *all* other sites; this operation is called **broadcast**. It is possible to perform a broadcast by simply sending separately as many single messages as there are sites in the network; in this case, the broadcast operation is the repetition of the basic message-sending operation. However, in several types of communication networks, broadcasting the same message is much less expensive than sending the same message many times. Indeed, there are communication networks in which the cost of broadcasting a message and the cost of sending it to just one site are practically the same.

2.2.1 Types of Communication Networks

There are several ways in which networks can be categorized; this section analyzes some of them. Consider, for example, the network of Figure 2.4a. The communication network is composed of a set of dedicated processors, called **IMP**s (interface message processors), which are pairwise connected by communication channels, for example telephone lines. Each site is connected to an IMP. When a site sends

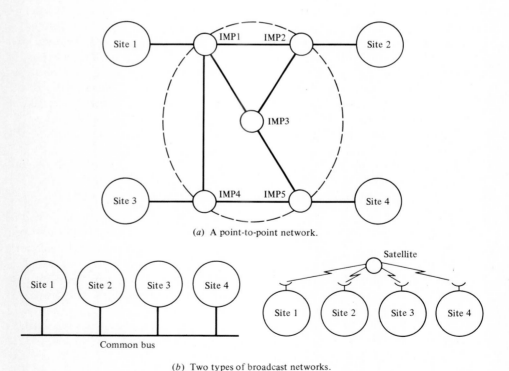

(*a*) A point-to-point network.

(*b*) Two types of broadcast networks.

Figure 2.4   Types of communication networks.

a message to another site, the message is delivered to an IMP, which stores it and then sends it to another IMP, which also stores it and then sends it to a further IMP, and so on, until the message finally reaches the IMP to which the destination site is connected. A network of this kind is called a **point-to-point** or **store-and-forward** network. In a point-to-point network, the IMPs have the responsibility of choosing the path along which a message is transmitted in the presence of alternatives. For example, in Figure 2.4a, if site 1 sends a message to site 4, the message can follow the IMP1-IMP3-IMP5 way, but also the IMP1-IMP2-IMP3-IMP5 way or several others. The function of choosing a path is called **routing**. In the definition of the basic facility provided by the communication network we implicitly require that the network be able to perform this routing function, because the sending sites simply specify the final destination of each message.

In a point-to-point network, the cost of broadcasting a message to many sites is equivalent to sending many separate messages. Finally, note that the separation between sites and IMPs is a logical one, not necessarily a physical one: the same computer could perform both functions.

Consider now the two examples of a network which are shown in Figure 2.4b: one is based on a common bus and the other on a satellite. The common characteristic of these two communication networks is that all sites receive all the messages which are sent by any other site; of course, there must be a mechanism which allows each site to recognize those messages which are directed to it, and discard the other ones. The typical mechanism consists of prefixing each message with the identification of the destination site. A communication network of this kind is called a **broadcast network**. In a broadcast network, broadcasting a message to many sites is not more expensive than sending a message to one site only.

Computer networks are also classified as **local** networks and **geographically distributed** (or long-haul) networks. This distinction depends on the fact that the types of communication channels which can be used if the distance between the sites is small are different from the communication channels which are used for long-distance communication. At today's state of the art, a typical local network does not exceed 1000 meters in distance. The sites of a local network typically belong to the same building or campus or factory. The communication channel can be implemented by a coaxial cable or by optical fibers. A throughput of 10 megabits per second and a very high reliability are achieved in this way. Local networks are typically broadcast networks.

Geographically distributed networks are still mainly based on telephone lines. With good dedicated telephone lines, a throughput of 50 to 100 kilobits per second can be achieved; however, the throughput is much lower in cases. Moreover, the reliability is much less than in local networks.

Finally, in some cases we have to distinguish networks on the basis of their **topology**. Although we have assumed that the routing function relieves us from knowing how the physical links which constitute the network are structured, in developing some algorithms it is extremely convenient to take advantage of this knowledge. The basic topologies shown in Figure 2.5 are the star, the hierarchical, the ring, the completely interconnected, and the irregular topology.

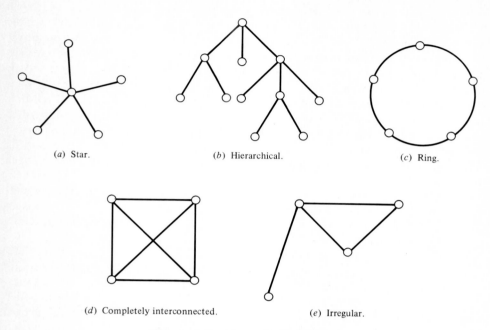

(a) Star.　　　　　　(b) Hierarchical.　　　　　　(c) Ring.

(d) Completely interconnected.　　　　(e) Irregular.

Figure 2.5　Network topologies.

2.2.2 Protocols and Sessions

Two processes which want to communicate by exchanging messages have to follow some rules in order to obtain a satisfactory communication. The rules which are followed by two (or more) processes for communicating are called a **protocol**. Typically, a protocol states how the sender and the receiver can reach an agreement on exchanging a message, how they can recognize and identify each other, how many messages they exchange, whether a message requires an answer or not, and similar aspects.

An example of a protocol which is very familiar to all of us is the set of rules which is required in order to make a phone call. These rules comprise dialing the number of the destination, recognizing the signals of the phone, saying "hello," identifying oneself, and so on. It is difficult to make a phone call without knowing these rules.

In a phone call, once that the caller and the called person have performed a set of preliminary operations, they can speak in turn until they have nothing more to say, and then they hang up. Consider now two processes at two different sites of the network, which also have to exchange some information by sending messages in turn. As with the two persons, it seems convenient that, once they have performed all the preliminary operations required for recognizing each other, they can exchange all the required messages without having to repeat these operations for each message. The concept of **session** was introduced for this purpose. A session is established between two processes which want to communicate and is held until all necessary messages have been exchanged. Closing a session is very similar to hanging up.

As with the telephone call between two persons, the duration of a session must take into account the following trade-off. As long as two persons are exchanging information continuously, it is not convenient to hang up. However, if one has to think about a problem before he or she can answer, it may be convenient to hang up and call again at a later time. Since sessions tie up resources, a similar trade-off has to be considered when some processes do not need to communicate for some time.

There are some fundamental differences between a phone call and a session between two processes. In the phone call example, establishing the communication consists not only in exchanging identification information between the involved persons, but also in establishing a physical connection between them. Consider instead the store-and-forward network of Figure 2.4a and two processes at sites 1 and 4. The two processes can establish a session, thus recognizing each other and deciding to exchange several messages, without a direct physical connection being established between them. In fact, the messages which are exchanged between processes during the same session can follow different paths depending on the decisions taken by the routing algorithm. The session concept is therefore a high level facility, which is provided by the communication network as a whole and does not imply the existence of a direct physical connection.

In some cases the exchange of messages between processes has an irregular pattern, so that it is not convenient to establish sessions; instead the whole introduction protocol is performed for each message which is sent. This approach is called **datagram**. In the same communication network, two processes can exchange information by establishing sessions and/or by sending datagram messages to each other. The choice depends on the expected pattern of communication.

2.2.3 The ISO/OSI Reference Architecture

A layered approach is typically used for simplifying the design and implementation of communication networks. The purpose of each layer is to offer a virtual communication facility to the higher-level layer. Different networks use different approaches to the layering of the network; we will briefly describe here the **ISO** (International Standards Organization) reference model called **OSI** (Open Systems Interconnection). Most existing networks are structured in a similar way, although often some layers are combined.

The ISO/OSI reference model is based on the seven layers shown in Figure 2.6. This figure shows that each layer is implemented in all communicating sites. At each level, two corresponding layers at two different sites communicate using the protocol of the corresponding level.

Most of the algorithms and protocols which are described in this book belong to the **application layer**. From the viewpoint of computer communication networks, a distributed database is in fact a particular application. Assuming this perspective,

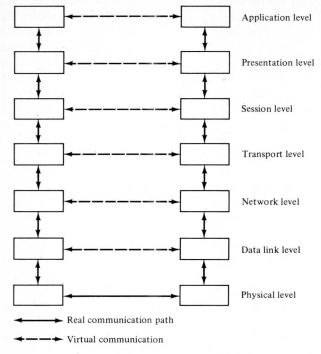

Figure 2.6 The ISO/OSI levels.

we can say that this book describes the techniques for implementing a specific kind of application layer. Of course, the ISO/OSI proposal does not specify any application protocol and leaves this to the users.

In order to implement an application layer, the underlying layers must provide several facilities. We have already defined the basic facility at the beginning of this section: the transmission of messages between processes at different sites. We will now descend the hierarchy of layers considering how this basic facility is obtained.

The **presentation layer** deals with the conversion of information between the different forms of data representation which can be used at each different site. A typical example of this function is the conversion of a message from the character code which is used at the sender site to the character code which is used at the destination site. In this way, the sender process sends a message coded in the form which it knows, and the receiver process receives the same message converted to its code.

The **session layer** has the responsibility of establishing and maintaining the sessions between processes. The importance of having sessions has already been shown.

The **transport layer** is the true source-to-destination layer. It implements a virtual point-to-point channel between the source and the destination. Messages which are sent by the source are delivered error-free and in the right order at the destination.

For performing this function in an efficient way, the transport layer uses the services of the underlying **network, data-link**, and **physical layers**. We are not interested in these lower level layers. They depend greatly on the kind of communication channels which are used and on other technical aspects of data communication.

Note that the units of data which are transmitted in the network are different from the logical messages which are sent from one process to another at the application level. A single message can be broken into several transmission units or several messages can be compacted into one unit. How these functions are performed is not relevant. The transport layer provides the higher layers with the basic facility of exchanging messages between sites, and therefore represents the lowest level layer which we may have to consider. The size of the messages which are used at the levels above the transport layer depends on their information content, while the size of the units which are transmitted at lower levels depends essentially on the characteristics of the communication channels.

Annotated Bibliography

References [2.1] to [2.5] are books on centralized databases. Reference [2.6] is the original presentation of the SQL language, which was originally called Sequel. References [2.7] and [2.8] are books on computer networks.

[2.1]   J. D. Ullman, *Principles of Database Systems*, 2d ed., Computer Science Press, 1983.

[2.2]   C. J. Date, *An Introduction to Database Systems*, 3d ed., Addison-Wesley, 1981.

[2.3]   J. T. Martin, *Computer Data-Base Organization*, Prentice-Hall, 1975.

[2.4]   G. Wiederhold, *Database Design*, 2d ed., McGraw-Hill, 1983.

[2.5]   D. C. Tsichritzis, F. H. Lochovsky, *Data Base Management Systems*, Academic Press, 1977.

[2.6]   D. D. Chamberlin et al., "Sequel 2: A Unified Approach to Data Definition, Manipulation, and Control," *IBM Journal of Research and Development* 1976.

[2.7]   A. S. Tanenbaum, *Computer Networks*, Prentice-Hall, 1981.

[2.8]   D. W. Davies et al., *Computer Networks and Their Protocols*, Wiley, 1979.

Principles
of Distributed Databases

Part I presents the principles of distributed databases.

Chapter 3 introduces a layered architecture of distributed databases and shows that the distributed database can be seen by an application programmer at different levels.

Chapter 4 describes the design of distributed databases; it discusses the techniques for determining the fragmentation and allocation of data at the different sites of the computer network.

Chapters 5 and 6 present the techniques for accessing efficiently a distributed database. Chapter 5 deals with the simplification of database applications by means of equivalence transformations. Chapter 6 deals with the optimization of the execution of applications, whose most important goal is the minimization of intersite transmissions.

Chapters 7, 8, and 9 deal with transaction management, i.e., supporting the efficient, reliable, and concurrent execution of transactions. Chapter 7 shows how the different aspects of transaction management are interrelated. Chapter 8 presents the techniques for distributed concurrency control. Chapter 9 presents the techniques for the recovery of the distributed database from failures.

Finally, Chapter 10 deals with the data administration function, the management of catalogs, and security in distributed databases.

Chapter 3

Levels of Distribution Transparency

This chapter deals with the different levels at which an application programmer views the distributed database, depending on how much distribution transparency is provided by the DDBMS. Distribution transparency has already been informally defined in Chapter 1 as the independence of the application program from the distribution of data, and has been considered to be conceptually equivalent to data independence in centralized databases.

In this chapter we show that there are several levels of distribution transparency. In order to do this, in Section 3.1 we define a layered reference architecture for a distributed database. This architecture allows us to determine easily different levels of distribution transparency. The levels are conceptually relevant in order to understand distributed databases, although specific systems may not implement them explicitly.

In Section 3.2 we show how the mapping between the different levels can be defined. We use for this purpose the relational model and relational algebra.

The remaining sections show how applications can be written at the different levels defined in the reference architecture. The applications are written using a Pascal-like language with embedded SQL statements. The SQL statements represent the distributed database access primitives; SQL was chosen as the data manipulation language because it expresses accesses to a database in a user-friendly, nonprocedural, set-oriented manner.

The emphasis in this chapter is on how applications view the database, i.e., how the SQL primitives reference the objects which constitute the database, and thus the emphasis is also on how much a modification of database distribution affects the application programs. We are not concerned here with the efficiency of database access strategies defined by applications. The problem of determining, evaluating, and choosing between different access strategies is dealt with in Chapters 5 and 6. However, we will show that the same application can be written in many different ways, and that the way in which an application is written can affect the possible access strategies.

Section 3.3 deals with read-only applications. It shows, first with a very simple application and then with a more complex one, the different levels of distribution transparency. Section 3.4 performs the same analysis as Section 3.3 on update applications. Both the above sections are based on applications which access the distributed database for retrieving or updating just a single tuple; in this way we can discuss distribution transparency without being concerned with the problems of accessing sets of tuples. In Section 3.5 we deal with the latter problem, and show that even at the highest level of distribution transparency the application programmer can control the power of the primitives which are issued to the DDBMS. Section 3.6 deals with integrity constraints and their enforcement in distributed databases.

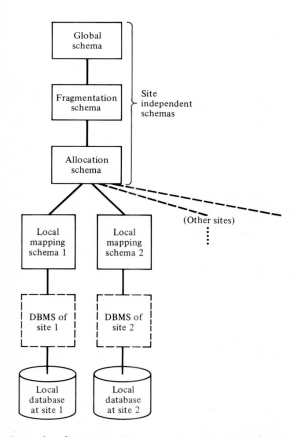

Figure 3.1   A reference architecture for distributed databases.

3.1 REFERENCE ARCHITECTURE FOR DISTRIBUTED DATABASES

Figure 3.1 shows a reference architecture for a distributed database. This reference architecture is not explicitly implemented in all distributed databases; however, its levels are conceptually relevant in order to understand the organization of any distributed database. We will therefore analyze and understand all the components of this reference architecture.

At the top level of Figure 3.1 is the **global schema**. The global schema defines all the data which are contained in the distributed database as if the database were not distributed at all. For this reason, the global schema can be defined exactly in the same way as in a nondistributed database. However, the data model which is used for the definition of a global schema should be convenient for the definition of the mapping to the other levels of the distributed database. We will use the relational model for this purpose. Using this model, the global schema consists of the definition of a set of **global relations**.

Each global relation can be split into several nonoverlapping portions which are called **fragments**. There are several different ways in which to perform the splitting operation; they are described in the next section. The mapping between global relations and fragments is defined in the **fragmentation schema**. This mapping is one to many; i.e., several fragments correspond to one global relation, but only one global relation corresponds to one fragment. Fragments are indicated by a global relation name with an index (fragment index); for example, R_i indicates the ith fragment of global relation R.

Fragments are logical portions of global relations which are physically located at one or several sites of the network. The **allocation schema** defines at which site(s) a fragment is located. Note that the type of mapping defined in the allocation schema determines whether the distributed database is **redundant** or **nonredundant**: in the former case the mapping is one to many, while in the latter case the mapping is one to one. All the fragments which correspond to the same global relation R and are located at the same site j constitute the **physical image** of global relation R at site j. There is therefore a one to one mapping between a physical image and a pair ⟨global relation, site⟩; physical images can be indicated by a global relation name and a site index. To distinguish them from fragments, we will use a superscript; for example, R^j indicates the physical image of the global relation R at site j.

An example of the relationship between the object types defined above is shown in Figure 3.2. A global relation R is split into four fragments R_1, R_2, R_3, and R_4. These four fragments are allocated redundantly at the three sites of a computer network, thus building three physical images R^1, R^2, and R^3.

To complete the terminology, we will refer to a **copy of a fragment** at a given site, and denote it using the global relation name and two indexes (a fragment index and a site index). For example, in Figure 3.2, the notation R_2^3 indicates the copy of fragment R_2 which is located at site 3.

Finally, note that two physical images can be identical. In this case we will

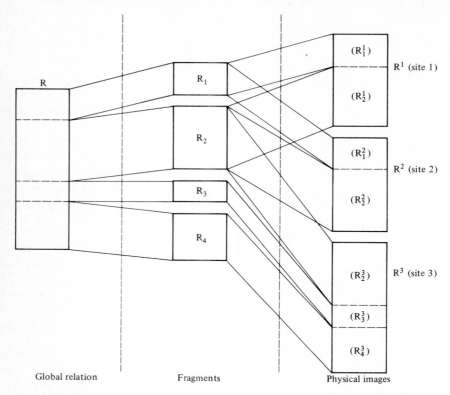

Figure 3.2 Fragments and physical images for a global relation.

say that a physical image is a copy of another physical image. For example, in Figure 3.2, R^1 is a copy of R^2.

Let us now go back to the reference architecture of Figure 3.1. We have already described the relationships between the objects at the three top levels of this architecture. These three levels are site independent; therefore, they do not depend on the data model of the local DBMSs. At a lower level, it is necessary to map the physical images to the objects which are manipulated by the local DBMSs. This mapping is called a **local mapping schema** and depends on the type of local DBMS; therefore in a heterogeneous system we have different types of local mappings at different sites.

This architecture provides a very general conceptual framework for understanding distributed databases. The three most important objectives which motivate the features of this architecture are the separation of data fragmentation and allocation, the control of redundancy, and the independence from local DBMSs.

1. *Separating the concept of data fragmentation from the concept of data allocation.* This separation allows us to distinguish two different levels of distribution transparency, namely **fragmentation transparency** and **location transparency**. Fragmentation transparency is the highest degree of

transparency and consists of the fact that the user or application programmer works on global relations. Location transparency is a lower degree of transparency and requires the user or application programmer to work on fragments instead of global relations; however, he or she does not know where the fragments are located. The separation between the concept of fragmentation and allocation is very convenient in distributed database design, because the determination of relevant portions of the data is thus distinguished from the problem of optimal allocation, as will be shown in the next chapter.

2. *Explicit control of redundancy.* The reference architecture provides explicit control of redundancy at the fragment level. For example, in Figure 3.2 the two physical images R^2 and R^3 are overlapping; i.e., they contain common data. The definition of disjoint fragments as building blocks of physical images allows us to refer explicitly to this overlapping part: the replicated fragment R_2. As we shall see, the explicit control over redundancy is useful in several aspects of distributed database management.

3. *Independence from local DBMSs.* This feature, called **local mapping transparency**, allows us to study several problems of distributed database management without having to take into account the specific data models of local DBMSs. Clearly, in a homogeneous system it is possible that the site-independent schemata are defined using the same data model as the local DBMSs, thus reducing the complexity of this mapping.

Another type of transparency which is strictly related to location transparency is **replication transparency**. Replication transparency means that the user is unaware of the replication of fragments. Clearly, replication transparency is implied by location transparency; however, in certain cases it is possible that the user has no location transparency but has replication transparency (thus, he or she uses one particular copy, and the system makes appropriate actions on the other copies). In this book, we do not further distinguish replication transparency from location transparency.

As a final remark on the reference architecture, we can say that it performs the same function as the ANSI/SPARC architecture in traditional DBMSs: it is not necessarily implemented by the existing systems, but it shows which levels and schemata are conceptually relevant.

3.2 TYPES OF DATA FRAGMENTATION

The decomposition of global relations into fragments can be performed by applying two different types of fragmentation: **horizontal fragmentation** and **vertical fragmentation**. We will first consider these two types of fragmentation separately and then consider the more complex fragmentation which can be obtained by applying a composition of both.

In all types of fragmentation, a fragment can be defined by an expression in a relational language (we will use relational algebra) which takes global relations as operands and produces the fragment as result. For example, if a global relation contains data about employees, a fragment which contains only data about employees who work at department D_1 can be obviously defined by a selection operation on the global relation.

There are, however, some rules which must be followed when defining fragments:

Completeness condition All the data of the global relation must be mapped into the fragments; i.e., it must not happen that a data item which belongs to a global relation does not belong to any fragment.

Reconstruction condition It must always be possible to reconstruct each global relation from its fragments. The necessity of this condition is obvious: in fact, only fragments are stored in the distributed database, and global 'atio. have to be built through this reconstruction operation if necessary.

Disjointness condition As we have discussed in the previous section, it is convenient that fragments be disjoint, so that the replication of data can be controlled explicitly at the allocation level. However, this condition is useful mainly with horizontal fragmentation, while for vertical fragmentation we will sometimes allow this condition to be violated. The reason for this exception will be discussed when dealing with vertical fragmentation.

We can now consider the fragmentation rules.

3.2.1 Horizontal Fragmentation

Horizontal fragmentation consists of partitioning the tuples of a global relation into subsets; this is clearly useful in distributed databases, where each subset can contain data which have common geographical properties. It can be defined by expressing each fragment as a selection operation on the global relation. For example, let a global relation be

$$SUPPLIER(SNUM,\ NAME,\ CITY)$$

Then the horizontal fragmentation can be defined in the following way:

$$SUPPLIER_1 = \mathbf{SL}_{CITY=\text{"SF"}}\ SUPPLIER$$
$$SUPPLIER_2 = \mathbf{SL}_{CITY=\text{"LA"}}\ SUPPLIER$$

The above fragmentation satisfies the completeness condition if "SF" and "LA" are the only possible values of the $CITY$ attribute; otherwise we would not know to which fragment the tuples with other $CITY$ values belong.

The reconstruction condition is easily verified, because it is always possible to reconstruct the $SUPPLIER$ global relation through the following operation:

$$SUPPLIER = SUPPLIER_1\ \mathbf{UN}\ SUPPLIER_2$$

The disjointness condition is clearly verified.

We will call the predicate which is used in the selection operation which defines a fragment its **qualification**. For instance, in the above example the qualifications are:

$$q_1 : CITY = \text{``SF''}$$
$$q_2 : CITY = \text{``LA''}$$

We can generalize from the above example that in order to satisfy the completeness condition, the set of qualifications of all fragments must be complete, at least with respect to the set of allowed values. The reconstruction condition is always satisfied through the union operation, and the disjointness condition requires that qualifications be mutually exclusive.

3.2.2 Derived Horizontal Fragmentation

In some cases, the horizontal fragmentation of a relation cannot be based on a property of its own attributes, but is derived from the horizontal fragmentation of another relation. Consider, for example, a global relation

$$SUPPLY(SNUM, PNUM, DEPTNUM, QUAN)$$

where $SNUM$ is a supplier number. It is meaningful to partition this relation so that a fragment contains the tuples for suppliers which are in a given city. However, city is not an attribute of the $SUPPLY$ relation, it is an attribute of the $SUPPLIER$ relation considered in the above example. Therefore we need a semi-join operation in order to determine the tuples of $SUPPLY$ which correspond to the suppliers in a given city. The derived fragmentation of $SUPPLY$ can be therefore defined as follows:

$$SUPPLY_1 = SUPPLY \, \mathbf{SJ}_{SNUM=SNUM} \, SUPPLIER_1$$
$$SUPPLY_2 = SUPPLY \, \mathbf{SJ}_{SNUM=SNUM} \, SUPPLIER_2$$

The effect of the semi-join operations is to select from $SUPPLY$ the tuples which satisfy the join condition between $SUPPLIER_1$ or $SUPPLIER_2$ and $SUPPLY$, thus determining those tuples of $SUPPLY$ which refer to suppliers in San Francisco or Los Angeles, respectively.

The reconstruction of the global relation $SUPPLY$ can be performed through the union operation as was shown for $SUPPLIER$.

When a global relation R has a derived fragmentation, the qualifications of its fragments cannot be expressed as predicates which use attributes from R; rather, the condition for a tuple t to belong to a given fragment R_i of R is the existence, in some other fragment S_i of S, of a tuple t' such that t and t' satisfy the semi-join specification of the derived fragmentation. Considering the above example, we give a simple representation of this condition (which should in fact include an existential quantifier) as follows:

$$q_1 : SUPPLY.SNUM = SUPPLIER.SNUM \, AND \, SUPPLIER.CITY = \text{``SF''}$$
$$q_2 : SUPPLY.SNUM = SUPPLIER.SNUM \, AND \, SUPPLIER.CITY = \text{``LA''}$$

The meaning of the above qualifications is to state, for any tuple of $SUPPLY_1$ ($SUPPLY_2$), the existence of a supplier from San Francisco (Los Angeles) with the same supplier number.

The completeness of the above fragmentation requires that there be no supplier numbers in the *SUPPLY* relation which are not contained also in the *SUPPLIER* relation. This is a typical, and reasonable, integrity constraint for this database, and usually is called the **referential integrity** constraint.

The disjointness condition is satisfied if a tuple of the *SUPPLY* relation does not correspond to two tuples of the *SUPPLIER* relation which belong to two different fragments. In this case this condition is easily verified, because the supplier numbers are unique keys of the *SUPPLIER* relation; however, in general it can be difficult to prove that this condition holds.

3.2.3 Vertical Fragmentation

The vertical fragmentation of a global relation is the subdivision of its attributes into groups; fragments are obtained by projecting the global relation over each group. This can be useful in distributed databases where each group of attributes can contain data which have common geographical properties. The fragmentation is correct if each attribute is mapped into at least one attribute of the fragments; moreover, it must be possible to reconstruct the original relation by joining the fragments together. Consider, for example, a global relation

$$EMP(EMPNUM, NAME, SAL, TAX, MGRNUM, DEPTNUM)$$

A vertical fragmentation of this relation can be defined as

$$EMP_1 = \mathbf{PJ}_{EMPNUM,NAME,MGRNUM,DEPTNUM}\ EMP$$
$$EMP_2 = \mathbf{PJ}_{EMPNUM,SAL,TAX}\ EMP$$

This fragmentation could, for instance, reflect an organization in which salaries and taxes are managed separately. The reconstruction of relation *EMP* can be obtained as

$$EMP = EMP_1\ \mathbf{JN}_{EMPNUM=EMPNUM}\ EMP_2$$

because *EMPNUM* is a key of *EMP*. In general, the inclusion of a key of the global relation into each fragment is the most straightforward way to guarantee that the reconstruction through a join operation is possible. An alternative way to provide the reconstruction property is to generate **tuple identifiers** which are used as system-controlled keys. This can be convenient in order to avoid the replication of large keys; moreover, tuple identifiers cannot be modified by users.

Notice that the above formula for the reconstruction of the global relation *EMP* is not complete, because the result of joining EMP_1 and EMP_2 contains the column *EMPNUM* twice. This undesired replication can be eliminated by a projection operation that we omit to indicate.

Let us finally consider the problem of fragment disjointness. First, we have seen that at least the key should be replicated in all fragments in order to allow reconstruction. In general, we can say that in vertical fragmentation the main motivation for having disjoint fragments (i.e., to control replication) is not as important as in horizontal fragmentation. In fact, if we include the same attribute in two different vertical fragments, we know exactly that the replicated data is constituted by the column which corresponds to this attribute; if instead we allow two horizontal fragments to overlap, by permitting nonmutually exclusive qualifications, then we cannot refer directly to the overlapping portion.

For example, consider the following vertical fragmentation of relation *EMP*:

$$EMP_1 = \mathbf{PJ}_{EMPNUM,NAME,MGRNUM,DEPTNUM} \; EMP$$
$$EMP_2 = \mathbf{PJ}_{EMPNUM,NAME,SAL,TAX} \; EMP$$

The attribute *NAME* is replicated in both fragments. We can explicitly eliminate this attribute when we reconstruct relation *EMP* through an additional projection operation:

$$EMP = EMP_1 \; \mathbf{JN}_{EMPNUM=EMPNUM} \; \mathbf{PJ}_{EMPNUM,SAL,TAX} \; EMP_2$$

3.2.4 Mixed Fragmentation

The fragments which are obtained by the above fragmentation operations are relations themselves, so that it is possible to apply the fragmentation operations recursively, provided that the correctness conditions are satisfied each time. The reconstruction can be obtained by applying the reconstruction rules in inverse order. The expressions which define fragments are more complex in this case; consider, for example, the same global relation

$$EMP(EMPNUM, \; NAME, \; SAL, \; TAX, \; MGRNUM, \; DEPTNUM)$$

The following is a mixed fragmentation which is obtained by applying the vertical fragmentation of the previous example, followed by a horizontal fragmentation on *DEPTNUM*:

$$EMP_1 = \mathbf{SL}_{DEPTNUM \leq 10} \mathbf{PJ}_{EMPNUM,NAME,MGRNUM,DEPTNUM} \; EMP$$
$$EMP_2 = \mathbf{SL}_{10 < DEPTNUM \leq 20} \mathbf{PJ}_{EMPNUM,NAME,MGRNUM,DEPTNUM} \; EMP$$
$$EMP_3 = \mathbf{SL}_{DEPTNUM > 20} \mathbf{PJ}_{EMPNUM,NAME,MGRNUM,DEPTNUM} \; EMP$$
$$EMP_4 = \mathbf{PJ}_{EMPNUM,NAME,SAL,TAX} \; EMP$$

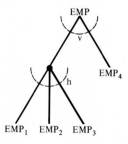

Figure 3.3 The fragmentation tree of relation *EMP*.

The reconstruction of relation EMP is defined by the following expression:

$$EMP = \mathbf{UN}\,(EMP_1, EMP_2, EMP_3)\mathbf{JN}_{EMPNUM=EMPNUM}$$
$$\mathbf{PJ}_{EMPNUM,SAL,TAX}\,EMP_4$$

Mixed fragmentation can be conveniently represented by a **fragmentation tree**. In a fragmentation tree, the root corresponds to a global relation, the leaves correspond to the fragments, and the intermediate nodes correspond to the intermediate results of the fragment-defining expressions. The set of nodes which are sons of a given node represent the decomposition of this node by a fragmentation operation (vertical or horizontal). For example, Figure 3.3 shows the fragmentation tree of relation EMP. The root (relation EMP) is vertically fragmented into two portions: one portion corresponds to a leaf node of the tree (EMP_4); the other portion is horizontally partitioned, thus generating the other three leaves, corresponding to fragments EMP_1, EMP_2, and EMP_3.

The EXAMPLE_DDB

Figure 3.4 shows the global and fragmentation schemata of EXAMPLE_DDB which will be used in the rest of this book for the development of examples. Most of the global relations of EXAMPLE_DDB and their fragmentation have been already introduced. A $DEPT$ relation, horizontally fragmented into three fragments on the value of the $DEPTNUM$ attribute, is added. The features of EXAMPLE_DDB will be discussed when they will be used to exemplify specific topics. Note, as a

Global schema

    EMP(EMPNUM, NAME, SAL, TAX, MGRNUM, DEPTNUM)

    DEPT(DEPTNUM, NAME, AREA, MGRNUM)

    SUPPLIER(SNUM, NAME, CITY)

    SUPPLY(SNUM, PNUM, DEPTNUM, QUAN)

Fragmentation schema

$EMP_1 = \mathbf{SL}_{DEPTNUM\leq 10}\mathbf{PJ}_{EMPNUM,NAME,MGRNUM,DEPTNUM}(EMP)$

$EMP_2 = \mathbf{SL}_{10<DEPTNUM\leq 20}\mathbf{PJ}_{EMPNUM,NAME,MGRNUM,DEPTNUM}(EMP)$

$EMP_3 = \mathbf{SL}_{DEPTNUM>20}\mathbf{PJ}_{EMPNUM,NAME,MGRNUM,DEPTNUM}(EMP)$

$EMP_4 = \mathbf{PJ}_{EMPNUM,NAME,SAL,TAX}(EMP)$

$DEPT_1 = \mathbf{SL}_{DEPTNUM\leq 10}(DEPT)$

$DEPT_2 = \mathbf{SL}_{10<DEPTNUM\leq 20}(DEPT)$

$DEPT_3 = \mathbf{SL}_{DEPTNUM>20}(DEPT)_{\text{,}}$

$SUPPLIER_1 = \mathbf{SL}_{CITY=\text{``SF''}}(SUPPLIER)$

$SUPPLIER_2 = \mathbf{SL}_{CITY=\text{``LA''}}(SUPPLIER)$

$SUPPLY_1 = SUPPLY\,\mathbf{SJ}_{SNUM=SNUM}SUPPLIER_1$

$SUPPLY_2 = SUPPLY\,\mathbf{SJ}_{SNUM=SNUM}SUPPLIER_2$

Figure 3.4   The global and fragmentation schemata of EXAMPLE_DDB.

general aspect, that the four global relations have several common attributes on which it is presumable that some applications will need to perform joins, in particular *DEPTNUM* in relations *EMP, DEPT,* and *SUPPLY; MGRNUM* in relations *EMP* and *DEPT;* and *SNUM* in relations *SUPPLIER* and *SUPPLY.* In all these cases, the same attribute name refers to semantically homogeneous relation domains. The same is not true for the *NAME* attribute, which denotes an employee name in relation *EMP*, a department name in relation *DEPT*, and a supplier name in relation *SUPPLIER.* Note also that the horizontal fragmentation of relation *DEPT* is the same as the horizontal fragmentation of one portion of relation *EMP*; likewise, the relation *SUPPLY* has a derived fragmentation from relation *SUPPLIER.* These facts are of great importance in the determination of convenient strategies for performing joins, as we shall see.

3.3 DISTRIBUTION TRANSPARENCY FOR READ-ONLY APPLICATIONS

In this section, we analyze the different levels of distribution transparency which can be provided by a DDBMS for read-only applications.

3.3.1 A Simple Application

We consider initially a simple example application, called SUPINQUIRY, which consists in accepting a supplier number from a terminal, finding the corresponding supplier name, and displaying it at the terminal. We will analyze how this application sees the database at decreasing levels of distribution transparency.

The application is written using a Pascal-like language with embedded SQL statements for database access. This combination of languages has been chosen because it gives the semantics of the programs easily, without requiring the reader to understand too many linguistic details. The few necessary details will be explained when they are used in the examples. We will omit the declaration of variables in our Pascal-like examples. All variables will be assumed to be strings (arrays) of characters. Input-output will be performed using the standard procedures "read(filename,variable)" and "write(filename,variable)." If input-output is performed at the terminal, the standard filename "terminal" will be used.

An SQL statement in this application language defines a required database access primitive; it can be interpreted as the invocation of a procedure which receives some input parameters from the Pascal-like program, accesses the database, and returns the result as an output parameter. In order to indicate the input and output parameters for these database access procedures, the Pascal variables which are used as parameters in the SQL statements are prefixed with a "$" symbol. Note that the input parameters of an SQL query appear in the where-clause, while the output parameters appear in the select-clause. For instance, the query

Select *NAME* into $NAME
from *SUPPLIER*
where *SNUM* = $SNUM

can be considered as a procedure which receives the variable $SNUM as an input parameter, selects the name of the supplier who has the current value of $SNUM as supplier number, and returns this name to the Pascal-like program in the variable $NAME. In Section 3.5, we will consider the general case in which the SQL statement returns sets (or relations) rather than variables.

In some cases, the application has also to communicate with the DDBMS in order to exchange some control information, for example information on the success or failure of a required database operation. The Pascal variables which are used for this type of communication are prefixed with the "#" symbol. For example, after an SQL query we will often test a boolean variable #FOUND which is true only if the result of the query is not empty. Another typical variable of this kind is #OK, which is true only if the operation has been performed correctly by the DDBMS (these variables are often called "condition codes" in DBMSs).

Level 1: Fragmentation transparency   The way in which the application accesses the database if the DDBMS provides fragmentation transparency is shown in Figure 3.5a. First, the application accepts a supplier number from the terminal; then it accesses the database. The whole SQL statement represents a single distributed database access primitive, which receives the variable $SUPNUM as input parameter and returns the variable $NAME as output parameter. The DDBMS interprets this primitive by accessing the databases at any one of the three sites in a way which is completely determined by the system. The problem of determining how to access the database will be discussed in Chapters 5 and 6. From the viewpoint of distribution transparency, notice that the application refers to the global relation name *SUPPLIER*, completely ignoring the fact that the database is distributed. In this way, the application is completely immune to any change which is applied to all schemata which are below the global schema in our reference architecture.

Level 2: Location Transparency   If the DDBMS provides location transparency but not fragmentation transparency, the same application can be written as shown in Figure 3.5b. The request for the supplier with the given number is first issued referring to fragment $SUPPLIER_1$, and if the DDBMS returns a negative answer in the control variable #FOUND, a similar request is issued with respect to fragment $SUPPLIER_2$. At this point, this naive implementation assumes that the supplier has been found and displays the result. Of course, several variations of this solution are possible, for instance, issuing both requests in parallel in order to exploit the parallelism of the distributed system; however, this does not change the distribution transparency characteristics. This application is clearly independent from changes in the allocation schema, but not from changes in the fragmentation schema, because the fragmentation structure is incorporated in the application. However, location transparency is by itself very useful, because it allows the application to ignore which copies exist of each fragment, therefore allowing copies to be moved from one site to another, and allowing the creation of new copies without affecting the applications.

When location transparency is provided without fragmentation transparency, it is very efficient to write applications which take explicit advantage of knowing the fragmentation structure. For example, the same application of Figure 3.5b can

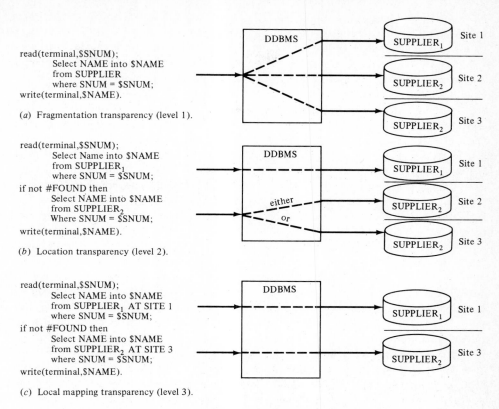

```
read(terminal,$SNUM);
        Select NAME into $NAME
        from SUPPLIER
        where SNUM = $SNUM;
write(terminal,$NAME).
```

(*a*) Fragmentation transparency (level 1).

```
read(terminal,$SNUM);
        Select Name into $NAME
        from SUPPLIER₁
        where SNUM = $SNUM;
if not #FOUND then
        Select NAME into $NAME
        from SUPPLIER₂
        Where SNUM = $SNUM;
write(terminal,$NAME).
```

(*b*) Location transparency (level 2).

```
read(terminal,$SNUM);
        Select NAME into $NAME
        from SUPPLIER₁ AT SITE 1
        where SNUM = $SNUM;
if not #FOUND then
        Select NAME into $NAME
        from SUPPLIER₂ AT SITE 3
        where SNUM = $SNUM;
write(terminal,$NAME).
```

(*c*) Local mapping transparency (level 3).

Figure 3.5 The read-only application SUPINQUIRY at different levels of distribution transparency.

be written in the following way:

> SUPINQUIRY:
> read (terminal, $SNUM);
> read (terminal, $CITY);
> case $CITY of
>   "SF": Select *NAME* into $NAME
>   from *SUPPLIER*₁
>   where *SNUM* = $SNUM;
>   "LA": Select *NAME* into $NAME
>   from *SUPPLIER*₂
>   where *SNUM* = $SNUM
> end;
> write (terminal, $NAME).

The database access primitives are in this case the same as in Figure 3.5*b*; however, only one of them is issued by the application. The application written in this way is based on the same level of distribution transparency provided by the DDBMS as the application of Figure 3.5b (i.e., location transparency); however, it is more dependent on the fragmentation schema, because it incorporates the constants "SF" and "LA", which are attribute values used in the fragmentation schema. Therefore, a change of these values affects this application, while it does not affect the application of Figure 3.5b.

Level 3: Local mapping transparency At this level, we assume that the application still refers to objects using names which are independent from the individual local systems; however, it has to specify at which site the objects reside. This is shown in Figure 3.5c. The site names are indicated in the SQL statements by adding an "at" clause to the "from" clause. Clearly, in this case each database access primitive is routed by the DDBMS to a specific site. However, these primitives use site-independent fragment names. If this mapping were not provided, the application would incorporate directly the filenames which are used by the local systems.

The most important aspect of local mapping transparency is not this name-mapping between fragment names and local filenames, but the mapping of the primitives used by the application program into the primitives used by the local DBMS. Therefore, local mapping transparency is an important feature in a heterogeneous DDBMS. Suppose, for example, that the local DBMS at site 1 is IMS and the local DBMS at site 3 is a Codasyl system. In order to provide local mapping transparency, the DDBMS has to transform the database access primitives issued by the application into corresponding IMS and Codasyl programs. Similar translation problems can be found also in a homogeneous DDBMS, because even in homogeneous systems there is a difference between the primitives which are useful at the global level and the primitives of the local DBMS.

Level 4: No transparency We have already shown that local mapping transparency is particularly important but difficult to obtain in a heterogeneous system. Let us therefore see how the application SUPINQUIRY can be written on the distributed database with IMS at site 1 and Codasyl at site 3 if the DDBMS does not support any type of distribution transparency. The application programmer has to code the IMS and Codasyl programs which implement the required functions and install these auxiliary programs at the sites where they are required; the application has to be written with a request for activating these remote auxiliary programs instead of the SQL statements, as shown in Figure 3.6. In this example, we have assumed that the DDBMS accepts an "execute" primitive which specifies which program must be run at which site and which parameters have to be passed. The details of the IMS and Codasyl programs are not shown, because this would require defining the local mapping schemata and entering into several unnecessary details of IMS and Codasyl systems. Note that the variable #FOUND, which was a condition code in the previous examples, has been changed into a parameter $FOUND. This change is motivated by the fact that in this case the DDBMS does not have enough information on the semantics of the primitives to return this type of condition code; the auxiliary application programs will have to determine these conditions and return them explicitly. Again, independently of linguistic details, this example shows another typical advantage of distribution transparency: the

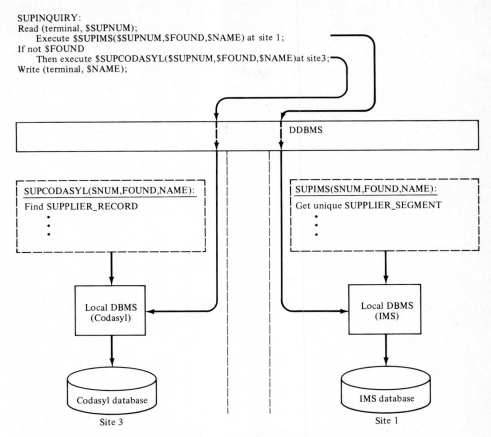

SUPINQUIRY:
Read (terminal, $SUPNUM);
    Execute $SUPIMS($SUPNUM,$FOUND,$NAME) at site 1;
If not $FOUND
      Then execute $SUPCODASYL($SUPNUM,$FOUND,$NAME)at site3;
Write (terminal, $NAME);

DDBMS

SUPCODASYL(SNUM,FOUND,NAME):
Find SUPPLIER_RECORD

SUPIMS(SNUM,FOUND,NAME):
Get unique SUPPLIER_SEGMENT

Local DBMS
(Codasyl)

Local DBMS
(IMS)

Codasyl database

IMS database

Site 3

Site 1

Figure 3.6   An application on a heterogeneous distributed
database without transparency.

DDBMS can determine and manage more conditions autonomously at higher levels
of transparency.

The DDBMS has in the above example the not completely trivial task of activating remote programs and passing parameters between programs which run
on different local DBMSs. Note that a DDBMS can be very useful in developing
distributed database applications even if it does not provide any distribution transparency.

3.3.2 A More Complex Application

The levels of distribution transparency for applications have been presented for a
very simple application which performed the retrieval of data from only one relation; the difference between different levels of distribution transparency is much
more evident if we consider a more complex application which performs a join
operation between two different relations. Let us therefore consider a second application, SUPOFPART, which retrieves the name of the supplier who supplies

a given part; the part number is entered by the user who requests the application. The application is written with the fundamental assumption that each part is supplied by only one supplier.

  Level 1: Fragmentation transparency The way in which the application is written at this level is shown in Figure 3.7a. There is nothing new with respect to the previous application at the same level, except for the fact that now the global query contains a join.

```
read(terminal, $PNUM);
Select NAME into $NAME
from SUPPLIER, SUPPLY
where SUPPLIER.SNUM=SUPPLY.SNUM
      and SUPPLY.PNUM=$PNUM;
write(terminal, $NAME).
```

(a) Fragmentation transparency (level 1)

```
read(terminal, $PNUM);
Select NAME into $NAME
from SUPPLIER, SUPPLY
where SUPPLIER₁.SNUM=SUPPLY₁.SNUM
and SUPPLY₁.PNUM=$PNUM;
if not #FOUND then
        Select NAME into $NAME
        from SUPPLIER₂,SUPPLY₂
        where SUPPLIER₂.SNUM=SUPPLY₂.SNUM
              and SUPPLY₂.PNUM=$PNUM;
write(terminal, $NAME).
```

(b) Location transparency (level 2)

```
read(terminal, $PNUM);
Select SNUM into $SNUM
from SUPPLY₁ at site 3
where PNUM=$PNUM;
if #FOUND then
        begin
            send $SNUM from site 3 to site 1;
            Select NAME into $NAME
            from SUPPLIER₁ at site 1
            where SNUM=$SNUM
        end
else begin
            Select SNUM into $SNUM
            from SUPPLY₂ at site 4
            where PNUM=$PNUM;
            send $SNUM from site 4 to site 2;
            Select NAME into $NAME
            from SUPPLIER₂ at site 2
            where SNUM=$SNUM
        end;
write(terminal, $NAME).
```

(c) Local mapping transparency (level 3)

Figure 3.7 The read-only application SUPOFPART
at different levels of distribution transparency.

Level 2: Location transparency If the system provides only location transparency, then the application can be written in several different ways, which are more or less efficient. A naive solution would consist of four different queries, one for each different pair of *SUPPLIER* and *SUPPLY* fragments, thus applying an exhaustive strategy: each *SUPPLY* fragment is joined with each *SUPPLIER* fragment in order to find the name of the supplier who supplies the requested part number.

A more "clever" solution, shown in Figure 3.7*b*, takes advantage of the information content of the fragmentation schema, namely from the fact that the suppliers of parts stored in $SUPPLY_1$ ($SUPPLY_2$) are stored in $SUPPLIER_1$ ($SUPPLIER_2$). In this way, only two SQL queries are needed instead of four. This program first reads a part number from the terminal, and then it joins fragment $SUPPLIER_1$ with the tuples of fragment $SUPPLY_1$ which have the required part number. If the result of this first query is empty (not #FOUND), then a similar operation is applied to fragments $SUPPLIER_2$ and $SUPPLY_2$. The application assumes at this point that the required supplier name has been found and displays it at the terminal.

This example shows that, in a system which does not provide fragmentation transparency, the application programmer defines the strategy for performing operations like joins (in this case the application programmer decided that two joins between fragments were required instead of four); conversely, the example shows that in order to provide fragmentation transparency, the system must be capable of choosing automatically between different access strategies. The really crucial problem in providing transparency is therefore not the interpretation of a mapping (the fragmentation schema), but the choice of a good access strategy. For example, a DDBMS which provides fragmentation transparency, and allows writing the application SUPOFPART as in Figure 3.7*a*, but then implements the required join by performing four joins between fragments, is very inefficient compared with the performance which can be obtained by a (clever) application programmer.

Level 3: Local mapping transparency Let us consider how the same application SUPOFPART is coded if the DDBMS does not provide location transparency. Assume that the allocation schema of the *SUPPLY* fragments is the following:

$$SUPPLIER_1 : \text{site } 1$$
$$SUPPLIER_2 : \text{site } 2$$
$$SUPPLY_1 : \text{site } 3$$
$$SUPPLY_2 : \text{site } 4$$

The application can now be written as shown in Figure 3.7*c*. This program reads a part number and looks for a supplier of this part in fragment $SUPPLY_1$ at site 3. If the supplier number is found (#FOUND), then the application sends ("send" statement) the supplier number to site 1 in order to find the supplier name in the copy of fragment $SUPPLIER_1$ which is located at site 1; if the supplier number was not found at site 3, then the same operations are repeated on fragment $SUPPLY_2$ at site 4 and on fragment $SUPPLIER_2$ at site 2.

Notice that the SQL queries used in the previous application example, which performed a join between two fragments possibly located at different sites, have been split in this example. In fact, in this example we have assumed that the DDBMS requires each primitive to be executed at only one site, and therefore it cannot perform a join between two fragments which reside at different sites; this is a reasonable assumption for a DDBMS which does not provide location transparency.

The "send" instructions are not strictly necessary; if send primitives were not defined explicitly, then we should assume that the $SNUM variables produced by the first query are implicitly returned to the application and then sent to the execution sites of the second query. The "send" instruction allows direct communication between the sites where the two queries are executed. This can be very important if the intermediate result ($SNUM in this case) is not a single variable but a whole file.

This last application is clearly very dependent on the content of the schemata; any change in the fragmentation and allocation of data requires the modification of the application.

We will not present the application SUPOFPART on a heterogeneous system without local mapping transparency, because this would require dealing with many linguistic details which are not very relevant here.

By comparing the first example application (SUPINQUIRY) with the second one (SUPOFPART) at the level of local mapping transparency, we note that distribution transparency is more important for the application involving a join. Having to rewrite applications like SUPOFPART as a consequence of the migration of a fragment is a very hard task, almost like writing a completely new application.

3.4 DISTRIBUTION TRANPARENCY FOR UPDATE APPLICATIONS

In the previous section, we have considered only applications which performed retrieval of data from the database. In this section we consider applications which also perform distributed database updates. The update problem is considered here only from the viewpoint of distribution transparency for the application programmmer, while the problems of guaranteeing the atomicity of update transactions will be treated in later chapters.

The same levels of distribution transparency which we have analyzed for read only applications can be considered also for update applications. However, an update must be performed on all copies of a data item, while retrieval can be performed on any one copy. This means that if a DDBMS does not provide location and replication transparency, the application programmer has the responsibility of performing all the required updates. Therefore location and replication transparency are even more important for update applications than for read-only applications.

In providing distribution transparency to update applications, there is another problem which is more complex than performing the updates on all copies of a data item. Consider for example what happens if the *CITY* attribute of a supplier is modified. Clearly, the supplier tuple must be moved from one fragment to another. Moreover, in our example database, the tuples of the *SUPPLY* relation which refer to the same supplier also must change fragment, because the *SUPPLY* relation

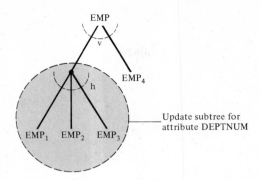

Figure 3.8   The update subtree of the attribute DEPTNUM
in the fragmentation tree of relation EMP.

has a derived fragmentation. It is intuitively clear that changing the value of an
attribute which is used in the definition of the fragmentation schema can have
rather complex effects. The degree to which these effects are managed by the
DDBMS characterizes the level of distribution transparency for updates.

In order to understand which data movement operations are required by an
update of a fragmentation attribute, it is useful to look at the fragmentation tree.

Consider an attribute A which is used in a selection predicate of a horizontal
fragmentation. The **update subtree** of A is the subtree having as root the node
representing the above horizontal fragmentation. For example, we indicate in
Figure 3.8 the update subtree for attribute $DEPTNUM$. The effects of a change of
an attribute are limited to the fragments which are leaves of its update subtree. For
example, a change of attribute $DEPTNUM$ affects only EMP_1, EMP_2, and EMP_3,
but not EMP_4. A tuple can migrate (change fragments) between two of the three
former fragments as a consequence of the update.

In general, the update subtree of an attribute A can be more complex than
the simple one shown in Figure 3.8, and the effect of changing a value of the
attribute A is therefore more complex. For example, suppose that relation EMP
has the fragmentation tree shown in Figure 3.9a. In this case the update subtree
of attribute $DEPTNUM$ is the same as the whole fragmentation tree. The effect
of changing the $DEPTNUM$ value of a tuple having $EMPNUM = 100$ from 3 to
15 is shown in Figure 3.9b. This update is such that the tuple, originally stored
in fragments belonging to the left subtree of Figure 3.9a, becomes then part of the
right subtree. We see that not only the data has been moved between fragments,
but the tuple has also been composed in a different way.

We can now consider the levels of distribution transparency for a simple update
application.

Level 1: Fragmentation transparency   At this level the application program performs its updates as if the database were not distributed; therefore the application programmer need not know whether an attribute is used in the definition
of the fragmentation schema or not. In order to change the $DEPTNUM$ of the

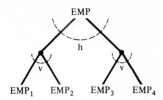

$$EMP_1 = PJ_{EMPNUM,NAME,SAL,TAX}SL_{DEPTNUM < 10}(EMP)$$
$$EMP_2 = PJ_{EMPNUM,MGRNUM,DEPTNUM}SL_{DEPTNUM < 10}(EMP)$$
$$EMP_3 = PJ_{EMPNUM,NAME,DEPTNUM}SL_{DEPTNUM > 10}(EMP)$$
$$EMP_4 = PJ_{EMPNUM,SAL,TAX,MGRNUM}SL_{DEPTNUM > 10}(EMP)$$

(*a*) A different fragmentation and fragmentation tree for relation EMP.

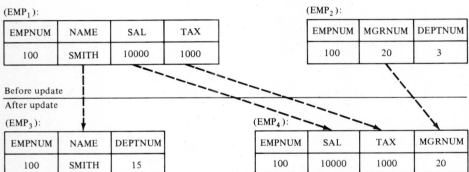

(*b*) Effect of updating DEPTNUM of employee with EMPNUM = 100.

Figure 3.9 An update application.

employee with $EMPNUM = 100$, the programmer writes the application program shown in Figure 3.10a. It is the system's responsibility to perform all the operations which are implicitly required by the fragmentation and allocation schema.

Level 2: Location transparency At this level the application programmer has to deal explicitly with fragments. Assuming the fragmentation of Figure 3.9, the same application is written as in Figure 3.10b. The first two select statements collect the required *EMP* tuple from the fragments where they are stored. The two insert statements compose the tuple in a different way and store it into the two other fragments. The two delete statements delete the old copy of the tuple. Note that the last four statements can be executed in parallel or in any arbitrary order.

The above application has been written under the very simplifying assumption that it has to change exactly the *DEPTNUM* of an employee having $EMPNUM = 100$; however, a real application might be parametric in the *EMPNUM* and *DEPTNUM*, performing something like: Read an employee number and a department number from the terminal and update the department number of the employee having this employee number. In this case the application would be more complex, having to find out in which fragment the tuple of the employee is stored, read the old *DEPTNUM* of the employee, determine whether the change in *DEPTNUM* is such that it changes the fragment to which the tuple belongs, and finally perform the required insertions and deletions. The required insertions and deletions are different for different initial and final fragments to which the tuple belongs, therefore the application has to contain the code for dealing with all the possible alternatives. This example shows how beneficial fragmentation transparency is for the application programmer in the case of update applications, but it shows also implicitly how complex it can be for a DDBMS to provide this feature.

Update *EMP*
set *DEPTNUM*=15
where *EMPNUM*=100.

(a) Fragmentation transparency (level 1)

Select *NAME, SAL, TAX* into $NAME, $SAL, $TAX
from *EMP*₁
where *EMPNUM*=100;
Select *MGRNUM* into $MGRNUM
from *EMP*₂
where *EMPNUM*=100;
Insert into *EMP*₃ (*EMPNUM, NAME, DEPTNUM*):
      (100, $NAME, 15);
Insert into *EMP*₄ (*EMPNUM, SAL, TAX, MGRNUM*):
      (100, $SAL, $TAX, $MGRNUM);
Delete *EMP*₁ where *EMPNUM*=100;
Delete *EMP*₂ where *EMPNUM*=100.

(b) Location transparency (level 2)

Select *NAME, SAL, TAX* into $NAME, $SAL, $TAX
from *EMP*₁ at site 1
where *EMPNUM*=100;
Select *MGRNUM* into $MGRNUM
from *EMP*₂ at site 2
where *EMPNUM*=100;
Insert into *EMP*₃ (*EMPNUM, NAME, DEPTNUM*)
      at site 3: (100, $NAME, 15);
Insert into *EMP*₃ (*EMPNUM, NAME, DEPTNUM*)
      at site 7: (100, $NAME, 15);
Insert into *EMP*₄ (*EMPNUM, SAL, TAX, MGRNUM*)
      at site 4: (100, $SAL, $TAX, $MGRNUM);
Insert into *EMP*₄ (*EMPNUM, SAL, TAX, MGRNUM*)
      at site 8: (100, $SAL, $TAX, $MGRNUM);
Delete *EMP*₁ at site 1 where *EMPNUM*=100;
Delete *EMP*₁ at site 5 where *EMPNUM*=100;
Delete *EMP*₂ at site 2 where *EMPNUM*=100;
Delete *EMP*₂ at site 6 where *EMPNUM*=100.

(c) Local mapping transparency (level 3)

Figure 3.10 An update application at different levels
of distribution transparency.

Level 3: Local mapping transparency At this level the application has to deal explicitly with the location of fragments. In the case of update applications this means that it must take into account replication. Assume that the fragments of relation *EMP* are allocated in the following way:

$$EMP_1 : \text{sites 1 and 5}$$
$$EMP_2 : \text{sites 2 and 6}$$
$$EMP_3 : \text{sites 3 and 7}$$
$$EMP_4 : \text{sites 4 and 8}$$

The above application has to be modified as shown in Figure 3.10c: the two initial selections include an "at" clause for choosing the sites at which to access EMP_1 and EMP_2; the two insert and the two delete statements are replicated in order to insert the new tuples into all copies of the fragment to which they belong and to delete the old tuples from all copies where they were stored.

Finally, we do not present an example for the case without local mapping transparency, since the same considerations that were made in the previous section apply to this case.

3.5 DISTRIBUTED DATABASE ACCESS PRIMITIVES

In the examples of the previous sections, we have always assumed that each database access primitive (query) returned a single value as a result, which was assigned to a simple Pascal variable. However, in general we want to use more powerful primitives, which return entire relations as a result; in this case, the procedural Pascal-like program and the SQL primitives exchange parameters which are not simple variables but whole files (parameter_files). In order to avoid the problem of declaring types, we will use the following approach in our examples: the parameters which have a name which terminates with the suffix "*REL*" will be considered of type "file" by the Pascal-like program and of type "relation" by the SQL statements. For instance, the SQL statement

Select *EMPNUM,NAME* into $EMP\_REL($EMPNUM, $NAME) from *EMP*

returns to the Pascal-like program a file of records; the file name is $EMP_REL, and the records consist of two fields, $EMPNUM and $NAME. The file $EMP_REL contains, of course, the projection of relation *EMP* on attributes *EMPNUM* and *NAME*.

Let us consider different ways in which the programmer can write the same application, and analyze the effect of these alternatives on the efficiency of the application execution. Consider the application which retrieves all parts which are supplied by a set of suppliers. The user specifies the set of suppliers by typing their numbers at the terminal. Assume that each supplier supplies many parts.

A first way of writing this application is shown in Figure 3.11a. The distributed database is accessed at each iteration of the external loop; for each supplier whose number $SNUM is typed by the user, the supplied parts are retrieved into the parameter_file $PNUM_REL. The inner loop scans this parameter_file and displays each part number $PNUM of the selected parts.

The same application can be written as shown in Figure 3.11b. This application first collects all the required supplier numbers and then accesses the database, thus retrieving at once a much larger parameter_file than in the previous example. In this way, the number of distributed database accesses is reduced, the same global amount of result data is transmitted, but less control messages are used. This

```
repeat
     read(terminal, $SNUM);
     Select PNUM into $PNUM_REL($PNUM)
     from SUPPLY
     where SNUM=$SNUM;
     repeat
          read($PNUM_REL, $PNUM);
          write(terminal, $PNUM)
     until END-OF-$PNUM_REL
until END-OF-TERMINAL-INPUT.
```

(a) The database is accessed for each $SNUM value

```
repeat
     read(terminal, $SNUM);
     write($SNUM_REL($SNUM), $SNUM)
until END-OF-TERMINAL-INPUT;
Select PNUM into $PNUM_REL($PNUM)
from SUPPLY, $SNUM_REL
where SUPPLY.SNUM=$SNUM_REL.$SNUM;
repeat
     read($PNUM_REL, $PNUM);
     write(terminal, $PNUM)
until END-OF-$PNUM_REL.
```

(b) The database is accessed after all the values of $SNUM have been collected

```
Select PNUM, SNUM into $TEMP_REL($TEMP_PNUM, $TEMP_SNUM)
from SUPPLY;
repeat
     read(terminal, $SNUM);
     Select $TEMP_PNUM into $TEMP2_REL($TEMP2_PNUM)
     from $TEMP_REL
     where $TEMP_PNUM=$SNUM;
     repeat
          read($TEMP2_REL, $TEMP2_PNUM);
          write(terminal, $TEMP2_PNUM)
     until END-OF-$TEMP2_REL
until END-OF-TERMINAL-INPUT.
```

(c) The database is accessed before collecting the values of $SNUM

Figure 3.11 Different ways of writing an application with fragmentation transparency.

example shows that the programmer can control to some extent the way in which the database is accessed even if he or she operates at the global level. The choice between the two above solutions depends on the number of parts supplied by each supplier and on the number of suppliers to which the application is applied. Clearly, a trade-off between response time and overall system overhead must be considered: if the minimization of the number of messages is desired, then the second solution is better; if rapid response is desired after each supplier number is entered, then the first solution is better. In other words, an application can access larger sets if it is more "batched" and less interactive; this trade-off between more batch and more online solutions is well known also in traditional database applications.

As a final solution, let us consider the one shown in Figure 3.11c. Here, the first query has no input parameters and retrieves into a temporary relation $TEMP\_REL$ all the data which are required to perform the whole application; this is done before knowing which suppliers will really be requested. Assuming that only a small number of *SUPPLY* tuples were retrieved in the two previous cases, this solution requires transmitting much more data. However, this solution can be useful if the application retrieves many *SUPPLY* tuples, because it performs only one distributed database access and then performs retrieval on the temporary relation for a long time. This is often adequate, if the application does not require that the data be completely up to date. The temporary relation represents in this case a static image of the database taken at a given (past) time, which is used for performing a local application. In reference [3.3] portions of the databases with these characteristics are called **snapshots**; they are stored at one site so that read only applications which are not update-sensitive can be executed locally.

A related problem in writing distributed database access primitives, discussed in reference [3.7], is the factorization of **common subexpressions**. Consider, for example, an application which has to retrieve the names of employees who work in the departments of a given area and the part numbers of parts which are stored at departments of the same area. Clearly, there is no relationship between the employee and the parts; therefore, the most natural way of writing this application would be to write two independent queries which are executed one after the other, with the same area as input parameter. This solution is shown in Figure 3.12a. The main disadvantage of this solution is that the set of departments which belong to a given area is determined twice and is possibly transmitted twice between sites. It is very hard to determine automatically from the program of Figure 3.12a that there is a common operation in executing both queries. To make such a determination, it is necessary to isolate the common expression and to determine that the $AREA variable has not changed its value between the two queries. This requires a complex analysis of the procedural program at compile time (note that the problem of finding common subexpressions in a *single* query is much simpler and will be discussed in Chapter 5).

In order to solve the above problem it is necessary to write the application in a different way, for example as shown in Figure 3.12b. The parameter $AREA is passed only once to the DDBMS and has therefore clearly only one common value for both queries. The first query in this solution performs the same retrieval which was performed by each query in the previous solution.

```
read(terminal, $AREA);
. . .
Select NAME into $NAME_REL($NAME)
from EMP, DEPT
where EMP.DEPTNUM=DEPT.DEPTNUM
and DEPT.AREA=$AREA;
. . .
Select PNUM into $PNUM_REL($PNUM)
from SUPPLY, DEPT
where SUPPLY.DEPTNUM=DEPT.DEPTNUM
and DEPT.AREA=$AREA;
. . .
```

(a) Independent queries

```
read(terminal, $AREA);
. . .
Select DEPTNUM into $NUM_REL($DEPTNUM)
from DEPT
where AREA=$AREA;
. . .
Select NAME into $NAME_REL($NAME)
from EMP, $NUM_REL
where EMP.DEPTNUM=$NUM_REL.$DEPTNUM;
. . .
Select PNUM into $PNUM_REL($PNUM)
from SUPPLY, $NUM_REL
where SUPPLY.DEPTNUM=$NUM_REL.$DEPTNUM;
. . .
```

(b) Queries with prior evaluation of a common subexpression

Figure 3.12   Use of common subexpressions in writing applications.

Finally, let us state that if the language interface of the DDBMS does not provide set-oriented, associative operations but only a procedural language, it is possible to attempt the so-called **decompilation**. Decompilation consists in transforming a program written in a procedural language into an equivalent set of nonprocedural queries. Decompilation is a very difficult problem, because it is necessary to derive from the static structure of the programs which data will be accessed at run time. An algorithm for decompiling a large class of Codasyl DML programs into relational queries is proposed in reference [3.6].

3.6 INTEGRITY CONSTRAINTS IN DISTRIBUTED DATABASES

In some database management systems it is possible to specify **integrity constraints**; i.e., assertions on the allowed values of data. Integrity constraints can indicate which data values are allowed (e.g., that ages are integers from 0 to 100) or which transitions are allowed (e.g., that ages cannot decrease); they can involve a single relation or multiple relations. When an update performed by a database application violates an integrity constraint, the application is rejected and thus the correctness of data is preserved.

A typical example of integrity constraint that we have already mentioned in this chapter is referential integrity, which requires that all values of a given attribute of a relation exist also in some other relation. This constraint is particularly useful in distributed databases, for ensuring the correctness of derived fragmentation. For instance, since the *SUPPLY* relation has a fragmentation which is derived from that of the *SUPPLIER* relation by means of a semi-join on the *SUPNUM* attribute, it is required that all values of *SUPNUM* in *SUPPLY* be present also in *SUPPLIER*.

Managing integrity constraints in centralized systems is very difficult and expensive. Therefore, very few systems have built-in capabilities for defining and enforcing integrity constraints; thus, it is often the application programmer's responsability to write applications which preserve the correctness of data. However, a clear specification of constraints can be useful, even if they are not directly supported by the systems, in order to write applications correctly.

Integrity constraints can be enforced automatically by adding to application programs some code for testing whether the constraint is violated. If so, the program execution is suspended and all actions already performed by it are cancelled, if necessary. Let us consider, for instance, the deletion of a tuple from the *SUPPLIER* relation. In SQL, we can express this application as:

> Delete *
> from *SUPPLIER*
> where *SNUM* = $SNUM

(* indicates the entire tuple). This operation could violate the above referential integrity constraint. In order to verify that the constraint is not violated, it is possible to modify the program as follows:

> Select $SNUM
> from *SUPPLY*
> where *SNUM* = $SNUM;
> if not #FOUND then
>   Delete *
>   from *SUPPLIER*
>   where *SNUM* = $SNUM

The first SQL query attempts to retrieve tuples from the *SUPPLY* relation with the same supplier number as the original application; if #FOUND is false, there are no tuples in the *SUPPLY* relation referring to the tuples to be deleted, so it is safe to proceed with deleting the specified tuples in the *SUPPLIER* relation as done unconditionally in the original application.

This example applies both to centralized databases and to distributed databases in which the system provides fragmentation transparency. In this case, integrity constraints are defined using global relations; the composition of application programs with the code for testing integrity is done at the global level. If, instead, global applications are written at lower levels of transparency, then this composition is more difficult and depends on the fragmentation and allocation of data.

One of the most serious disadvantages of integrity constraints is the loss in performance which is due to the execution of the integrity tests; this loss is very important in distributed databases. Assume, for instance, that *SUPPLY* and *SUPPLIER* are allocated as described in Section 3.3.2 (application SUPOFPART); then, the SQL query which is added for performing the test, operating on *SUPPLY*, must be transmitted to sites 3 and 4, while the original application would require accessing only the relation *SUPPLIER* at sites 1 and 2.

The management of integrity constraints in distributed databases has not yet been fully investigated; most likely, the techniques which are required for a distributed environment are not very different from those which are required in a centralized system, especially if the distributed database provides fragmentation transparency (and it is very unreasonable to attempt developing integrity constraints at a lower level of transparency). The major problem in applying integrity checking to distributed databases is the overall performance of the system. Since testing integrity might increase the need of accessing remote sites (as the above example shows), it is necessary to consider also integrity checking in the design of the distribution of the database.

CONCLUSIONS

Distribution transparency provides the independence of programs from the distribution of the database. Different levels of distribution transparency can be provided by a DDBMS; at each level, different aspects of the real distribution of data are hidden from the application programmers. At the highest level, called fragmentation transparency, a modification of data distribution does not require rewriting programs. Providing distribution transparency for update applications is more complex than for read-only applications, because update applications can modify the values of fragmentation attributes; in this case, a rather complex restructuring of affected data might be required.

EXERCISES

3.1   Consider the global relations:

PATIENT(NUMBER, NAME, SSN, AMOUNT-DUE, DEPT,
DOCTOR, MED-TREATMENT)

DEPARTMENT(DEPT, LOCATION, DIRECTOR)

STAFF(STAFFNUM, DIRECTOR, TASK)

Define their fragmentation as follows:

(a) DEPARTMENT has a horizontal fragmentation by LOCATION, with two locations; each department is conducted by one DIRECTOR.

(b) There are several staffs members for each department, led by the department's director. STAFF has a horizontal fragmentation derived from that of DEPARTMENT and a semi-join on the DIRECTOR attribute. Which assumption is required in order to assure completeness? And disjointness?

(c) PATIENT has a mixed fragmentation: attributes NUMBER, NAME, SSN, and AMOUNT-DUE constitute a vertical fragment used for accounting purposes; attributes NUMBER, NAME, DEPT, DOCTOR, and MED-TREATMENT constitute a vertical fragment used for describing cares. This last fragment has a horizontal fragmentation derived from that of DEPARTMENT and a semi-join on the DEPT attribute. Which assumption is required in order to assure completeness? And disjointness?

Give also the reconstruction of global relations from fragments.

3.2 Consider the following global, fragmentation, and allocation schemata:

Global schema : STUDENT(NUMBER, NAME, DEPT)

Fragmentation schema : $STUDENT_1 = \mathbf{SL}_{DEPT=\text{“EE”}}\ STUDENT$

$STUDENT_2 = \mathbf{SL}_{DEPT=\text{“CS”}}\ STUDENT$

Allocation schema : $STUDENT_1$ at sites 1,2

$STUDENT_2$ at sites 3,4

(Assume that "EE" and "CS" are the only possible values for DEPT).

(a) Write an application that requires the student number from the terminal and outputs the name and department, at levels 1, 2, and 3 of transparency.

(b) Write an application that moves the student having number 232 from department "EE" to department "CS", at levels 1, 2, and 3 of transparency.

(c) Write an application that moves a student whose number and department are given at the terminal to the other department, at level 2 of transparency.

(d) Consider the case in which application 1 is repeated for many possible values of the student number. Write the application

* Accessing the database for each student number given at the terminal
* Accessing the database after having collected several inputs from the terminal
* Accessing the database before collecting inputs from the terminal

(e) Write application (a) for a heterogeneous database, using (at least) two database languages that you know. Describe the local schemata, the local applications, and the global application.

3.3 Write, at level 2 of transparency, the application on EXAMPLE_DDB which moves supplier 157 from "SF" to "LA". (Hint: Consider also SUPPLY information; use the SQL statement: "INSERT INTO relation-name : QUERY".)

Annotated Bibliography

This chapter is inspired by the approaches which have been proposed in several distributed database systems. In particular, the SDD-1 and R* systems deal with the problems of fragmentation, transparency, and user interfaces. References [3.1] and [3.2] illustrate their approaches to these problems. Reference [3.4] is on the problem of distribution transparency for update applications. Reference [3.6] deals with decompilation. References [3.8] and [3.9] deal with integrity constraints in distributed databases.

[3.1]   J. B. Rothnie et al., "Introduction to a System for Distributed Databases (SDD-1)," *ACM-TODS*, **5**:1, 1980.

[3.2]   B. G. Lindsay, "Object Naming and Catalog Management for a Distributed Database Manager," *Proc. Second Int. Conf. on Distributed Computing Systems*, Paris, 1981.

[3.3]   M. Adiba and B. G. Lindsay, "Database Snapshots," *Sixth VLDB*, Montreal, 1980.

This paper describes the use of database snapshots, i.e. of selected portions of the database which are evaluated at a given time and stored into temporary relations. Queries can be addressed to snaphots; in this case, the query views the database "as of" an earlier time. Snapshots can be "refreshed" (or reevaluated) periodically; moreover, it is possible to keep them up to date by applying the updates to the original relations also to them. Snapshots are extremely useful in distributed databases, because the cost of maintaining replicated data up to date and consistent is high; many applications do not require reading the latest version of the database, and can read data from local snapshots.

[3.4]   E. Bertino, C. Meghini, G. Pelagatti, and C. Thanos, "The Update Problem in the Distributed System Hermes/1," *Proc. Second ICOD Conf.*, London, 1983.

[3.5]   S. Ceri and G. Pelagatti, "Correctness of Query Execution Strategies in Distributed Databases," *ACM-TODS*, **8**:4, 1983.

This paper deals with translation problems from the user application to an access plan and will be described in detail in Chapter 5 (as reference [5.6]); however, it includes also a treatment of fragmentation which is very similar to the one in this chapter.

[3.6]   R. H. Katz and E. Wong, "Decompiling Codasyl DML into Relational Queries," *ACM-TODS*, **7**:1, 1982.

[3.7]   S. Finkelstein, "Common Expression Analysis in Database Applications," *ACM-SIGMOD*, 1982.

This paper analyzes in depth the usage of temporaries for answering multiple queries. For instance, the paper considers the possibility of using the answer to a query about ships in the Mediterranean for answering a query about French ships in the Mediterranean. The answer to the first query can be "further restricted" to generate the answer of the second one; a formal model is presented that allows relating queries and determining when one of them is an "upper bound" of another; i.e., the former can be used for answering the latter. Of course, it is possible to take advantage of this notion if the result of the former query is stored in a temporary relation.

[3.8]   R. El-Masri, "Semantic Integrity in DDTS (Distributed Database Testbed System)," Honeywell CCSC, Tech. Rep. HR-80-274, Bloomington, Minnesota, 1980.

[3.9]   C. Parent, "Integrity in Distributed Databases," *Proc. AICA 77*, Pisa, 1977.

Chapter 4

Distributed Database Design

Since distributed databases are now at an early stage, very little experience exists about how they should be designed. However, it is clear that designing a distributed database is very difficult, since many technical and organizational issues, which are crucial in the design of single-site databases, become more difficult in a multiple-site system. From the technical viewpoint, new problems arise such as the interconnection of sites by a computer network and the optimal distribution of data and applications to the sites for meeting the requirements of applications and for optimizing performances. From the organizational viewpoint, the issue of decentralization is crucial, since distributed systems typically substitute for large, centralized systems, and in this case distributing an application has a major impact on the organization.

In spite of limited experiences in the design of distributed systems, this problem has been extensively studied as an advanced research area, mostly from a technical viewpoint, and many contributions can be found in the literature. The mathematical problem of optimally distributing data over a computer network has been widely analyzed in the context of distributed file systems and, more recently, in the context of distributed databases. The major outcomes of this research are twofold:

1. Several design criteria have been established about how data can be conveniently distributed.

2. Mathematical foundation has been given to "design aids" that, in the near future, will help the designer in determining data distribution.

This chapter is organized as follows: In Section 4.1 we introduce a framework for the design of distributed databases, by stressing *what* should be designed. We also indicate the *objectives* of the design of data distribution, and we present a top-down and a bottom-up approach. In the rest of the chapter, we will concentrate on the top-down approach.

In Section 4.2 we deal with the design of horizontal and vertical fragments, giving empirical criteria that can lead to determining them; in this context, we introduce the notion of a distributed join between fragmented relations, and we show that the choice of fragmentation criteria can be very useful for simplifying distributed joins.

In Section 4.3 we deal with the allocation of fragments; in terms of our reference model, this problem corresponds to determining the mapping between fragments and physical images. We present the principles and concepts in fragment allocation, followed by simple formulas for evaluating costs and benefits of allocations; reference to existing models for optimal data allocation can be found in the annotated bibliography.

4.1 A FRAMEWORK FOR DISTRIBUTED DATABASE DESIGN

The term "distributed database design" has a very broad and unprecise meaning. In this chapter, we concentrate on those aspects which are peculiar to distributed databases, while we do not present design problems which are faced also in the design of centralized databases. The design of a centralized database amounts to:

1. Designing the "conceptual schema" which describes the integrated database (i.e., all the data which are used by the database applications).
2. Designing the "physical database," i.e., mapping the conceptual schema to storage areas and determining appropriate access methods.

In a distributed database these two problems become the design of the global schema and the design of the local physical databases at each site; the techniques which can be applied to these problems are the same as in centralized databases (an overview of these techniques can be found in reference [4.1]). The distribution of the database adds to the above problems two new ones:

3. Designing the fragmentation, i.e., determining how global relations are subdivided into horizontal, vertical, or mixed fragments.
4. Designing the allocation of fragments, i.e., determining how fragments are mapped to physical images; in this way, also the replication of fragments is determined.

These two problems fully characterize the design of data distribution. Fragmentation design has been studied only in recent times, since fragmentation has been established as a distinguishing feature of distributed databases; it had, however, been partially analyzed in the context of centralized systems with multiple storage devices. The allocation problem has instead been studied extensively since the development of distributed file systems, and is typically regarded in the literature as the "file allocation problem."

The distinction between these two problems is conceptually relevant, since the first one deals with the "logical criteria" which motivate the fragmentation of a global relation, while the second one deals with the "physical" placement of data at the various sites. However, this distinction must be introduced with extreme care;

in general, it is not possible to determine the optimal fragmentation and allocation by solving the two problems independently, since they are interrelated.

Although the design of application programs is made after the design of schemata, the knowledge of application requirements influences schema design, since schemata must be able to support applications efficiently. Thus, in the design of a distributed database, sufficiently precise knowledge of application requirements is needed; clearly, this knowledge is required only for the more "important" applications, i.e., those which will be executed frequently or whose performances are critical. In the application requirements we include:

1.   The site from which the application is issued (also called **site of origin** of the application).
2.   The frequency of activation of the application (i.e., the number of activation requests in the unit time); in the general case of applications which can be issued at multiple sites, we need to know the frequency of activation of each application at each site.
3.   The number, type, and the statistical distribution of accesses made by each application to each required data "object."

Characterizing these features is not trivial; moreover, consider that these data are typically given for global relations and must be properly translated into terms which apply to fragments; since fragmentation is produced as a result of design and is not known a priori, these data must be known for all fragmentation alternatives which are considered during design.

4.1.1 Objectives of the Design of Data Distribution

In the design of data distribution, the following objectives should be taken into account:

Processing locality   Distributing data to maximize processing locality corresponds to the simple principle of placing data as close as possible to the applications which use them. In Chapter 1, we have indicated that achieving processing locality is one of the major goals of a distributed database. The simplest way of characterizing processing locality is to consider two types of references to data: "local" references and "remote" references. Clearly, once the sites of origin of applications are known, locality and remoteness of references depend only on data distribution.

Designing data distribution for maximizing processing locality (or, conversely, for minimizing remote references) can be done by adding the number of local and remote references corresponding to each candidate fragmentation and fragment allocation, and selecting the best solution among them.

An extension to this simple optimization criterion is to take into account when an application has **complete locality**. We use this term to designate those applications which can be completely executed at their sites of origin. The advantage of complete locality is not only the reduction of remote accesses, but also the increased simplicity in controlling the execution of the application.

Availability and reliability of distributed data In Chapter 1 we have indicated availability and reliability as advantages of distributed systems versus nondistributed ones. A high degree of availability for read-only applications is achieved by storing multiple copies of the same information; the system must be able to switch to an alternative copy when the one that should be accessed under normal conditions is not available.

Reliability is also achieved by storing multiple copies of the same information, since it is possible to recover from crashes or from the physical destruction of one of the copies by using the other, still available copies. Since physical destruction can be caused by events which have nothing to do with computer crashes (such as fire, earthquake, or sabotage), it is relevant to store replicated copies in geographically dispersed locations.

Workload distribution Distributing the workload over the sites is an important feature of distributed computer systems. Workload distribution is done in order to take advantage of the different powers or utilizations of computers at each site, and to maximize the degree of parallelism of execution of applications. Since workload distribution might negatively affect processing locality, it is necessary to consider the trade-off between them in the design of data distribution.

Storage costs and availability Database distribution should reflect the cost and availability of storage at the different sites. It is possible to have specialized sites in the network for data storage, or conversely to have sites which do not support mass storage at all. Typically, the cost of data storage is not relevant if compared with CPU, I/O, and transmission costs of applications, but the limitation of available storage at each site must be considered.

Using all the above criteria at the same time is extremely difficult, since this leads to complex optimization models. It is possible to consider some of the above features as constraints, rather than objectives (for instance, it is possible to formulate constraints on the maximum amount of workload or the maximum available storage at each site). Alternatively, it is possible to consider the most important criterion in the initial design and to introduce other criteria in the postoptimization.

In the following, we will use the simple approach of maximizing processing locality; this objective is adequate to indicate design criteria which are general and of practical use.

4.1.2 Top-Down and Bottom-Up Approaches to the Design of Data Distribution

There are two alternative approaches to the design of data distribution, the top-down and the bottom-up approaches.

In the top-down approach, we start by designing the global schema, and we proceed by designing the fragmentation of the database, and then by allocating the fragments to the sites, creating the physical images. The approach is completed by performing, at each site, the "physical design" of the data which are allocated to it.

This approach is the most attractive for systems which are developed from scratch, since it allows performing the design rationally. Therefore, this approach will be followed in the rest of this chapter. However, we will not discuss the techniques which can be used for designing a global and a physical schema, since they are not peculiar to a distributed database. We will deal instead with the design of fragmentation and the allocation of fragments in Sections 4.2 and 4.3.

When the distributed database is developed as the aggregation of existing databases, it is not easy to follow the top-down approach. In fact, in this case the global schema is often produced as a compromise between existing data descriptions. It is even possible that each pair of existing databases is independently interfaced using a different translation schema, without the notion of a global schema; this, however, leads to systems which are different in conception from our reference architecture.

When existing databases are aggregated, a bottom-up approach to the design of data distribution can be used. This approach is based on the **integration** of existing schemata into a single, global schema. By integration, we mean the merging of common data definitions and the resolution of conflicts among different representations given to the same data.

It should be noticed that the bottom-up approach lends itself less easily to the development of horizontally fragmented relations. In fact, horizontal fragments of a same global relation must have the same relation schema; this feature is easily enforced in a top-down design, while it is difficult to "discover" it a posteriori, on independently designed databases which are then integrated. Since horizontal fragments are a relevant and useful feature of a distributed database, the integration process should attempt to modify the definitions of local relations, so that they can be regarded as horizontal fragments of a common, global relation.

When existing databases are aggregated into a distributed database, it is possible that they use different DBMSs. As we have briefly discussed in Chapters 1 and 3, a heterogeneous system adds to the complexity of data integration the need for a **translation** between different representations. In this case, it is possible to make a one-to-one translation between each pair of different DBMSs; however, the approach which is mostly used in the prototypes of heterogeneous systems is to select a common data model, and then to translate into this unique representation all the different schemata of the involved DBMSs.

In summary, the bottom-up design of a distributed database requires:

1. The **selection of a common database model** for describing the global schema of the database.
2. The **translation** of each local schema into the common data model.
3. The **integration** of the local schemata into a common global schema.

Thus, the bottom-up approach requires solving three problems which are not peculiar to distributed databases, but are present also in centralized systems; references [4.2] to [4.8] deal with these problems in a nondistributed environment. Therefore, the bottom-up design is not treated in this chapter. However, since the above three problems are particularly important in heterogeneous distributed systems, they will be briefly reviewed in Chapter 15, which deals with heterogeneous DDBMSs.

4.2 THE DESIGN OF DATABASE FRAGMENTATION

The design of fragmentation is the first problem that must be solved in the top-down design of data distribution. The purpose of fragmentation design is to determine nonoverlapping fragments which are "logical units of allocation," i.e., that are appropriate startpoints for the following data allocation problem.

Clearly, tuples or attributes of relations cannot be considered as individual "units of allocation," since the allocation problem would become unmanageable. Designing fragments consists in grouping tuples (in the case of horizontal fragmentation) or attributes (in the case of vertical fragmentation) which have the "same properties" from the viewpoint of their allocation. Each group of tuples or attributes having the "same properties" will constitute a fragment. The basic idea is that if any two elements of the same fragment have the "same properties" from the viewpoint of their allocation, any method used for allocating data will put them together; thus, the fragments which are obtained in this way are appropriate units of allocation. We must now make clear what we mean by "same properties" of the elements of fragments.

Example 4.1
Consider the determination of horizontal fragments for a global relation *EMP*. Assume that the important applications of this distributed database require information from relation *EMP* about employees who are members of projects. Let each department be a site of the distributed database.

Applications can be issued at any department; however, when they are issued at a given department, they reference the tuples of employees of that department with higher probability than the tuples of other employees. This happens because existing employees are distributed in departments, because each project is made in one department, and because information about projects is typically requested by employees who work in the project. Then, in this simple case, fragments are designed by collecting in each fragment the tuples of employees who work at the same department; these tuples have the same properties from the viewpoint of their allocation.

Let us introduce also a simple example of a vertical fragmentation for relation *EMP*. Assume that attributes *SAL* and *TAX* are used only by administrative applications, which always use these attributes together. Then, the pair *SAL,TAX* is an appropriate vertical fragment.

Notice that the site of origin of each application is relevant for determining the locality properties for an appropriate definition of fragments; we therefore regard applications issued at different sites as different applications, even if they perform the same function.

In the following, we examine horizontal, vertical, and mixed fragmentation independently. As we have already observed, it is conceptually correct first to determine fragmentation and then to allocate fragments; however, we will be able to follow this approach "neatly" only in horizontal fragmentation, while we will need to take into account also the final allocation in performing vertical fragmentation.

4.2.1 Horizontal Fragmentation

In Chapter 3, we have introduced two types of horizontal fragmentation, called primary and derived; derived fragmentation is defined in terms of primary fragmentation; therefore we deal with primary fragmentation first.

Determining the horizontal fragmentation of a database amounts to determining both "logical" properties of data, such as the fragmentation predicates, and "statistical" properties of data, such as the number of references of applications to fragments; this coordination of logical and statistical aspects is rather difficult.

4.2.1.1 Primary fragmentation   Recall that primary horizontal fragments are defined using selections on global relations; the correctness of primary fragmentation requires that each tuple of the global relation be selected in one and only one fragment. Thus, determining the primary fragmentation of a global relation requires determining a set of disjoint and complete selection predicates. The property that we require for each fragment is that the elements of them must be referenced homogeneously by all the applications.

Let R be the global relation for which we want to produce a horizontal primary fragmentation. We introduce the following definitions:

1.　A **simple predicate** is a predicate of the type:

$$\text{Attribute} = \text{value}$$

2.　A **minterm predicate** y for a set P of simple predicates is the conjunction of *all* predicates appearing in P, either taken in natural form or negated, provided that this expression is not a contradiction. Thus:

$$y = \bigwedge_{p_i \in p} p_i^*$$

where $(p_i^* = p_i$ or $p_i^* = \text{NOT } p_i)$ and $y \neq \text{false}$

3.　A **fragment** is the set of all tuples for which a minterm predicate holds.

4.　A simple predicate p_i is **relevant** with respect to a set P of simple predicates if there exist at least two minterm predicates of P whose expression differs only in the predicate p_i itself (which appears in the natural form in one case and negated in the other one) such that the corresponding fragments are referenced in a different way by at least one application.

Example 4.2
Consider Example 4.1 on horizontal fragmentation. Assume that some important applications require, as in Example 4.1, information about employees who are members of projects; assume that there are also other important applications which require only the data of employees who are programmers; these last applications can be issued at any site of the distributed database, and reference all programmers with the same probability. Let us assume for simplicity that there are only two departments, 1 and 2; thus, $DEPT = 1$ is equivalent to $DEPT \neq 2$, and vice

versa. Two simple predicates for this example are $DEPT = 1$ and $JOB =$ "P" (programmer). The minterm predicates for these two predicates are

$$DEPT = 1 \text{ AND } JOB = \text{ "P"}$$
$$DEPT = 1 \text{ AND } JOB \neq \text{ "P"}$$
$$DEPT \neq 1 \text{ AND } JOB = \text{ "P"}$$
$$DEPT \neq 1 \text{ AND } JOB \neq \text{ "P"}$$

All the above simple predicates are relevant, while, for instance, $SAL > 50$ is not a relevant predicate; in fact, if we partition any of the fragments corresponding to one of the above minterm predicates in two parts having either $SAL > 50$ or $SAL \leq 50$, then each one of the two fragments obtained in this way is referenced in the same way by all applications.

The above definitions are not constructive; we still don't know how to build fragmentation. Unfortunately, the selection of predicates cannot be helped too much by precise rules, since understanding that a predicate is useful for describing fragmentation relies mostly on the intuition of the database designer. However, we can define two properties which characterize an appropriate fragmentation.

Let $P = \{p_1, p_2, \ldots, p_n\}$ be a set of simple predicates. In order for P to represent fragmentation correctly and efficiently, P must be complete and minimal.

1. We say that a set P of predicates is **complete** if and only if any two tuples belonging to the same fragment are referenced with the same probability by any application.
2. We say that the set P is **minimal** if all its predicates are relevant.

Example 4.3
The previous Examples 4.1 and 4.2 can be used for clarifying these definitions. $P_1 = \{DEPT = 1\}$ is not complete, since the applications reference tuples of programmers with a greater probability within each fragment produced by P_1. The set $P_2 = \{DEPT = 1, JOB = \text{"P"}\}$ is complete and minimal. The set $P_3 = \{DEPT = 1, JOB = \text{"P"}, SAL > 50\}$ is complete but not minimal, since $SAL > 50$ is not relevant.

Fragmentation can be produced with the following method:

Basis Consider a predicate p_1 which partitions the tuples of R into two parts which are referenced differently by at least one application. Let $P = p_1$.

Method Consider a new simple predicate p_i which partitions at least one fragment of P into two parts which are referenced in a different way by at least one application. Set $P \leftarrow P \bigcup p_i$. Eliminate nonrelevant predicates from P. Repeat this step until the set of the minterm fragments of P is complete.

Example 4.4
This example is the continuation of Examples 4.1, 4.2, and 4.3; its purpose is to show an application of the above method, and also to show that the elimination of nonrelevant predicates from P, required by the method, is in fact necessary in some cases.

Let us consider as the first predicate $SAL > 50$; we can assume that programmers have, on the average, a salary greater than 50, and therefore this predicate determines two sets of employees who are referenced differently by the applications (notice that we are asserting the relevance of the predicate $SAL > 50$ with respect to the set $P1 = \{SAL > 50\}$).

We consider then $DEPT = 1$; this predicate is relevant and is added to the previous one, giving the set $P2 = \{SAL > 50, DEPT = 1\}$.

Finally, we consider $JOB = $ "P". The predicate is relevant, and we build initially the set $P3 = \{SAL > 50, DEPT = 1, JOB = $ "P"$\}$. We then discover that $SAL > 50$ is not relevant in $P3$ (see Example 4.2); thus, we obtain the final set $P4 = \{DEPT = 1, JOB = $ "P"$\}$, which is complete and minimal.

Notice that determining a complete set of predicates might be too expensive in some cases; for instance, this happens when predicates introduced for describing references by different applications use different criteria. In this case, fragments correspond to the cross-products of the criteria. In fact, this search for a complete set of predicates must be done in a "reasonable" way, by:

1. Concentrating on a few important applications
2. Not distinguishing fragments whose features are very similar

General example

In this and the next subsections we develop a general example, based on the global relations of EXAMPLE_DDB of Chapter 3. Consider the distributed database for a company in California having three sites at San Francisco (site 1), Fresno (site 2), and Los Angeles (site 3); Fresno is located about halfway between San Francisco and Los Angeles. There are 30 departments, physically grouped as follows: the first 10 are close to San Francisco, departments between 11 and 20 are close to Fresno, and departments over 20 are close to Los Angeles. Suppliers of the company are all either in the city of San Francisco or in the city of Los Angeles; there is also the notion of areas into which the company is divided; the area "North" includes San Francisco, the area "South" includes Los Angeles, and Fresno falls exactly on the border, with some departments close to Fresno in the northern area and some in the southern. Figure 4.1 represents this example.

The global schema is that of EXAMPLE_DDB, including relations *EMP*, *DEPT*, *SUPPLIER*, and *SUPPLY*. We design the fragmentation of *SUPPLIER* and *DEPT* with a primary fragmentation.

We start by analyzing the relation *SUPPLIER(SNUM,NAME,CITY)*. City assumes just two values, "SF" and "LA"; *SUPPLIERS* in "SF" or "LA" are about the same in number. Let us assume that there is just one important application, requiring the *NAME* of suppliers with a given number *SNUM*. A SQL query for this application is:

Select *NAME*
from *SUPPLIER*
where *SNUM* = $X

This application is issued at any one of the sites; if it is issued at site 1, it references *SUPPLIERS* whose *CITY* is "SF" with 80 percent probability; if it is issued at site 2, it references *SUPPLIERS* of "SF" and "LA" with equal probability; if it is issued at site 3, it references *SUPPLIERS* of "LA" with 80 percent probability. This comes from the fact that departments around one city tend to use suppliers which are close to them.

Figure 4.1 A geographically distributed company.

We can apply to this simple case the method for producing the predicates:

- $p_1 : CITY = $ "SF"
- $p_2 : CITY = $ "LA"

Since the set $\{ p_1, p_2 \}$ is complete and minimal, the search is terminated.

Though simple, this example shows two important features:

1. The predicates which are relevant for describing this fragmentation cannot be deduced by analyzing the code of an application; in our example, the values of $CITY$ generate the predicates, and there is no reference to them in the query.

2. Implications between predicates reduce the number of fragments. In this case, we should consider as fragments those which correspond to the following minterm predicates:

$$y_1 : (CITY = \text{“SF”}) \text{ AND } (CITY = \text{“LA”})$$
$$y_2 : (CITY = \text{“SF”}) \text{ AND NOT } (CITY = \text{“LA”})$$
$$y_3 : \text{NOT} (CITY = \text{“SF”}) \text{ AND } (CITY = \text{“LA”})$$
$$y_4 : \text{NOT} (CITY = \text{“SF”}) \text{ AND NOT } (CITY = \text{“LA”})$$

but we know that:

$$(CITY = \text{“LA”}) \Rightarrow \text{NOT}(CITY = \text{“SF”})$$

and

$$(CITY = \text{“SF”}) \Rightarrow \text{NOT}(CITY = \text{“LA”})$$

and therefore we can infer that y_1 and y_4 are contradictions, and y_2 and y_3 reduce to the two predicates p_1 and p_2.

Let us consider now the global relation:

$$DEPT(DEPTNUM, NAME, AREA, MGRNUM)$$

We concentrate on the following important applications:

1. Administrative applications, which are issued only at sites 1 and 3; administrative applications about departments in the northern area are issued at site 1; those about departments in the southern area are issued at site 3.
2. Applications about work conducted at each department; they can be issued at any department, but they reference tuples of the departments which are closer to their site of origin with higher probability than the tuples of other departments.

By applying the same method, we produce the following set of predicates:

$$p_1 : DEPTNUM \le 10$$
$$p_2 : 10 < DEPTNUM \le 20$$
$$p_3 : DEPTNUM > 20$$
$$p_4 : AREA = \text{``North''}$$
$$p_5 : AREA = \text{``South''}$$

There are a number of implications between them (for instance, $AREA = $ "North" implies that $DEPTNUM > 20$ is false); thus, the fragmentation that they introduce reduces to four fragments:

$$y_1 : DEPTNUM \le 10$$
$$y_2 : (10 < DEPTNUM \le 20)\,\text{AND}\,(AREA = \text{``North''})$$
$$y_3 : (10 < DEPTNUM \le 20)\,\text{AND}\,(AREA = \text{``South''})$$
$$y_4 : DEPTNUM > 20$$

	p_4: $AREA = $ "North"	p_5: $AREA = $ "South"
p_1: $DEPTNUM \le 10$	y_1	FALSE
p_2: $10 < DEPTNUM \le 20$	y_2	y_3
p_3: $DEPTNUM > 20$	FALSE	y_4

Figure 4.2 Fragmentation of relation $DEPT$.

This fragmentation is represented in Figure 4.2, where rows have predicates p_1, p_2, and p_3 and columns have predicates p_4 and p_5. Areas represent the conjunction of predicates; four of them correspond to the above fragments, while two of them correspond to contradictions.

As a final remark on this example, let us anticipate the discussion about fragment allocation; clearly, fragments corresponding to y_1 and y_4 can be easily allocated at sites 1 and 3. The allocation of fragments y_2 and y_3 presents instead a trade-off between administrative applications, which would like fragments to be allocated at site 1 or 3, and applications about department work, which would like fragments to be allocated at site 2. The trade-off will be solved in the next section, which deals with fragment allocation. We stress again that fragments y_2 and y_3 are appropriate "units" for the allocation problem.

4.2.1.2 Derived horizontal fragmentation
The derived horizontal fragmentation of a global relation R is not based on properties of its own attributes, but is derived from the horizontal fragmentation of another relation. Derived fragmentation is used to facilitate the join between fragments.

A **distributed join** is a join between horizontally fragmented relations. When an application requires the join between two global relations R and S, all the tuples of R and S need to be compared; thus, in principle, it is necessary to compare all the fragments R_i of R with all the fragments S_j of S. However, sometimes it is possible to deduce that some of the partial joins R_i **JN** S_j are intrinsically empty. This happens when, for a given data distribution, values of the join attribute in R_i and S_j are disjoint.

A distributed join is represented efficiently using **join graphs**. The join graph G of the distributed join R **JN** S is a graph $\langle N, E \rangle$, where nodes N represent fragments of R and S and nondirected edges between nodes represent joins between fragments which are not intrinsically empty. For simplicity, we do not include in N those fragments of R or S which have an empty join with all fragments of the other relation. An example of a join graph is presented in Figure 4.3a.

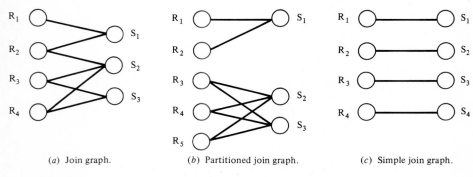

    (a) Join graph.   (b) Partitioned join graph.   (c) Simple join graph.

Figure 4.3   Join graphs.

We say that a join graph is **total** when it contains all possible edges between fragments of R and S; it is **reduced** when some of the edges between fragments of R and fragments of S are missing. Two types of reduced join graphs are particularly relevant:

1.   A reduced join graph is **partitioned** if the graph is composed of two or more subgraphs without edges between them (Figure 4.3b).

2. A reduced join graph is **simple** if it is partitioned and each subgraph has just one edge (Figure 4.3c).

Determining that a join has a simple join graph is very important in database design. A pair of fragments which are connected by an edge in a simple join graph have a common set of values of join attributes. Therefore, if it is possible to determine the fragmentation and allocation of the two operand relations R and S so that the join graph is simple and corresponding pairs of fragments are allocated at the same site, then the join can be performed in a distributed way, by locally joining pairs of fragments and then collecting the results of these partial joins. Therefore, it is important to design the distributed database so that joins which are performed very often have a simple join graph.

We can now consider derived fragmentation in this respect. Consider a global relation R whose fragments R_i are derived from the fragmentation of S by a semi-join, as we have shown in Chapter 3:

$$R_i = R \, \mathbf{SJ}_F \, S_i$$

Let the conditions of Chapter 3 about disjointness and completeness of fragmentation hold. Then, the join $R \, \mathbf{JN}_F \, S$ is simple. Thus, the basic idea is to consider derived fragmentation of relations as an alternative to primary fragmentation; this is extremely convenient when the derivation is made with a semi-join condition F that is the same as that of a join used by many applications.

Also partitioned join graphs have useful properties, because they can be optimized more easily using the techniques which will be presented in Chapter 6. It is therefore convenient to define fragmentation so that joins which are performed very often, and for which it is not possible to have a simple join graph, have a partitioned join graph.

General example (continued)

Consider now the relation $SUPPLY$ ($SNUM, PNUM, DEPTNUM, QUAN$). Let the applications which use this relation be such that $SUPPLY$ is always used together with another relation; more precisely:

* Some applications require information about supplies of given suppliers; thus, they join $SUPPLY$ and $SUPPLIER$ on the $SNUM$ attribute.
* The other applications require information about supplies at a given department; thus, they join $SUPPLY$ and $DEPT$ on the $DEPTNUM$ attribute.

Let us assume that global relation $DEPT$ is horizontally fragmented according to values taken by the attribute $DEPTNUM$ and that $SUPPLIER$ is horizontally fragmented according to values taken by the attribute $SNUM$. There are two possible derived fragmentations for relation $SUPPLY$: one through the semi-join with $SUPPLIER$ on $SNUM$ and one through the semi-join with $DEPT$ on $DEPTNUM$; both of them are correct. The selection between these alternatives should take into account which one of the two corresponding joins is more used by applications.

4.2.2 Vertical Fragmentation

Determining the vertical fragmentation of a global relation R requires grouping into sets attributes which are referenced "in the same way" by applications. We distinguish the **vertical partitioning** problem, in which sets must be disjoint, from the **vertical clustering** problem, in which sets can overlap. The correctness conditions for vertical partitioning require that each attribute of R belong to at least one set and that each set include either a key of R or a "tuple identifier."

The purpose of vertical fragmentation is to identify fragments R_i such that many applications can be executed using just one fragment. Let us consider a global relation R which is vertically partitioned into R_1 and R_2. An application takes advantage of this vertical partitioning if it can be executed using one of R_1 or R_2, since in this case the access to the (larger) relation R is avoided; however, if an application requires *both* R_1 and R_2, then the fragmentation is not beneficial, since an additional join is required for reconstructing R. This criterion applies also to nondistributed databases; in distributed databases, the advantage of vertical partitioning is greater when many applications which use R_1 and many applications which use R_2 are issued at different sites. In this case, placing R at one of the sites would penalize the applications at the other site, while fragmenting R allows satisfying both.

Determining a fragmentation for a global relation R is not easy, since the number of possible partitionings grows combinatorially with the number of attributes of R, and the number of possible clusters is even larger. Thus, in the presence of a large relation, heuristic approaches are necessary to determine the partitions or clusters; we briefly indicate how such methods operate.

Two alternative approaches are possible for attribute partitioning:

1. The **split approach** in which global relations are progressively split into fragments
2. The **grouping approach** in which attributes are progressively aggregated to constitute fragments

Both approaches can be classified as *greedy heuristics*, since they proceed by making at each iteration the "best" possible choice. In both cases, formulas are used to indicate which is the "best" possible splitting or grouping. Some form of backtracking can be made, by trying to move attributes from one set to another on the final partitioning.

Vertical clustering introduces **replication** within fragments, since values of overlapping attributes are replicated. Let us introduce here the discussion on the effects of replication, which will be completed in the next section. Replication has a different effect on read-only and update applications. Read-only applications take *advantage* of replication, because it is more likely that they can reference data locally. For update applications replication is *not convenient*, since they must update all copies in order to preserve consistency.

Let us consider what happens when two fragments R_1 and R_2 are overlapping; i.e., there exists a set of attributes I which belong to both R_1 and R_2. Assume that R_1 and R_2 are at sites 1 and 2. Then read applications at site 1, using attributes of I together with other attributes of R_1, are local to site 1; likewise, read applications at site 2, using attributes of I together with other attributes of R_2, are local to site 2. However, update applications which change the value of attributes of I must reference them at both sites.

Therefore, in evaluating the convenience of vertical clustering, it is important that overlapping attributes are not heavily updated.

General example (continued)

Consider now the global relation:

$$EMP(EMPNUM, NAME, SAL, TAX, MGRNUM, DEPTNUM)$$

Assume that the following applications use relation *EMP*:

1. Administrative applications, concentrated at site 3, requiring *NAME*, *SAL*, and *TAX* of employees.
2. Applications about work conducted at each department, requiring *NAME*, *MGRNUM*, and *DEPTNUM* of employees; these applications are issued at all sites, and reference tuples of employees in the same group of departments with 80 percent probability.

Thus, the vertical fragmentation of *EMP* in two fragments collecting "administrative" and "work-descriptive" attributes is rather natural. Let us include the key *EMPNUM* in both fragments. If we use vertical partitioning, then we must decide which of the two fragments has the attribute *NAME*. In this simple case, a vertical partitioning would not be efficient, since one of the two applications would have to make one join and several nonlocal references. Since the attribute *NAME* is relatively stable (because employees do not change their names often!), the vertical clustering is preferred, determining the following fragmentation:

$$EMP_1(EMPNUM, NAME, TAX, SAL)$$
$$EMP_2(EMPNUM, NAME, MGRNUM, DEPT)$$

4.2.3 Mixed Fragmentation

Finally, we examine mixed fragmentation. Few references ([4.9] and [4.14]) deal with this problem; the simplest ways for building mixed fragmentation consist of:

1. Applying horizontal fragmentation to vertical fragments
2. Applying vertical fragmentation to horizontal fragments

Although these operations can be recursively repeated, generating fragmentation trees of any complexity, it seems that having more than two levels of fragmentation is not of practical interest. Solutions 1 and 2 allow both fragmentations to be considered for each relation, and thus to be taken advantage of. Notice that the second fragmentation can be applied to subsets of the fragments produced by the first one; for instance, Figures 4.4a and b show examples in which:

1. Horizontal fragmentation is applied just to one fragment produced by vertical fragmentation.
2. Vertical fragmentation is applied just to one fragment produced by horizontal fragmentation.

The order in which horizontal and vertical fragmentations are applied can affect the final fragmentation.

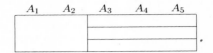

(a) Vertical fragmentation followed by horizontal fragmentation

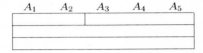

(b) Horizontal fragmentation followed by vertical fragmentation

Figure 4.4   Mixed fragmentation of relation $R(A_1, A_2, A_3, A_4, A_5)$.

General example (conclusion)

Let us consider again global relation *EMP*, vertically fragmented into EMP_1 and EMP_2. Let us assume that the applications about the work which is conducted at departments, which use fragment EMP_2, reference with 80 percent probability the tuples of the departments located around the site where they are issued; thus, EMP_2 can be further horizontally partitioned by department groups. The final, mixed fragmentation of *EMP*, described in Chapter 3, has the same structure as that shown in Figure 4.4a. Notice that, by effect of this decision, the join between global relations *DEPT* and *EMP* on attribute *DEPTNUM* has a simple join graph.

4.3 THE ALLOCATION OF FRAGMENTS

The data allocation problem has been widely analyzed in the context of the "file allocation problem"; references [4.18] to [4.31] describe several analytical models which build the optimal allocation of files under very different assumptions and with different objectives. The easiest way to apply this work to the fragment allocation problem is to consider each fragment as a separate file; however, this approach is not convenient for the following reasons:

1.   Fragments are not properly modeled as individual files, since in this way we do not take into account the fact that they have the same structure or behavior.
2.   There are many more fragments than original global relations, and many analytic models cannot compute the solution of problems involving too many variables.
3.   Modeling application behavior in file systems is very simple (typically, applications make a "remote file access"), while in distributed databases applications can make a sophisticated use of data.

Some of these problems have not yet been solved satisfactorily; for instance, problem 3 is particularly difficult, since the correct approach would be to evaluate data distribution measuring how "optimized" applications should behave with it. This, however, requires optimizing all the important applications for each possible data allocation; solving query optimization as a subproblem of data allocation is probably too hard, since it requires either an excessive amount of simulation or an excessively complex analytic computation.

We do not present in this section any of the models for file allocation (short descriptions of some of them can be found in the annotated bibliography). There are, however, some general criteria that can be used for allocating fragments; we concentrate on them, and we give empirical, simple measures to evaluate costs and benefits of fragmentation.

4.3.1 General Criteria for Fragment Allocation

In determining the allocation of fragments, it is important to distinguish whether we design a final **nonredundant** or **redundant** allocation.

Determining a nonredundant final allocation is easier. The simplest method is a "best-fit" approach; a measure is associated with each possible allocation, and the site with the best measure is selected. This approach gives a solution which disregards the "mutual" effect of placing a fragment at a given site if a related fragment is also at that site.

Replication introduces further complexity in the design, because:

1. The degree of replication of each fragment becomes a variable of the problem.
2. Modeling read applications is complicated by the fact that the applications can now select among several alternative sites for accessing fragments.

For determining the redundant allocation of fragments, either of the following two methods can be used:

1. Determine the set of all sites where the benefit of allocating one copy of the fragment is higher than the cost, and allocate a copy of the fragment to each element of this set; this method selects "all beneficial sites."
2. Determine first the solution of the nonreplicated problem, and then progressively introduce replicated copies starting from the most beneficial; the process is terminated when no "additional replication" is beneficial.

Both methods have some disadvantages. In the "all beneficial sites" method, quantifying costs and benefits for each individual fragment allocation is more critical than in the nonredundant case, because it disregards the "mutual" effects of allocating different copies of the same fragment. The "additional replication" method is a typical heuristic approach; with this method, it is possible to take into account that the increase in the degree of redundancy is progressively less beneficial. Both the reliability and availability of the system increase if there are two or three copies of the fragment, but further copies give a less than proportional increase.

4.3.2 Measure of Costs and Benefits of Fragment Allocation

Finally, we give very simple formulas for evaluating costs and benefits of the allocation of fragments of a global relation R. Let us first introduce some definitions:

i is the fragment index

j is the site index

k is the application index

f_{kj} is the frequency of application k at site j

r_{ki} is the number of retrieval references of application k to fragment i

u_{ki} is the number of update references of application k to fragment i

$n_{ki} = r_{ki} + u_{ki}$

4.3.2.1 Horizontal fragmentation

1. Using the "best-fit" approach for a nonreplicated allocation, we place R_i at the site where the number of references to R_i is maximum. The number of local references of R_i at site j is

$$B_{ij} = \sum_k f_{kj} n_{ki}$$

R_i is allocated at site j^* such that B_{ij^*} is maximum.

2. Using the "all beneficial sites" method for replicated allocation, we place R_i at all sites j where the cost of retrieval references of applications is larger than the cost of update references to R_i from applications at any other site. B_{ij} is evaluated as the difference:

$$B_{ij} = \sum_k f_{kj} r_{ki} - C \times \sum_k \sum_{j' \neq j} f_{kj'} u_{ki}$$

C is a constant which measures the ratio between the cost of an update and a retrieval access; typically, update accesses are more expensive, since they require a larger number of control messages and local operations (thus, $C \geq 1$).

   R_i is allocated at all sites j^* such that B_{ij^*} is positive; when all B_{ij} are negative, a single copy of R_i is placed at the site such that B_{ij^*} is maximum.

3. Using the "additional replication" method for replicated allocation, we can measure the benefit of placing a new copy of R_i in terms of increased reliability and availability of the system. As we have stated, this benefit does not grow proportionally to the degree of redundancy of R_i. Let d_i denote the degree of redundancy of R_i, and let F_i denote the benefit of having R_i fully replicated at each site. In reference [4.11] the following function $\beta(d_i)$ was introduced

to measure this benefit:

$$\beta(d_i) = (1 - 2^{1-d_i})F_i$$

Note that $\beta(1) = 0$, $\beta(2) = F_i/2$, $\beta(3) = 3F_i/4$, and so on. Then, we evaluate the benefit of introducing a new copy of R_i at site j by modifying the formula of case 2 as follows:

$$B_{ij} = \sum_k f_{kj}r_{ki} - C \times \sum_k \sum_{j' \neq j} f_{kj'}u_{ki} + \beta(d_i)$$

This formula takes into account the degree of replication.

4.3.2.2 Vertical fragmentation

Here we measure the benefit of vertically partitioning a fragment R_i, allocated at site r, into two fragments R_s and R_t, allocated at sites s and t. By the effect of this partitioning:

1. There are two sets A_s and A_t of applications, issued at sites s or t, which use only attributes of R_s or R_t and become local to sites s and t, respectively; these applications save one remote reference.
2. There is a set A_1 of applications formerly local to r which use only attributes of R_s or R_t; these applications now need to make an additional remote reference.
3. There is a set A_2 of applications formerly local to r which reference attributes of both R_s and R_t; these applications make two additional remote references.
4. There is a set A_3 of applications at sites different than r, s, or t which reference attributes of both R_s and R_t; these applications make one additional remote reference.

We evaluate the benefit of this partitioning as

$$B_{ist} = \sum_{k \in A_s} f_{ks}n_{ki} + \sum_{k \in A_t} f_{kt}n_{ki} - \sum_{k \in A_1} f_{kr}n_{ki}$$
$$- \sum_{k \in A_2} 2 \times f_{kr}n_{ki} - \sum_{k \in A_3} \sum_{j \notin r,s,t} f_{kj}n_{ki}$$

For simplicity, this formula counts the number of accesses; in order to distinguish between retrieval and update accesses, taking into account their different costs, it is sufficient to use $(r_{ki} + C \times u_{ki})$ instead of n_{ki}.

This formula can be used within an exhaustive "splitting" algorithm to determine whether splitting R_i at site i into R_s at site s and R_t at site t is convenient by trying all possible combinations of sites s and t; some care must be used when $r = s$ or $r = t$.

4.3.2.3 Vertical clustering

We measure the benefit of the vertical clustering of a fragment R_i, allocated at site r, into two fragments R_s and R_t, allocated at sites s and t, with overlapping attributes I. The clustering requires reconsidering the groups of applications introduced for vertical partitioning:

1. A_s includes applications which are local to site s because they either:
   - Read any attribute of R_s, or
   - Update attributes of R_s which are not in the overlapping part I
   The same holds for A_t.
2. A_2 includes update applications formerly local to r which make an update to attributes of I, since now they need to access both R_s and R_t.
3. A_3 includes the applications at sites different than r, s, or t which update attributes of I, which also need to access both R_s and R_t.

We evaluate the benefit of this clustering using the above expression for B_{ist}.

CONCLUSIONS

The design of a distributed database consists of four phases: the design of the global schema; the design of fragmentation; the design of allocation; and the design of the physical structures at each site. The global schema and the physical structures can be designed using the same methods as for the design of the conceptual and physical schema in a centralized database. Therefore, the peculiar aspects of distributed database design are the design of fragmentation and the design of allocation.

The determination of a convenient primary horizontal fragmentation is based on the determination of a complete and minimal set of predicates. The determination of a convenient derived horizontal fragmentation requires the determination of the most important join operations performed by the applications. The design of vertical fragments requires us to determine how different applications access sets of attributes. Finally, the allocation of fragments has the primary goal of minimizing the number of remote accesses which are performed by applications.

EXERCISES

4.1   Give an example of a bank application, accessing a database which is distributed over the branches of the bank, in which the relevant predicates for data distribution are not in the text of the application program.

4.2   Consider the following two allocations of fragments:
   1: R_1 at site 1; R_2 at site 2; R_3 at site 3
   2: R_1 and R_2 at site 1; R_2 and R_3 at site 3
with the following applications (all with the same frequency of activation):
   A1, issued at site 1, reads 5 records of R_1 and 5 records of R_2
   A2, issued at site 3, reads 5 records of R_3 and 5 records of R_2
   A3, issued at site 2, reads 10 records of R_2

(a)   If we take locality of references as objective, which solution is the best?

(b)   If we take complete locality of applications as objective, which solution is the best?

(c)   Assume now that A3 updates 10 records of R_2. Taking the locality of references as objective, which solution is the best?

4.3   Consider the following global and fragmentation schemata:

Global schema:

$$DOCTOR(DNUM,\ NAME,\ DEPT)$$
$$PATIENT(PNUM,\ NAME,\ DEPT,\ TREAT,\ DNUM)$$
$$CARE(PNUM,\ DRUG,\ QUAN)$$

Fragmentation schema:

$DOCTOR_1 = \mathbf{SL}_{DEPT=\text{"SURGERY"}}\,DOCTOR$

$DOCTOR_2 = \mathbf{SL}_{DEPT=\text{"PEDIATRICS"}}\,DOCTOR$

$DOCTOR_3 = \mathbf{SL}_{DEPT\neq\text{"SURGERY"}\ \text{AND}\ DEPT\neq\text{"PEDIATRICS"}}\,DOCTOR$

$PATIENT_1 = \mathbf{SL}_{DEPT=\text{"SURGERY"}\ \text{AND}\ TREAT=\text{"INTENSIVE"}}\,PATIENT$

$PATIENT_2 = \mathbf{SL}_{DEPT=\text{"SURGERY"}\ \text{AND}\ TREAT\neq\text{"INTENSIVE"}}\,PATIENT$

$PATIENT_3 = \mathbf{SL}_{DEPT\neq\text{"SURGERY"}}\,PATIENT$

$CARE_1 = CARE\,\mathbf{SJ}_{PNUM=PNUM}PATIENT_1$

$CARE_2 = CARE\,\mathbf{SJ}_{PNUM=PNUM}PATIENT_2$

$CARE_3 = CARE\,\mathbf{SJ}_{PNUM=PNUM}PATIENT_3$

Assume that a patient is always assigned to the same department as his or her doctor. Classify the join graphs of the following joins:

(a) $DOCTOR\ \mathbf{JN}_{DNUM=DNUM}\ PATIENT$

(b) $DOCTOR\ \mathbf{JN}_{NAME=NAME}\ PATIENT$

(c) $DOCTOR\ \mathbf{JN}_{DEPT=DEPT}\ PATIENT$

(d) $PATIENT\ \mathbf{NJN}\ CARE$

4.4   Consider an airline reservation database. The following information is required:

(a)   Flight description, including flight number, departure and arrival place and time, number of seats available, number of seats reserved, and cost (assume only one fare)

(b)   Passenger description, including code, name, address, and phone number

(c)   Reservation description, including passenger's code, flight number, and seat reserved

Consider the following two important applications, and disregard all other applications:

(a)   A request about flight availability; at the terminal, all information about flights is shown.

(b)   A request about reservations, which includes:

1.   Checking whether the passenger's data are already available, and if they are not, inserting the passenger's data

2.   Checking whether there are seats available (assume no overbooking)

3.   Inserting the reservation description

What is required in order for application 2 to be correct?

Distribute the database over four sites which are geographically located at New York, Atlanta, Denver, and Los Angeles. Give the statistics about the application that you consider appropriate for justifying your design. Include in the design:

(a) The definition of the global schema.

(b) The definition of the fragmentation schema; in case of primary horizontal fragmentation, give a complete and minimal set of predicates.

(c) The definition of the allocation schema.

(d) The reconstruction of global relations from fragments.

Annotated Bibliography

References [4.1] to [4.8] deal with database design in centralized systems, references [4.9] to [4.17] deal with determining data fragmentation, and references [4.18] to [4.31] (chronologically ordered) deal with the "file allocation" problem.

[4.1]   V. Lum et al., "1978 New Orleans Data Base Design Workshop Report," IBM Report RJ2554(33154), 7/13/79, IBM Res. Lab., San Jose, CA; part of this report is also published in the *Fifth VLDB*, Rio de Janeiro, 1979.

In this report, problems in the design of centralized databases are systematically analyzed. The major contribution of this work is the development of a decomposition of the design process into phases:

1.   The "requirement analysis" phase, in which database designers understand the requirement of the database application.
2.   The "view modeling" and "view integration" phases, in which a conceptual, high-level representation of the enterprise schema is produced.
3.   The "implementation design" phase, in which the conceptual representation is translated into statements of a DDL language of a peculiar DBMS.
4.   The "physical design" phase, in which the storage structures (or internal schemata) are designed.

[4.2]   *Data Base Design Techniques, Proc. NYU Symp. on Database Design*, New York, 1978, S. B. Yao, S. B. Navathe, J. L. Weldon, and T. L. Kunii, eds., Springer-Verlag, 1982.

[4.3]   T. J. Teorey and J. P. Fry, *Design of Database Structures*, Prentice-Hall, 1982.

[4.4]   G. Wiederhold: *Database Design*, 2d ed., McGraw-Hill, 1983.

[4.5]   *Methodology and Tools for Data Base Design*, S. Ceri, ed., North-Holland, 1983.

References [4.2] to [4.5] are recent books on the design of centralized databases.

[4.6]   S. B. Navathe and S. G. Gadgil, "A Methodology for View Integration in Logical Database Design," *Eighth VLDB*, Mexico City, 1982.

[4.7]   R. Elmasri and G. Wiederhold, "Data Model Integration Using the Structural Model," *ACM-SIGMOD*, 1979.

[4.8]   C. Batini, M. Lenzerini, and M. Moscarini, "Views Integration," in *Methodology and Tools for Database Design*, S. Ceri, ed., North-Holland, 1983.

References [4.6] to [4.8] are papers which analyze the specific problem of schema integration in the context of centralized database design.

[4.9]   S. Ceri and S. B. Navathe, "A Methodology for the Distribution Design of Databases," *Proc. Compcon 83*, San Francisco, March 1983.

[4.10]   S. Ceri, M. Negri, and G. Pelagatti, "Horizontal Partitioning in Database Design," *ACM-SIGMOD*, 1982.

This paper describes logical and statistical properties of primary horizontal fragmentation; it includes the definitions of Section 4.2.1. The paper also contains:

1.   An analytic method for computing the references to minterm predicates, given the number of references to simple predicates and making appropriate assumptions about the correlation between data and applications
2.   Simple formulas for fragment allocation (similar to those of Section 4.3.2) in the context of centralized and distributed databases

[4.11]   S. Ceri, S. B. Navathe, and G. Wiederhold, "Distribution Design of Logical Database Schemas," *IEEE-TSE*, **SE-9**:4, 1983.

This paper presents an integer programming model for selecting the optimal nonredundant allocation of horizontal fragments; for each global relation, only a limited subset of candidate fragmentations is considered; the candidates include primary or derived fragmentations. The convenience of derived fragmentation is measured by the number of remote references which are saved by performing a simple join. A method is presented for decomposing a large optimization problem into several smaller problems which disregard the effect of those joins which are least used by applications. Finally, a greedy heuristic method is presented for introducing "additional replication," starting from the nonredundant allocation.

[4.12]   S.B. Navathe, S. Ceri, G. Wiederhold, and J. Dou, "Vertical Partitioning for Physical and Distribution Design of Databases," Report No. STAN-CS-82-957, Stanford University, Stanford, 1982.

This paper contains a method for determining the partitioning or clustering of attributes of a relation R in the context of physical design of centralized databases and of the design of distribution. The method requires measuring the "affinity" of two attributes as the number of references to tuples in which both attributes are used; this number is evaluated by considering all important applications. A well-known technique of operations research, called the "bond energy algorithm," is used to permute attributes of R in such a way that the matrix of affinity coefficients determined by permutations is in semi/block diagonal form. As result, "affine" attributes are placed contiguously in a list. Then, binary partitionings or splittings are determined by progressively splitting this list in two nonoverlapping or overlapping sublists. The process is recursively applied to sublists, until no splitting is profitable; formulas are given to evaluate the advantage of binary splittings in different design contexts. In the context of distributed databases, the binary splitting of R, allocated at a given site, into R_1 and R_2 is profitable if there exist two different sites such that, by allocating R_1 and R_2 at them, applications make a greater number of local references.

[4.13]   S. Ceri, G. Gottlob, and G. Pelagatti, "Joining Fragmented Relations in Distributed Databases," Report No. DEPM-83-9, Dept. of Electronics, Politecnico, Milano, 1983.

This paper introduces the notion of join graph, used in Chapters 4, 5, and 6. The paper includes:

1.   The definition of a formal model for describing database fragmentation
2.   A complete classification of join graphs (including total, reduced, partitioned, monotonic, hierarchic, and simple join graphs)
3.   Necessary and sufficient conditions for determining the class of the join graph, given the fragmentation properties of the relations which are joined
4.   Sufficient conditions for deducing the class of the join graph from semantic properties of the operand relations, such as functional or order dependencies

[4.14]   S. K. Chang and W. H. Cheng, "A Methodology for Structured Database Decomposition," *IEEE-TSE*, **SE-6**:2, 1980.

This paper deals with horizontal and vertical fragmentation of relations. It is somehow misleading that the authors use the terms "vertical concatenation" for horizontal fragmentation and "horizontal concatenation" for vertical fragmentation. This paper considers as advantages for structured relation decomposition the efficiency in database retrieval and storage, the increased security, and the possibility of parallel processing. The paper gives a hashing technique which applies to decomposed relations, and an iterative procedure for constructing a structured decomposition; the main problem in following this procedure is that the assignment of costs or savings due to decomposition is not explained.

[4.15]   M. Hammer and B. Niamir, "A Heuristic Approach to Attribute Partitioning," *ACM-SIGMOD*, 1979.

[4.16]   J. A. Hoffer and D. G. Severance, "The Use of Cluster Analysis in Physical Database Design," *First VLDB*, 1975.

[4.17]   M. J. Eisner and D. G. Severance, "Mathematical Techniques for Efficient Record Segmentation in Large Shared Databases," *Journal of the ACM*, **23**:4, 1976.

Papers [4.15] to [4.17] address the problem of vertically partitioning a file in centralized databases. Reference [4.15] defines the "grouping" approach, reference [4.16] defines the "splitting" approach. In [4.17] the problem is considered of partitioning a file into a "primary" and a "secondary" memory; the idea is that about 80 percent of applications address about 20 percent of data; thus partitioning of a file into "heavily used" attributes and all other attributes and storing the "heavily used" attributes in a faster memory can be profitable.

[4.18]   L. W. Dowdy and D. V. Foster, "Comparative Models of the File Assignment Problem," *ACM Computing Surveys*, **14**:2, 1982.

This is an excellent survey of the literature on the file allocation problem. In the paper, 12 models for file assignment are surveyed and compared. Models 1 to 3 address the placement of single files and seek to minimize a cost objective. Models 4 to 5 address the placement of multiple files. Models 6 to 12 seek to optimize some performance measure, depending on the "load" at each site, using queuing models.

[4.19]   W. W. Chu, "Optimal File Allocation in a Multiple Computer System," *IEEE-TC*, **C-18**:10, 1969.

[4.20]   R. G. Casey, "Allocation of Copies of a File in an Information Network," *Proc. 1972 Spring Joint Computer Conference*, AFIPS, 1972.

[4.21]   K. P. Eswaran, "Placement of Records in a File and File Allocation in a Computer Network," *Proc. IFIP Congress*, North-Holland, 1974.

Papers [4.19] to [4.21] are the pioneers in the area of file allocation. Chu, in [4.19], developed a model for determining the minimum overall operating cost subject to constraints on the expected delay of applications and on the storage capacity at each site, assuming a fixed number of copies of each file. Casey, in [4.20], let the number of copies of each file be determined as a result of the optimization; he stressed that the convenience of replication increases with the increase of the query-update ratio. Eswaran, in [4.21], showed that Casey's formulation was NP-complete.

[4.22]   S. Mahmoud and J. S. Riordon, "Optimal Allocation of Resources in Distributed Information Networks," *ACM-TODS*, **1**:1, 1976.

This paper presents a model in which file allocation and the capacity of communication channels are designed together; the design takes into account network topology and the reliability of sites and links.

[4.23]   H. L. Morgan and J. D. Levin, "Optimal Program and Data Locations in Computer Networks," *Communications of the ACM*, **20**:5, 1977.

This paper examines the allocation of both applications and data within a generalized, ARPA-like network.

[4.24]   C. V. Ramamoorthy and B. W. Wah, "The Placement of Relations in a Distributed Relational Database," *Proc. First Int. Conf. on Distributed Computing Systems*, 1979.

[4.25]   P. P. S. Chen and J. Akoka, "Optimal Design of Distributed Information Systems," *IEEE-TC*, **C-29**:12, 1980.

[4.26]   M. L. Fisher and D. S. Hochbaum, "Database Location in Computer Networks," *Journal of the ACM*, **27**:4, 1980.

[4.27]   K. S. Trivedi, R. A. Wagner, and T. M. Sigmon, "Optimal Selection of CPU Speed, Device Capacities and File Assignment," *Journal of the ACM*, **7**:3, 1980.

[4.28]   P. P. S. Chen and J. Akoka, "Optimal Design of Distributed Information Systems," *IEEE-TC*, **C-29**:12, 1980.

[4.29]   K. B. Irani and N. G. Khabbaz, "A Methodology for the Design of Communication Networks and the Distribution of Data in Distributed Supercomputer Systems," *IEEE-TC*, **C-31**:5, 1982.

[4.30]   S. Ceri, G. Martella, and G. Pelagatti, "Optimal File Allocation in a Computer Network: a Solution Method Based on the Knapsack Problem," *Computer Networks,* **6**:5, 1982.

[4.31]   S. Ceri and G. Pelagatti, "A Solution Method for the Non-Additive Resource Allocation Problem in Distributed System Design," *Information Processing Letters,* **15**:4, 1982.

This paper presents a model for resource allocation in distributed systems which aims at distributing resources so that many applications become completely local. These applications do not just save some remote access, because their management and control are much simpler. A nonlinearity is introduced to distinguish completely local applications from applications that need to use at least one remote resource.

Chapter 5

Translation of Global Queries to Fragment Queries

We have seen in Chapter 3 that an access operation issued by an application can be expressed as a query which references global relations. The DDBMS has to transform this query into simpler queries which refer only to fragments. This chapter deals with this transformation.

In general, there are several different ways to transform a query over global relations (called a **global query**) into queries over fragments (called **fragment queries**). These different transformations produce fragment queries which are equivalent, in the sense that they produce the same result. For this reason, this chapter deals also with equivalence transformations, i.e., the rules that can be applied to a query in order to rewrite it into an equivalent expression.

The equivalence rules are used for simplifying the query expression: for instance, common subexpressions are identified (and eliminated), and operations are "distributed" to fragments. However, the emphasis in this chapter is on the *completeness* and *correctness* of the translation; our objective is to present a set of equivalence and translation rules which cover all the aspects relevant to query translation. The *quantitative* evaluation among a set of correct query expressions, to select the one which corresponds to the best value of a specific goal function, will be the subject of Chapter 6.

Section 5.1 is a reminder of the techniques which are used in centralized systems for query transformation. We first give a representation of the query using a query tree, then we present a systematic approach to equivalence transformations, and finally show how to transform a query tree into a query graph for determining common subexpressions within a query. We give this reminder here because it is highly coherent with what follows; moreover, these aspects are more crucial in distributed databases than in centralized databases because of the higher importance that query transformation takes in distributed environments.

In Section 5.2 we show how global queries are mapped into fragment queries. We introduce a canonical mapping and show that the canonical mapping is correct; then we use the equivalence transformations of Section 5.1 to transform the canonical expression of the query. The rationale behind these transformations is to apply algebraic operations, such as projection and selection, which reduce the size of their operands as much as possible on each fragment before transmitting any data among sites. We also introduce the notion of a semi-join program as an equivalence transformation for the join operation, which also has the property of (possibly) reducing the required data transmissions.

In Section 5.3 we deal with queries involving the evaluation of partial groupings (the group-by clause of SQL) and aggregate functions. We extend relational algebra to cover these aspects, and then present some equivalence transformations which apply to the new operations. The rationale behind these operations is again to distribute the processing to fragments.

In Section 5.4 we deal with parametric queries, i.e., those queries in which selection conditions include parameters whose value is specified at execution time. The queries are the typical access primitives issued by parametric applications as shown in Chapter 3. We show how equivalence transformations can be used for improving their efficiency.

5.1 EQUIVALENCE TRANSFORMATIONS FOR QUERIES

A relational query can be expressed using different languages; in this book, we use relational algebra and SQL for this purpose. As already stated in Chapter 2, it is possible to transform most SQL queries into equivalent expressions of relational algebra and vice versa; therefore, any of the above languages can be used for expressing the semantics of the query. However, we can interpret an expression of relational algebra not only as the specification of the semantics of a query, but also as the specification of a **sequence of operations**. From this viewpoint, two expressions with the same semantics can describe two different sequences of operations. For example,

$$\mathbf{PJ}_{NAME,DEPTNUM}\mathbf{SL}_{DEPTNUM=15} \; EMP$$

and

$$\mathbf{SL}_{DEPTNUM=15}\mathbf{PJ}_{NAME,DEPTNUM} \; EMP$$

are equivalent expressions but define two different sequences of operations. Since in this chapter we are interested in the order of execution of operations, we use expressions of relational algebra as the starting point, and we analyze their equivalence transformations.

5.1.1 Operator Tree of a Query

In order to have a more practical representation of queries, in which expression manipulation is easier to follow, we introduce **operator trees**. Let us consider query Q1, which requires the supplier number of suppliers that have issued a supply order in the North area of our company. Query Q1 corresponds to the following expression of the relational algebra:

$$Q1 : \textbf{PJ}_{SNUM} \; \textbf{SL}_{AREA=\text{“North”}} (SUPPLY \; \textbf{JN}_{DEPTNUM=DEPTNUM} \; DEPT)$$

An example of an operator tree for query Q1 is shown in Figure 5.1. Notice that the leaves of the tree are global relations and that each node represents a unary or binary operation. A tree defines a partial order in which operations must be applied in order to produce the result of the query; thus, in this case, the join is applied first, followed by a selection and a projection. We can informally notice that the selection operation applies more properly to the global relation *DEPT* (since *AREA* is an attribute of *DEPT*); thus, a different ordering of operations, corresponding to a different operator tree, could be selection (applied to the *DEPT* leaf), join, projection. This inversion in the order of nodes of an operator tree corresponds to an equivalence transformation.

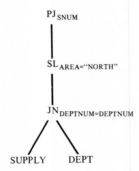

Figure 5.1   An operator tree for query Q1.

The operator tree of an expression of relational algebra can be regarded as the parse tree of the expression itself, assuming the following grammar:

$$R \rightarrow \text{identifier}$$
$$R \rightarrow (R)$$
$$R \rightarrow un\_op \; R$$
$$R \rightarrow R \; bin\_op \; R$$
$$un\_op \rightarrow \textbf{SL}_F \mid \textbf{PJ}_A$$
$$bin\_op \rightarrow \textbf{CP} \mid \textbf{UN} \mid \textbf{DF} \mid \textbf{JN}_F \mid \textbf{NJN}_F \mid \textbf{SJ}_F \mid \textbf{NSJ}_F$$

For ease of representation, we eliminate from the parse tree the parentheses generated by the second production, which are subsumed in the operator tree structure.

5.1.2 Equivalence Transformations for the Relational Algebra

Before giving equivalence transformations, we need to clarify our notion of **equivalence**; we use here the same notion as in reference [5.4]. Recall that we have adopted a nonpositional definition of relations, i.e., a definition in which the order of attributes within the attribute schema is immaterial. Thus, two relations are equivalent when their tuples represent the same mapping from attribute names to values, even if the order of attributes is different.

Let us now consider two expressions E_1 and E_2 of relational algebra. The relation names that appear in each expression correspond to relation variables; we say that the two expressions are equivalent, written $E_1 \leftrightarrow E_2$, if, substituting the same relations for identical names in the two expressions, we get equivalent results.

Equivalence transformations can be given systematically for small expressions, i.e., expressions of two or three operand relations. These transformations are classified into categories according to the type of the operators involved. Let U and B denote unary and binary algebraic operations, respectively. We have:

- **Commutativity** of unary operations:

$$U_1 \, U_2 \, R \leftrightarrow U_2 \, U_1 \, R$$

- **Commutativity** of operands of binary operations:

$$R \, B \, S \leftrightarrow S \, B \, R$$

- **Associativity** of binary operations:

$$R \, B \, (S \, B \, T) \leftrightarrow (R \, B \, S) \, B \, T$$

- **Idempotence** of unary operations:

$$U \, R \leftrightarrow U_1 \, U_2 R$$

- **Distributivity** of unary operations with respect to binary operations:

$$U(R \, B \, S) \to U(R) \, B \, U(S)$$

- **Factorization** of unary operations (this transformation is the inverse of distributivity):

$$U(R) \, B \, U(S) \to U(R \, B \, S)$$

These properties are summarized in Tables 5.1 to 5.5, giving all possible combinations of operations to which they can be applied. We indicate with $Attr(F)$ the attributes which appear in a formula F, with $Attr(R)$ the set of attributes of a relation R.

The tables contain in each position a **validity indicator**. A validity indicator "Y" means that the property can always be applied; "N" means that it cannot be applied. For example, the validity indicator "Y" in the first row and first column of Table 5.1 means that the following transformation is correct

$$\mathbf{SL}_{F1}\,\mathbf{SL}_{F2}R \rightarrow \mathbf{SL}_{F2}\mathbf{SL}_{F1}R$$

where $F1$ and $F2$ are two generic selection specifications.

Validity indicators can also be "SNC," specifying a condition which is necessary and sufficient for the application of the property. For example, the validity indicator SNC_1 in the second row and first column of Table 5.1 means that the transformation

$$\mathbf{PJ}_{A1}\mathbf{SL}_{F2}R \rightarrow \mathbf{SL}_{F2}\mathbf{PJ}_{A1}R$$

is correct only if the specifications $A1$ and $F2$ satisfy the condition SNC_1, which is defined at the bottom of Table 5.1. The condition SNC_1 expresses the requirement that the $\mathbf{PJ}_{A1}$ operation does not eliminate the attributes which are needed to evaluate the formula $F2$. This fact is expressed by requiring that the attributes which are used in formula $F2$ are contained in the specification $A1$.

Table 5.1   Commutativity of unary operations

	SL_{F2}	PJ_{A2}
$\mathbf{SL}_{F1}(*(R))$ $\rightarrow *(\mathbf{SL}_{F1}(R))$	Y	Y
$\mathbf{PJ}_{A1}(*(R))$ $\rightarrow *(\mathbf{PJ}_{A1}(R))$	SNC_1	SNC_2

$$SNC_1 : Attr(F2) \subseteq A1$$
$$SNC_2 : A1 \equiv A2$$

Table 5.2   Commutativity of operands and associativity of binary operations

	UN	DF	CP	JN_F	SJ_F
$R * S$ $\rightarrow S * R$	Y	N	Y	Y	N
$(R * S) * T$ $\rightarrow R * (S * T)$	Y	N	Y	SNC_1	N

SNC_1 for $(R\,\mathbf{JN}_{F1}\,S)\mathbf{JN}_{F2}\,T \rightarrow R\,\mathbf{JN}_{F1}(S\,\mathbf{JN}_{F2}\,T) : Attr(F2) \subseteq Attr(S) \cup Attr(T)$

Table 5.3   Idempotence of unary operations

$$\mathbf{PJ}_A(R) \rightarrow \mathbf{PJ}_{A1}\,\mathbf{PJ}_{A2}(R) \qquad SNC : A \equiv A1, A \subseteq A2$$

$$\mathbf{SL}_F(R) \rightarrow \mathbf{SL}_{F1}\,\mathbf{SL}_{F2}(R) \qquad SNC : F = F1 \wedge F2$$

Table 5.4 Distributivity of unary operations with respect to binary operations

	UN	DF	CP	JN_{F3}	SJ_{F3}
$SL_F(R * S) \rightarrow$	Y	Y	SNC_1	SNC_1	Y
$SL_{FR}(R) * SL_{FS}(S)$	$FR = F, FS = F$	$FR = F, FS = F$	$FR = F1, FS = F2$	$FR = F1, FS = F2$	$FR = F, FS = \text{true}$
$PJ_A(R * S) \rightarrow$	Y	N	SNC_2	SNC_2	SNC_2
$PJ_{AR}(R) * PJ_{AS}(S)$	$AR = A, AS = A$		$AR = A - Attr(S)$ $AS = A - Attr(R)$	$AR = A - Attr(S)$ $AS = A - Attr(R)$	$AR = A - Attr(S)$ $AS = Attr(S) \cap Attr(F3)$

$SNC_1 : \exists F1, F2 : (F = F1 \wedge F2) \wedge (Attr(F1) \subseteq Attr(R)) \wedge (Attr(F2) \subseteq Attr(S))$

$SNC_2 : Attr(F3) \subseteq A$

Table 5.5 Factorization of unary operations from binary operations

	UN	DF	CP	JN_{F1}	SJ_{F1}
$SL_{FR}(R) * SL_{FS}(S)$ $\rightarrow SL_F(R * S)$	SNC_1	SNC_2	Y	Y	SNC_4
	$F = FR = FS$	$F = FR$	$F = FR \wedge FS$	$F = FR \wedge FS$	$F = FR$
$PJ_{AR}(R) * PJ_{AS}(S)$ $\rightarrow PJ_A(R * S)$	SNC_3	N	Y	Y	Y
	$A = AR = AS$		$A = AR \cup AS$	$A = AR \cup AS$	$A = AR$

$SNC_1 : FR = FS$

$SNC_2 : FR \Rightarrow FS$

$SNC_3 : Attr(R) = Attr(S)$

$SNC_4 : FS = \text{true}$

Notice that if we consider the inverse transformation

$$\mathbf{SL}_{F1}\mathbf{PJ}_{A2}R \rightarrow \mathbf{PJ}_{A2}\mathbf{SL}_{F1}R$$

we find a "Y" validity indicator (first row, second column of Table 5.1). This means that indicators are not always symmetric; therefore equivalence rules are specified for each direction independently.

The validity indicators specify conditions which apply to the LHS (left-hand side) of an equivalence rule, and more precisely to the specification parts of its operands; in some cases, it is also necessary to give **generation rules**, which indicate how the specification part of the RHS should be derived from the specification part of the LHS. Generation rules are omitted when the specification parts of LHS and RHS are the same.

Generation rules are indicated in Tables 5.4 and 5.5 below the corresponding validity indicators. For example, consider the second row, third column of Table 5.4. The validity indicator "Y" and the generation rule mean that the transformation

$$\mathbf{PJ}_A(R\ \mathbf{CP}\ S) \rightarrow \mathbf{PJ}_{AR}(R)\ \mathbf{CP}\ \mathbf{PJ}_{AS}\ (S)$$

is correct, provided that AR and AS are determined as

$$AR = A - Attr(S), AS = A - Attr(R)$$

In addition to the transformations defined in Tables 5.1 to 5.5, the following commutativity rule between the binary operations join and union is correct and extremely useful (we do not give a full table of commutativity between binary operations, since most binary operations do not commute):

$$(R'\mathbf{UN}R'')\mathbf{JN}_F(S'\mathbf{UN}S'') \leftrightarrow \mathbf{UN}((R'\mathbf{JN}_F S'), (R'\mathbf{JN}_F S''),$$
$$(R''\mathbf{JN}_F S'), (R''\mathbf{JN}_F S''))$$

The property is shown here with two binary unions in the LHS, which gives rise to a union with four operands in the RHS, but it can be extended to unions having any number of operands; in particular, it holds also if one of the operands of the join in the LHS is a single relation.

We will see the practical application of this rule in the context of fragmentation, where R' and R'' are fragments of the same relation R.

The proof of the validity indicators and generation rules is omitted. We rely on reference [5.4] for most of the proofs; in reference [5.6] the proof is given of similar equivalence transformations applied to a more complex model of relations in distributed databases, called **multirelations** (see the annotated bibliography).

In nondistributed databases, general criteria have been given for applying equivalence transformations for the purpose of simplifying the execution of queries:

Criterion 1.   Use idempotence of selection and projection to generate appropriate selections and projections for each operand relation.

Criterion 2.   Push selections and projections down in the tree as far as possible.

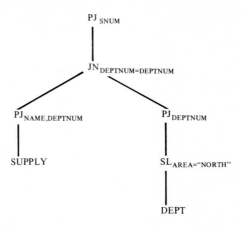

Figure 5.2   A modified operator tree for query Q1.

These criteria descend from the consideration that binary operations, and specifically joins, are the most expensive operations of database systems, and therefore it is convenient to reduce the sizes of operands of binary operations before performing them. In distributed databases, these criteria are even more important: binary operations require the comparison of operands that could be allocated at different sites. Transmission of data is one of the major components of the costs and delays associated with query execution. Thus, reducing the size of operands of binary operations is a major concern.

Figure 5.2 shows a modified operator tree for query Q1, in which the following transformations have been applied:

1. The selection is distributed with respect to the join; thus, the selection is applied directly to the *DEPT* relation.
2. Two new projection operations are generated and are distributed with respect to the join.

Notice that criterion 1 (use of idempotence) has been applied to the projection operation before distributing it; the selection operation, instead, has been directly moved to the *DEPT* relation.

5.1.3 Operator Graph and Determination of Common Subexpressions

An important issue in applying transformations to a query expression is to discover its common subexpressions; i.e., subexpressions which appear more than once in the query; clearly, there is a saving if common subexpressions are evaluated only once. A method for recognizing them consists in transforming the corresponding operator tree in an operator graph by first merging identical leaves of the tree (i.e., identical operand relations), and then merging other intermediate nodes of the tree corresponding to the same operations and having the same operands.

We use an example to illustrate this method. Consider query Q2: give the names of employees who work in a department whose manager has number 373 but who do not earn more than \$35,000. An expression for this query is:

$$Q2 : \textbf{PJ}_{EMP.NAME}((EMP\ \textbf{JN}_{DEPTNUM=DEPTNUM}\ \textbf{SL}_{MGRNUM=373}DEPT)\textbf{DF}$$
$$(\textbf{SL}_{SAL>35000}EMP\ \textbf{JN}_{DEPTNUM=DEPTNUM}\textbf{SL}_{MGRNUM=373}DEPT))$$

The corresponding operator tree is shown in Figure 5.3a. We start by merging leaves corresponding to *EMP* and *DEPT* relations. Then we factorize the selection on *SAL* with respect to join (in doing this, we move the selection upward). Now, we can merge the nodes corresponding to the selection on *MGRNUM* and finally the node corresponding to the join; we come to the operator tree of Figure 5.3b. We recognize the following subexpression:

$$EMP\ \textbf{JN}_{DEPTNUM=DEPTNUM}\ \textbf{SL}_{MGRNUM=373}\ DEPT$$

Once common subexpressions are identified, we can use the following properties to further simplify an operator tree:

$$R\ \textbf{NJN}\ R \leftrightarrow R$$
$$R\ \textbf{UN}\ R \leftrightarrow R$$
$$R\ \textbf{DF}\ R \leftrightarrow \emptyset$$

$$R\ \textbf{NJN}\ \textbf{SL}_F\ R \leftrightarrow \textbf{SL}_F\ R$$
$$R\ \textbf{UN}\ \textbf{SL}_F\ R \leftrightarrow R$$
$$R\ \textbf{DF}\ \textbf{SL}_F\ R \leftrightarrow \textbf{SL}_{\text{NOT}\ F}\ R$$

$$(\textbf{SL}_{F_1}\ R)\ \textbf{NJN}\ (\textbf{SL}_{F_2}\ R) \leftrightarrow \textbf{SL}_{F_1\ \text{AND}\ F_2}\ R$$
$$(\textbf{SL}_{F_1}\ R)\ \textbf{UN}\ (\textbf{SL}_{F_2}\ R) \leftrightarrow \textbf{SL}_{F_1\ \text{OR}\ F_2}\ R$$
$$(\textbf{SL}_{F_1}\ R)\ \textbf{DF}\ (\textbf{SL}_{F_2}\ R) \leftrightarrow \textbf{SL}_{F_1\ \text{AND}\ \text{NOT}\ F_2}\ R$$

We can apply to our example the sixth property in the list, reducing the operator tree to that in Figure 5.3c; finally, we can apply idempotence to projection and push selections and projections toward the leaves of the tree, generating the operator tree of Figure 5.3d. Notice that this new operator tree corresponds to a query that could have been given initially by an expert programmer; transformations which have been presented in this section have therefore the purpose of simplifying the specification of a query not immediately written in its best form.

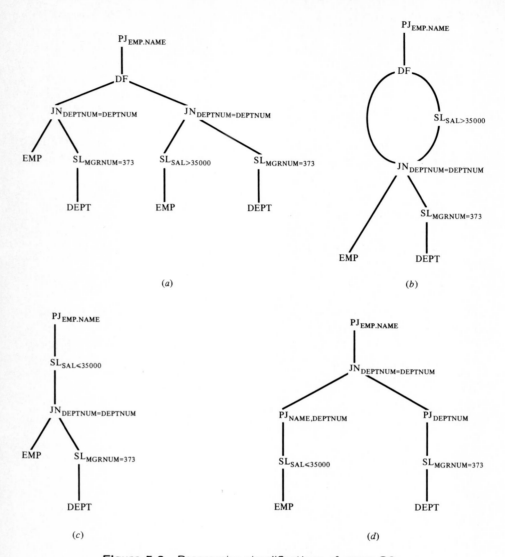

Figure 5.3 Progressive simplifications of query Q2.

5.2 TRANSFORMING GLOBAL QUERIES INTO FRAGMENT QUERIES

We now turn to aspects which are peculiar of distributed databases. In Chapter 3 we have introduced fragmentation as a relevant feature of distributed databases; in this section we give a standard transformation which maps an algebraic expression over the global schema into an algebraic expression over the fragmentation schema; then we give the relevant properties of these expressions.

5.2.1 Canonical Expression of a Fragment Query

Given an algebraic expression over the global schema, its **canonical expression** is obtained by substituting, for each global relation name appearing in it, the algebraic expression giving the reconstruction of global relations from fragments. In the same way, we map an operator tree on the global schema to an operator tree on the fragmentation schema by substituting for the leaves of the first tree the corresponding expressions of the inverse of the fragmentation schema.

Recall that the inverse of the fragmentation schema gives the rule for reconstructing a global relation from its fragments; therefore the new expression (over the fragmentation schema) will produce the same result as the old expression (over the global schema). The important fact is that the leaves of the operator tree of the canonical expression are now fragments rather than global relations.

Figure 5.4a shows the transformation of the operator tree of query Q1 represented in Figure 5.2 into the operator tree of the canonical expression of Q1. In Figure 5.4a the two circled subtrees substitute the global relations *SUPPLY* and *DEPT* of Figure 5.2.

A canonical expression corresponds to a conservative way of performing a query, consisting first in collecting the fragments of all global relations into temporary relations and then applying to these temporaries the global query. Clearly, this is not an efficient approach. Thus, probably the canonical expression is also the worst for a given query; but a canonical expression is an algebraic expression, and we can apply to it any equivalence transformation. In particular, we will use the distribution of selection and projection with respect to union and join in order to distribute the processing to the fragments; therefore, criteria 1 and 2 of Section 5.1.2 gain further relevance in the context of queries over the fragmentation schema. Figure 5.4b shows the application of these two criteria to the operator tree of Figure 5.4a.

In Chapter 3, when we introduced horizontal fragments, we also introduced fragment qualification, i.e., a predicate which expresses a property of all the tuples within the fragment. We now turn to the use of qualifications in simplifying distributed queries.

5.2.2 Algebra of Qualified Relations

A qualified relation is a relation extended by a qualification; the qualification can be seen as an intensional property possessed by all the tuples of the relation. We denote a **qualified relation** as a pair $[R : q_R]$, where R is a relation called the **body** of the qualified relation and q_R is a predicate called the **qualification** of the qualified relation. Horizontal fragments are typical examples of qualified relations, in which the qualification corresponds to the partitioning predicate.

We do not require that the qualification of a relation be evaluated on the tuples of the relation; however, if the qualification can be evaluated, we require that the qualification be true. Typically, a qualification cannot be evaluated when we project out some of the attributes used in the qualification expression.

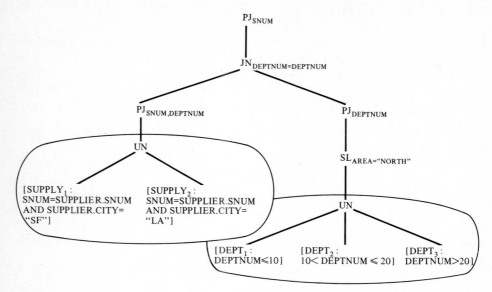

(*a*) Canonical form of query Q1.

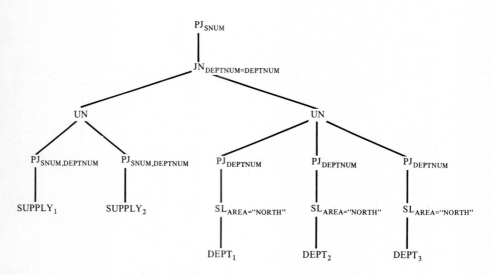

(*b*) Pushing selections and projections down in the operator tree.

Figure 5.4 Further transformations of the operator tree of query Q1.

The algebra of qualified relations is an extension of relational algebra which uses qualified relations as operands. Clearly, this algebra requires manipulating qualifications as well as relations. The following rules define the result of applying the operations of relational algebra to qualified relations.

Rule 1 $\qquad\qquad \mathbf{SL}_F[R : q_R] \Rightarrow [\mathbf{SL}_F R : F \text{ AND } q_R]$

This rule states that the application of a selection $\mathbf{SL}_F$ to a qualified relation $[R : q_R]$ produces a qualified relation having the relation $\mathbf{SL}_F R$ as its body and the predicate F AND q_R as its qualification. The extension of the qualification to F AND q_R after a selection reflects the fact that F holds on all the selected tuples as well as q_R.

Rule 2 $$\mathbf{PJ}_A[R : q_R] \Rightarrow [\mathbf{PJ}_A R : q_R]$$

The qualification of the result of a projection remains unchanged, even if the projection eliminates some of the attributes upon which the qualification was evaluated. The reason is in the nature of qualifications; qualifications bear intensional information, rather than extensive information. Therefore, it is correct to eliminate attributes used for expressing the qualification, without eliminating the qualification itself.

Rule 3 $$[R : q_R] \, \mathbf{CP} \, [S : q_S] \Rightarrow [R \, \mathbf{CP} \, S : q_R \text{ AND } q_S]$$

The extension of the qualification to q_R AND q_S is rather intuitive; notice that the two qualifications apply to disjoint attributes of $R \, \mathbf{CP} \, S$.

Rule 4 $$[R : q_R] \, \mathbf{DF} \, [S : q_S] \Rightarrow [R \, \mathbf{DF} \, S : q_R]$$

The extension of difference is rather unintuitive; when we subtract tuples of a relation S from a relation R, the qualification of the result remains the same as the qualification of R. It would be not correct to change it to q_R AND NOT q_s, because there could be tuples of R for which q_R AND NOT q_s does not hold, but that remain in the result just because S does not contain those tuples.

However, the following problem arises with rule 4: consider the intersection operation of traditional relational algebra, defined as $R \, \mathbf{IN} \, S = R \, \mathbf{DF} \, (R \, \mathbf{DF} \, S)$. From the definition, it is easy to show that intersection is commutative; i.e.,

$$R \, \mathbf{IN} \, S = S \, \mathbf{IN} \, R.$$

If we apply the definition of extended algebra, we come to a surprising result:

$$[R : q_R] \, \mathbf{IN} \, [S : q_S] \Rightarrow [R : q_R] \, \mathbf{DF} \, ([R : q_R] \, \mathbf{DF} \, [S : q_S]) \Rightarrow$$
$$[R : q_R] \, \mathbf{DF} \, [R \, \mathbf{DF} \, S : q_R] \Rightarrow [R \, \mathbf{DF} \, (R \, \mathbf{DF} \, S) : q_R] \Rightarrow$$
$$[R \, \mathbf{IN} \, S : q_R] \tag{5.4a}$$

$$[S : q_S] \, \mathbf{IN} \, [R : q_R] \Rightarrow [S : q_S] \, \mathbf{DF} \, ([S : q_S] \, \mathbf{DF} \, [R : q_R]) \Rightarrow$$
$$[S : q_S] \, \mathbf{DF} \, [S \, \mathbf{DF} \, R : q_S] \Rightarrow [S \, \mathbf{DF} \, (S \, \mathbf{DF} \, R) : q_S] \Rightarrow$$
$$[S \, \mathbf{IN} \, R : q_S] \tag{5.4b}$$

In fact, the result that we would like to find is

$$[R \, \mathbf{IN} \, S : q_R \text{ AND } q_S]$$

because the tuples of the intersection are those which belong to both relations, for which both q_R and q_S hold. Note that q_R AND q_S implies both q_R and q_S; thus, results (5.4a) and (5.4b) are not wrong, but certainly some information is lost; we do not obtain the most restricted predicate which is satisfied by all the tuples of R IN S.

Rule 5 $\qquad\qquad [R : q_R]\, \mathbf{UN}\, [S : q_S] \Rightarrow [R\, \mathbf{UN}\, S : q_R\, \text{OR}\, q_S]$

The union is extended by taking the disjunction of qualifications.

Given the above rules, let us see how derived operations of algebra, such as join and semi-joins, are extended. We have two additional rules:

Rule 6 $\qquad [R : q_R]\, \mathbf{JN}_F\, [S : q_S] \Rightarrow [R\, \mathbf{JN}_F\, S : q_R\, \text{AND}\, q_S\, \text{AND}\, F]$

Rule 7 $\qquad [R : q_R]\, \mathbf{SJ}_F\, [S : q_S] \Rightarrow [R\, \mathbf{SJ}_F\, S : q_R\, \text{AND}\, q_S\, \text{AND}\, F]$

The proof of these two rules is instructive for learning how to manipulate qualified relations.

Proof of rule 6 (Recall that join is derived from the use of selection and cartesian product).

$$[R : q_R]\, \mathbf{JN}_F\, [S : q_S] \Rightarrow$$
$$\mathbf{SL}_F([R : q_R]\mathbf{CP}[S : q_S]) \Rightarrow$$
$$\mathbf{SL}_F[RCPS : q_R\, \text{AND}\, q_s] \Rightarrow$$
$$[\mathbf{SL}_F(RCPS) : q_R AND q_S\, \text{AND}\, F] \Rightarrow$$
$$[RJN_F S : q_R\, \text{AND}\, q_S\, \text{AND}\, F]$$

Proof of rule 7 (Recall that semi-join is derived from the use of projection and join).

$$[R : q_R]\, \mathbf{SJ}_F\, [S : q_S] \Rightarrow$$
$$\mathbf{PJ}_{Attr(R)}([R : q_R]\mathbf{JN}_F\, [S : q_S]) \Rightarrow$$
$$\mathbf{PJ}_{Attr(R)}[R\, \mathbf{JN}_F\, S : q_R\, \text{AND}\, q_S\, \text{AND}\, F] \Rightarrow$$
$$[\mathbf{PJ}_{Attr(R)}(R\, \mathbf{JN}_F\, S) : q_R\, \text{AND}\, q_S\, \text{AND}\, F] \Rightarrow$$
$$[R\, \mathbf{SJ}_F\, S : q_R\, \text{AND}\, q_S\, \text{AND}\, F]$$

Having defined the algebra of qualified relations, we now give the extension of equivalence transformations for it. Two qualified relations are equivalent if their bodies are equivalent relations and their qualifications represent the same truth function (i.e., if we apply both qualification to the same tuple, we obtain the same truth value). The following proposition applies to the algebra of qualified relations: all equivalence transformations of relational algebra hold also for the algebra of qualified relations. The proof of this proposition is left as an exercise to the reader. A proof for a similar extension of algebra can be found in reference [5.6].

We use qualifications for *eliminating fragments* which are not involved in the query. Consider the qualification that is produced after a selection or a join; in these cases, the qualification includes a conjunction of predicates. This qualification could be contradictory. An example of a contradictory qualification is $DEPTNUM = 1$

AND *DEPTNUM* = 5. Qualified relations with contradictory qualifications are intrinsically empty. This knowledge is much more useful than discovering, when the query is executed, that the result of an expression is empty; in fact, the contradiction descends from intensional properties of fragments, and can be used during query compilation.

Given the above use of qualifications, the algebra of qualified relations will give consistent results provided that the qualifications of its operands are given correctly, and will instead behave unpredictably if qualifications are not correct. Since we apply this algebra to fragments of relations, this warning points out that qualifications of fragments need to be given appropriately.

Examples of subexpressions that reduce to the empty relation are:

$$\mathbf{SL}_{CITY=\text{``LA''}}[SUPPLIER_1 : CITY = \text{``SF''}]$$

or

$$[DEPT_1 : DEPTNUM \leq 10]\mathbf{JN}_{DEPTNUM=DEPTNUM}[EMP_3 : DEPTNUM > 20]$$

Recognizing that one of the subexpressions of a query is intrinsically empty leads to substantial simplifications of the query tree; the following equivalence transformations, in which R can be regarded either as a usual relation or as a qualified relation, are useful:

$$\mathbf{SL}_F(\emptyset) \leftrightarrow \emptyset$$
$$\mathbf{PJ}_A(\emptyset) \leftrightarrow \emptyset$$
$$R \mathbf{CP} \emptyset \leftrightarrow \emptyset$$
$$R \mathbf{UN} \emptyset \leftrightarrow R$$
$$R \mathbf{DF} \emptyset \leftrightarrow R$$
$$\emptyset \mathbf{DF} R \leftrightarrow \emptyset$$
$$R \mathbf{JN}_F \emptyset \leftrightarrow \emptyset$$
$$R \mathbf{SJ}_F \emptyset \leftrightarrow \emptyset$$
$$\emptyset \mathbf{SJ}_F R \leftrightarrow \emptyset$$

We now give new criteria for simplifying expressions over a fragmentation schema; they should be used together with criteria 1 and 2 of Section 5.1.2. The new criteria are:

Criterion 3.   Push selections down to the leaves of the tree, and then apply them using the algebra of qualified relations; substitute the selection result with the empty relation if the qualification of the result is contradictory.

Criterion 4.   Use the algebra of qualified relations to evaluate the qualification of operands of joins; substitute the subtree, including the join and its operands, with the empty relation if the qualification of the result of the join is contradictory.

The above criteria are used in the next two subsections to simplify horizontally fragmented relations and to simplify joins between horizontally fragmented relations.

5.2.3 Simplifications of Horizontally Fragmented Relations

We show this kind of simplification with an example. Let us consider query Q3 on relation *DEPT*, which is horizontally fragmented:

$$Q3 : \mathbf{SL}_{DEPTNUM=1} \; DEPT$$

The canonical form of the query is shown in Figure 5.5a. We push the selection toward the leaves by distributing it with respect to union. Then we apply selections according to criterion 3; the qualification of results of the selections on $DEPT_2$ and $DEPT_3$ is a contradiction; thus these two subexpressions are substituted in the tree with the empty relation. Finally, we simplify the union operation; the final result is the simple operator tree of Figure 5.5b.

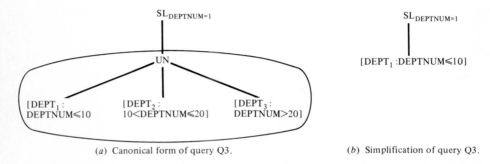

(a) Canonical form of query Q3.   (b) Simplification of query Q3.

Figure 5.5   Simplification of horizontally fragmented relations.

Notice that if global relations are properly fragmented horizontally, the above simplification should apply to most of the queries operating on them.

5.2.4 Simplification of Joins between Horizontally Fragmented Relations

Let us consider, for simplicity, the join between two fragmented relations R and S. There are two distinct possibilities of joining them; the first one requires collecting all the fragments of R and S before performing the join. The second one consists of performing the join between fragments and then collecting all the results into the same result relation; we refer to this second case as "distributed join." Neither of the above possibilities dominates the other. Very generally, we prefer the first solution if conditions on fragments are highly selective; the second solution is preferred if the join between fragments involves few pairs of fragments.

We have already discussed, in Chapter 4, the criteria that allow designing the fragmentation of relations in order to make an efficient distributed join. The properties are summarized in join graphs which show, for given joins, which are the fragments that need to be joined together. Join graphs help the design of fragmentation, but we also need to show how it is possible to *build* join graphs for specific queries; any attempt to perform a good design would be worthless if we do not give such construction rules when we map global queries over the fragmentation schema.

The following equivalence transformation allows the transformation of a query processed without distributed joins into a query processed with them: joins appearing in the global query must be distributed with respect to unions representing the collection of fragments. Notice that this corresponds to pushing the union up in the operator tree, i.e., delaying the union of fragments. We can summarize this transformation into criterion 5:

Criterion 5.   In order to distribute joins which appear in the global query, unions (representing fragment collections) must be pushed up, beyond the joins that we want to distribute.

Building a join graph requires, then, applying criterion 5 (for distributing the join) followed by criterion 4 (for eliminating joins between fragments that do not give any contribution to the result). The join graph, as defined in Chapter 4, is given by all pairs of fragments from R and S that "survive" in the operator tree.

Let us show an example of a distributed join. We start from query Q4 which requires the number $SNUM$ of all suppliers having a supply order. The algebraic expression of the query over the global schema is

$$Q4 : \textbf{PJ}_{SNUM} \, (SUPPLY \, \textbf{NJN} \, SUPPLIER)$$

Figure 5.6*a* shows the canonical form of the query. We recall that the fragmentation of $SUPPLY$ is derived from the fragmentation of $SUPPLIER$; i.e., each tuple of $SUPPLY$ is stored either in fragment $SUPPLY_1$, if it refers to a supplier of San Francisco, or in fragment $SUPPLY_2$, if it refers to a supplier of Los Angeles. Applying criterion 5, we push the two unions up beyond the join; thus, we generate four joins between fragments. We then apply criterion 4, and we discover that two of them are intrinsically empty because their qualification is contradictory. The empty joins are those of $SUPPLIER_1$ (in "SF") with $SUPPLY_2$ (of "LA" suppliers), and likewise of $SUPPLIER_2$ (in "LA") with $SUPPLY_1$ (of "SF" suppliers). Thus, the operator tree reduces to that of Figure 5.6*b*. Assuming that fragments with the same index are placed at the same site (i.e., that data about $SUPPLY$ are stored together with data about $SUPPLIERS$), this operator tree corresponds to an efficient way of evaluating the query, because each join is local to one site.

Notice that this distributed join has a join graph which was classified as "simple" in Chapter 4; the join graph is

$$SUPPLIER_1 \, \text{---------} \, SUPPLY_1$$

$$SUPPLIER_2 \, \text{---------} \, SUPPLY_2$$

Finally, notice that this same example was presented in Chapter 3, and the emphasis was placed on how the application could be written by a programmer; here, instead, we show how the distributed join strategy can be determined by query transformations.

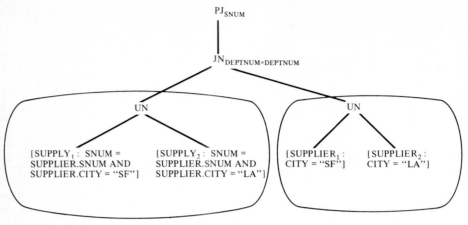

(*a*) Canonical form of query Q4.

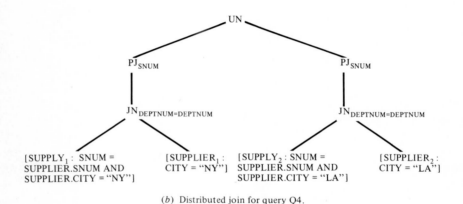

(*b*) Distributed join for query Q4.

Figure 5.6 Simplification of joins between horizontally fragmented relations.

5.2.5 Using Inference for Further Simplifications

The previous subsections have shown that the determination of contradictions between selection criteria of queries and qualifications of fragments is extremely useful. The contradictions of the above cases are very easy to detect, as they amount to discovering that values required by a query for an attribute or group of attributes are not compatible with respect to fragmentation criteria also expressed on the same attribute or group of attributes. Simple tests can be sufficient for this purpose. However, determining that a formula is a contradiction can be done using more sophisticated intensional information and requires, in general, the usage of a theorem prover.

We just want to give examples of how additional information could be used for simplifying queries. Let us consider again query Q1 that requires the supplier number of those suppliers having a supply order issued in the North area, for which we have developed the operator tree in Figure 5.4. Assume that the following knowledge is available to the query optimizer:

1. The North area includes only departments 1 to 10.
2. Orders from departments 1 to 10 are all addressed to suppliers of San Francisco.

We use the above knowledge to "infer" contradictions that allow eliminating subexpressions.

a. From 1 above, we can write the following implications:

$$AREA = \text{``North''} \Rightarrow NOT\,(10 < DEPTNUM \leq 20)$$
$$AREA = \text{``North''} \Rightarrow NOT\,(DEPTNUM > 20)$$

Using criterion 3, we apply the selection to fragments $DEPT_1$, $DEPT_2$, and $DEPT_3$ and evaluate the qualification of the results. By virtue of the above implications, two of them are contradictory. This allows us to eliminate the subexpressions for fragments $DEPT_2$ and $DEPT_3$. Thus, the operator tree of Figure 5.4b reduces to that of Figure 5.7a.

b. We then apply criterion 5 for distributing the join; in principle, we would need to join the subtree including $DEPT_1$ with both subtrees including $SUPPLY_1$ and $SUPPLY_2$. But from 1 above, we know that:

$$AREA = \text{``North''} \Rightarrow DEPTNUM \leq 10$$

and from 2 above we know that:

$$DEPTNUM \leq 10 \Rightarrow$$
$$NOT\,(SNUM = SUPPLIER.SNUM\,AND\,SUPPLIER.CITY = \text{``LA''})$$

By applying criterion 4, it is possible to deduce that only the subtree including $SUPPLY_1$ needs to be joined. The final operator tree for query Q1 is shown in Figure 5.7b.

It is instructive to reflect on the progressive simplifications that have been applied to the operator tree of query Q1, which now involves only two fragments (possibly stored at the same site).

5.2.6 Simplification of Vertically Fragmented Relations

We now turn to the simplification of vertically fragmented relations, which is dual to the simplification of horizontally fragmented ones. The rationale behind this simplification is to determine a proper subset of the fragments which is sufficient for answering the query, and then to eliminate all other fragments from the query expression, as well as the joins which are used in the inverse of the fragmentation schema for reconstructing the global relations. In particular, if the fragments which

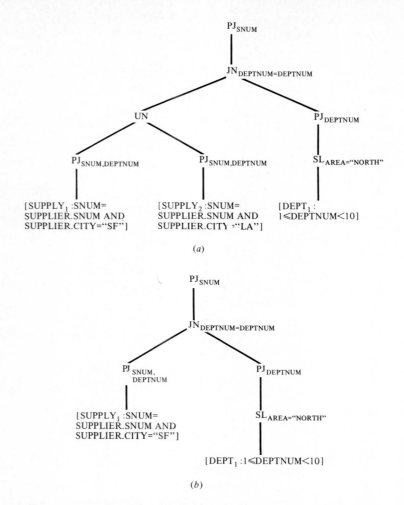

Figure 5.7 Simplification of an operator tree using inference.

are required reduce to only one fragment, there is no need of performing join operations.

We show the simplification with an example. Consider query Q5, which requires names and salaries of employees. The query on the global schema is simply

$$Q5 : \mathbf{PJ}_{NAME,SAL} \; EMP$$

The canonical operator tree of the expression is shown in Figure 5.8a. Recall that *EMP* is first vertically partitioned into fragment EMP_4 (describing the management of employees' salaries) and a second fragment, which is further partitioned horizontally into EMP_1, EMP_2, and EMP_3. We notice that the attributes of EMP_4 include *NAME* and *SAL*, which are required by the query. Then it is possible to answer

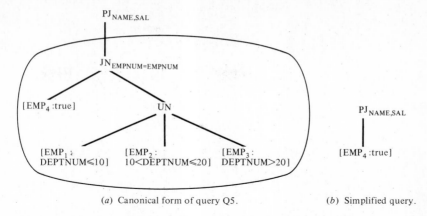

(a) Canonical form of query Q5.   (b) Simplified query.

Figure 5.8   Simplification of vertically fragmented relations.

the query using only the fragment EMP_4, and the operator tree can be simplified by disregarding the other fragments and the join operation. The final operator tree for query Q5 is shown in Figure 5.8b.

Notice that if the design of vertical fragmentation is done properly, the above simplification should apply to most of the queries operating on them.

5.2.7 Semi-join Programs

A semi-join is a derived operation of relational algebra which takes particular relevance in the optimization of distributed queries. In this section, we show how it is possible, given a join operation, to map it into a **semi-join program**, i.e., a set of operations which produce the same result as the join. We also give an intuitive explanation of why semi-joins can be profitable. In the next chapter, we will consider the optimization of queries using semi-join programs.

Given an equi-join $R \: \mathbf{JN}_{A=B} \: S$, where A and B are attributes (or, more generally, sets of attributes) of R and S, the semi-join program for it is given by

$$S \: \mathbf{JN}_{A=B} \: (R \: \mathbf{SJ}_{A=B} \: \mathbf{PJ}_B \: S)$$

Notice that relation S appears twice in this expression; by merging leaves corresponding to S into the same node, we obtain the operator graph of the semi-join program shown in Figure 5.9. The proof that the semi-join program is equivalent to the join is left to the reader (the proof can be found in reference [5.4]).

In order to understand intuitively why semi-join programs are useful, assume that R and S are on different sites. Executing the semi-join program consists in projecting B from S and sending the result of the projection to the site of R; performing the semi-join on the site of R; sending the result of the semi-join to the site of S; and performing the join there. The important aspect of a semi-join program is that only a subset of the tuples of R will "survive" the semi-join; only these tuples of R, which will contribute to the result of the final join, need to be transmitted between sites.

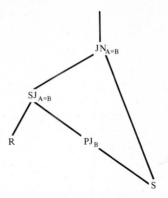

Figure 5.9 Operator graph of a semi-join program.

5.3 DISTRIBUTED GROUPING AND AGGREGATE FUNCTION EVALUATION

Database applications often require performing database access operations that cannot be expressed with relational algebra. Therefore, query languages for relational databases typically allow the formulation of queries that cannot be reduced to expressions of relational algebra. The most important of these additional features are the possibility of **grouping** tuples into disjoint subsets of relations and of evaluating **aggregate functions** over them. In this section we show how, by introducing suitable properties, these queries can be handled efficiently in a distributed database.

We first give some examples, using SQL, of queries which use the above features.

> Q6: Select AVG($QUAN$)
> from $SUPPLY$
> where $PNUM =$ "P1"

This query retrieves into a result relation having one attribute and one tuple the average quantity of supply orders for product "P1."

> Q7: Select $PNUM, SNUM,$ SUM($QUAN$)
> from $SUPPLY$
> group by $SNUM, PNUM$

This query corresponds to partitioning the relation $SUPPLY$ into groups having the same value of $SNUM$ and $PNUM$ (but different values of $DEPTNUM$ and $QUAN$), evaluating for each such group the sum of the quantities, and retrieving $SNUM$, $PNUM$, and the sum of the quantities of each group into the result relation.

> Q8: Select $SNUM, PNUM,$ SUM($QUAN$)
> from $SUPPLY$
> group by $SNUM, PNUM$
> having SUM($QUAN$) > 300

This query again partitions the relation *SUPPLY* into groups, but only those groups are kept in which the sum of quantities is greater than 300; then the same information as in the second query is retrieved.

We have already noticed that it is not possible to express these queries directly using relational algebra; thus, we need to extend relational algebra before dealing with them.

5.3.1 Extension of Relational Algebra

Relational algebra is extended with the following **group-by GB**$_{G,AF}$ R such that:

- G are the attributes which determine the grouping of R.
- AF are aggregate functions to be evaluated on each group.
- **GB**$_{G,AF}R$ is a relation having:
  A relation schema made by the attributes of G and the aggregate functions of AF.
  As many tuples as there are groups in R; attributes of G take the grouping value; attributes of AF take the value of the aggregate functions evaluated on the group.
- Either G or AF may be unspecified.

With the above operation, it is possible to write in algebra queries Q6, Q7, and Q8. We have

$$Q6 : \mathbf{GB}_{AVG(QUAN)} \, \mathbf{SL}_{PNUM=\text{``P1''}} \, SUPPLY$$

$$Q7 : \mathbf{GB}_{SNUM,PNUM,SUM(QUAN)} \, SUPPLY$$

$$Q8 : \mathbf{SL}_{SUM(QUANT)>300} \, \mathbf{GB}_{SNUM,PNUM,SUM(QUAN)} \, SUPPLY$$

Some comments are in order. The G part corresponds to the "group-by" clause, and the AF part corresponds to the aggregate functions whose computation is required. Typically in these queries attributes upon which grouping is made are also retrieved; thus, the attributes which appear in the "group-by" clause also appear in the "select" clause.

In query Q6, the G part is left empty, as the function is applied to all the tuples of *SUPPLY*. In query Q8, the usual selection operation is applied to the result of the **GB** operation; this selection corresponds to the "having" clause of SQL.

5.3.2 Properties of the Group-by Operation

In this section, we give an equivalence property for the new operation, and we discuss, in general, the possibility of evaluating aggregate functions in a distributed way.

The property in which we are interested is the distributivity of **GB** with respect to union:

$$\mathbf{GB}_{G,AF}(R_1 \, \mathbf{UN} \, R_2) \rightarrow (\mathbf{GB}_{G,AF} R_1)\mathbf{UN}(\mathbf{GB}_{G,AF} R_2), \qquad \text{Val. ind.: } SNC$$

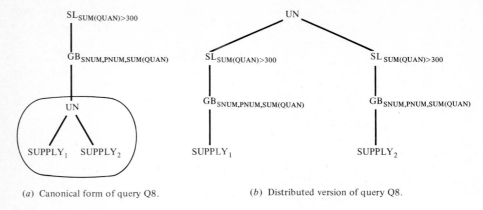

(a) Canonical form of query Q8.   (b) Distributed version of query Q8.

Figure 5.10   A query with grouping and aggregate functions.

The sufficient and necessary condition for this property requires that each group G_i either is contained or has no intersection with every operand R_j:

$$SNC : \text{For every } i, j \text{ either } (G_i \subseteq R_j) \text{ or } (G_i \cap R_j = \emptyset)$$

The interpretation of this condition is that each group must be entirely contained within a fragment, i.e., that grouping is finer than fragmentation. Then, clearly, performing the group-by operation on the operands of union and then the union of their results is equivalent to performing the group-by operation directly on the result of the union (a proof of a similar property can be found in reference [5.6]). It is evident that the distributivity of group-by leads to a distributed evaluation of the query which is extremely profitable, as (small) results of group-by operations are collected instead of (large) global relations. We can now state a new criterion that applies to the above transformation:

Criterion 6.   In order to distribute grouping and aggregate function evaluations appearing in a global query, unions (representing fragment collections) must be pushed up, beyond the corresponding group-by operation.

This criterion applies successfully to queries Q7 and Q8; we show query Q8. The canonical form of the query is in Figure 5.10a. Tuples of *SUPPLY* must be grouped for different values of the attributes *SNUM* and *PNUM*, and we know, from the fragmentation of *SUPPLY*, that equal values of *SNUM* fall into the same fragment; then we can apply the transformation required by criterion 6 to push the union up with respect to the **GB** operation. We distribute the selection with respect to the union. The final operator tree for query Q8 is shown in Figure 5.10b. Notice that the **GB** operation is separately applied to each fragment and that the selection operation is applied to the result.

By means of the above transformation and criterion it is possible to simplify many queries, but we still have to consider those to which the above *SNC* condition does not apply. This is, for instance, the case of query Q6, in which no grouping is required. It is possible to introduce another property, which holds on some aggregate functions.

We say that an aggregate function F has a distributed computation if for any multiset S and any decomposition of S into multisets $S_1, S_2, \ldots, S_n$, it is possible to determine a set of aggregate functions $F_1, \ldots, F_m$ and an expression $E(F_1, \ldots, F_m)$ such that

$$F(S) = E(F_1(S_1), \ldots, F_1(S_n), F_2(S_1), \ldots, F_2(S_n), \ldots, F_m(S_1), \ldots, F_m(S_n))$$

We recall that a multiset has replicated elements; in the above definition, the decomposition of S must be such that each element of S is mapped to one and only one element of one of the multisets $S_1, \ldots, S_n$ (i.e., that the degree of replication of elements of S does not change). This notion of decomposition holds when $S_1, S_2, \ldots, S_n$ are multisets given by the values of a given column on fragments $R_1, R_2, \ldots, R_n$, and S is the multiset given by the values of that column on the global relation R.

An aggregate function for which it is possible to find the functions F_i and the expression $E(F_i)$ is the function average

$$\text{AVG}(S) = \frac{\text{SUM}(\text{SUM}(S_1), \text{SUM}(S_2), \ldots, \text{SUM}(S_n))}{\text{SUM}(\text{COUNT}(S_1), \text{COUNT}(S_2), \ldots, \text{COUNT}(S_n))}$$

Similarly, we have

$$\text{MIN}(S) = \text{MIN}(\text{MIN}(S_1), \text{MIN}(S_2), \ldots, \text{MIN}(S_n))$$
$$\text{MAX}(S) = \text{MAX}(\text{MAX}(S_1), \text{MAX}(S_2), \ldots, \text{MAX}(S_n))$$
$$\text{COUNT}(S) = \text{SUM}(\text{COUNT}(S_1), \text{COUNT}(S_2), \ldots, \text{COUNT}(S_n))$$
$$\text{SUM}(S) = \text{SUM}(\text{SUM}(S_1), \text{SUM}(S_2), \ldots, \text{SUM}(S_n))$$

The distributed computation of aggregate functions is an important property in distributed databases, because the partial results of the functions $F_1(S_1), \ldots, F_m(S_n)$ can be transmitted to a common site, where the expression E can be evaluated, instead of transmitting all the data to that site and computing the aggregate function there.

The above property can be applied to query Q6. The canonical form of the query is shown in Figure 5.11a. In this case, it is not possible to apply criterion 6, because the SNC condition does not hold. To solve the query, we generate two independent subqueries, operating on the two fragments $SUPPLY_1$ and $SUPPLY_2$:

$$\mathbf{GB}_{\text{SUM}(SAL),\text{COUNT}}\mathbf{SL}_{PNUM=\text{``P1''}}SUPPLY_i, \quad \text{for } i = 1, 2$$

Let S_1 and C_1 be the values returned into SUM(SAL) and COUNT attributes of the expression over $SUPPLY_1$, and S_2 and C_2 be the corresponding values over $SUPPLY_2$. Then, the average value of salaries, AVG(SAL), is given by $(S_1 + S_2)/(C_1 + C_2)$. Thus, S_1, S_2, C_1, and C_2 are transmitted to the site where the result of the query must be produced, and the value of AVG(SAL) is computed there.

In the absence of this transformation, the nondistributed evaluation of the function would require collecting on the same site the actual tuples from fragments $SUPPLY_1$ and $SUPPLY_2$.

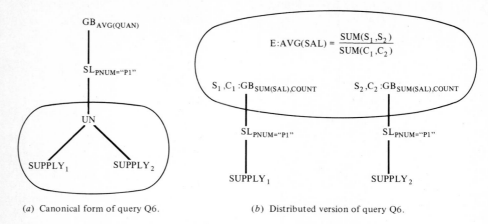

(a) Canonical form of query Q6.   (b) Distributed version of query Q6.

Figure 5.11   Distributed evaluation of aggregate functions.

5.4 PARAMETRIC QUERIES

We now turn our attention to parametric queries. By this term, we mean queries in which the formulas in the selection criteria of queries include parameters whose values are not known when the query is compiled. When parametric queries are executed, the user provides values which are bound to (substituted for) parameters; thus, parametric queries allow the repeated execution of queries for different values of the parameters, which, of course, return different results at each execution.

Parametric queries are very important. We have seen in Chapter 3 that all repetitive, compiled applications use parametric queries for accessing the distributed database. The following transformations are important for understanding how application programs should be written; typically, these transformations are not part of a query optimizer, but are instead used by application programmers for determining the queries which implement their applications correctly.

5.4.1 Simplification of Parametric Queries and Extension of Algebra

As an example of a parametric query, let us consider query Q9, selecting tuples of the global relation *DEPT* having given department numbers. Let the selection on *DEPTNUM* be parametric:

$$Q9 : \mathbf{SL}_{DEPTNUM=\$X \; OR \; DEPTNUM=\$Y} \; SUPPLY$$

At run time, the actual values are assigned to the parameters $X and $Y by the program which issues the query.

The simplification of parametric queries has some distinguishing features. Consider the above query, whose canonical form is shown in Figure 5.12a. At compile

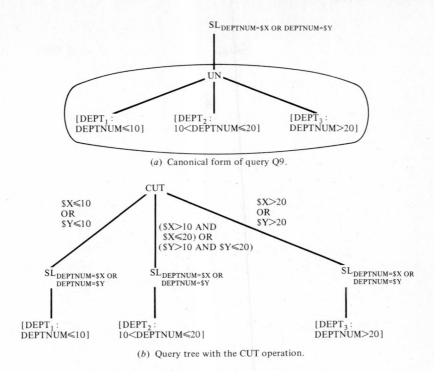

(a) Canonical form of query Q9.

(b) Query tree with the CUT operation.

Figure 5.12 Use of **CUT** in a parametric query.

time, we don't know which of the fragments of the global relation *DEPT* will be addressed. However, we know that *at most two* of them will be involved in the query. At run time, when the query will be activated, it will also be possible to know, given the value of the parameters, which ones of the fragments will be involved in the query. This shows that part of the simplification of a parametric query can be done at compile time, but part of it needs to be done at run time.

Notice that the simplification of parametric queries involves the application of the algebra of qualified relations in order to determine if qualifications of subexpressions are contradictory. In the above example, let us assume that when the query is issued, parameters are bound to the following values: $X = 1$ and $Y = 13$. Then, it is possible to simplify at run time the subtree of $DEPT_3$ because the selection formula "$DEPTNUM = 1$ OR $DEPTNUM = 13$" contradicts its qualification. Thus, in principle, there is no need for dealing with run time simplifications differently than with compile time simplifications. However, we expect that most of the optimization is done at compile time, especially for parametric queries that are often activated. Also, we do not expect to use sophisticated techniques (like applying theorem provers) at run time, for efficiency reasons. Therefore, it seems appropriate to limit run time optimization to simple tests which, when satisfied, allow simplifying the execution of the query. Obtaining the expressions for these tests requires some algebraic manipulations on qualifiers and selection conditions which are more properly done at compile time than at run time.

The run time optimization has the same effect as eliminating subexpressions from the operator tree produced at compile time. In order to represent on the operator tree the presence of tests for run time simplification, we substitute union operators with a new n-ary operator, called **CUT**; the new operator performs the union of only *some* of its operands. The **CUT** operator has a specification which contains, for each of the operands, a formula which uses the parameters of the query and the qualification of fragments. Each formula is prepared at compile time and evaluated at run time; if the formula returns true, then the corresponding operand is included in the union; if it returns false, then the corresponding operand is eliminated from the tree. Notice that the whole subtree which produces the operand needs not to be executed in this case; therefore, it is convenient to evaluate the formulas as soon as the parameters are available, so that the operator tree is simplified before beginning the actual execution. Each formula, in practice, requires that the corresponding subexpression have a qualification which is *not* a contradiction.

Figure 5.12b shows the new operator tree for the parametric query. In this example, the selection is pushed below the union operation, applying criterion 2, and then the union is substituted by the **CUT** operation. The three formulas for the **CUT** operation (one for each operand of the union operation) are

$$F1 : \$X \leq 10 \text{ OR } \$Y \leq 10$$
$$F2 : (\$X > 10 \text{ AND } \$X \leq 20) \text{ OR } (\$Y > 10 \text{ AND } \$Y \leq 20)$$
$$F3 : \$X > 20 \text{ OR } \$Y > 20$$

$F1$, $F2$, and $F3$ are prepared at compile time by determining the formulas which must be satisfied by the query parameters in order for the qualification of the corresponding operands not to be contradictory. We leave to the reader the verification of the above three formulas; it is required to compare the query predicate and the qualification of subexpressions, which is evaluated using the algebra of qualified relations.

At run time, the **CUT** operation is the first one to be evaluated; the query, for $\$X = 1$ and $\$Y = 13$, reduces to the first and second branch of the operator tree; for $\$X = 1$ and $\$Y = 5$, the query reduces to the first branch of the tree.

5.4.2 Using Temporaries in Multiple Activations of Parametric Queries

Parametric queries are characterized by the fact that they are repeatedly used, for different values of the parameters. In certain cases, repeated executions are concentrated within short time intervals; this happens, for instance, when the query is part of a loop of an application program which, at each iteration, requires a new value and binds it to the query's parameter.

As we have already seen in Chapter 3, repeating the execution of the query at each activation has a certain cost; to lower this cost, it might be useful to build temporary relations at the site of origin of the query, which store a superset of the data required by each iteration. We do not enter in the rather complex problem

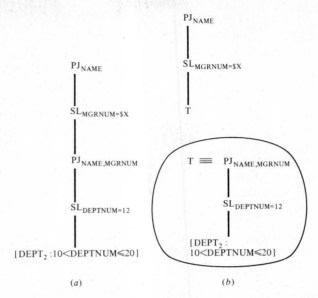

Figure 5.13 Use of temporary relations for parametric queries.

of evaluating the convenience of creating temporary copies of the information (see reference [3.7]). We instead show, on an example, how it is possible to build a useful temporary relation by manipulating the operator tree of the query. Let us consider query Q10, requiring the name of employees working in department 12 who have manager \$X (i. e., the manager number is the parameter of the query). We have

$$Q10 : \mathbf{PJ}_{NAME} \, \mathbf{SL}_{MGRNUM=\$X \text{ AND } DEPTNUM=12} \, EMP$$

First, we modify the query so that the operator tree of Figure 5.13a is obtained. The general goal of this transformation is to insulate subtrees which are **not parametric**, as they will constitute the required temporaries.

In the example, we have used idempotence to generate two distinct selections; one of them, on *MGRNUM*, is parametric; the other one, on *DEPTNUM*, is not parametric. We also used idempotence to generate a projection on *NAME* and *MGRNUM*. The selection on *DEPTNUM* and the projection are pushed toward the leaves of the operator tree as usual, while the selection on *MGRNUM* is pushed up. Thus, we have insulated a subtree which is not parametric, corresponding to the expression

$$\mathbf{PJ}_{NAME,MGRNUM} \, \mathbf{SL}_{DEPTNUM=12} \, EMP$$

We then call T the temporary given by the above expression, and divide the operator tree into two pieces in correspondence to T (see Figure 5.13b). T represents the temporary relation that will be used for repeated executions of query Q10.

CONCLUSIONS

Before executing a query which operates on global relations it is necessary to transform it into a query which operates on fragments. The most straightforward way of performing this transformation is to substitute the global relations which appear in the global query with the inverse of their fragmentation expressions. The resulting query, which operates on fragments, is called the canonical expression of the global query.

The canonical expression could be directly executed on the distributed database; however, in general, it represents a very inefficient execution of the query. It is therefore convenient to modify the canonical expression by applying equivalence transformations to it. Several heuristic criteria suggest the transformations which should be applied in order to obtain simpler expressions.

It is also possible to take advantage of the information on fragmentation in order to eliminate from the query expression those subexpressions which do not give any contribution to the final result. The concept of qualified relations and the algebra of qualified relations have been developed to this purpose.

EXERCISES

5.1 Determine common subexpressions in the following global queries (global relations are taken from the EXAMPLE_DDB). Do step-by-step transformations, indicating which rule is applied at each step. Apply criteria 1 and 2 to simplify the global queries.

(a) $\quad \mathbf{PJ}_{NAME, TAX}((EMP \ \mathbf{JN}_{DEPTNUM=DEPTNUM}\mathbf{SL}_{AREA=\text{"North"}} DEPT)$
$\qquad \mathbf{DF}(EMP \ \mathbf{JN}_{DEPTNUM=DEPTNUM}\mathbf{SL}_{DEPTNUM<10} DEPT))$

(b) $\quad (\mathbf{SL}_{DEPTNUM=10}DEPT \ \mathbf{NJN}(\mathbf{SL}_{PNUM=\text{"P1"}}$
$\qquad SUPPLY \ \mathbf{DF} \ \mathbf{SL}_{PNUM=\text{"P2"}} SUPPLY))$
$\qquad \mathbf{UN} \ (\mathbf{SL}_{DEPTNUM=\text{"10"}} DEPT \ \mathbf{NJN} \ \mathbf{SL}_{PNUM=\text{"P1"}} SUPPLY)$

5.2 Assume the global and fragmentation schema of Exercise 4.3. Translate the following global queries into fragment queries and use criteria 1 to 6 to simplify them. Use the algebra of qualified relations when this leads to the elimination of fragments which are not required by the query.

(a) List patients who use aspirin in their care:

$$\mathbf{PJ}_{NAME} (PATIENT \ \mathbf{NJN} \ \mathbf{SL}_{DRUG=\text{"ASPIRIN"}} \ CARE)$$

(b) List doctors who have prescribed aspirin to patients undergoing intensive treatment:

$$\mathbf{PJ}_{NAME} \ \mathbf{SL}_{DRUG=\text{"ASPIRIN"} \ AND \ TREAT=\text{"INTENSIVE"}}$$
$$(DOCTOR \ \mathbf{JN}_{DNUM=DNUM} \ PATIENT \ \mathbf{NJN} \ CARE)$$

(*c*) List the average quantity of aspirin prescribed to patients undergoing intensive care who have aspirin in their prescription:

$$\mathbf{GB}_{AVG(QUAN)}\mathbf{SL}_{DRUG=\text{``ASPIRIN''}}$$
$$(CARE \ \mathbf{NJN} \ \mathbf{SL}_{TREAT=\text{``INTENSIVE''}} \ PATIENT)$$

(*d*) List the average salary of doctors who prescribe aspirin, grouped by department:

$$\mathbf{GB}_{DEPTNUM,AVG(SAL)}\mathbf{SL}_{DRUG=\text{``ASPIRIN''}}$$
$$(DOCTOR \ \mathbf{JN}_{DNUM=DNUM} \ PATIENT \ \mathbf{NJN} \ CARE)$$

5.3 With the same global relations and fragments of Exercises 4.4 and 5.2, determine the smallest temporary relations that can be used for repeated executions of the following parametric queries:

(*a*) List doctors and patients of department pediatrics to which the drug $X is prescribed:

$$\mathbf{PJ}_{DOCTOR.NAME,PATIENT.NAME} \ \mathbf{SL}_{DRUG=\$X \ AND \ DEPT=\text{``PEDIATRICS''}}$$
$$(DOCTOR \ \mathbf{JN}_{DNUM=DNUM} \ PATIENT \ \mathbf{NJN} \ CARE)$$

(*b*) List all drugs prescribed to patient $X in the immunology department:

$$\mathbf{PJ}_{DRUG} \ \mathbf{SL}_{PNUN=\$X \ AND \ DEPT=\text{``IMMUNOLOGY''}} \ (PATIENT \ \mathbf{NJN} \ CARE)$$

5.4 Assume that the fragmentation of a global relation $R(A, B, C)$ is described by the following predicates:

$$p1 : (1 \leq A \leq 4)$$
$$p2 : (5 \leq A \leq 7) \ \text{AND} \ (1 \leq B \leq 5)$$
$$p3 : (5 \leq A \leq 7) \ \text{AND} \ (6 \leq B \leq 10)$$
$$p4 : (8 \leq A \leq 10) \ \text{AND} \ (1 \leq C \leq 5)$$
$$p5 : (8 \leq A \leq 10) \ \text{AND} \ (6 \leq C \leq 10)$$

Introduce the **CUT** operation in the following parametric queries:

(*a*) $\mathbf{SL}_{A=\$X \ AND \ B<\$Y}R$
(*b*) $\mathbf{SL}_{C=\$X \ AND \ B=\$Y}R$
(*c*) $\mathbf{SL}_{A>\$X \ OR \ C=\$Y}R$

5.5 Give an example of global schema, fragmentation schema, and additional semantic knowledge, such that all this information can be used for deducing the simplification of a query.

5.6 Consider the possibility of commuting $\mathbf{SL}_F$ and $\mathbf{GB}_{G,AF}$. Give the validity indicator (*Y, N, SNC, SC*) for this transformation; justify your answer.

5.7 Compute the following expression, using the algebra of qualified relations:

$$\mathbf{SL}_{NOT \, b}((([R1 : a] \ \mathbf{JN}_F \ [S1 : b]) \ \mathbf{UN} \ ([R2 : NOT \ a] \ \mathbf{JN}_F \ [S1 : b]))$$
$$\mathbf{DF} \ ([T1 : c] \ \mathbf{JN}_F \ [S2 : \ NOT \ b]))$$

Annotated Bibliography

References [5.1] to [5.5] are concerned with traditional relational algebra; references [5.6] to [5.8] are concerned with extensions to algebra which have inspired those covered in this chapter. Notice that, consistent with the distribution of the material about query processing in Chapters 5 and 6, references on query optimization will be found in the annotated bibliography of the next chapter.

[5.1]   J. M. Smith and P. Y. T. Chang, "Optimizing the Performance of a Relational Algebra Database Interface," *Communications of the ACM*, **18**:10, October 1975.

This paper introduces the use of "query trees" and query tree transformations for optimizing expressions of relational algebra, which are applied to a "smart query interface for a relational algebra" (SQIRAL). The interface assumes queries written in relational algebra; the corresponding operator tree is first simplified (typically, by pushing unary operations down in the tree); then nodes are mapped by a tree transformer to internal nodes which describe the implementation of operations. For instance, a pair selection-projection over the same operand is merged into one node called COMPOUND RESTRICT; joins can be mapped to several internal nodes, corresponding to different join methods. The transformation takes into account sorting and the presence of indexes.

[5.2]   P. A. V. Hall, "Optimization of a Single Relational Expression in a Relational Database System," *IBM Journal of Research and Development*, **20**:3, 1976.

[5.3]   F. P. Palermo, "A Data Base Search Problem," *Information Systems: COINS IV*, J. T. Tou, ed., Plenum Press, 1974.

The above two papers belong, as does the first one, to the early literature on relational algebra optimization. They are mentioned here because reference [5.2] introduced first the determination and elimination of common subexpressions, redundant expressions, and trivial selection formulas; reference [5.3] was the first to show the convenience of executing selections early and developed a method for joining relations which is similar to using semi-joins.

[5.4]   J. D. Ullman, *Principles of Database Systems*, 2d ed., Computer Science Press, 1983.

[5.5]   D. Maier, *The Theory of Relational Databases*, Computer Science Press, 1983.

The above two references are books about database systems which have recently appeared; they each have a large section on query processing for centralized database systems and a small section on distributed query processing. In particular, Ullman's book describes a method for simplifying queries over horizontally fragmented relations which is similar to that of Section 5.2.3 (he uses the term "guard" instead of "qualification" for the predicate distinguishing each fragment).

[5.6]   S. Ceri and G. Pelagatti, "Correctness of Query Execution Strategies in Distributed Databases," *ACM TODS*, **8**:4, 1983.

The material of this chapter comes largely from this paper; however, the notation used in the paper is very different. The paper introduces **multirelations** for describing horizontally fragmented relations. A multirelation is a set of extended relations; each extended relation represents a fragment and is constituted by a triple:

1. A relation called the **body** of the fragment
2. A predicate called the **qualification** of the fragment
3. A relation with one tuple which contains the value of the aggregate functions evaluated on the fragment, called the **functional qualification**

Correctness of multirelations requires that all the bodies of the same multirelation have the same relation schema; the same constraint applies to all the functional qualifications. Algebra of multirelations (MRA) contains, beyond the natural extension to multirelations of operations of standard algebra, some original features:

1. The partition operation, which can be applied to a global relation for the initial partitioning or to any multirelation for changing its partitioning criteria
2. The collection operation, for merging all extended relations into a single one
3. The selection on qualifiers, for eliminating extended relations whose qualifiers are contradictory with query conditions
4. The evaluation of aggregate functions for each extended relation
5. The extraction of functional qualifications, which fill the body of a new multirelation having only one extended relation (this allows manipulating algebraically the results of function evaluations)

Clearly, MRA has inspired several features of this chapter, such as the algebra of qualified relations (in Section 5.2.2) and the new operations **GB** and **CUT**.

The paper develops the tables of equivalence transformations between expressions of extended algebra organized as those of Section 5.1.2, and then shows the usage of extended algebra for proving that a query processing strategy is correct and for generating efficient query processing strategies.

[5.7]   M. Adiba, "Derived Relations: a Unified Mechanisms for Views, Snapshots and Distributed Data," *Seventh VLDB*, 1981.

[5.8]   A. L. Furtado and L. Kerschberg, "An Algebra of Quotient Relations," *ACM-SIGMOD*, 1977.

The above two papers present extensions to relational algebra which go in the direction of partitioning relations into fragments.

In reference [5.7] partitioned relations are called **derived relations** (DERELs); operations of standard algebra are extended to DERELs (in a way similar to that of reference [5.6]). The emphasis of this paper is on the application of DERELs in the definition of views, snapshots, and distributed data; a language is introduced for defining and manipulating DERELs.

In [5.8] partitioned relations are called **quotient relations**; they are produced by selecting some of the attributes and dividing relations into subsets having the same values of these attributes. The paper presents a formal model of algebraic operations on quotient relations; while this formal model seems adequate to describe the effect of operations such as the GROUP BY of SQL [2.6], it does not adequately represent fragments of distributed databases, because their definition requires more general predicates.

[5.9]   F. Crivellari, F. Dalla Libera, S. Frasson, and F. A. Schreiber, "Computation of Statistical Functions in Distributed Information Systems," *Information Systems*, **8**:4, 1983.

This paper analyzes the distributed evaluation of aggregate and statistical functions in distributed databases, which we have described in Section 5.3. Functions are distinguished into two classes: **homogeneously decomposable**, whose result can be obtained by applying the function itself to each fragment of a horizontally partitioned relation, and **nonhomogeneously decomposable**, in which the synthesis of the result requires the application of some other functions to the fragments. Functions include the typical aggregate functions and the statistical functions (such as moments and indexes); for each function, the distributed computation is shown.

[5.10]   J. J. King, "QUIST: A System for Semantic Query Optimization in Relational Data Bases," *Seventh VLDB*, 1982.

This paper presents the use of semantic information for improving query execution used by a system called QUIST. The system can improve the execution of the query by making inferences involving the selection conditions and the semantic rules of the database. The basic idea is exemplified as follows: Given a query about the destination of a cargo whose capacity exceeds 350 tons, we only have to search through the ports with offshore load/discharge capabilities, because such a cargo needs these facilities; this is stated by a semantic rule. The approach presented in this paper is a generalization of what is done in this chapter for selecting the fragments to which queries must be addressed.

Chapter 6

Optimization
of Access Strategies

In the previous chapter, we have shown how it is possible to "ameliorate" a query by suitable modifications. In this chapter, we attempt the "optimization" of access strategies, i.e., the selection, among alternative possibilities, of the one which corresponds to the minimum cost. In fact, the term "optimization" is rather inaccurate, since the techniques for optimizing the execution typically do not obtain optimality and just look for "good" access strategies; moreover, they rely on simplifying assumptions about the processing environment. Therefore, any claim of optimality must be carefully considered. We will, however, keep the term "optimization," since it is commonly used in the literature.

Most of the transformations shown in the previous chapter, while constituting a fundamental premise to query optimization, do not really require a selection among alternatives, because they are certainly beneficial. Factoring common subexpressions and eliminating subexpressions not required by the query are examples of modifications which are certainly beneficial. Also pushing the unary operations toward the leaves of operator trees is beneficial, because this allows the reduction in size of the operands "at the earliest time"; this is beneficial in nondistributed environments (where the critical cost factors are related to the execution of joins), and is especially beneficial in distributed environments (where we add the costs of data transmission). The important fact is that the transformations of Chapter 5 are made on a logical basis and do not require any assumption on the processing environment.

There are two major exceptions:

1. The commutativity of joins and unions
2. The transformation of joins into semi-join programs

These transformations generate alternative query processing strategies which must be compared on a cost basis; these transformations, therefore, belong properly to both Chapter 5 and Chapter 6, and we will deal with them again.

6.1 A FRAMEWORK FOR QUERY OPTIMIZATION

In this section, we give a classification of query processing problems, of the assumptions which are required for modeling and solving them, and of the criteria that are used in the optimization. We then build a new model of queries and introduce all the relevant quantitative parameters which are part of the model.

6.1.1 Problems in Query Optimization

The selection of a query processing strategy involves:

1. Determining the physical copies of the fragments upon which to execute the query, given a query expression over fragments. The term **materialization** is typically used in the literature to denote a nonredundant copy of the entire distributed database upon which the query is executed. In terms of the reference model of Chapter 3, a materialization corresponds to the selection, for each fragment, of one of the fragment's copies. Notice that different queries will use, in general, different materializations.

    The selection of a materialization for a query is by itself a limitation on the general formulation of the problem, as there is no reason, in principle, to select a different copy of each fragment for executing the same query. For instance, different subexpressions requiring the same fragment could be executed over different copies of it. However, most query processing algorithms operate in the context of a materialization.

2. Selecting the order of execution of operations; as we will see, this involves the determination of a "good" sequence of join, semi-join, and union operations, since determining the order of execution of the other operations is not difficult. It is worth noticing that the operator tree produced after the query tranformations of Chapter 5 implicitly defines a partial ordering of operations, consisting in executing them ascending from the leaves to the root. However, this does not completely define a solution of the optimization problem, since it is required to indicate also the ordering of the evaluation of subexpressions which are executed at the same level of the tree; moreover, ascending from the leaves to the root does not necessarily produce the best solution.

3. Selecting the method for executing each operation; this involves the choice of performing some algebraic operations together within the same database access (for instance, executing selections and projections on the same operand at the same time), and the selection of a method for executing each database access among the various available methods. Typically, the most difficult problem is to determine the best method for evaluating joins. This last problem is peculiar to each individual system, and we will not attempt to

give a general solution to it; in Section 6.2.4 we will show the methods for evaluating joins which are supported by the R* prototype. In general, we consider all the sequences of operations which are applied to operands stored at the same database site as constituting a single program, but we do not indicate how to perform the corresponding database accesses.

The above problems are not independent: for instance, the choice of the best materialization for a query depends on the order in which operations are executed; therefore, proceeding by solving them independently introduces errors. However, a typical simplification which is made by optimization methods consists exactly in considering the three problems as independent; thus:

1. A materialization is assumed for a given query.
2. The order of execution of operations is optimized.
3. Operations are clustered into local programs.

In practice, the first problem is often bypassed (by taking a materialization as granted), the third problem is also disregarded (because it is system-dependent), and the emphasis is placed on the second problem; we will follow the same approach.

As we concentrate on the problem of determining the order of execution of operations, queries can still be modeled in terms of fragments, as in Chapter 5; within a materialization, each fragment gets mapped to one of its physical copies within the physical images; we can think of "allocated fragments." The selection of an optimal materialization for a given query requires instead a complete knowledge of the mapping between fragments and physical images.

6.1.2 Objectives in Query Processing Optimization

The selection of alternative query execution strategies, in both a centralized and a distributed environment, is made by measuring their expected performances. The typical measures which are assumed in centralized databases are the number of I/O operations and the use of a CPU which is required to perform the query. In distributed databases, also the amount of data transmission between sites must be considered. However, there is no agreement on the relative importance of cost of transmission versus local I/O. In some papers, like references [6.5] and [6.9], we find the statement that the minimization of transmission costs is the only important goal. In general, these papers make this statement because the communication network bandwidth is *orders of magnitude lower* than transfer rates between disks and main memory. These references typically consider as a communication network the ARPANET, whose bandwidth is about 10 kilobits per second.

However, other authors have a different opinion; in reference [6.10], for example, it is stated that "doing complex work in a distributed database environment as opposed to a centralized database, adds only a relatively small overhead (e.g., 15 to 30 percent) to the cost of performing any significant amount of database work, whereas response time for small amounts of work will increase considerably when data is remote." These authors used for their experiences a communication system with a bandwidth of about 50 kilobits per second.

These two opinions reflect different assumptions about the processing environment. Considering only transmission costs appears more coherent with the assumption of a geographically dispersed distributed database, where limitations in bandwidth are severe; in local networks, instead, we can have an intersite bandwidth which is closer to that of local I/O operations, and therefore intersite communication becomes a resource comparable to local I/O and CPU operations.

Considering only transmission requirements is extremely appealing, because:

1. Transmission requirements are neutral with respect to systems; they are typically a function of the amount of data transmitted between sites (the same consideration does not apply, for instance, to I/O measures, which depend on the method used for performing operations).

2. The optimization of a distributed query can be partitioned into two independent problems: the distribution of the access strategy among sites, which is done considering transmission only, and the determination of local access strategies at each site, which uses traditional methods of centralized databases. The two problems are solved in sequence, since the former is much more important than the latter.

In this chapter, we will, in general, assume that global optimization can be performed independently from local optimization, and that it can be based only on transmission costs, with the exception of Section 6.2.4, in which we will discuss a query optimization algorithm that also includes the selection of local access methods and considers I/O and CPU costs for the optimization.

However, the rationale behind the query processing methods presented in this chapter remains valid if we drop the above assumption. In this case, we might think of having a complex model of query processing strategies available, but the basic structure of algorithms presented in this chapter would not change.

Transmission requirements can be evaluated in terms of costs and delays:

1. When costs are considered, the measure of performance for an application is given by the sum of all the transmission costs of each required transmission. This approach corresponds to the minimization of the overall transmission overhead in the communication network.

2. When delays are considered, the measure of performance for an application is given by the elapsed time between activation and completion of the application. Reducing delays amounts to increasing the degree of parallelism in the execution and does not necessarily correspond to the minimization of the overall transmission overhead.

Transmission costs TC and transmission delays TD for a single transmission are typically modeled by a function which is linear in the size x of transmitted data:

$$TC(x) = C_0 + x \times C_1$$
$$TD(x) = D_0 + x \times D_1$$

where C_0, C_1, D_0, and D_1 are system-dependent constants; C_0 corresponds to the fixed cost of initiating a transmission among two sites; C_1 is the networkwide unitary transmission cost; D_0 is the fixed time for establishing a connection; and D_1 is the networkwide unitary transfer rate.

Other models assume a more detailed characterization of costs and delays by associating different coefficients to each pair of sites. In this case, we have

$$TC(x) = C_0^{ij} + x \times C_1^{ij}$$
$$TD(x) = D_0^{ij} + x \times D_1^{ij}$$

where the two indexes i and j denote the source and the destination of the transmission, respectively. This detailed characterization adds little significant information, since:

1. In geographically dispersed networks, costs and delays depend on routings (i.e., sequences of sites connecting the source and the destination) which are dynamically determined; thus, it is hard to assign precise values to the above coefficients.
2. In local networks, intersite communication is typically done using homogeneous links, and therefore it is not useful to give independent intersite unitary costs.

In some cases, different intersite unitary costs are more convincing:

1. When costs are charged to the users of the distributed database system on a distance basis (then, a good optimizer should probably help the user in saving money).
2. When the network topology helps in distinguishing between classes of intersite connections (for instance, in a star network, we distinguish intersite communications between those involving the central site and a remote site or those between two distinct remote sites).

6.1.3 A New Model of Queries

In the previous section, we have given a tree representation of queries in which the nodes of the tree represented a variety of operations (including traditional algebraic operations and extensions of algebra). We have also converted trees into graphs because of the need to determine common subexpressions. In this section, we give a simpler representation of queries by considering only critical operations for query processing. We also add to this model all the quantitative information which can be useful for evaluating alternative query processing strategies.

6.1.3.1 Database profiles   Let us begin by defining the statistical description of the database which is required for a quantitative analysis. We use for this description the term **profile**, as in reference [6.5]. Profiles describe fragments and contain the following information:

1.   The number of tuples of each fragment R_i, denoted card(R_i).
2.   The size (i.e., the number of bytes) of each attribute A, denoted size(A) (for simplicity, attributes with the same name in the database schema are assumed to be of the same size); the size of a fragment, size(R_i), is given by the sum of the sizes of its attributes.
3.   For each attribute A in each fragment R_i, the number of distinct values appearing in R_i, denoted val($A[R_i]$). When the fragment R_i is clear from the context, it can be omitted from this expression.

This information can be specified for global relations rather than for fragments; for example, Figure 6.1a shows the profiles of two global relations and Figure 6.1b shows the profiles of two fragments. As shown in Figure 6.1b, in the examples of this chapter the characterization of each fragment R_i includes not only its profile but also its allocation, denoted site(R_i).

card($SUPPLY$) = 50,000

	SNUM	PNUM	DEPTNUM	QUAN
size	6	7	2	10
val	3000	1000	30	500

card($DEPT$) = 30

	DEPTNUM	NAME	AREA	MGRNUM
size	2	15	1	7
val	30	30	6	30

(a) Profiles of global relations $SUPPLY$ and $DEPT$

card($SUPPLY_1$) = 30,000
site($SUPPLY_1$) = 1

	SNUM	PNUM	DEPTNUM	QUAN
size	6	7	2	10
val	1800	1000	20	500

card($DEPT_1$) = 10
site($DEPT_1$) = 2

	DEPTNUM	NAME	AREA	MGRNUM
size	2	15	1	7
val	10	10	2	10

(b) Profiles of fragments $SUPPLY_1$ and $DEPT_1$

Figure 6.1   Examples of profiles.

6.1.3.2 Estimating profiles of results of algebraic operations

The estimation of the profiles of the results of algebraic operations is useful for evaluating the effect of applying alternative operations during the optimization; it is also useful for evaluating the profiles of fragments, given the profiles of global relations. Let

S denote the result of performing a unary operation over a relation R, and let T denote the result of applying a binary operation to two relations R and S.

Selection

1. *Cardinality.* To each selection we associate a selectivity ρ which is the fraction of tuples satisfying it. In simple selections *attribute = value* $(A = v)$, ρ can be estimated as $1/\mathrm{val}(A[R])$, under the assumptions that values are homogeneously distributed and that the value v appears in R. We have

$$\mathrm{card}(S) = \rho \times \mathrm{card}(R)$$

2. *Size.* Selection does not affect the size of relations:

$$\mathrm{size}(S) = \mathrm{size}(R)$$

3. *Distinct values.* Consider an attribute B which is not used in the selection formula. Under the assumptions of independence of B with respect to selection criteria and of homogeneous distribution of values, the determination of $\mathrm{val}(B[S])$ is reconducted to the following statistical problem: Given $n = \mathrm{card}(R)$ objects uniformly distributed over $m = \mathrm{val}(B[R_i])$ colors, how many different colors $c = \mathrm{val}(B[R_i])$ are selected if we take just $r = \mathrm{card}(R_i)$ objects?

This problem has been solved by using different mathematical approximations (see references [6.5], [6.14b], and [6.15]); we give here a practical approximation of the value $c(n, m, r)$, assumed also in reference [6.5]:

$$c(n, m, r) = \begin{cases} r, & \text{for } r < m/2 \\ (r + m)/3, & \text{for } m/2 \leq r < 2m \\ m, & \text{for } r \geq 2m \end{cases} \qquad (6.1)$$

Sometimes, the assumptions of independence and of homogeneous distribution of values are wrong, and the use of formula (6.1) would be unacceptable. In particular, for the attributes which are used in the selection formula a completely different evaluation must be done; for example, in the important case of simple selection on A, $\mathrm{val}(A[S]) = 1$. The extension to more complex selections is straightforward.

Projection

1. *Cardinality.* Projection affects the cardinality of operands, since duplicates are eliminated from the result. This effect is difficult to evaluate; the following three rules can be applied:

   - If the projection involves a single attribute A, set

$$\mathrm{card}(S) = \mathrm{val}(A[R])$$

   - If the product $\prod_{A_i \in Attr(S)} \mathrm{val}(A_i(R))$ is less than $\mathrm{card}(R)$, where $Attr(S)$ are the attributes in the result of the projection, set

$$\text{card}(S) = \prod_{A_i \in Attr(S)} \text{val}(A_i(R))$$

- If the projection includes a key of R, set

$$\text{card}(S) = \text{card}(R)$$

Notice that some systems do not perform the elimination of duplicates after the projection. In this case, the cardinality of the result is the same as the cardinality of the operand relation.

2. *Size.* The size of the result of a projection is reduced to the sum of the sizes of attributes in its specification.

3. *Distinct values.* The distinct values of projected attributes are the same as in the operand relation.

Group-by (Recall that the operation $\mathbf{GB}_{G,AF}$ was introduced for performing the partitioning of relations into groups and the evaluation of aggregate functions over them; G indicates the attributes on which the grouping is performed, AF indicates the aggregate functions to be evaluated.)

1. *Cardinality.* We give an upper bound on the cardinality of S:

$$\text{card}(S) \leq \prod_{A_i \in G} \text{val}(A[R])$$

This upper bound corresponds to the case in which each value of a given attribute of the group by specification combines with every value of all other attributes in the specification.

2. *Size.* For all attributes A appearing in G

$$\text{size}(R.A) = \text{size}(S.A)$$

The size of S is given by the sum of the sizes of attributes in G and AF.

3. *Distinct values.* For all attributes A appearing in G

$$\text{val}(A[S]) = \text{val}(A[R])$$

Union

1. *Cardinality.* We have

$$\text{card}(T) \leq \text{card}(R) + \text{card}(S)$$

Equality holds when duplicate tuples are not eliminated.

2. *Size.* We have

$$\text{size}(T) = \text{size}(R) = \text{size}(S)$$

since the union applies to relations with the same attribute schema.

3. *Distinct values.* An upper bound is

$$\text{val}(A[T]) \leq \text{val}(A[R]) + \text{val}(A[S])$$

Difference

1. *Cardinality.* We have

$$\max(0, \text{card}(R) - \text{card}(S)) \le \text{card}(T) \le \text{card}(R)$$

2. *Size.* We have

$$\text{size}(T) = \text{size}(R) = \text{size}(S)$$

since the difference applies to relations with the same attribute schema.

3. *Distinct values.* An upper bound is

$$\text{val}(A[T]) \le \text{val}(A[R])$$

Cartesian product

1. *Cardinality.* We have

$$\text{card}(T) = \text{card}(R) \times \text{card}(S)$$

2. *Size.* We have

$$\text{size}(T) = \text{size}(R) + \text{size}(S)$$

3. *Distinct values.* The distinct values of attributes are the same as in the operand relations.

Join   Consider the join $T = R \text{ } \mathbf{JN}_{A=B} \text{ } S$.

1. *Cardinality.* Estimating precisely the cardinality of T is quite complex; we can give an upper bound to $\text{card}(T)$ because $\text{card}(T) \le \text{card}(R) \times \text{card}(S)$, but this value is usually much higher than the actual cardinality. Assuming that all the values of A in R appear also as values of B in S and vice versa (with $\text{val}(A[R]) = \text{val}(B[S])$) and that the two attributes are both uniformly distributed over the tuples of R and S, we have

$$\text{card}(T) = (\text{card}(R) \times \text{card}(S))/\text{val}(A[R])$$

Also under the above assumptions, if one of the two attributes, say A, is a key of R, then

$$\text{card}(T) = \text{card}(S)$$

These values can be considered as upper bounds if the above assumptions do not hold.

2. *Size.* We have

$$\text{size}(T) = \text{size}(R) + \text{size}(S)$$

In the case of natural join, since the natural join also eliminates one of the join attributes, the size of this attribute must be subtracted from the size of the result.

3. *Distinct values.* We can give an upper bound to the number of distinct values generated by a join. If A is a join attribute, we have

$$\text{val}(A[T]) \le \min(\text{val}(A[R]), \text{val}(B[S]))$$

If A is not a join attribute, we have

$$\text{val}(A[T]) \le \text{val}(A[R]) + \text{val}(B[S])$$

Semi-join   Consider the semi-join $T = R\,\mathbf{SJ}_{A=B}\,S$.

1.   *Cardinality.* The estimation of the cardinality of T is similar to that of a selection operation; we denote with ρ the selectivity of the semi-join operation, which measures the fraction of the tuples of R which belong to the result. In references [6.5] and [6.6], the following estimation is proposed:

$$\rho = \mathrm{val}(A[S])/\mathrm{val}(\mathrm{dom}(A))$$

where $\mathrm{val}(\mathrm{dom}(A))$ denotes the number of distinct values in A's domain. Given ρ, we determine $\mathrm{card}(T)$ as

$$\mathrm{card}(T) = \rho \times \mathrm{card}(R)$$

2.   *Size.* The size of the result of a semi-join is the same as the size of its first operand.

3.   *Distinct values.* The number of distinct values of attributes which do not belong to the semi-join specification can be estimated using formula (6.1), with $n = \mathrm{card}(R)$, $m = \mathrm{val}(A[R])$ and $r = \mathrm{card}(T)$. If A is the only attribute appearing in the semi-join specification, then

$$\mathrm{val}(A[T]) = \rho \times \mathrm{val}(A[R])$$

In Figure 6.1b, the profiles of horizontal fragments $SUPPLY_1$ and $DEPT_1$ are shown; since they correspond to selections of global relations $SUPPLY$ and $DEPT$ respectively, profiles are evaluated with the rules which apply to the selection operation, assuming $\rho(SUPPLY_1) = 0.6$ and $\rho(DEPT_1) = 0.33$. Notice that the assumption of independence of the attributes with respect to the selection criteria does not hold in the evaluation of the number of distinct values of attributes $SNUM$, $AREA$, and $DEPTNUM$. In this case, distinct values have been assumed proportional to the selectivities of selections.

6.1.3.3 A model for query optimization   We develop now a new model of a query, which is more convenient than the operator tree model for describing query optimization. In this new model, we include only those operations which are *critical* for the query optimization problem; we consider only the subset of the most commonly used queries.

Unary operations are not critical, because they have the effect of reducing their operands both in cardinality and in size, without requiring any data transmission; thus, unary operations must be performed as early as possible. Unary operations which apply to the same fragment are collected into programs called **fragment reducers**. Reducers are applied to fragments before performing binary operations; the modification to a fragment profile which is caused by applying a reducer program can be computed using the rules of the previous section.

Binary operations are critical, because they involve the comparison of two operands; thus, when operands are not at the same site, they require data transmission. We do not consider in this chapter the cartesian product and the difference, which appear rarely in the user's queries. We also assume that semi-join operations are not part of the user's query; however, they are introduced during query optimization. Thus, we need to consider only the binary operations join and union.

Since we restrict the binary operations to joins and unions, while unary operations are not relevant in the query optimization problem, it is convenient to introduce a new model of query, at a higher abstraction level. This model is called **optimization graph**. In optimization graphs, nodes represent reduced fragments, joins are represented by edges between nodes which are labeled with the join specification, and unions are represented by hypernodes enclosing their operands.

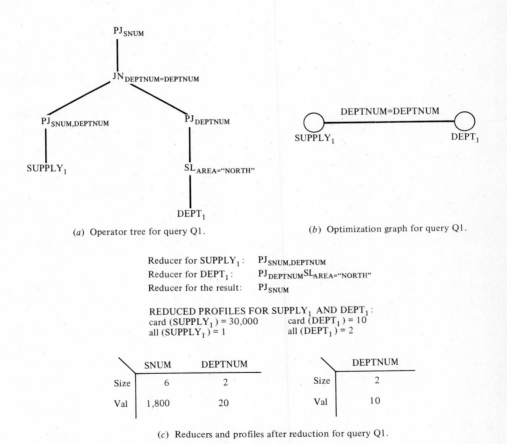

(a) Operator tree for query Q1.

(b) Optimization graph for query Q1.

Reducer for SUPPLY$_1$:   PJ$_{SNUM,DEPTNUM}$
Reducer for DEPT$_1$:   PJ$_{DEPTNUM}$SL$_{AREA="NORTH"}$
Reducer for the result: PJ$_{SNUM}$

REDUCED PROFILES FOR SUPPLY$_1$ AND DEPT$_1$:
card (SUPPLY$_1$) = 30,000   card (DEPT$_1$) = 10
all (SUPPLY$_1$) = 1   all (DEPT$_1$) = 2

	SNUM	DEPTNUM			DEPTNUM
Size	6	2		Size	2
Val	1,800	20		Val	10

(c) Reducers and profiles after reduction for query Q1.

Figure 6.2   Transformation of a query tree into an optimization graph with the reducer programs and the profiles of fragments.

Figure 6.2a shows the operator tree of query Q1 after all the transformations done in Chapter 5. The optimization graph of the same query is shown in Figure 6.2b; the graph includes only two nodes connected by an edge, which represents the required join. The reducer programs for the two fragments of this query are shown in Figure 6.2c; before starting to consider the optimization problem, it is required to evaluate the profiles of the fragments *as if* reducer programs were applied. These profiles are also shown in Figure 6.2c.

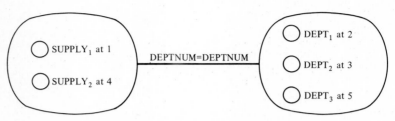

(*a*) Optimization graph for the first version of query Q1.

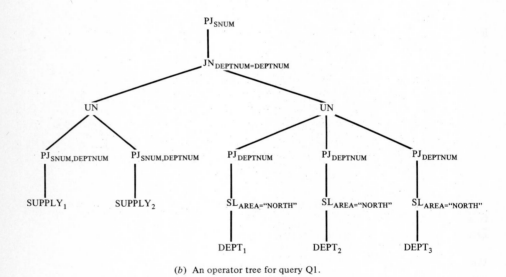

(*b*) An operator tree for query Q1.

Figure 6.3 Optimization graphs for query Q1.

Figure 6.3*a* shows a more complex example of optimization graph, corresponding to the operator tree of Figure 5.4, which is reproduced also in Figure 6.3*b*. This operator tree refers to the same query Q1, before the simplifications of Chapter 5. The optimization graph of Figure 6.3*a* shows two union operations followed by a join operation.

The use of operator trees would be ackward in query optimization, because once that the "operations have been pushed to the leaves," there is really no interest in maintaining partial orders between nodes. Instead, optimization graphs are simpler and more neutral, i.e., without the partial orders which are implicit in the tree structure.

6.1.4 Summary of the Assumptions for Distributed Query Optimization

We summarize here the assumptions used in this chapter; this summary is also a guide to the sections which follow.

1. For each query, we assume a materialization as given, and we operate upon allocated fragments.

2. We consider initially (Sections 6.2.1 and 6.2.2) only transmission requirements and minimize transmission costs; transmission delays are minimized in Section 6.2.3, and a more comprehensive cost model is assumed in Section 6.2.4.

3. Transmission costs do not depend on the sites between which each transmission occurs.

4. In order to evaluate the profiles, we make, when required, the assumption that values are uniformly distributed over the tuples of fragments, and that all attributes are independent.

5. We do not consider queries which include the cartesian product and the difference.

6. In Section 6.2 we examine **join queries**, i.e., queries whose optimization graph includes only join operations without unions. This assumption is abandoned in Section 6.3, where we address the more complex case of queries whose optimization graph includes both joins and unions. The reason for dealing with join queries separately is that this class of queries has been largely studied in the literature and several techniques exist for their optimization (join queries are often called "select-project-join" queries in the literature, since clearly also unary operations can be used in their expression).

6.1.5 Importance of Query Optimization in Distributed Databases

We complete this introductory section on query optimization by stressing its importance in a distributed environment. We want to show that the development of a "good" query processing strategy is mandatory in this environment, as there exist also "very bad" query processing strategies that must be avoided. Thus, the efficiency of the final system relies very much upon the quality of the query optimizer or, in the absence of the optimizer, upon the skill of the application programmer. Recall that all the transformations of query expressions shown in Chapter 5 and some of the algorithms of this chapter must become part of the optimizers in a system which provides distribution transparency, and constitute a guide to application programmers in writing efficient queries for systems with lower degrees of transparency.

Let us take query Q1 of Chapter 5 as a working example. The query asks for suppliers that have issued a supply order in the North area of the company; let the result be required at site 2. Let us analyze the transmission requirements for different execution strategies of this query; for simplicity, we disregard C_0 and D_0 in the expression of costs and delays. The following discussion is based on the operator trees, optimization graphs, and profiles of the query Q1 shown in Figures 5.1, 5.4, 5.7, 6.1, 6.2, and 6.3.

Strategy 1 A first, "very bad" execution strategy consists in performing operations in the same order as they are indicated in the query (and represented in Figure 5.4a), without any simplification and optimization; Figure 6.3a shows the optimization graph for this case, Figure 6.1 gives the profiles of $SUPPLY_1$ and $DEPT_1$; assume that the profiles of $SUPPLY_2$, $DEPT_2$, and $DEPT_3$ are similar, with $\text{card}(SUPPLY_2) = 20{,}000$, $\text{card}(DEPT_2) = \text{card}(DEPT_3) = 10$. Let us collect all the fragments at site 2 in order to execute the query there, and let the collection be made in parallel. Then, $DEPT_1$ needs not to be transmitted; $SUPPLY_1$ amounts to $30{,}000 \times 25 \times 8$ bits, $SUPPLY_2$ to $20{,}000 \times 25 \times 8$ bits, and $DEPT_1$ and $DEPT_3$ to $10 \times 25 \times 8$ bits. Thus, we have a transmission cost of $10{,}002{,}000 \times C_1$ and a transmission delay of $6{,}000{,}000 \times D_1$ (corresponding to the transmission of the largest fragment, $SUPPLY_1$). If D_1 amounts to 10,000 bits per second, as in the ARPANET, this execution strategy requires 10 minutes.

Strategy 2 A second execution strategy consists in performing local processing on fragments (i.e., applying fragment reducers) and then sending all the reduced fragments to site 2, where the query is executed. The operator tree corresponding to this query transformation is shown in Figure 6.3b; the optimization graph remains that of the previous case, shown in Figure 6.3a. $SUPPLY_1$ and $SUPPLY_2$ are reduced by a projection to $30{,}000 \times 8 \times 8$ bits and $20{,}000 \times 8 \times 8$ bits, respectively; fragments of $DEPT$ are reduced drastically by a selection and a projection. They can be disregarded in the computation of costs and delays. Thus, the total cost and delay reduce to about $3{,}200{,}000 \times C_1$ and $1{,}920{,}000 \times D_1$, respectively; still, we need about 3 minutes to execute the query.

Strategy 3 A third execution strategy uses the further simplifications that were inferred for query Q1 in Section 5.2.5; the operator tree is that of Figure 6.2a, and the optimization graph reduces to that in Figure 6.2b. We have discovered that only fragments $SUPPLY_1$ and $DEPT_1$ give a contribution to the query; again, we transmit all required fragments (i.e., only $SUPPLY_1$) to site 2, where the query is performed. The total cost is therefore reduced to $1{,}920{,}000 \times C_1$ with respect to the previous strategy. The delay is still $1{,}920{,}000 \times D_1$, since unfortunately the elimination of the transmission of $SUPPLY_2$ has no effect on the delay, which is determined by the largest fragment $SUPPLY_1$.

Strategies 2 and 3 are still considered "bad" execution strategies because they move fragment $SUPPLY_1$ before reducing its cardinality.

Strategy 4 A fourth execution strategy reflects the improvement that is obtained through query optimization, and consists of a different order of execution of operations; precisely, the reduced fragment $DEPT_1$ is sent to site 1, the join is performed there, and the result of the query is sent back to site 2. Clearly, the optimization graph is the same as in strategy 3. Since $DEPT_1$ consists only of the join attribute, this method falls into the category of semi-joins. In order to measure the required transmissions, we need to evaluate the profile of the result of the semi-join and of the projection on the attribute $SNUM$; applying the formulas of Section 6.1.3.2, we obtain card($DEPT_1$) = 5, card($RESULT$) = 1800 (i.e., card($RESULT$) = val($SNUM[SUPPLY_1]$)). Then, the transmission requirements amount to 1800 × 2 × 8 bits; the transmission costs and delays are 28,800 × C_1 and 28,800 × D_1, respectively; the required time is 2.88 seconds.

The delay of strategy 1 is more than 200 times the delay of strategy 4 for executing the same query. This example shows the importance of selecting a good execution strategy in distributed databases.

6.2 JOIN QUERIES

In this section, we restrict our analysis to join queries, i.e., queries whose optimization graph includes only joins. The algorithms which are presented in this section do not consider explicitly the fragmentation of relations. Thus, in this section we do not use the notion of fragmentation, and we use the generic term "relation" to denote either fragments or nonfragmented relations which appear as nodes of the optimization graphs. Optimization algorithms can be classified in two classes:

1. Algorithms which use semi-joins for reducing relations before transmitting them
2. Algorithms which do not consider semi-joins

We first present the general foundation of algorithms which use semi-joins, and then we show two specific approaches to optimization which use them. Both these approaches consider only transmission costs as the goal function. Finally, we show an approach to query optimization which does not use semi-joins, and which takes into account also local processing costs.

The optimization graph of a join query consists only of nodes, which represent relations, and edges, which represent joins; this kind of representation was already introduced in Chapter 4 and called a **join graph**. Since we allow more than one join specification between any two relations, a join graph is, in fact, a multigraph.

6.2.1 Use of Semi-join Programs for Join Queries

Let us start by considering a simple example of a semi-join program and its transmission cost. We recall from Section 5.2.7 that a semi-join program between two relations R and S over two attributes A and B is defined as $(R\,\mathbf{SJ}_{A=B}\,S)\,\mathbf{JN}_{A=B}\,S$, and is equivalent to $R\,\mathbf{JN}_{A=B}\,S$. Assume that R and S are allocated at sites r and s, respectively. Then, performing the semi-join program corresponds to:

1. Sending $\mathbf{PJ}_B\,(S)$ to site r, at a cost:

$$C_0 + C_1 \times \text{size}(B) \times \text{val}(B[S])$$

2. Computing the semi-join on r, at a null cost; let

$$R' = R\,\mathbf{SJ}_{A=B}\,S$$

3. Sending R' to s, at a cost:

$$C_0 + C_1 \times \text{size}(R) \times \text{card}(R')$$

4. Computing the join on s, at a null cost

The overall cost is

$$C_{\mathbf{SJ}} = 2 \times C_0 + C_1 \times (\text{size}(B) \times \text{val}(B[S]) + \text{size}(R) \times \text{card}(R'))$$

Semi-join is not symmetric, and clearly the other semi-join program $(S\,\mathbf{SJ}\,R)\,\mathbf{JN}\,R$ has a different cost. Comparing their two costs solves the problem of determining the optimal semi-join program for the join of R and S. Notice that the two programs produce results which are allocated on different sites; thus, the possible difference in cost in the transmission of the results also should be taken into consideration.

Moreover, it is important to verify that the semi-join program is profitable with respect to the use of joins as a query processing tactic, which consists in executing the join directly, without previous semi-joins. The cost of using joins as a query processing tactic is that of transmitting one of the operands to the site of the other one. If we perform the join at site s, the corresponding cost is

$$C_{\mathbf{JN}} = C_0 + C_1 \times \text{size}(R) \times \text{card}(R)$$

Comparing $C_{\mathbf{JN}}$ and $C_{\mathbf{SJ}}$, the semi-join program is profitable if

$$C_0 + C_1 \times (\text{size}(B) \times \text{val}(B[S]) + \text{size}(R) \times \text{card}(R')) < C_1 \times \text{size}(R) \times \text{card}(R)$$

In many cases the above inequality holds, because $\text{size}(B)$ and $\text{val}(B[S])$ are small while $\text{card}(R)$ is larger than $\text{card}(R')$. Therefore, the algorithms which are presented in Sections 6.2.2 and 6.2.3 simply ignore the use of joins as a query processing tactic.

6.2.1.1 Reduction of relations using semi-joins Semi-joins can be regarded as **reducers**, i.e. operations that can be applied, similarly to unary operations, to reduce the cardinality of their operands. Clearly, for any R and S that can be semi-joined, we have $R \supseteq (R' \equiv R\,\mathbf{SJ}\,S)$. Extending this property to the case of a query with three relations that allow semi-joins between each possible pair, we have, for any R, S, and T,

$$R \supseteq (R' \equiv R\,\mathbf{SJ}\,(S\,\mathbf{SJ}\,T))$$

but also

$$R \supseteq (R'' \equiv R\,\mathbf{SJ}\,(T\,\mathbf{SJ}\,S))$$

We will call **reducer programs** for R a chain of semi-joins, like R' and R''.

Let $RED(Q, R)$ denote the set of reducer programs that can be built for a given relation R in a given query Q. Then, clearly, there is one reducer program, element of $RED(Q, R)$, which reduces R more than all other elements; we call this reducer program a **full reducer** of R. An interesting problem is therefore to determine full reducers for the relations of a query. Notice, however, that this does not solve the problem of determining the best strategy for a query, because the cost of a full reducer program, in terms of transmissions, can be higher than its advantage.

The determination of full reducers is a difficult task. The example of Figure 6.4 shows that, in general, it is not even possible to give an upper limit to the length of the full reducer program, i.e., the number of semi-joins involved in the program. In this example, each relation can be reduced to the empty relation; this, however, requires a reducer program whose length grows linearly with the number of tuples of the relations [precisely, if m is that number, then the length is $3 \times (m - 1)$]. Notice that it is required to store into temporary relations the results of each partial semi-join.

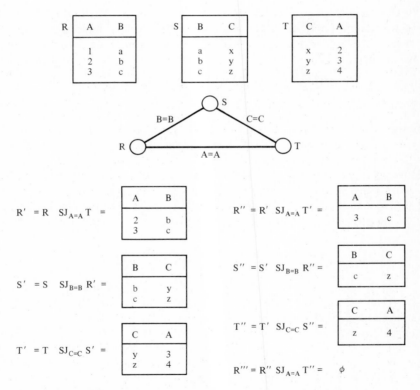

Figure 6.4 A full reducer program for relation R.

Given the above example, the following question arises immediately: Is it possible to give a limitation to the length of the full reducer, at least for a limited class of queries? The answer to this question is positive. In reference [6.1] it is shown that there exists a limitation for those queries whose join graph is a tree, called **tree queries** (as it is well-known, trees are special cases of graphs without cycles). The limitation on the length of the full reducer amounts to $n-1$, where n is the number of nodes of the tree. A second theorem of reference [6.1], which can be deduced intuitively from the example of Figure 6.4, states that in the general case of cyclic queries, the length of the "best" reducer is linearly bound by the number of tuples of some relations in the query. Moreover, there is no assurance about the efficiency of reducer programs; i.e., the "best" reducer does not necessarily reduce each operand relation to the tuples that will give a contribution to the final result; for instance, in a join which produces as a result the empty relation, it might be possible not to find any reducer for any of the operands which returns the empty relation. Thus, the idea of a "full" reducer program is much weaker in the context of cyclic queries.

We now need to decide whether a join graph can be considered a tree. Inspecting the graph for cycles could lead to erroneous decisions, since there are cases in which cycles can be broken without changing the meaning of the query. These cases are:

1. In the cycle $(R.A = S.B)$, $(S.B = T.C)$, $(T.C = R.A)$, in which R, S, T are relation names and A, B, C are attribute names, any one of the edges can be dropped, as any edge can be obtained from the remaining ones by transitivity.
2. In the cycle $(R.A = S.B)$, $(S.B = T.C)$, $(T.C = R.D)$, we can substitute $(R.A = R.D)$ for $(T.C = R.D)$ because, by transitivity, $T.C$ must equal $R.A$; the remaining graph contains two edges $\langle R, S \rangle$ and $\langle S, T \rangle$ and is acyclic, because an interrelation clause has been substituted by an intrarelation clause.

A theorem of reference [6.1] asserts that testing if a query graph can be reduced to a query tree by the above types of simplification has a complexity which is linear with the number of nodes. As a conclusion, the search of full reducers, which are probably also "good" query execution strategies, has a high probability of success if we deal with tree queries rather than with cyclic queries.

There is a method for transforming cyclic queries into tree queries by making use of **generalized semi-joins**. Generalized semi-joins are defined as

$$R \, \mathbf{GSJ}_{X,F} \, S = \mathbf{PJ}_{Attr(R),X} \, (R \, \mathbf{JN}_F \, S)$$

where $Attr(R)$ denotes the attributes of R, and X is a set of attributes of S. Notice that the result of a generalized semi-join has more attributes than R. Generalized semi-joins can be conveniently applied to cyclic queries.

Consider again the cyclic join graph of Figure 6.4, with edges corresponding to the joins: $R.B = S.B$, $S.C = T.C$, $T.A = R.A$. The method consists in selecting one edge of the graph whose removal transforms the query to a tree query (say, the edge $\langle S, T \rangle$, corresponding to the join on attribute C), and sending the join attribute C of relation T to the other relations. Sending the attribute C corresponds to performing a generalized semi-join, in which attribute X of the definition corresponds to attribute C. In the simple example of Figure 6.4, the use of one generalized semi-join suffices to discover that the result of the join is empty; it is

$$R' = R \, \mathbf{GSJ}_{C,A=A} \, T$$
$$S' = S \, \mathbf{SJ}_{B=B \, \text{AND} \, C=C} \, R' = \emptyset$$

We leave as an exercise the verification of the above result and the use of different semi-join programs for the same purpose. The generalization of this method to more complex cyclic queries can be found in reference [6.3].

The above discussion has shown that a reasonable starting point for executing a query consists of determining reducer programs based on semi-joins for each involved relation in the query. Therefore, it is relevant to know how many of such programs exist and what is the complexity of an algorithm which searches for the best one among them. Unfortunately, there is a combinatorial explosion of programs when the number of relations becomes large. The general formulation of the problem is NP-complete, and only a limited class of queries admits a polynomial solution. This is a good reason for disregarding exhaustive approaches to the selection of semi-join programs, and for concentrating instead on heuristic algorithms.

6.2.2 Determination of Semi-join Programs in SDD-1

The algorithm used by the SDD-1 optimizer for determining a "good" query processing strategy is presented in reference [6.5]. In the SDD-1 approach, semi-joins are used for reducing cardinalities of relations; when they have been applied to the maximum extent, all relations are collected at the same site, where the query can be executed. The algorithm does not consider the cost of the final transmission of the result from the site selected for processing to the site of origin of the query.

The SDD-1 approach consists of a basic algorithm for first determining an inefficient but feasible execution strategy and then using postoptimization criteria for ameliorating it.

6.2.2.1 Basic SDD-1 algorithm   The basic SDD-1 algorithm constructs reducer programs for relations; reducers consist of unary operations and semi-joins, which are selected on the basis of their cost. When a new operation is included within the reducer of a relation, the profile of the relation is modified. Clearly, unary operations have no cost and become immediately part of the reducer programs; the order in which they appear in the reducer programs is not relevant, since, when the algorithm is applied, all local operations will have been inserted in reducers, and profiles will have been modified correspondingly.

Let us consider the semi-join $R \, \mathbf{SJ}_{A=B} \, S$; it has no cost when R and S are stored at the same site; when the sites of R and S are different, we recall that the cost can be evaluated as

$$\text{cost}(R \, \mathbf{SJ}_{A=B} \, S) = C_0 + \text{val}(B[S]) \times \text{size}(B) \times C_1$$

The benefit of a semi-join program can be evaluated in terms of "avoided" future transmissions:

$$\text{benefit}(R \, \mathbf{SJ}_{A=B} \, S) = (1 - \rho) \times \text{size}(R) \times \text{card}(R) \times C_1$$

where ρ is the selectivity of the semi-join. Given the set of all possible semi-joins, these values allow constructing a set P of **profitable** semi-joins, i.e., semi-joins

Join graph

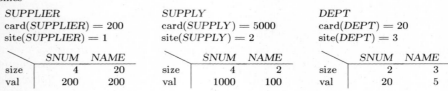

	SUPPLIER		SUPPLY		DEPT
	SNUM	NAME			

Profiles

SUPPLIER
card(*SUPPLIER*) = 200
site(*SUPPLIER*) = 1

	SNUM	NAME
size	4	20
val	200	200

SUPPLY
card(*SUPPLY*) = 5000
site(*SUPPLY*) = 2

	SNUM	NAME
size	4	2
val	1000	100

DEPT
card(*DEPT*) = 20
site(*DEPT*) = 3

	SNUM	NAME
size	2	3
val	20	5

Assumptions
All values of *SNUM* in *SUPPLIER* are present in *SUPPLY*
All values of *DEPTNUM* in *DEPT* are present in *SUPPLY*
$C_0 = 0$, $C_1 = 1$

(a) Definition of the optimization problem.

Semi-joins	Selectivity	Benefit	Cost
p1: *SUPPLY* **NSJ** *SUPPLIER*	$\rho(p1) = 0.2$	$0.8 \times 6 \times 5000$	4×200
p2: *SUPPLY* **NSJ** *DEPT*	$\rho(p2) = 0.2$	$0.8 \times 6 \times 5000$	2×20
p3: *SUPPLIER* **NSJ** *SUPPLY*	$\rho(p3) = 1$	–	4×1000
p4: *DEPT* **NSJ** *SUPPLY*	$\rho(p4) = 1$	–	2×100

Profitable semi-joins: p1, p2

(b) Description of all possible semi-joins.

Iteration 1: p2 selected

Effect on the profile of *SUPPLY*
card(*SUPPLY*) = 1000
site(*SUPPLY*) = 2

	SNUM	DEPTNUM
size	4	2
val	666†	20

† $c(n, m, r)$ used for *SNUM*, with $n = 5000$, $r = 1000$, $m = $ val(*SNUM*[*SUPPLY*]) = 1000.

Effect on other semi-joins	Selectivity	Benefit	Cost
p1: *SUPPLY* **NSJ** *SUPPLIER*	$\rho(p1) = 0.2$	$0.8 \times 6 \times 1000$	4×200
p3: *SUPPLIER* **NSJ** *SUPPLY*	$\rho(p3) = 0.666$†	$0.333 \times 24 \times 200$	4×666
p4: *DEPT* **NSJ** *SUPPLY*	$\rho(p4) = 1$‡	–	2×20

† Since 666 out of 1000 values of *SNUM* have been selected
‡ Since all *DEPTNUM* values of *SUPPLY* are also in *DEPT*
Profitable semi-joins: p1, p3

(c) cont.

Iteration 2: p1 selected

Effect on the profile of *SUPPLY*
card($SUPPLY$) = 200
site($SUPPLY$) = 2

	SNUM	DEPTNUM
size	4	2
val	123	20†

† $c(n, m, r)$ used for *DEPTNUM*, with $n = 1000$, $r = 200$, $m = $ val($DEPTNUM[SUPPLY']$) = 20.

Effect on other semi-joins	Selectivity	Benefit	Cost
p3: *SUPPLY* **NSJ** *SUPPLY*	$\rho(p3) = 0.666$†	$0.333 \times 24 \times 200$	4×123
p4: *SUPPLIER* **NSJ** *DEPT*	$\rho(p4) = 1$	–	2×20

† In the reduction of *SUPPLY*, the selectivity is just 0.666, since all *DEPTNUM* values of *SUPPLY* are also in *DEPT*.
Profitable semi-joins: *p3*

Iteration 3: p3 selected

Effect on the profile of *SUPPLIER*
card($SUPPLIER$) = 123
site($SUPPLIER$) = 1

	SNUM	NAME
size	4	20
val	123	123

Effect on other semi-joins	Selectivity	Benefit	Cost
p4: *SUPPLY* **NSJ** *DEPT*	$\rho(p4) = 1$	–	2×20

No other profitable semi-joins exist, thus the semi-join selection is terminated.

Selection of the site for collecting all the relations

Cost(site 1) = $6 \times 200 + 5 \times 20 = 1300$
Cost(site 2) = $123 \times 24 + 5 \times 20 = 3052$
Cost(site 3) = $123 \times 24 + 6 \times 200 = 4152$

Site 1 is selected

(*c*) The basic SDD-1 algorithm.

Postoptimization
Since semi-join *p3* has the only effect of reducing relation *SUPPLIER*, which is at the selected site 1, *p3* is no longer useful.

Summary
DEPT is sent to site 1 without semi-join reduction, at a cost of 100. *SUPPLY* is reduced by the two semi-joins with *SUPPLIER* and *DEPT*, at a cost of 840, then sent to site 1, at a cost of 1200. The total transmission cost is 2140.

(*d*) Postoptimization and summary.

Figure 6.5 Query optimization using the SDD-1 algorithm.

whose benefit exceeds the cost. The main loop of the algorithm selects the order of application of the profitable semi-joins.

The algorithm selects, at each iteration, the **most profitable** semi-join in P. This semi-join becomes part of the reducer of R; the profile of R and the cost of semi-joins using attributes of R are modified. Moreover, all other semi-joins are analyzed to see if some of them have become profitable. The iterations are terminated when profitable semi-joins have been exhausted. We have shown in the example of Figure 6.4 that repeating the execution of a semi-join could be profitable for cyclic queries; this, however, might lead to inefficient solutions with very long reducers. It is possible to avoid this danger by imposing the constraint that each semi-join be executed no more than once.

Finally, the algorithm selects the most convenient site for collecting the reduced relations; this is done simply by evaluating the one which requires the most limited amount of transmissions.

Notice that it would be also possible to select at each iteration the **cheapest** semi-join instead of the most profitable one. This alternative choice is also reasonable, because the most profitable semi-join, say SJ, could be highly expensive and placing it in the reducer corresponds to paying its cost. If other cheaper semi-joins are performed first, the cost of SJ might be reduced in later iterations.

We can now summarize the algorithm as follows:

1. *Basis.* A join graph G is given. All local reductions to relations appearing in G have been applied already.

2. *Method.* While there are profitable semi-joins, include either the most profitable or the cheapest one in the reducer program of the relation to which it applies; reevaluate benefits and costs of affected semi-joins.

3. *Termination.* The site which requires less transmissions is selected for collecting all the relations.

Example 6.1

Consider the optimization problem defined in Figure 6.5a, which shows the join graph, the profiles of relations, and some basic assumptions on attribute values. Assume that the profiles of Figure 6.5a take care of the effect of local reducers (i.e., the reducers consisting of unary operations), so that we can consider them as the starting point for the SDD-1 optimization algorithm.

There are four possible semi-joins, which are shown in Figure 6.5b, but only two of them are profitable, those which reduce the (larger) relation *SUPPLY*. Figure 6.5c shows the development of the computation of cardinalities, sizes, and distinct values of relations after the selection of a new semi-join at each iteration, and consequently the modifications of costs and benefits of other semi-joins. For the sake of simplicity, the assumption is made that all the values of *SNUM* in *SUPPLIER* and of *DEPTNUM* in *DEPT* are present in *SUPPLY*; this simplifies the evaluation of the selectivities $\rho(p_i)$. When a semi-join is selected, it is eliminated from the set of semi-joins which are considered at the next iteration.

The basic algorithm includes as a result of its first two iterations the two profitable semi-joins of Figure 6.5b in the reducer of *SUPPLY*. As a consequence of the reduction of the *SUPPLY* relation, a third semi-join *SUPPLIER* **SJ** *SUPPLY* becomes profitable; it is selected at the third iteration.

Finally, one site must be selected for executing the query. The transmission costs associated with each choice are shown in Figure 6.5c; site 1 is selected since its cost is minimal.

6.2.2.2 Postoptimization   The SDD-1 algorithm applies a greedy heuristic, because it searches, at each iteration, for the best improvement without taking into account the consequences on future iterations. To improve the obtained solution, a postoptimization can be made. The postoptimization obeys two criteria:

1.   Eliminating the semi-joins whose only effect is to reduce relations that are already on the site selected for executing the query.
2.   Delaying expensive semi-joins R **SJ** S after the reduction of S by means of other semi-joins; this requires changing the order of application of semi-join operations.

The first postoptimization can be applied to Example 6.1.

Example 6.1 (continued)
The semi-join *SUPPLIER* **SJ** *SUPPLY* is dropped, since the relation *SUPPLIER*, which would be reduced by the semi-join, is stored at site 1, where all relations are collected. The final result of the whole optimization of query Q1 is shown in Figure 6.5d.

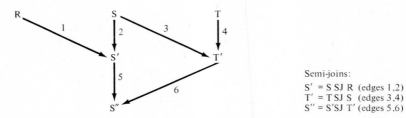

Semi-joins:

S' = S SJ R (edges 1,2)
T' = T SJ S (edges 3,4)
S'' = S'SJ T' (edges 5,6)

Nodes represent relations, edges represent operands of semi-join operations (the first operand is connected to the result by a vertical edge).

(*a*) Semi-join programs before applying criterion 2 of post-optimization.

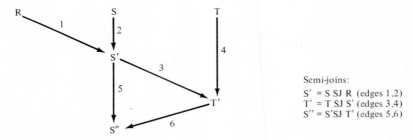

Semi-joins:

S' = S SJ R (edges 1,2)
T' = T SJ S' (edges 3,4)
S'' = S'SJ T' (edges 5,6)

(*b*) Semi-join programs after applying criterion 2 of post-optimization.

Figure 6.6   Postoptimization in the SDD-1 algorithm.

The second postoptimization is done by constructing, during the main iterations of the basic algorithm, a flow graph which shows the order in which semi-joins are selected; progressively reduced relations correspond to nodes, and semi-joins correspond to edges of the flow graph. The postoptimization algorithm consists of selecting on the flow graph the expensive semi-joins and delaying them if possible.

More formally, let $\langle T, S \rangle$ be an arc of the flow graph describing that a semi-join T **SJ** S takes place, and let S' be any node representing the reduction of S; the postoptimization consists in replacing $\langle T, S \rangle$ by $\langle T, S' \rangle$, provided that it does not introduce cycles in the graph (a graph with cycles corresponds to a nonexecutable program). This simplification is shown in Figure 6.6. The advantage of this simplification is twofold:

1. Fewer tuples are sent from S to T, since S is reduced to S'.
2. The selectivity of the semi-join T **SJ** S is increased by effect of the previous semi-join S **SJ** R.

6.2.3 Determination of Semi-join Programs by Algorithms of Apers, Hevner, and Yao

A different heuristic approach is the basis of the algorithms that are presented in this section. This approach is based on the decomposition of the query into simpler subqueries that can be solved easily and optimally. Thus, several subproblems are solved independently, and then their results are integrated into complete strategies (possibly not in an optimal way). This approach was first proposed in reference [6.6], improved in references [6.7] and [6.8], and then revised by Apers, Hevner, and Yao in reference [6.9]. We follow the latter approach, concentrating on principles rather than on the details of algorithms.

The **AHY** (Apers-Hevner-Yao) approach is suited to both cost and delay minimization; since we have already described a method for cost minimization (the SDD-1 algorithm), we present in this section only delay minimization. The AHY approach consists of performing local processing on relations, then reducing relations using semi-joins, and finally performing the evaluation of the query on a single site, which is called the **execution site** of the query. Determining a query processing strategy in this approach consists of producing **schedules** for each relation in the join graph.

The schedule of a relation T is a precedence tree in which all nodes except the root and the root's unique son correspond to attributes of relations; they are labeled $R.A$ (where R is a relation name and A is an attribute name). The special node directly connected to the root of the tree corresponds to the relation T itself and is labeled T. The root represents the execution site of the query, and is not labeled.

Each directed edge connecting any node other than the root to the node T corresponds to a semi-join operation applied to T. For instance, the edge $\langle R.A, T \rangle$ represents the fact that a semi-join T **SJ**$_{A=A}$ R is done. When schedules have a depth which is greater than 2, this means that chains of semi-joins are used; for instance, an edge $\langle U.C, R.A \rangle$ represents the fact that a semi-join R **SJ**$_{C=C} U$ is done for reducing R before projecting the attribute A from it and using it in subsequent semi-joins. Edges are labeled with the delays of data transmissions required for performing the corresponding semi-joins; the special edge between T and the root is labeled by the delay which is required to transmit the reduced relation T to the execution site.

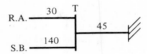

Figure 6.7 Schedule for relation T.

For instance, consider the schedule for relation T represented in Figure 6.7. T is reduced using two semi-joins with relations R and S on attributes A and B, respectively. Then, the tuples of T which are selected by the two semi-joins are sent to the execution site of the query.

This schedule corresponds to:

1. A total cost of 205 units (given by the sum of all costs)
2. A total delay of 185 units (considering the longest path to the root)

Let us denote by **simple schedule** for T the schedule consisting of only two nodes, T and the root, and one edge between them, labeled by the cost of transmitting T without reduction. This schedule corresponds to sending the relation T directly to the execution site.

A fixed selectivity, called the **incoming selectivity**, is associated to each attribute which can be used for performing semi-joins. For instance, let the incoming selectivity of attributes $R.A$ and $S.B$ be ρ_A and ρ_B, respectively. Since both semi-joins are applied to T, under the assumption of independence of the two attributes, the incoming selectivity for T is $\rho_A \times \rho_B$.

For simplicity, in the AHY approach all relations are assumed to be at a different site; dropping this assumption requires considering in the algorithm also the allocation of relations, because semi-joins between relations at the same site have no cost.

6.2.3.1 Simple queries A simple query is a query in which, after initial local processing, relations contain only one attribute, which is used for joining them. Simple queries are used for the decomposition of the problem; they can be optimally solved by very simple algorithms. Notice that simple queries certainly belong to the class of tree queries, even if their join graph is cyclic, because it is always possible to eliminate some of their edges and reduce them to tree queries.

Let us associate to each relation R_i appearing in the join graph the total number of bytes of R_i, denoted as s_i:

$$s_i = \text{card}(R_i) \times \text{size}(R_i).$$

The algorithm PARALLEL proceeds as follows:

1. *Basis.* Consider relations in ascending order of s_i; let us assume for simplicity that the relation index i reflects this order (i.e., $i < j$ means that $s_i < s_j$). Select the simple schedule for R_1.

2. *Method.* At iteration j $(j > 1)$, build the schedule for R_j by choosing the schedule with minimum delay among:

    a. The simple schedule for R_j
    b. For each $i < j$, the schedule constructed as the composition of:

    -   The schedule selected, at previous iterations, for R_i, in which we put the relation R_j instead of the root
    -   All the schedules selected, at previous iterations, for R_k (with $k < i$), in which we also put the relation R_j instead of the root
    -   The edge between R_j and the root, labeled by the transmission cost of of R_j reduced by the incoming selectivities of all semi-joins applied to it.

The rationale behind the basis is that the simple schedule is certainly the best possible schedule for the relation which has the shortest simple schedule. Thus, relation R_1 is sent to the execution node without reduction. For relations $R_2, \dots, R_n$ there is instead the possibility of improving the simple schedule by using semi-joins.

The rationale behind rule (b) is that, if we include the schedule of R_i as part of the schedule of R_j, the composition of it with any of the schedules of R_k, which are shorter by construction, produces an additional incoming selectivity for R without increasing the delay, and therefore must be added.

In evaluating the profiles of relations, the AHY algorithm makes the assumption of independence among join attributes, and evaluates incoming selectivities due to many semi-joins upon the same attribute as the product of their incoming selectivities.

Example 6.2

Let us exemplify the PARALLEL algorithm; the example is taken from reference [6.6] with minor modifications. We need to introduce a new relation

$$PROJECT(SNUM, DEPTNUM, PROJNUM)$$

Consider the following query

$$\mathbf{PJ}_{SUPPLIER.NAME, PROJNUM}(SUPPLIER \ \mathbf{NJN} \ SUPPLY \ \mathbf{NJN} \ PROJECT)$$

The initial profiles of relations after the initial processing and the join graph of this query are shown in Figure 6.8a. Profiles include the incoming selectivity of attributes, i.e., the selectivity ρ of semi-joins that can be applied if these attributes are transmitted. Though the graph is cyclic, it is easy to see that this is a tree query, as any one of the edges labeled with *SNUM* can be eliminated.

Let us now consider the join attributes individually; thus, we insulate from this query two simple subqueries. For ease of notation, we do not indicate in the schedules of simple queries the corresponding attribute name. We apply first the PARALLEL algorithm to the simple query built for attribute *SNUM*. We start by ordering relations *SUPPLY*, *PROJECT*, and *SUPPLIER*, which all have the attribute *SNUM*, by increasing values of s_i (see the table in Figure 6.8a); notice that

$$s_i = \text{size}(SNUM) \times \text{val}(SNUM)$$

in all three relations. Then we build the simple schedules for the smaller relations *PROJECT* and *SUPPLY*, according to the basis of the PARALLEL algorithm. Notice that the edges of the simple schedules are both labelled 420, since we have a total transmission delay of

$$D_0 + 400 \times D_1 = 420$$

We consider then the schedule of *SUPPLIER*, and we discover that the simple schedule for it corresponds to a delay of 920 units. Let us consider the schedule which uses the semi-joins with *PROJECT* and *SUPPLY*. This schedule is obtained by composing the schedules for *PROJECT* and *SUPPLY* with the edge connecting the *SUPPLIER* node to the root. Incoming selectivities due to these semi-joins are shown at the bottom of the *SUPPLIER* node. The delay of the transmission of the reduced relation *SUPPLIER* to the execution site is evaluated as:

$$D_0 + 900 \times 0.16 \times D_1 = 164 \text{ units}$$

This schedule is shorter than the simple schedule, since it corresponds to a total delay of 584 units; therefore it is selected, and algorithm PARALLEL is terminated.

The algorithm PARALLEL applies similarly to the attribute *DEPTNUM*; the result of its application is also shown in Figure 6.8a. *PROJECT.DEPTNUM* is reduced by the incoming selectivity $\rho = 0.2$ before being transmitted.

It is important to notice that the algorithm PARALLEL evaluates the cost of transmitting a relation constituted of a single attribute, by effect of reductions due to semi-joins on that attribute. Thus, the solutions that we have obtained are very different from the solution of the original problem. However, nothing is decided at this point; we have simply built the input data for the following integration of the schedules.

6.2.3.2 Integration of schedules   We concentrate now upon the integration of schedules for the minimization of delay. Delay minimization is obtained by applying algorithm RESPONSE, which is very similar to algorithm PARALLEL.

The algorithm RESPONSE applies to each relation of the join graph individually and produces the shortest schedule for it; the schedule includes the final transmission of the relation to the execution site. The algorithm, applied to a relation R, proceeds as follows:

1. *Basis.* Consider all the joining attributes available for R. Order them according to the delay which is required in order to receive the join attributes at the site of R. Let S_j represent the corresponding schedule.
2. *Method.* Build the schedule for R by choosing the schedule with minimum delay among:
    a.   The simple schedule for R
    b.   For $j \geq 1$, the schedule constructed as the composition of:

INITIAL PROFILES

SUPPLIER

card=225   site=1

SUPPLY

card=100   site=2

PROJECT

card=1000   site=3

	SNUM	NAME
Size	4	20
Val	225	225
ρ	0.9	—

	SNUM	DEPTNUM	QTY
	4	5	7
	100	20	50
	0.4	0.2	—

	SNUM	DEPTNUM	PROJECT
	4	5	4
	100	90	30
	0.4	0.9	—

JOIN GRAPH:

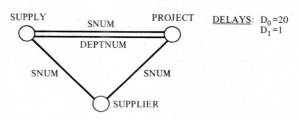

DELAYS: D_0=20
         D_1=1

ALGORITHM PARALLEL ON SNUM

RELATION	S
SUPPLY	400
PROJECT	400
SUPPLIER	900

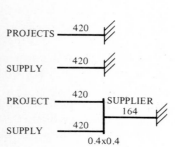

ALGORITHM PARALLEL ON DEPTNUM

RELATION	S
SUPPLY	100
PROJECT	450

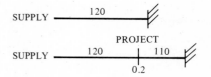

Figure 6.8   Query optimization using the AHY algorithm (continued).

- The schedule S_j in which we put the relation R instead of the root
- All the schedules S_k, with $k < j$, in which we also put the relation R instead of the root
- The edge between R and the root, labeled by the transmission cost of R reduced by the incoming selectivities of all semi-joins applied to it

SCHEDULES FOR SUPPLY	DELAY	SELECTIVITY
PROJECT.DEPTNUM	230	0.9
PROJECT.SNUM	420	0.4
SUPPLIER.SNUM	584	0.16

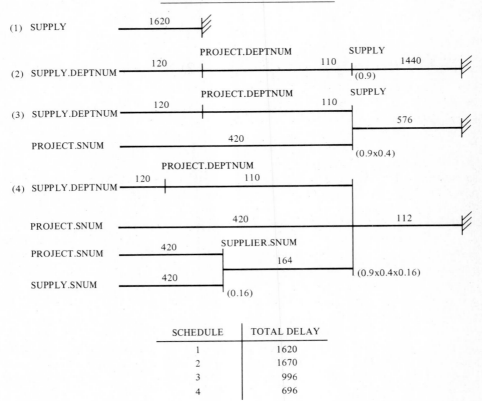

ALGORITHM RESPONSE FOR SUPPLY

SCHEDULE	TOTAL DELAY
1	1620
2	1670
3	996
4	696

Figure 6.8 Query optimization using the AHY algorithm.

The rationale behind rule (*b*) of this algorithm is again that any parallel transmission of a shorter schedule S_k produces an additional incoming selectivity without increasing the delay, and therefore must be added.

The final part of the AHY approach, similar to the SDD-1 approach, consists in determining the execution site, by selecting the one with the longest associated schedule; once this schedule and site are determined, the transmissions corresponding to it are no longer required, and the total delay associated with the query becomes that of the second longest schedule.

Example 6.2 (continued)

In Figure 6.8*b* we show the application of algorithm RESPONSE to the relation *SUPPLY*. The possible attributes for a semi-join reduction of *SUPPLY* are *DEPTNUM* and *SNUM*; they can both be transmitted from relations *PROJECT*, while relation *SUPPLIER* can transmit only attribute *SNUM*. From the schedules of *PROJECT.DEPTNUM*, *PROJECT.SNUM*, and *SUPPLIER.SNUM* in Figure 6.8*a* we know the required delays. Then we develop:

1. The simple schedule for *SUPPLY*
2. The schedule which uses the attribute *PROJECT.DEPTNUM*, with the shortest delay, to reduce *SUPPLY* (the incoming selectivity is 0.9)
3. The schedule which uses both *PROJECT.DEPTNUM* and *PROJECT.SNUM* to reduce *SUPPLY* (the total incoming selectivity is 0.36)
4. The schedule using all the attributes to reduce *SUPPLY* (the total incoming selectivity is 0.057)

Among them, the fourth schedule amounts to the shortest delay (696 units) and is selected.

6.2.4 Use of Joins as a Query Processing Tactic

The query optimization methods which we have presented are based on the distinction of three phases: first, local processing is performed; next, semi-joins are used for reducing the sizes of relations, which are sent to a common site; finally, the query is performed upon the reduced relations. A different approach consists in alternating local operations and some data transmissions. Thus, a query involving the join of three relations which are stored at different sites is solved by first sending the first relation to the second one, then computing their join, then sending its result to the third relation, and finally computing their join and producing the query result. This method uses joins as a query processing tactic.

The choice between using semi-joins or joins as a query processing tactic depends also on the assumptions on the relative costs of transmission and local processing; in general, the advantage of using semi-joins is greater if transmission costs are considered important and local processing costs are considered relatively negligible. If we consider also the cost of local processing in evaluating alternative query processing strategies, then the use of joins as a query processing tactic is often more convenient than the use of semi-joins. A semi-join $R \, \mathbf{SJ}_{A=B} \, S$ for reducing R requires:

1. Performing the projection from S of semi-join attributes
2. Eliminating duplicates from this projection before transmitting them (typically, this requires the sorting of the projected attributes)
3. Computing an extra-join (i.e., a join which does not appear in the query) $R' = R \, \mathbf{JN} \, \mathbf{PJ}_B \, S$ for reducing the size of R.

Semi-join reduction is convenient only if the amount of saved transmissions exceeds all these costs.

It is possible, though not very likely, that joins perform better than semi-joins also when only transmission costs are considered. Typically, in this case the following conditions are verified:

1. There are few attributes in the target list of the query (i.e., attributes which appear in the result relation) which do not appear also as join attributes of some join.
2. Semi-joins have a low selectivity (i.e., they do not perform reductions efficiently).

The above considerations have shown that joins and semi-joins as query processing techniques should be considered together; in the above example of a query with three relations, semi-joins could be used for reducing just one of the operands of the first join, and the remainder of the processing could be performed using joins. However, there are few optimizers which combine the use of joins and semi-joins (probably, because this optimization problem is too complex).

6.2.4.1 Join Queries in the R* approach   A system which uses joins as a query processing tactic is R*; the query optimization of R* takes also local processing costs into account. The approach of R* to query optimization is described in references [6.10] to [6.13]. We deal here with joins of multiple relations; in the above references, it is also described how to optimize queries over single relations (for instance, determining an access method for performing selections using available indexes).

Since the R* optimizer considers also local processing costs, we have to examine which methods are available for joining locally two relations and to evaluate their cost. One of the two relations is regarded as the **outer** relation O, and the other one as the **inner** relation I, depending on the order in which they are scanned; the outer relation can be the result of a previous join. The fundamental methods are two:

1. *Nested-loop method.* The outer relation O is sequentially scanned; for each tuple of O, the inner relation is scanned, searching for tuples which agree on the join attribute. Matching tuples are composed and become part of the join result. This method requires one full scan of O and card(O) searches of matching tuples of I; let N_{out} be the number of pages fetched for scanning O, and let N_{in} be the average number of pages of I fetched for each tuple of O. Assume that I/O costs are proportional to the number of pages fetched and that CPU costs are proportional to the cardinality of the result of the join. Then the cost of the nested-loop method is

$$C(\text{nested-loop}) = (N_{out} + \text{card}(O) \times N_{in}) \times C_{I/O} + \text{card}(RESULT) \times C_{CPU}$$

2. *Merge-scan method.* Both relations are scanned in join attribute order; matching tuples become part of the join result. The tuples of the inner relation with the same value are buffered, so that if the subsequent records of O have the same join value, matching tuples can be composed without repeating any page fetch. This method requires the sorting of both relations; the cost of sorting depends on the available access methods. The cost of the merge-scan method is

$$C(\text{merge-scan}) = (N_{out} + N_{in}) \times C_{I/O} + C_{sort}(I) + C_{sort}(O)$$
$$+ \text{card}(RESULT) \times C_{CPU}$$

In R*, a join of relations I and O which are stored at different sites can be performed at the site of O, at the site of I, or at a third site. Transmission costs must be added to the local costs for determining the best join method; they are measured in terms of exchanged messages between sites. This measure is more detailed than the measure based on C_0 and C_1; it is at the same level as I/O and CPU measures. The R* optimizer considers two methods for transmitting relations:

1. *"Shipped whole."* The transmission cost is given by the number of required messages, which is roughly proportional to the number of bytes of the relation. If the inner relation is transmitted, it must be stored into a temporary relation at its destination; if the outer relation is transmitted, the inner relation can use the incoming tuples as they arrive and does not need to store them.

2. *"Fetched as needed."* In this case, the remote site coordinates the transfer of tuples and uses them directly, without temporary storage; the transmission cost is higher as each fetch requires an exchange of messages. We have already noticed that a "tuple-at-a-time" processing is reasonable in networks with high bandwidth (such as local networks) and is unrealistic in geographically dispersed networks; the R* prototype operates in the former environment.

If relations are shipped whole, they can just be locally restricted; if, instead, they are fetched as needed, the incoming message can contain a value of the join attribute, and the fetch operation is then restricted to the tuples which match that value. In practice, the effect is obtained of performing a tuple-at-a-time semi-join. However, there is an important distinction between this method and the semi-join approach; while the former is mainly used for synchronizing the processing of the inner and outer relations and typically requires more transmissions, the latter is done exactly for saving transmissions and typically requires more local processing.

While in principle each transmission method could be used in the context of each join method, there are practical considerations that make only a few combinations attractive for R*. For instance, in the nested-loop method, the transmission of I as a whole is excluded, because I must be scanned card(O) times, and this is efficient only if there are efficient access methods to the join attribute; shipping the relation would destroy such methods. This and similar considerations restrict the possible cases to:

1. *Nested-loop, outer "shipped whole and not stored."* The cost is the sum of the local join cost with this method and the transmission of O:

$$C_1 = C(\text{nested-loop}) + C_{\text{mes}} \times \text{ceil}[\text{card}(O) \times \text{size}(O)/m]$$

where C_{mes} is the unitary cost of sending a message and m is the size in bytes of data shipped within each message; ceil returns the upper integer of a real number.

2. *Merge-scan, outer "shipped whole and not stored."* Similarly, it is

$$C_2 = C(\text{merge-scan}) + C_{\text{mes}} \times \text{ceil}[\text{card}(O) \times \text{size}(O)/m]$$

3. *Nested-loop, inner "fetched as needed."* In this case, for each tuple of O we send a request to I, and NI tuples which (on the average) satisfy the request

are sent back; we have

$$C_3 = C(\text{nested-loop}) + C_{\text{mes}} \times \text{card}(O) \times (1 + \text{ceil}[NI \times \text{size}(I)/m])$$

4. *Merge-scan, inner "fetched as needed."* We assume here that we send a request message from O to I for each different value of the join attribute, and that all matching tuples of I are sent back; these assumptions contrast with what is done in R*, where one message is sent for any tuple of O. If A is the join attribute on O, we have

$$C_4 = C(\text{merge-scan}) + C_{\text{mes}} \times \text{val}(A[O]) \times (1 + \text{ceil}[NI \times \text{size}(I)/m])$$

5. *Merge-scan, inner "shipped whole and stored before use."* In this case, we pay an additional cost for storing and retrieving the I relation at the remote site:

$$C_5 = C(\text{merge-scan}) + C_{\text{mes}} \times \text{ceil}[\text{card}(I) \times \text{size}(I)/m] + 2 \times N_{\text{in}} \times C_{\text{I/O}}$$

6. *Shipping both relations to a third site.* In this case, the transmission costs are given by the sum of transmitting both inner to outer and outer to inner; the join cost is either $C(\text{merge-scan})$ or $C(\text{nested-loop})$.

The R* optimizer enumerates exhaustively all possible sequences of joins with all possible join methods and allocated joins at each possible site; thus, it determines the cheapest access plan for a join query. Dynamic programming is applied to speed up the computation, since the cost computation satisfies the applicability rules for this technique.

6.3 GENERAL QUERIES

In this section, we turn our attention to the general case of queries with joins and unions in their optimization graph. Very few works in the literature address these queries; however, we show that the extension from join queries to general queries is not trivial, and that a great number of very different execution strategies can be found for the same general query. The basic transformation which is used is the commutativity of join and union (i.e., criterion 5 of the previous chapter) for generating distributed joins. We concentrate on the problem of a single join between fragmented relations; multiple joins can be dealt with by applying the following considerations in sequence.

Determining the strategy for performing a union is easy, as there is no concern about the order in which tuples from the operands are collected into the result relation. Thus, transmissions of nonlocal fragments to the sites where the union is performed can be done in parallel. In terms of transmission requirements, union has the delay associated with the transmission of the largest fragment, and the cost given by the sum of all transmission costs.

6.3.1 Effect of Commuting Joins and Unions

The commutation of joins and unions is represented in Figure 6.9, which represents three different optimization graphs of the same query. In Figure 6.9 and in all other figures in this section, circles represent the fragments of relation R, and squares represent the fragments of relation S. Consider first the two optimization graphs of Figure 6.9a and b. In Figure 6.9a, fragments are first collected and then joined; in Figure 6.9b fragments are first joined and then collected. We call the first approach a nondistributed join and the second a distributed join. The two cases give rise to very different optimization issues:

1.   *Nondistributed join.* This optimization problem is simpler; it reduces to deter-mining a pair of sites (possibly the same site) at which the union operations are performed. If the two sites are different, then the query is reduced to a simple join query between two relations, which can be optimized as shown in the previous section.

2.   *Distributed join.* This optimization problem is much harder. Notice that in Figure 6.9b we find the join graph of the join between R and S within the hypernode representing the union operation. The knowledge of fragmenta-tion criteria must be used for eliminating edges from the join graph which correspond to empty joins, as it was shown in Section 5.2.4. Once that a minimal join graph has been determined, the execution of the joins appearing in the join graph must be optimized using the techniques developed in the previous section. Finally, join results are sent to the same site for performing the union. The optimization graph of Figure 6.9b shows a distributed join in which the union is performed after all the joins. However, it is also possible to perform **partial unions**, which involve some of the fragments of the same relation, before performing joins. An example is shown in Figure 6.9c.

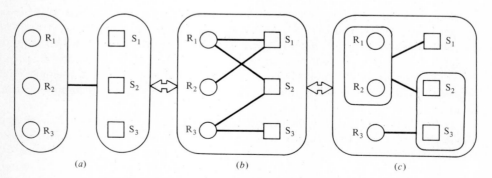

(a)   (b)   (c)

Figure 6.9 Commuting join and union.

In building the optimization graph G' of Figure 6.9c, starting from the optimization graph G of Figure 6.9b, the following rules have been applied:

1. Fragments on which partial unions are performed are enclosed into a hypernode (in the example, this rule applies to $\{R_1, R_2\}$ and to $\{S_2, S_3\}$).
2. If two fragments R_i and S_j are connected by an arc in G, then the (hyper)nodes to which they belong are also connected by an arc in G' (for example, the edge between R_1 and S_2 in G generates the edge between $\{R_1, R_2\}$ and $\{S_2, S_3\}$ in G').

Partitioned join graphs are a relevant class of join graphs from the viewpoint of the optimization of their execution. Recall from Chapter 4 that in a partitioned join graph we can distinguish disconnected subgraphs; each such subgraph can be independently optimized. This property is independent of the method which is used for computing query performances, and is due to the following facts:

1. The optimization of joins of disconnected subgraphs can be performed independently.
2. The union operation is not affected by the order in which operands are collected.

For instance, in Figure 6.10a we have a partitioned join graph; the optimization problem can be decomposed into the two problems involving fragments $\{R_1, R_2, S_1, S_2\}$ and $\{R_3, S_3\}$. In Figure 6.10b we show a possible final optimization graph for the query, consisting in making partial unions of $\{R_1, R_2\}$ and $\{S_1, S_2\}$, the joins between them, the join between R_3 and S_3, and the final union of the join results.

The convenience of the transformation from the optimization graph of Figure 6.10a to that of Figure 6.10b depends on the allocation and sizes of the fragments. Consider the following example: Assume a network with three sites, let the ith fragment be at site i; let the result be required at site 1; and let the operands and results of each partial join have the same size. Then it is convenient to perform

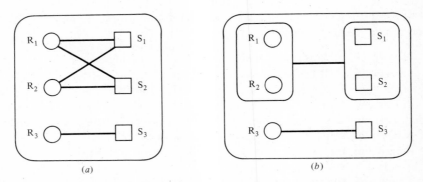

(a)   (b)

Figure 6.10 Independent optimization of a partitioned join graph.

the partial collection at site 1, the join between R_3 and S_3 at site 3, and the final union at site 1.

The above properties allow the building of a variety of strategies involving partial unions for each partition in the join graph; searching for the best execution strategy of a given query requires:

1. Generating all the possible query optimization graphs.
2. Applying join query methods to optimize joins, and adding the costs of unions; thus, each query graph is associated with an optimal query strategy and a cost.
3. Selecting the best query processing strategy within the above ones.

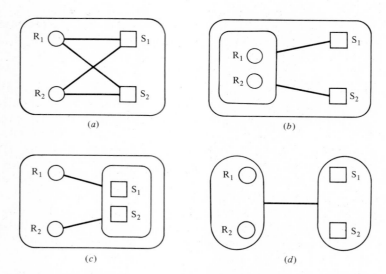

Figure 6.11 Alternative optimization graphs for the same query.

We conclude this section by exemplifying, in Figure 6.11a to d, four alternative ways of computing the cost for a fully connected join graph of two relations R and S having two fragments each.

1. Performing the distributed join. This problem reduces to performing the four joins of Figure 6.11a and collecting their results. Notice that the optimization of the four joins cannot be done separately, since, for instance, the reduction in the size of one of the fragments could be useful for more than one join.
2. Performing the partial collection of fragments of R; the problem reduces to performing two joins, and is shown in Figure 6.11b.
3. Performing the partial collection of two fragments of S; the problem is symmetrical, and is shown in Figure 6.11c.
4. Performing the union of fragments, followed by their joins; this corresponds to a nondistributed execution of the join, shown in Figure 6.11d.

6.3.2 Methods for the Optimization of General Queries

The literature reports few attempts to optimize general queries; however, this is an area in which we expect new developments in the near future. We describe here an approach that was developed in the context of the R* project and the method used by the distributed database DDM.

Global optimization was studied in the context of the R* system by Selinger and Adiba in reference [6.10], but global optimization is not included in the specification of the R* prototype, since presently the system does not support fragmentation. A query is represented by an operator tree similar to those described in Chapter 5. This tree includes not only the specification of algebraic operations, but also the method used for their computation (such as merge-scan or nested-loop), and the indication of required transmissions. Trees also include CHOOSE nodes for selecting between strategies which use different copies of the same fragment.

There is a noticeable distinction between the model of fragmentation in reference [6.10] and the one used in this book. The model in reference [6.10] allows overlapping fragments; in this book we deal with redundancy by replicating whole fragments. Thus, in our model CHOOSE nodes should be immediately above fragments; in the approach of reference [6.10], entire subtrees can return the same result obtained by operating on different, possibly overlapping fragments, and therefore CHOOSE nodes can be at any level of the tree. Optimization consists of analyzing the operator tree bottom-up, computing the cost of alternative methods for evaluating subtrees and appropriately selecting the best one. Since the commutation of joins and unions is not considered, there are limited possibilities for tree manipulations; these strategies are examined exaustively. Simple rules are developed for dealing with UNION and CHOOSE nodes:

1. At each UNION node, substitute for it the sum of all costs of its subtrees and all costs of performing the union.
2. At each CHOOSE node, substitute for it the minimum of all costs of its subtrees and consider the corresponding strategy as selected, disregarding all others.

Global optimization is done also by DDM, a distributed data manager described in Chapter 14 and in reference [14.5]. Query optimization in DDM is performed on a relational expression which is obtained after "decompiling" an initial procedural statement (recall Chapter 3). In DDM, the possibility of commuting joins and unions is actually taken into account. Thus, in the case described in Figure 6.11, all four possible alternatives would be considered.

The overall optimization method used in DDM is summarized as follows: First, selections are distributed over unions and joins, and applied locally to fragments. Next, joins which can be performed at the same site are clustered. Then, a partial order of execution of joins is determined by a hill-climbing search strategy. For a given partial order and for each join between horizontally fragmented relations, the distributed execution of the join is considered; if it is cost-effective, it is selected. Finally, one site is selected for executing each operation, and at this time the effectiveness of performing semi-join reductions before moving relations or fragments is considered.

CONCLUSIONS

The goal of query optimization is to find an execution strategy which minimizes the cost of a query, given by the sum of the transmission costs and of the local processing costs. Depending on the characteristics of the communication network and of the local systems, local processing costs can be disregarded in the optimization of the execution strategy of the query. This is typically the case of large geographical networks with low bandwidth, which have transfer rates of an order of magnitude lower than the disk-to-memory transfer rate. On the opposite, on fast local networks also local processing costs must be considered.

The above alternative on the cost assumption has a major impact on the approach which is taken in the optimization of join queries (i.e., of queries whose expression contains only unary operations and joins). If only transmission costs are considered, then the use of semi-joins is convenient and query optimization consists of determining the best sequence of semi-joins for reducing relations before transmitting them. If instead also local processing costs are considered relevant, then joins are used as query processing tactic, and query optimization consists of selecting the best technique for executing joins. These considerations are used for simplifying the general query optimization problem, which would be not manageable otherwise because of its extreme complexity.

Although join queries are the most extensively studied, some systems attempt the optimization also of general queries (whose expression includes the union). The relevant techniques used in the optimization of general queries consist of commuting joins and unions and in performing partial unions.

EXERCISES

6.1 Construct a reducer for R using semi-join programs having the join graph in the figure:

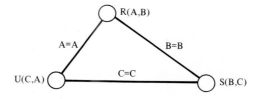

with:
$$R = \langle 0, 1 \rangle, \langle 3, 4 \rangle, \langle 6, 7 \rangle, \langle 7, 1 \rangle$$
$$S = \langle 1, 2 \rangle, \langle 4, 5 \rangle, \langle 6, 6 \rangle, \langle 7, 7 \rangle$$
$$U = \langle 2, 3 \rangle, \langle 5, 0 \rangle, \langle 6, 6 \rangle, \langle 7, 7 \rangle$$

Discuss the good or bad properties of your reducer program.

6.2 Explain the rationale of semi-join reduction in distributed databases.

6.3   Is the join graph in the figure cyclic? (Show your reasoning.)

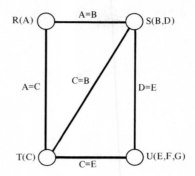

6.4   Consider the join $R \mathbf{JN}_{A=B} S$; assume that R and S are at different sites, and disregard the cost of collecting the result of the join. Let $C_0 = 0$ and $C_1 = 1$. The following profiles are given:

$$\text{size}(R) = 50; \text{card}(R) = 100; \text{val}(A[R]) = 50; \text{size}(A) = 3$$
$$\text{size}(S) = 5; \text{card}(S) = 50; \text{val}(B[S]) = 50; \text{size}(B) = 3$$

$$R \mathbf{SJ}_{A=B} S \text{ has selectivity } \rho = 0.2$$
$$S \mathbf{SJ}_{B=A} R \text{ has selectivity } \rho = 0.8$$

Give the transmission cost of:
(a)   Performing the join at the site of R using semi-join reduction
(b)   Performing the join at the site of S using semi-join reduction
(c)   Performing the join at the site of R without semi-join reduction
(d)   Performing the join at the site of S without semi-join reduction
Which is the best solution?

6.5   Consider the join graph:

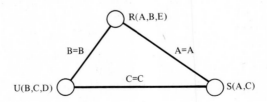

and assume the following profiles:

R			
card = 5000, site = 1			

	A	B	E
size	3	4	25
val	100	50	500

S		
card = 20, site = 2		

	A	C
size	3	2
val	20	5

U		
card = 100, site = 3		

	B	C	D
size	4	2	20
val	20	10	100

(a) Determine the semi-join reducers of the relations involved in the semi-join using the SDD-1 algorithm (recall that in the SDD-1 algorithm the most beneficial semi-join is selected at each iteration). For evaluating semi-join selectivities, assume that all the values of $S.A$ are also in $R.A$, that all the values of $U.B$ are also in $R.B$, and that all the values of $S.C$ are also in $U.C$. (*Hint:* There are six possible semi-joins. You are not expected to use each semi-join more than once. Therefore, the maximum number of iterations is six; moreover, some semi-joins are certainly not profitable.)

(b) Select the final site for executing the query, and apply simplification criterion 2.

(c) Assume then that the relations are collected, for some reason, at site number 4. Perform postoptimization using criterion 1.

(d) What would happen if the less expensive semi-join were selected at each iteration, instead of the most beneficial one?

6.6 Consider the join graph:

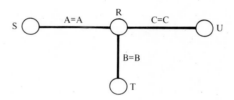

and consider the following profiles:

S site = 1			T site = 2		U site = 3		R card = 100, site = 4				
	A			B		C		A	B	C	D
size	4		size	3	size	2	size	4	3	2	21
val	20		val	30	val	100	val	20	30	100	100
ρ	0.2		ρ	0.5	ρ	0.8	ρ	–	–	–	–

Build a schedule for R using the AHY algorithm for delay minimization. (*Hint:* All attributes give a separate contribution. You must use only algorithm RESPONSE.)

6.7 Consider the optimization of a join query between two relations I and O in System R*. Let I be the inner relation and O be the outer relation. Let A be the name of the join attribute. Assume the following parameters:

Outer relation:
size = 100; card = 1000; val($A[O]$) = 50; N_{out} = 100; C_{sort} = 2000 × $C_{I/O}$

Inner relation:
size = 100; card = 100; val($A[I]$) = 50; N_{in} = 10, A_{in} = 1; C_{sort} = 0; NI = 10

Let m = 100 and C_{CPU} = 0. Determine which method is used by the R* optimizer for joining the two tables for different values of the ratio $C_{I/O}/C_{mes}$.

6.8   Consider the following partitioned join graph:

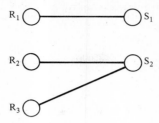

Let the following information about profiles be known:

$$\text{size}(R) = \text{size}(S) = 100; \text{size}(R \textbf{ JN } S) = 2 \times \text{size}(R)$$
$$\text{card}(R_i) = 20; \text{card}(S_j) = 100; \text{card}(R_i \textbf{ JN } S_j) = 20$$
$$\text{site}(R_i) = i; \text{site}(S_j) = j$$

Assume that the result has to be shipped at site 4, with $C_0 = 0$ and $C_1 = 1$. Give a "good" solution to this problem, without using semi-joins.

Annotated Bibliography

Many of the references in the annotated bibliography have been dealt with extensively in this chapter. The first three references are related to the theory of semi-joins, and in particular reference [6.1] contributed to most of the material of Section 6.2.1; references [6.4] to [6.5] cover the SDD-1 approach of Section 6.2.2, references [6.6] to [6.9] cover the AHY approach of Section 6.2.3; references [6.10] to [6.13] describe the R* approach of Section 6.2.4 and the global optimization of Section 6.3.3.

[6.1]   P. A. Bernstein and D. M. Chiu, "Using Semi-joins to Solve Relational Queries," *Journal of the ACM*, **28**:1, 1981.

See Section 6.2.1.1.

[6.2]   D. M. Chiu and Y. C. Ho, "A Methodology for Interpreting Tree Queries into Optimal Semi-join Expressions," *ACM-SIGMOD*, 1980.

The relevant contribution of this work is a generalized formula which computes the optimal cost for evaluating a tree query. The formula is independent of the method used for evaluating semi-join costs and is a recursive rule which gives the cost associated with a node in the query tree on the basis of the knowledge of costs associated with the node's children. Eventually, the solution associated with the root yields the solution of the query optimization problem. Though this problem can be solved using dynamic programming, the direct application of the formula is of very limited practical relevance because of its very high computational complexity. However, for limited classes of queries, the method allows a simpler enumeration of solutions. These classes include simple queries (as dealt with in Section 6.2.3) and **chain queries**. Chain queries have a join tree which is in fact a chain; i.e., each relation is joined with one predecessor and one successor, with the exception of the leaf (on which typically selections are made) and the root (which represents the final result of the query); they differ from simple queries because any one relation can use a different attribute for joining with the predecessor and the successor.

[6.3]   Y. Kambayashi, M. Yoshikawa, and S. Yajima, "Query Processing for Distributed Databases using Generalized Semi-joins," *ACM-SIGMOD*, 1982.

This paper describes the use of generalized semi-joins for solving cyclic queries, which we introduced in Section 6.2.1. The solution method amounts to the determination of a spanning tree within the join graph, i.e., a tree connecting all the nodes of the graph. Each edge of the original graph which does not belong to the spanning tree is treated using generalized semi-joins. The method also includes a compression of join attributes to be transmitted in the generalized semi-join by means of the conversion of their values into integer values.

[6.4]   E. Wong, "Retrieving Dispersed Data from SDD-1: A System for Distributed Databases," *Second Int. Berkeley Workshop on Distributed Data Management and Computer Networks*, 1977.

This is a pioneer work in the area of distributed query processing. The method consists of translating a query into a sequence of **moves of relations** and of **local processing actions**. The algorithm proceeds by selecting one site s to which all relations are sent as the initial feasible solution (which therefore has all "moves" before all processing actions); this solution is improved by recursively replacing individual moves by sequences of "moves and actions," using a hill-climbing heuristic, until no move can be replaced with profit. The major weakness of the algorithms is the a priori selection of an initial feasible solution, which does not allow reaching those points within the solution space which are too far from it.

[6.5]   N. Goodman, P. A. Bernstein, E. Wong, C. L. Reeve, and J. B. Rothnie, "Query Processing in SDD-1: A System for Distributed Databases," *ACM-TODS*, **6**:4, 1981.

See Section 6.2.2.

[6.6]   A. R. Hevner and S. B. Yao, "Query Processing in Distributed Database Systems," *IEEE-TSE*, **SE-5**:3, 1979.

[6.7]   P. M. G. Apers, "Distributed Query Processing: Minimum Response Time Schedules for Relations," Vrjie Univ., Amsterdam, The Netherlands, 1979.

[6.8]   T. Y. Cheung, "A Method for Equijoin Queries in Distributed Relational Databases," *IEEE-TC*, **C-31**:8, 1982.

[6.9]   P. M. G. Apers, A. R. Hevner, and S. B. Yao, "Optimization Algorithms for Distributed Queries," *IEEE-TSE*, **SE-9**:1, 1983.

Papers [6.6] to [6.9] are built within the same framework, which was introduced in [6.6]. The earlier paper [6.6] proposed the decomposition of the optimization problem into two parts, the independent optimization of simple queries and the integration of them within schedules for relations. Algorithm PARALLEL in Section 6.2.3 is from reference [6.6]; this paper also presents algorithm G for schedule integration with both cost and delay minimization.

Apers, in reference [6.7], introduced a variation to algorithm G for delay minimization, which improved it substantially; this variation is an early version of algorithm RESPONSE described in Section 6.2.3. Cheung, in reference [6.8], was instead able to improve algorithm G for total time minimization.

Taking into account such independent improvements, the authors of reference [6.9] present a procedure RESPONSE for delay minimization and prove that it achieves the optimum. They also present two other procedures for total cost minimization, which are heuristic in nature, and show that total time minimization is a harder problem than delay minimization.

[6.10] P. G. Selinger and M. Adiba, "Access Path Selection in Distributed Data Base Management Systems," *Proc. of the First Int. Conf. on Data Bases*, S. M. Deen and P. Hammersley, eds., Aberdeen, 1980.

[6.11] D. Daniels et al., "An Introduction to Distributed Query Compilation in R*," *Distributed Data Bases*, H. J. Schneider, ed., North-Holland, 1982.

[6.12] D. Daniels, "Query Compilation in a Distributed Database System," IBM Rep. RJ3423, IBM Res. Lab., San Jose, CA, 1982.

[6.13] P. Ng, "Distributed Compilation and Recompilation of Database Queries," IBM Rep. RJ3375, IBM Res. Lab., San Jose, CA, 1982.

Papers [6.10] to [6.13] deal with query compilation in the R* system; the material of Section 6.2.4 comes mostly from references [6.11] and [6.12]. In reference [6.10], it is possible to find a quantitative analysis of the relative costs of CPU, I/O, and messages. Reference [6.11] gives a synthetic overview, while reports [6.12] and [6.13] are extended master's theses. The two reports cover similar material; the emphasis in the former is more on the determination of efficient query compilation; in the latter it is upon the efficient "recompilation" of the query when part of the access plan for it becomes invalid.

[6.14] Special Issue on Query Processing, *Database Engineering*, **5**:3; in particular:

[6.14a] C. W. Chung and K. Irani, "A Methodology for Query Optimization in Distributed Database Systems."

[6.14b] S. Christodoulakis, "Issues in Query Evaluation."

This special issue of *Database Engineering* contains 12 short papers on query optimization; among them, six deal with distributed query optimization and the remaining ones with centralized systems and special machine architectures. We indicate, among others, references [a] and [b] because both of them address the important argument of improving the estimations of cardinalities of reduced relations.

[6.15] G. Pelagatti and F. A. Schreiber, "A Model of an Access Strategy in a Distributed Database," *Proc. IFIP TC-2 Working Conference on Data Base Architecture*, G. Bracchi and G. M. Njissen, eds., North-Holland, 1979.

[6.16] S. Ceri and G. Pelagatti, "Allocation of Operations in Distributed Database Access," *IEEE-TC*, **C-31**:2, 1982.

[6.17] S. Ceri and G. Pelagatti, "An Upper Bound on the Number of Execution Nodes for a Distributed Join," *Information Processing Letters*, **12**:1, 1981.

Papers [6.15] to [6.17] deal with the optimization of queries over fragmented relations involving selections, projections, and joins; they constitute, together with reference [5.6], the foundations of Chapters 5 and 6. In reference [6.15], a structured approach to query compilation was presented; the following phases were recognized:

- Determination of a "logical strategy"; this involves equivalence transformations of the operator tree over the global schema.
- Determination of a "distribution strategy"; each global relation is now considered a fragmented relation, and global queries are translated to fragment queries.
- Determination of an "execution strategy"; this involves the determination of nodes upon which each operation is executed and of transmissions required for "moving" operands.

These phases are made in cascade and with feedbacks between them; the last problem involves the solution of a linear integer program. It is possible either to make an exhaustive analysis or to perform the optimization of execution strategies just for the most promising solutions of the first two problems.

Let E be a set of sites upon which an algebraic operation is performed; we say that a relation is **completely distributed** over E if each of its fragments is present on at least one of the sites of E and that a relation is **completely replicated** over E if each of its fragments is present at all the sites of E. Then, the execution sites of distributed operations are constrained by the following rules:

- *Selection and projection.* Fragments must be completely distributed on E.
- *Join.* One of the two operands must be completely distributed on E; the other one must be completely replicated on E.

The above condition on the join execution is not necessary; however, there are classes of execution strategies in which the condition is reasonable; it allows formulating the problem of optimally determining the execution sites of operations as an integer program, shown to be equivalent to the warehouse location problem.

In reference [6.16], the special features of the problem are used for solving it more efficiently. Optimality is measured by the amount of transmissions required, and different transmission costs C_{ij} for each pair of sites are considered. The method includes the determination of one materialization for the query. The efficiency of the computation is improved by the development of a theoretical upper bound to the size of E, which depends on the size of the operands. Intuitively, when operands have about the same size, there is little convenience in having many execution sites, while when one relation is "very big" and the other one is "very small," the first one is likely to be distributed and the other one to be replicated, possibly to all the sites of the big relation. This bound is demonstrated in reference [6.17].

[6.18]   C. Baldissera, G. Bracchi, and S. Ceri, "A Query Processing Strategy for Distributed Databases," *Proc. EURO-IFIP Congress*, North-Holland, 1979.

This paper presents a heuristic method for solving tree queries which makes use of semi-joins. The start point for the optimization is an operator tree of the type shown in Chapter 5. A recursive algorithm "prunes" the tree by removing subtrees; removing a subtree means deciding how its operations are performed. Choices are made at each "branch" node (or diramation) of the tree, where the children of the branch node can be reduced using semi-joins; the method determines at each branch the cheapest sequence of semi-joins. The algorithm is also able to reduce a "chain" of the tree (similar to a chain query) by computing the associated cost.

[6.19]   R. Epstein, M. Stonebraker, and E. Wong, "Distributed Query Processing in a Relational Database System," *ACM-SIGMOD*, 1980.

This paper extends to Distributed INGRES the query processing algorithm which is used in centralized INGRES; see Section 14.2 of Part II.

[6.20]   R. Epstein and M. Stonebraker, "Analysis of Distributed Data Base Processing Strategies," *Sixth VLDB*, 1980.

This paper reports the results of experiments conducted over one sample database for comparing different features of query optimization methods. These features are:

1.   The type of information available for estimating sizes of intermediate results and the estimating technique used.
2.   The search among a limited subset of solutions using heuristics versus the use of an exhaustive method which enumerates all possible solutions.
3.   The use of static (compile time) versus dynamic (run time) decisions.

The experiment was conducted on a query over four relations; exhaustive enumeration of solutions required processing 1215 cases. The major results are that:

- Maximum size estimates, typically used for sizes of intermediate relations, are too pessimistic, and practical approximations such as maximum size divided by 2 or 10 behave better in many cases.
- Methods which search among a limited subset of solutions do not always perform well, and especially for simple queries of few relations it could be worth paying the CPU cost of exhaustive search.
- Dynamic decision making for correcting initial estimates may be beneficial, but the greater cost of decision making at run-time might make these decisions unprofitable.

[6.21]   E. Wong, "Dynamic Re-Materialization: Processing Distributed Queries using Redundant Data," *Fifth Int. Berkeley Workshop on Distributed Data Management and Computer Networks*, 1981.

In this paper, a framework is provided for optimization methods in the context of relation fragmentation. We restate Wong's notation in terms of our reference architecture. Selecting a materialization for a given query means selecting, for each fragment involved, one of its physical copies within the image relations, or the results produced (into temporary relations) by operations which have already been performed. A materialization M is said to be **self-sufficient** for a query Q if there are queries Q_i that can be executed locally to sites, such that the result of Q is the union of the results of the Q_i. An additional **minimal redundancy** property requires that, by eliminating instances of the materialization, the self-sufficiency property does not hold any more.

Given these definitions, an algorithm for query processing can be represented as a sequence of states: (Q_i, M_i), in which the terminal state is required to be self-sufficient and equivalent to the first state (Q_0, M_0); this state is built using actual relation images. Transitions between two states are of two types: **redistribution**, involving data movements, and **local derivations**, involving local processing. Measuring τ as the delay required for the query and C as its cost, the above problem can be restated as one of optimal control. The major contribution of this paper was in the above definitions, rather than in the proposal of solutions which take advantage of them.

[6.22]   L. Kerschberg, P. D. Ting, and S. B. Yao, "Query Optimization in Star Computer Networks," *ACM-TODS*, **7**:4, 1982.

This paper assumes a star network topology and develops for this environment a more precise and complex optimization model. Local processing costs, and particularly page fetches, are taken into consideration; the model selects the most profitable copy for accessing among replicas of the same information. For instance, the paper gives criteria for selecting between local or remote processing of selections and projections, based on the existence of indexes on local and remote copies. Similarly, the paper develops a model of join processing which includes both costs due to sorting or building indexes for the operands of the join and costs due to filtering tuples of its result, along with the cost of operand transmissions.

[6.23]   W. W. Chu and P. Hurley, "Optimal Query Processing for Distributed Database Systems," *IEEE-TC*, **C-31**:9, Sept. 1982.

This paper shows the separation between "query translation and amelioration" and "query optimization" which we have used for distributing the material presented in Chapters 5 and 6. Thus, query processing amounts initially to manipulating query trees using equivalence transformations and then concentrating on the "more promising" query trees; for each of them, several "query processing graphs" are obtained by merging contiguous operations which are performed at the same site into a single node; as each operation can be allocated to several sites, many different groupings are possible (in fact, there is an exponential growth going from trees to graph representations). Finally, a formula is given for evaluating the cost, in terms of file transmissions, of each such grouping. The first part, describing equivalence transformations, is not systematic and does not include semi-join as a relevant transformation.

Chapter 7

The Management
of Distributed
Transactions

The management of distributed transactions requires dealing with several problems which are strictly interconnected, like reliability, concurrency control, and the efficient utilization of the resources of the whole system. Most of the existing research literature is dedicated to the solution of one specific problem, especially in the fields of distributed transaction recovery and concurrency control. However, for understanding distributed transaction management it is necessary to understand the relationship between concurrency control, recovery mechanisms, and the overall structure of the system.

Since many of the techniques which have been proposed in the research literature have not been implemented in real systems, it is not clear how they affect each other and how they perform. Therefore, in this chapter we consider only the most well-known techniques, used in building most of the commercial systems and research prototypes: 2-phase-commitment for recovery, and 2-phase-locking for concurrency control. An extensive presentation of the research on distributed concurrency control and on distributed recovery is instead deferred to Chapters 8 and 9, respectively. We also defer to the following chapters the discussion of some advanced features of 2-phase-commitment and 2-phase-locking which are not required to understand the basic aspects of distributed transaction management.

In Section 7.1, we present a framework for transaction management, discussing the properties, goals, and structure of distributed transactions. Section 7.2 deals with atomicity of distributed transactions, and presents the 2-phase-commitment

173

protocol. We also derive a reference model of a distributed transaction manager which can be used for describing recovery algorithms. Section 7.3 deals with concurrency control for distributed transactions; we present 2-phase-locking and extend our reference model for the description of concurrency control. Finally, in Section 7.4 several architectural aspects of the distributed transaction manager are presented. The relationship to the local operating systems and to the functionalities which are provided by the communication network are also considered.

7.1 A FRAMEWORK FOR TRANSACTION MANAGEMENT

In this section, we define the properties of transactions, state the goals of distributed transaction management, and present a model of a distributed transaction.

7.1.1 Properties of Transactions

As we have seen in Chapter 2, a transaction is an application or part of an application which is characterized by the following properties:

Atomicity Either all or none of the transaction's operations are performed. Atomicity requires that if a transaction is interrupted by a failure, its partial results are undone.

There are two typical reasons why a transaction is not completed: **transaction aborts** and **system crashes**. The abort of a transaction can be requested by the transaction itself (or by its user) because some of its inputs are wrong or because some conditions are recognized that make transaction completion inappropriate or useless. A transaction abort can also be forced by the system for system-dependent reasons, typically system overloads and deadlocks. The activity of ensuring atomicity in the presence of transaction aborts is called **transaction recovery**, and the activity of ensuring atomicity in the presence of system crashes is called **crash recovery**.

The completion of a transaction is called **commitment**. We will assume that each transaction begins with a **begin_transaction** primitive and ends with a **commit** primitive or an **abort** primitive. Taking also the abort forced by the system into consideration, the ways in which a transaction can terminate are those which are shown in Figure 7.1.

Durability Once a transaction has committed, the system must guarantee that the results of its operations will never be lost, independent of subsequent failures. Since the results of a transaction which must be preserved by the system

Figure 7.1 Types of transaction termination.

are stored in the database, the activity of providing the transaction's durability is called **database recovery**.

Serializability   If several transactions are executed concurrently, the result must be the same as if they were executed serially in some order. The activity of guaranteeing transactions' serializability is called **concurrency control**. If a system provides concurrency control, the programmer can write the transaction as if it were executed alone.

Isolation   An incomplete transaction cannot reveal its results to other transactions before its commitment. This property is needed in order to avoid the problem of **cascading aborts** (also called the domino effect), i.e., the necessity to abort all the transactions which have observed the partial results of a transaction which was later aborted. Note that if some of these transactions had already committed, we would have to undo already committed transactions, thus violating the transaction durability property. For this reason, transaction isolation is a very important property in order to implement the transaction notion effectively.

> **Example 7.1**
> As an example, consider the accounting system of a bank and a transaction T1 which credits $1000 to an account with $0 initially. A second transaction T2 reads the $1000 balance which has been written by T1 before the commitment of T1 and debits $1000 to the same account. T2 commits, and $1000 cash is given to the user who invoked T2. Suppose now that T1 aborts because a subsequent control makes the credit operation invalid. The aborting of T1 requires the aborting of T2, because the operation performed by T2 was based on the operation performed by T1; however, aborting T2 is not possible because the effect of T2 on the *real world* cannot be undone by the system. This example shows sufficiently why isolation is a very desirable property.

7.1.2 Goals of Transaction Management

After having considered the characteristics of transactions, let us return to the goals of transaction management: the efficient, reliable, and concurrent execution of transactions. These three goals are strongly interrelated; moreover, there is a trade-off between them, because the effort which is required in order to implement in a reliable way the properties of transactions causes an obvious performance penalty.

Recall that in Chapters 5 and 6 we considered the main aspects which determine the efficiency of an access plan to a distributed database; the aspects considered in those chapters were completely dependent on the characteristics of the data and of the required application. In this chapter we assume that the best access plan in the sense of Chapters 5 and 6 has been determined, and we consider different, and in several cases equally important, efficiency aspects.

CPU and main memory utilization   This aspect is common to both centralized and distributed databases. Although typical database applications are I/O bound (i.e., they spend much of their time waiting for I/O operations and perform only simple computations), the concurrent execution of many of them (tens or hundreds) in a large system can reveal a bottleneck in main memory or in CPU time. If the operating system has to create a process for each active transaction, most of these processes will be swapped in and out of main memory. Moreover, a lot of context switching will be required. In order to reduce this overhead, transaction managers apply specialized techniques which take advantage of the typical characteristics of database applications, and avoid considering them in the same way as the generalized processes which are dealt with by a general-purpose operating system.

Control messages   In a distributed database we have to consider also another aspect of efficiency: the number of control messages which are exchanged between sites. A control message is not used to transfer data but is needed in order to control the execution of the application. This aspect is not independent of the previous one, because the cost of a message is constituted not only by its transmission cost, but also by the nontrivial amount of instructions which the CPU has to execute in order to send a message. In many large systems this cost has been estimated to be somewhere between 5,000 and 10,000 instructions. There is agreement on this estimate, although it is not clear why messages are so CPU-expensive. This latter cost is paid even if the message is exchanged between processes at the same site, without any transmission cost.

Recall that in the minimization of communication costs which we considered in Chapter 6, only data transfers were considered, not control messages. This approach was correct for two reasons: First, data transfers can be much larger than control messages, especially if no effort is spent in designing a good access plan. Second, data transfer depends only on the required application, while the minimization of control messages is to a large extent dependent on the mechanisms which are provided by the system. This latter reason means that query optimization can be performed to a large extent independent of the problems which are treated in this chapter; however, if two alternative solutions which are obtained with the techniques of Chapters 5 and 6 have comparable costs, then it is worthwhile to compare them also with respect to the efficiency aspects which are related to transaction management.

Response time   As a third important efficiency aspect, we have to consider the response time of each individual transaction. Clearly, obtaining an acceptable response time can be more critical for distributed applications than for local applications, because of the additional time which is required for communication between different sites.

Availability   Another aspect which must be considered by the transaction manager of a distributed database is the availability of the whole sytem.   Of course, in a distributed system it is not acceptable for the failure of one site to stop the whole system's operation. Therefore, the algorithms implemented by the transaction manager must not block the execution of those transactions which do not strictly need to access a site which is not operational. As we shall see, the effort of increasing the system's availability in the presence of site failures is a significant characteristic of the algorithms which are used for transaction recovery and concurrency control in distributed databases.

Let us summarize the whole discussion of the last two sections as follows: The goal of transaction management in a distributed database is to control the execution of transactions so that:

1. Transactions have atomicity, durability, serializability, and isolation properties.
2. Their cost in terms of main memory, CPU, and number of transmitted control messages and their response time are minimized.
3. The availability of the system is maximized.

7.1.3 Distributed Transactions

A transaction is always part of an application. When a user types an application code, he or she requests the execution of an application, which does not have the properties of atomicity, durability, serializability, and isolation. At some time after its invocation by the user, the application issues a **begin_transaction** primitive; from this moment, all actions which are performed by the application, until a **commit** or an **abort** primitive is issued, are to be considered part of the same transaction. In some systems, the beginning of a transaction is implicitly associated with the beginning of the application, and the commit primitive ends a transaction and automatically begins a new one, so that the explicit begin_transaction primitive is not necessary. However, the model with explicit primitives which is assumed here is more general.

In order to perform functions at different sites, a distributed application has to execute several processes at these sites. We will call these processes the **agents** of the application. An agent is therefore a local process which performs some actions on behalf of an application.

Note that in the definition of agent we are not interested in knowing whether the agent executes a program written by the application programmer or a primitive function of the system; we have seen in Chapters 1 and 3 that the programmer can request the execution of a remote primitive or write an auxiliary program, install it at a remote site, and then invoke its execution. We have also discussed the difference between these two approaches from the viewpoint of the application programmer; however, if we consider the *execution* of the application, there will be some code which is executed at the remote site in order to perform the required function, and it makes little difference for the purpose of this chapter to know how this code is produced. In both cases this code constitutes an agent of the distributed application.

In order to cooperate in the execution of the global operation required by the application, the agents have to communicate. As they are resident at different sites, the communication between agents is performed through messages.

There are different ways in which the agents can be organized to build a structure of cooperating processes. These alternatives will be discussed in a later section. For the purpose of the discussion of atomicity we will assume that:

1. There exists a **root agent** which starts the whole transaction, so that when the user requests the execution of an application, the root agent is started; the site of the root agent is called the **site of origin** of the transaction.

2.   The root agent has the responsibility of issuing the begin_transaction, commit, and abort primitives.

3.   Only the root agent can request the creation of a new agent.

   While assumption 1 is intrinsic to the definition of root agent, the other two assumptions are made only for simplifying the presentation of this section and will not apply in later sections. In fact, assumption 2 is adopted by most systems, while only a few systems adopt assumption 3.

FUND_TRANSFER:
Read(terminal, $AMOUNT, $FROM_ACC, $TO_ACC);
Begin_transaction;
Select *AMOUNT* into $FROM_AMOUNT
from *ACCOUNT*
where *ACCOUNT_NUMBER*=$FROM_ACC;
if $FROM_AMOUNT − $AMOUNT < 0 then *abort*
else begin
       Update *ACCOUNT*
       set *AMOUNT*=*AMOUNT* − $AMOUNT
       where *ACCOUNT*=$FROM_ACC;
       Update *ACCOUNT*
       set *AMOUNT*=*AMOUNT* + $AMOUNT
       where *ACCOUNT*=$TO_ACC;
       Commit
   end

(*a*) The FUND_TRANSFER transaction at the global level

ROOT-AGENT:
Read(terminal,$AMOUNT, $FROM_ACC, $TO_ACC);
Begin_transaction;
Select *AMOUNT* into $FROM_$AMOUNT
from *ACCOUNT*
where *ACCOUNT_NUMBER*=$FROM_ACCOUNT;
If $FROM_AMOUNT − $AMOUNT < 0 then *abort*
else begin
       Update *ACCOUNT*
       set *AMOUNT*=*AMOUNT* − $AMOUNT
       where *ACCOUNT*=$FROM_ACC;
       Create AGENT$_1$;
       Send to AGENT$_1$($AMOUNT, $TO_ACC);
       Commit
   end

AGENT$_1$:
Receive from ROOT_AGENT ($AMOUNT, $TO_ACC);
Update *ACCOUNT*
set *AMOUNT*=*AMOUNT* + $AMOUNT
where *ACCOUNT*=$TO_ACC;

(*b*) The FUND_TRANSFER transaction constituted by two agents

Figure 7.2   FUND_TRANSFER application.

Example 7.2

Let us consider an example of a distributed transaction. Figure 7.2a shows how a transaction is written by a programmer at the global level. The transaction performs a "fund transfer" operation between two accounts. It operates on a global relation *ACCOUNT(ACCOUNT_NUMBER, AMOUNT)*. The application starts reading from the terminal the amount which has to be transferred ($AMOUNT) and the account numbers from which the amount must be taken and to which it must be credited ($FROM_ACC and $TO_ACC, respectively). Then the application issues a begin_transaction primitive, and from this time on, the properties of transactions must be preserved by the system. The remaining code of the transaction is straightforward: if the from_account has an amount which is smaller than the amount which has to be transferred, the transaction is aborted; otherwise the two amounts are both updated, and the transaction commits (note that this is a very simplified transaction logic: typically, many other conditions can cause an abort, such as a wrong account number).

If we assume now that the accounts are distributed at different sites of a network (e.g., the branches of the bank), at execution time the transaction will be performed by several cooperating agents. For example, in Figure 7.2b two agents are shown. One of the two is the root agent. In Figure 7.2b we assume that the "from account" is located at the root agent site and that the "to account" is located at a different site, where the agent $AGENT_1$ is executed. When the root agent needs the execution of $AGENT_1$, it issues the Create $AGENT_1$ primitive; then it sends the parameters to $AGENT_1$. It would be possible to perform both operations with one primitive; however, they have been split because conceptually they are very different: the first one is a request to the system to create a remote process, and the second one is a communication between two agents.

The root agent also issues the begin_transaction, commit, and abort primitives. It is important to notice that these primitives have not only a local validity at the root agent's site, because the transaction's atomicity property requires that if $AGENT_1$ fails, then the transaction as a whole has no effect. Suppose, for example, that the transaction is executed up to the point at which the root agent issues the "send" command, and that the site of $AGENT_1$ crashes. In this case, the transaction as a whole must be aborted. This means that the update of the from_account which has been performed at the root agent's site must be undone.

Let us state again the most important principle which we have derived from this example: *The begin_transaction, commit, and abort primitives which are issued by the root agent of a distributed transaction are not local; they affect all the agents of the transaction.*

7.2 SUPPORTING ATOMICITY OF DISTRIBUTED TRANSACTIONS

The global primitives begin_transaction, commit, and abort must be implemented by executing a set of appropriate local actions at the sites where the distributed transaction is executed. In order to build a distributed transaction manager which implements the above primitives for distributed transactions, it is convenient to assume that we have at each site a **local transaction manager (LTM)** which is capable of implementing local transactions. In this way we take advantage of the existing techniques and systems for implementing nondistributed transactions. Therefore, we briefly review the main recovery techniques which are used by local, nondistributed transaction managers and then show how a distributed transaction manager is built.

7.2.1 Recovery in Centralized Systems

Recovery mechanisms are built for allowing the return to normal operations of a database system after a failure; thus, before discussing recovery, we must analyze the kinds of failures which can occur in a centralized database.

7.2.1.1 A model of failures in centralized databases From the viewpoint of local recovery, the most important characteristic of failures is the amount of information which is lost because of the failure. Therefore, in the classification of failures we consider essentially the memory component. From this viewpoint, failures can be classified as follows:

1. *Failures without loss of information.* In these failures, all the information stored in memory is available for the recovery. These failures include, for example, the abort of transactions because an error condition is discovered, like an arithmetic overflow or a division by zero.

2. *Failures with loss of volatile storage.* In these failures, the content of main memory is lost; however, all the information which is recorded on disks is not affected by the failure. Typical failures of this kind are system crashes.

3. *Failures with loss of nonvolatile storage.* In these failures, called **media failures**, also the content of disk storage is lost. Typical failures of this kind are head crashes.

   The probability of failures of the third type is less than that of the other two types. Moreover, it is possible to make the probability of the failures of the third type arbitrarily small by replicating the information on several disks having **independent failure modes**. Two disks have independent failure modes if the probability of failure of one of them does not depend on the operational status of the other one.

   This idea is the basis for the development of **stable storage**. Stable storage is the most resilient storage medium available in the system. Stable storage is typically implemented by replicating the same information on several disks with independent failure modes and using the so-called **careful replacement strategy**: at every update operation, first one copy of the information is updated, then the correctness of the update is verified, and finally the second copy is updated.

   Having introduced stable storage, we can introduce a new type of failure:

4. *Failures with loss of stable storage.* In these failures, some information stored in stable storage is lost because of several, simultaneous failures of the third type. Although we can make the probability of failures of stable storage arbitrarily small by using more replication and careful replacement strategies, it is impossible to reduce this probability to zero.

7.2.1.2 Logs   The basic technique for implementing transactions in presence of failures is based on the use of logs. A **log** contains information for undoing or redoing all actions which are performed by transactions. To **undo** the actions of a transaction means to reconstruct the database as prior to its execution. To **redo** the actions of a transaction means to perform again its actions. Before considering how logs are implemented, let us review why it is sometimes necessary to undo or to redo the actions of transactions.

The necessity of undoing the actions of a transaction which fails before the commitment is obvious: since transactions are atomic, if the commitment is not possible then the database must remain the same as if the transaction were not executed at all; hence partial actions must be undone.

For understanding the necessity to redo the actions of a transaction, we have to consider a failure with the loss of volatile storage (failure of type 2). It is possible that when the failure occurs some of the actions performed by an already committed transaction have not yet been written to stable storage (for instance, the loss of volatile storage might include the loss of buffers which have to be written to stable storage). In this case, the recovery mechanism has to redo the actions of the committed transaction in order to ensure that these actions are all recorded in the database.

Notice that the undo and redo operations must be *idempotent*, i.e., performing them several times should be equivalent to performing them once. Therefore,

$$\text{UNDO(UNDO(UNDO}(\ldots(\text{action})\ldots))) = \text{UNDO(action)}$$
$$\text{REDO(REDO(REDO}(\ldots(\text{action})\ldots))) = \text{REDO(action)}$$

This feature is required because the recovery procedure might fail and be restarted several times. Moreover, this feature is very convenient, since we are relieved from the need of knowing whether an action that we want to undo or redo was already undone or redone.

A log record contains the required information for undoing or redoing actions. Whenever a transaction performs an action on the database, a log record is written in the log file. The log record contains:

1.   The identifier of the transaction
2.   The identifier of the record
3.   The type of action (insert, delete, modify)
4.   The old record value (required for the undo)
5.   The new record value (required for the redo)
6.   Auxiliary information for the recovery procedure (typically, a pointer to the previous log record of the same transaction)

Moreover, when a transaction is started, committed, or aborted, a begin_transaction, commit, or abort record is written in the log.

The writing of a database update and the writing of the corresponding log record are two distinct operations; therefore, it is possible that a failure occurs between them. In this case, if the database update were performed before writing the log record, the recovery procedure would be unable of undoing the update; the corresponding log record would in fact not be available. In order to avoid this problem, the **log write-ahead protocol** is used, which consists of two basic rules:

1. Before performing a database update, at least the undo portion of the corresponding log record must have been already recorded on stable storage
2. Before committing a transaction, all log records of the transaction must have already been recorded on stable storage

7.2.1.3 Recovery procedures When a failure with loss of volatile storage occurs, a recovery procedure reads the log file and performs the following operations:

1. Determine all noncommitted transactions that have to be undone. Noncommitted transactions are recognized because they have a begin_transaction record in the log file, without having a commit or abort record.
2. Determine all transactions which need to be redone. In principle, this set includes all transactions which have a commit record in the log file. In practice, most of them were safely stored in stable storage before the failure, hence they do not need to be redone. In order to distinguish transactions which need to be redone from those which do not, **checkpoints** are used.
3. Undo the transactions determined at step 1, and redo the transactions determined at step 2.

Checkpoints are operations which are periodically performed (typically, every few minutes) in order to simplify the first two steps of the recovery procedure. Performing a checkpoint requires the following operations:

a. Writing to stable storage all log records and all database updates which are still in volatile storage (thus, after a checkpoint all transactions have all their actions recorded in stable storage).
b. Writing to stable storage a checkpoint record. A checkpoint record in the log contains the indication of transactions which are active at the time when the checkpoint is done (a transaction is active when its begin_transaction record belongs to the log but not a commit or abort record).

The existence of checkpoints facilitates the recovery procedure. Steps 1 and 2 of the recovery procedure are substituted by the following:

1. Find and read the last checkpoint record.
2. Put all transactions written in the checkpoint record into the undo set, which contains the transactions to be undone. The redo set, which contains the transactions to be redone, is initially empty.
3. Read the log file starting from the checkpoint record until its end. If a begin_transaction record is found, put the corresponding transaction in the undo set. If a commit record is found, move the corresponding transaction from the undo set to the redo set.

The above discussion of checkpoints allows us to consider other aspects of logs. Conceptually, a log contains the whole history of the database. However, only the latest portion refers to transactions which might be undone or redone. Therefore, only this latest portion of the log must be kept online, while the remainder of the log can be kept in offline storage (tape).

So far, we have considered only the recovery from failures without loss of stable storage. Since this latter event is also possible, recovery techniques have been developed also for this case. It is convenient to distinguish two possibilities:

1. Failures in which database information is lost, but logs are safe
2. Failures in which log information is lost

In the first case, the basic recovery technique consists of performing a redo of all committed transactions using the log. The redo is performed after having reset the database to a **dump**, i.e., an image of a previous state which was stored on offline storage. Taking a dump is of course an expensive and lengthy process which is performed only at predefined time intervals, possibly when the database is not active.

In the second case, since log information is lost, it is in general impossible to completely restore the most recent database state, and thus transaction durability is violated. This is a catastrophic event and should never happen in certain systems (for instance, bank systems). In this case, an older state is reestablished, by resetting the database to the last dump and by applying the portion of the log which is not damaged.

We will not consider centralized recovery in further detail. The basic principles which we have seen allow us to understand recovery problems. However, in the actual implementation of systems several other mechanisms are used for reducing the cost and increasing the performance of the whole recovery process.

7.2.2 Communication Failures in Distributed Databases

In the previous Section 7.2.1.1 we have examined the failures which can occur at each site (called **site failures**). Recovery mechanisms for distributed transactions require understanding also the failures which may occur in the communications between sites. In this section, we classify the main types of communication failures, and state some basic assumptions on the communication network which are relevant in this chapter and in Chapter 9.

When a message is sent from site X to site Y, we require from a communication network the following behavior:

1. X receives a positive acknowledgment after a delay which is less then some maximum delay DMAX.
2. The message is delivered at Y in proper sequence with respect to other X–Y messages.
3. The message is correct.

There is a great variety of possible failures with respect to the above specification; for example, the message might not be correct, the message might be out of order, X might not receive the acknowledgment with the message being delivered, X might receive the acknowledgment without the message being delivered, and so on. Most communication networks are capable of eliminating most of these errors, so that we can assume that:

1. If a message from X to Y is delivered at Y, then the message is correct and is in sequence with respect to other X–Y messages.
2. If X receives an acknowledgment, then the message has been delivered.

Note, however, that *if, after a delay DMAX, site X has not received an acknowledgment, X cannot know whether the message has been delivered or not*. This uncertainty is due to the fact that a lack of acknowledgment can mean two things: either the original message is lost (not delivered), and hence no acknowledgment is returned; or the original message is delivered, but the acknowledgment message is lost. Although this uncertainty is very inconvenient, there is no way to eliminate it with a finite protocol, i.e., with a protocol which requires a finite number of messages and terminates in a finite time. Therefore, X will typically try to send the message a finite number of times and then assume that the communication network or the site Y has failed.

With modern communication networks, which are capable of routing messages, the following assumption about the network is also reasonable: if site X cannot communicate with site Y but can communicate with site Z, then site Z cannot communicate with site Y either. In this case, when two operating sites X and Y cannot communicate, this means that no communication path is available between them, and the network is **partitioned** into two or more completely disconnected subnetworks, one including X, and the other one including Y. All the operational sites which belong to the same subnetwork can communicate with each other; however, they cannot communicate with sites which belong to a different subnetwork until the partition is repaired.

We can now summarize the above discussion in the following way. There are two basic types of possible communication errors: lost messages and partitions. When a site X does not receive an acknowledgment of a message from a site Y within a predefined time interval, X is uncertain about the following things:

1. Did a failure occur at all, or is the system simply slow?
2. If a failure occurred, was it a communication failure, or a crash of site Y?
3. Has the message been delivered at Y or not?

The answer to question 3 does not depend on the answer to question 2, because either the communication failure or the crash can have happened before or after the delivery of the message.

Dealing with network partitions is a harder problem than dealing with site crashes or lost messages. Fortunately, in many computer networks partitions are much less frequent than site crashes. Therefore, several levels of reliability algorithms can be designed, which are capable of dealing with the following failures, in order of increasing difficulty:

Class 1.   Site failures only.
Class 2.   Site failures and lost messages, but no partitions.
Class 3.   Site failures, lost messages, and partitions.

The algorithms of class 1 consider the communication network completely reliable and deal with site failures under this assumption. Hence, if a communication failure occurs, the system behaves in an erroneous way. We will call **catastrophic failures** for a reliability mechanism all the failures which cannot be dealt with by it. A network partition is a catastrophic failure for the algorithms of classes 1 and 2.

Multiple failures and K-resiliency Unfortunately failures do not occur one at a time. A system which can tolerate K failures is called K-**resilient**. In distributed databases, this concept is applied to site failures and/or partitions. With respect to site failures, an algorithm is said to be K-resilient if it works properly even if K sites are down. With respect to partitions, K-resiliency refers to the number of subpartitions which have been generated. An extreme case of multiple failure is a **total failure**, where all sites are down. Many algorithms do not deal with this case, as it is considered extremely rare.

7.2.3 Recovery of Distributed Transactions

We can now consider the recovery problem in a distributed database. We assume that at each site a local transaction manager is available, and that it can use the techniques described in Section 7.2.1 for local recovery.

Each agent can therefore issue begin_transaction, commit, and abort primitives to its LTM. After having issued a begin_transaction to its LTM, an agent will possess the properties of a local transaction. We will call an agent which has issued a begin_transaction primitive to its local transaction manager a **subtransaction**, in order to reflect the fact that it is not an autonomous transaction. Moreover, in order to distinguish the begin_transaction, commit, and abort primitives of the distributed transaction from the local primitives issued by each agent to its LTM, we will call the latter **local_begin**, **local_commit**, and **local_abort**.

For the purpose of building a distributed transaction manager (DTM), we require that the LTM has the capabilities of:

1. Ensuring the atomicity of a subtransaction
2. Writing some records on stable storage on behalf of the distributed transaction manager

We need capability 2 because, in implementing a DTM, some additional information (new types of log records) must also be recorded in such a way that they will survive a failure.

The fact that all agents which participate in performing a distributed transaction are local subtransactions is not sufficient to guarantee the properties of a distributed transaction. In other words, the fact that local transaction managers provide atomicity for subtransactions is by itself not sufficient to provide atomicity at the distributed level. The reason for this fact is simple. In order to make sure that either all actions of a distributed transaction are performed or none is performed at all, two conditions are necessary:

1. At *each* site either all actions are performed or none is performed
2. *All* sites must take the *same* decision with respect to the commitment or abort of subtransactions (and must be really capable of performing it)

The existence of local transaction managers, although not sufficient by itself for the implementation of a distributed transaction, is very useful because it allows us to concentrate on the peculiar problem of distributed transaction management,

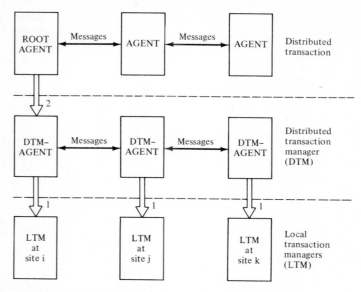

Interface 1: Local_begin, Local_Commit, Local_Abort, Local_Create
Interface 2: Begin_Transaction, Commit, Abort, Create

Figure 7.3 A reference model of distributed transaction recovery.

i.e., *making sure that all local managers take the same decision*, and relieves us from the problem of implementing this decision at each site.

The relationship between distributed transaction management and local transaction management is represented in the reference model of a distributed transaction manager shown in Figure 7.3. At the bottom level we have the local transaction managers, which do not need communication between them. The LTMs implement interface (1): local_begin, local_commit, and local_abort. An additional local_create primitive is indicated as part of interface (1), because the creation of a process (agent) is a function of the local systems, although not strictly related to the implementation of the transaction properties.

At the next higher level we have the distributed transaction manager. DTM is by its nature a distributed layer; DTM will be implemented by a set of local DTM-agents which exchange messages between them. DTM as a whole implements interface (2): begin_transaction, commit, abort, and (remote) create. The creation of a new agent is a primitive which must be issued to the DTM, because the DTM must have a notion of which agents constitute a distributed transaction.

At the next higher level we have the distributed transaction, constituted by the root agent and the other agents. Since we have assumed that only the root agent can issue the begin_transaction, commit, and abort primitives, interface (2) is used only by the root agent.

A word of caution is necessary: this reference model must not be considered as the run-time organization of a distributed transaction; in fact most systems do not implement explicitly all these layers at run time, but reduce them for performance reasons. Typically, some primitives are translated at compile time and are not interpreted at run time. Therefore, the reference model is a conceptual model for understanding how the algorithms work and to which level an operation belongs, and is not necessarily an implementation structure.

We can now analyze how the distributed transaction manager implements the primitives of interface (2) of Figure 7.3.

Begin_transaction When a begin_transaction is issued by the root agent, the DTM will have to issue a local_begin primitive to the LTM at the site of origin and at all the sites at which there are already active agents of the same application, thus transforming all agents into subtransactions; from this time on the activation of a new agent by the same distributed transaction requires that the local_begin be issued to the LTM where the agent is activated, so that the new agent is created as a subtransaction.

As an example, in Figure 7.4 the primitives and messages are shown which are issued by the various components of the reference model for the execution of the distributed FUND_TRANSFER transaction of Figure 7.2 up to the point where the parameters are sent from the root agent to AGENT$_1$. The numbers in Figure 7.4 indicate the order in which actions are performed and messages are sent.

Abort When an abort is issued by the root agent, all existing subtransactions must be aborted. This is performed by issuing local_aborts to the LTMs at all sites where there is an active subtransaction. Clearly, by aborting all subtransactions, the effect of a global abort is obtained, because all actions performed by the agents since the (global) begin_transaction are undone by the LTMs.

Commit The implementation of the commit primitive is the most difficult and expensive. The main difficulty originates from the fact that the correct commitment of a distributed transaction requires that all its subtransactions commit locally even in the case of failures. It is therefore not acceptable that a subtransaction is locally aborted because of a failure and the other subtransactions commit. In order to implement this primitive for a distributed transaction, the general idea of **2-phase-commitment (2PC)** has been developed. The basic 2-phase-commitment protocol is described in the next section. There are, however, several variations of this basic protocol which have been developed to increase its efficiency and availability. These variations will be described in later sections.

7.2.4 The 2-Phase-Commitment Protocol

In the basic 2-phase-commitment protocol, there is one agent (a DTM-agent in our reference model) which has a special role. This agent is called the **coordinator**; all the other agents which must commit together are called **participants**. The coordinator is responsible of taking the final commit or abort decision. Each participant corresponds to a subtransaction which has performed some write action; it is responsible for performing the write action at its local database. We assume that each participant is at a different site. Note that when the transaction performs some write action at the site of its coordinator, then the coordinator and one

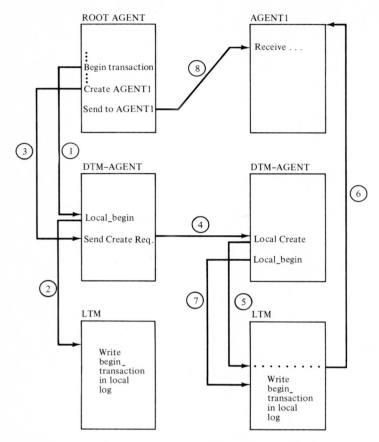

Figure 7.4 Actions and messages during the first part of the FUND_TRANSFER transaction.

participant are at the same site; though they don't need to communicate using the network, we assume that they follow the protocol as if they were at different sites.

The basic idea of 2PC is to determine a unique decision for all participants with respect to committing or aborting all the local subtransactions. If a participant is unable to locally commit its subtransaction, then all participants must locally abort. The protocol consist of two phases. The goal of the first phase of the protocol is to reach a common decision; the goal of the second phase is to implement this decision. We first present the protocol in absence of failures, and then we discuss the recovery from all possible types of failures. The protocol proceeds as follows (see Figure 7.5).

Phase one There is a **first phase** during which the coordinator asks all the participants to **prepare for commitment**; each participant answers READY if it is ready to commit and willing to do so. Before sending the first prepare for

Coordinator: Write "prepare" record in the log;
Send PREPARE message and activate timeout

Participant: Wait for PREPARE message;
If the participant is willing to commit then
   begin
         Write subtransaction's records in the log;
         Write "ready" record in the log;
         Send READY answer message to coordinator
   end
else begin
         Write "abort" record in the log;
         Send ABORT answer message to coordinator
   end

Coordinator: Wait for ANSWER message (READY or ABORT) from all participants
   or timeout;
If timeout expired or some answer message is ABORT then
   begin
         Write "global_abort" record in the log;
         Send ABORT command message to all participants
   end
else (* all answers arrived and were READY *)
   begin
         Write "global_commit" record in the log;
         Send COMMIT command message to all participants
   end

Participant: Wait for command message;
Write "abort" or "commit" record in the log;
Send the ACK message to coordinator;
Execute command

Coordinator: Wait for ACK messages from all participants;
Write "complete" record in the log

Figure 7.5 Basic 2-phase-commitment protocol.

commitment message, the coordinator records on stable storage a log record of a new type, called a "prepare" log record, in which the identifiers of all subtransactions participating to the 2-phase-commitment are recorded. The coordinator also activates a **timeout** mechanism, which will interrupt the coordinator after that a given time interval is expired.

When a participant answers READY, it ensures that it will be able to commit the subtransaction even if failures occur at its site. In practice, this means that each participant has to record on stable storage two things:

1. All the information which is required for locally committing the subtransaction. This means that all the log records of the subtransaction must be recorded on stable storage.

2. The fact that this subtransaction has declared to be ready to commit. This means that a log record of a new type, called a "ready" log record, must be recorded on stable storage.

The coordinator decides whether to commit or abort the transaction as a result of the answers which it has received from the participants. If *all* participants have answered READY, it decides to commit the transaction. If instead some participant has answered ABORT or has not yet answered when the timeout expires, it decides to abort the transaction.

Phase two   The coordinator begins the **second phase** of 2PC by recording on stable storage its decision. This corresponds to writing a "global_commit" or "global_abort" record in the log (these are two new types of log records). The fact that the coordinator records its decision on stable storage means that the distributed transaction will eventually be committed or aborted, in spite of failures. Then the coordinator informs all participants of its decision, by sending them the command message.

All the participants write a commit or abort record in the log, based on the command message received from the coordinator. From this moment, the local recovery procedure is capable of ensuring that the effect of the subtransaction will not be lost. As in centralized databases, all log records related to the subtransaction can be taken offline after the next checkpoint.

Finally, all participants send a final acknowledgment (ACK) message to the coordinator, and perform the actions required for committing or aborting the subtransaction. When the coordinator has received an ACK message from all participants, he or she writes a log record of a new type, called a "complete" record. After having written this record, the coordinator can forget the outcome of the transaction; thus, all records related to this transaction can be taken offline after the next checkpoint.

Note that the ACK message is not simply an acknowledgment that a command message has been received, but it is a regular message of the protocol, informing that the command has been recorded in stable storage. Therefore, even if the communication network automatically returns acknowledgments, an explicit ACK message is required.

The 2-phase-commitment protocol is resilient to all failures in which no log information is lost. The behavior of the protocol in the presence of different kinds of failures is now analyzed.

1.   *Site failures*

   a.   *A participant fails before having written the ready record in the log.* In this case, the coordinator's timeout expires, and it takes the abort decision. All operational participants abort their subtransactions. When the failed participant recovers, the restart procedure simply aborts the transaction, without having to collect information from other sites.

   b.   *A participant fails after having written the ready record in the log.* In this case, the operational sites correctly terminate the transaction (commit or abort). When the failed site recovers, the restart procedure has to ask the coordinator or some other participant about the outcome of the transaction, and then perform the appropriate action (commit or abort). In this case, access to remote recovery information is required. In the above discussion, we have considered writing the log and sending the message as an atomic action. However, in a real system a failure can occur after the log has been written and before the message is sent. In this case the coordinator and all other operational participants would behave as in the above point (1a), while the failed participant would perform restart as described here. The outcome is correct in this case also. In the following we will normally assume that writing the log and sending the message constitute an atomic action.

c. *The coordinator fails after having written the prepare record in the log, but before having written a global_commit or global_abort record in the log.* In this case all participants which have already answered READY must wait for the recovery of the coordinator. The restart procedure of the coordinator resumes the commitment protocol from the beginning, reading the identity of participants from the prepare record in the log, and sending again the PREPARE message to them. Each ready participant must recognize that the new PREPARE message is a repetition of the previous one.

d. *The coordinator fails after having written a global_commit or global_abort record in the log, but before having written the complete record in the log.* In this case, the coordinator at restart must send to all participants the decision again; all participants which have not received the command have to wait until the coordinator recovers. As before, participants should not be affected by receiving the command message twice.

e. *The coordinator fails after having written the complete record in the log.* In this case, the transaction was already concluded, and no action is required at restart.

2. *Lost messages*

a. *An answer message (READY or ABORT) from a participant is lost.* In this case the coordinator's timeout expires, and the whole transaction is aborted. Note that this failure is observed only by the coordinator, and from the coordinator's viewpoint it is exactly like a participant's failure. However, from the participant's viewpoint the situation is different; the participant does not consider itself failed and does not execute a restart procedure.

b. *A PREPARE message is lost.* In this case the participant remains in wait. The global result is the same as in the previous case, because the coordinator does not receive an answer.

c. *A command message (COMMIT or ABORT) is lost.* With the protocol of Figure 7.5, the destination participant remains uncertain about the decision. It is very simple to eliminate this problem by introducing a timeout in the participant; if no command has been received after the timeout interval from the answer, a request for a repetition of the command is sent.

d. *An ACK message is lost.* With the protocol of Figure 7.5, the coordinator remains uncertain about the fact that the participant has received the command message. This problem can be eliminated by introducing a timeout in the coordinator; if no ACK message is received after the timeout interval from the transmission of the command, the coordinator will send the command again. The best way of dealing with this case at the participant's site is to send again the ACK message, even if the subtransaction was completed in the meantime and is no longer active.

3. *Network partitions*
   Let us suppose that a simple partition occurs, dividing the sites in two groups; the group which contains the coordinator is called the **coordinator-group**; the other the **participant-group**. From the viewpoint of the coordinator, the partition is equivalent to a multiple failure of a set of participants, and the situation is similar to that of points (1a) and (1b) above: the coordinator takes a decision and sends the command to all participants of the coordinator-group, so that these sites can terminate correctly the transaction. From the viewpoint of the members of the participant-group, the partition is equivalent to a coordinator failure and the situation is similar to the above cases (1c) and (1d).

Notice that the recovery procedure for a site which is involved in processing a distributed transaction is more complex than that for a centralized database. In centralized databases, just two cases are possible: transactions are either committed or noncommitted, and the recovery mechanism performs the corresponding redo or undo actions. In distributed databases, additional cases are possible:

1. A participant is ready (case 1b). This situation is recognized by the recovery mechanism because the ready record is in the log, but not a commit or abort record.
2. A coordinator has initiated phase one (case 1c). This situation is recognized by the recovery mechanism because a prepare record is in the log, but not a global_commit or global_abort record.
3. A coordinator has initiated phase two (case 1d). The situation is recognized by the recovery mechanism because the prepare and a global_commit or global_abort record are in the log, but not a complete record.

7.2.5 Some Comments on the 2-Phase-Commitment Protocol

Unilateral abort capability   An important feature of the 2PC protocol is that each site is authorized to **unilaterally abort** its subtransaction until it has answered READY to the prepare message; this site autonomy characteristic is very useful in the management of each local system. However, after a subtransaction has entered the ready state, this type of site autonomy is lost.

Blocking   A problem with the basic 2-phase-commitment protocol is that a subtransaction which has entered its ready state could be **blocked**. A typical reason for blocking is a failure of the coordinator or of the communication network. The blocked subtransactions must keep all their resources until they receive the final command during the recovery from the failure, because they must be able of eventually commiting or aborting. Therefore, blocking reduces the availability of the system in case of failures. Several commit protocols have been studied in order to reduce the probability of blocking; they are presented in Chapter 9.

Elimination of the PREPARE message   In describing the basic 2-phase-commitment protocol, we have assumed that the whole process is started by the coordinator when the main execution of the transaction is terminated. This is not necessary and the first phase of these protocols can be incorporated in the transaction execution. When agents finish performing their operations, they can return the READY message immediately, without waiting for a PREPARE message. In fact, when the root agent knows that all required operations have been performed and the transaction was not unilaterally aborted, it also knows that all agents are ready to commit. With this assumption the 2-phase-commitment protocol (without the final ACK message) becomes:

Coordinator:

>   Write prepare record in the log;
>   Request operations from participants, and activate timeout;
>   Wait for completion of participants (READY message)
>   or timeout expired;
>   Write global_commit or global_abort record in the log;
>   Send command message to all participants.

Participant:

>   Receive request for operation;
>   Perform local processing and write log records;
>   Send READY message and write ready record in the log;
>   Wait for command message;
>   Write commit or abort records in the log;
>   Execute command.

This approach eliminates the PREPARE messages and the first phase by incorporating them in the main execution. It has, however, a serious disadvantage: once a participant declares to be ready to commit, it will remain in this state until the whole transaction is terminated. This is the situation in which the participant has abandoned its right to unilaterally abort the transaction, and a failure of the coordinator can block it. Therefore, in this way a higher probability of blocking exists, and site autonomy is reduced.

Increase of efficiency by using defaults   Variations to the basic 2-phase-commitment protocol have been designed with the purpose of improving their performances in terms of messages exchanged and of records written on logs. The modified protocols are based on the idea of assuming by default that a transaction is committed (or aborted) if no information about it is found in the log. These protocols are called "presumed commit" and "presumed abort"; they are used by the R* system, and they are described in Sections 13.5.1 and 13.5.2.

The remote recovery information problem   We have seen that with 2-phase-commitment the remote recovery information problem arises if a participant fails after having answered READY and before having received the command or if the command message gets lost. In both cases, the participant has to send an inquiry in order to know the outcome of the transaction. The most straightforward solution is that the participant sends its inquiry to the coordinator. However, the coordinator might have failed when the participant recovers. It is possible to let the participant wait and later retry the inquiry; however, with this solution the participant remains blocked. Two more complex alternatives exist:

1. *Redirecting the inquiry*   The inquiry can be sent from the recovering site to other participants. If at least one participant has received the decision, then all other participants can find out the decision from it. This means that, in the case of a network partition, all the participant-groups in which at least one participant has received the command can complete the transaction. This solution requires that information about terminated transactions be maintained also at the participants' sites.

2. *Spooling the command message*   This approach consists in assigning to each site i a set of spooling sites $S(i)$. A spooling site has the responsibility of receiving and storing the messages which are directed to site i while it is down. When site i recovers, it receives from one of the sites of $S(i)$ all messages which were directed to it.

    With this method, the coordinator sends the command message for a crashed participant to all its spoolers, and receives the ACK messages from them. When the participant recovers, it receives the decision from the spoolers and does not interact with the coordinator. If K spoolers are used, K-resiliency is obtained, independently of the number of participants. This method is used by the SDD-1 system; it is further discussed in Chapter 12.

7.3 CONCURRENCY CONTROL FOR DISTRIBUTED TRANSACTIONS

In this section we analyze the fundamental problems which are due to the concurrent execution of transactions. We discuss concurrency control based on locking. First, the 2-phase-locking protocol in centralized databases is presented; then, 2-phase-locking is extended to distributed databases, and the problems which arise in this environment are discussed.

7.3.1 Concurrency Control Based on Locking in Centralized Databases

The basic idea of locking is that whenever a transaction accesses a data item, it locks it, and that a transaction which wants to lock a data item which is already locked by another transaction must *wait* until the other transaction has released the lock (unlock).

In fact, typical locking mechanisms are more complex, because they have the notion of **lock mode**: a transaction locks a data item in **shared mode** if it wants only to read the data item and in **exclusive mode** if it wants to write the data item. A transaction is **well-formed** if it always locks a data item in shared mode before reading it, and it always locks a data item in exclusive mode before writing it. The correctness of locking mechanisms is based on the assumption that all transactions are well-formed.

The following compatibility rules exist between lock modes:

1. A transaction can lock a data item in shared mode if it is not locked at all or it is locked in shared mode by another transaction.
2. A transaction can lock a data item in exclusive mode only if it is not locked at all.

Two transactions are in **conflict** if they want to lock the same data item with two incompatible modes; we have shared-exclusive (or read-write) conflicts and exclusive-exclusive (or write-write) conflicts.

Another relevant aspect is the **granularity** of locking. This term relates to the size of the objects which are locked with a single lock operation. In general, it is possible to lock at a "record level" (i.e, to lock individual tuples) or at a "file level" (i.e., to lock entire fragments or relations). In the former case conflicts between transactions arise when two transactions want to access the same record. In the latter case, conflicts are instead determined when two transactions need to access the same file. Since the former case occurs with much less probability, locking at the record level allows much more concurrency than locking at the file level. Therefore, most database management systems provide locking at the record level.

In reference [7.3] it has been proved that the concurrent execution of transactions is correct provided that the following rules are observed:

1. Transactions are well-formed.
2. Compatibility rules for locking are observed.
3. Each transaction does not request new locks after it has released a lock.

The latter condition is expressed also by saying that the transactions are **2-phase-locked (2PL)**, because for each transaction there is a first phase during which new locks are acquired (growing phase) and a second phase during which locks are only released (shrinking phase).

Although 2-phase-locking is sufficient to preserve the serializability of transactions, it is not sufficient to guarantee isolation, because a transaction can release its exclusive locks at any time during the shrinking phase and a different transaction can therefore observe its results before its commitment. In order to guarantee isolation we must therefore require that *transactions hold all their exclusive locks until commitment.*

It is beyond the scope of this book to discuss centralized locking schemes in further detail. We will simply assume here that all transactions are performed according to the following scheme:

> (Begin application)
> Begin transaction
> Acquire locks before reading or writing
> Commit
> Release locks
> (End application)

In this way transactions are well-formed, 2-phase-locked, and isolated.

An important problem which must be considered in using locking mechanisms for concurrency control is **deadlock**. A deadlock between two transactions arises if each transaction has locked a data item and is waiting to lock a different data item which has already been locked by the other transaction with a conflicting lock mode. Both transactions will wait forever in this situation, and system intervention is required to unblock the situation. The system must first discover the deadlock situation and then force one transaction to release its locks, so that the other one can proceed. In general, this means that one transaction is aborted.

The above method is called **deadlock detection**. Other techniques, based on a priori avoidance of deadlocks, are less frequently used, especially in distributed systems.

7.3.2 Concurrency Control Based on Locking in Distributed Databases

Let us now turn our attention to the peculiar aspects of using a locking mechanism for a distributed database. We will assume, as in the previous section, that we can (and want to) use the facilities which are provided by the local systems in order to build the distributed mechanisms. Clearly, local systems (LTMs) allow a local agent to lock and unlock local data items. We extend therefore the interfaces which have been shown in Figure 7.3 in the way which is shown in Figure 7.6: the LTMs interpret local locking primitives (local-lock-shared, local-lock-exclusive, and local-unlock), while the agents of the transaction issue global primitives (lock-shared, lock-exclusive, and unlock). Understanding the peculiar aspects of distributed concurrency control is tantamount to understanding what the DTM has to do in order to guarantee that the global transaction has the required characteristics of serializability and isolation. The most important result for distributed databases is the following:

> If distributed transactions are well-formed and 2-phase-locked (i.e., they acquire locks in the growing phase and release locks in the shrinking phase), then 2-phase-locking is a correct locking mechanism in distributed databases as well as in centralized databases.

This statement will be proved in the next chapter.

We will now analyze separately the main problems which the DTM has to solve:

Dealing with multiple copies of data   Locking mechanisms have been developed for centralized databases with the implicit assumption that only one copy of each data item exists; thus, a transaction discovers that another transaction is

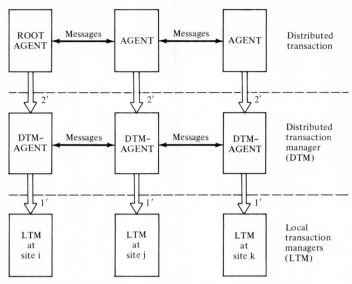

Interface 1': Local_lock_shared, Local_lock_exclusive, Local_unlock
Interface 2': Lock_shared, Lock_exclusive, Unlock

Figure 7.6 A reference model for distributed concurrency control.

working on a data item by finding it locked. In distributed databases, redundancy between data items which are stored at different sites is often desired, and in this case two transactions which hold conflicting locks on two copies of the same data item stored at different sites could be unaware of their mutual existence. In this case locking would be completely useless.

In order to avoid this problem, the DTM has to translate the lock primitive issued by an agent on a data item in such a way that it is impossible for a conflicting transaction to be unaware of this lock. The simplest way of doing this is to issue local locks to all LTMs at all sites where a local copy of the data item is stored; in this way, a lock primitive is translated into as many lock primitives as there are copies of the locked data item. This approach would work, because two conflicting transactions would discover their conflict at all sites where they request locks. Clearly, this approach is redundant, because it is enough to discover the conflict at one site. Therefore, we can try to find alternative schemes which guarantee that conflicts are discovered at least at one site and reduce the amount of overhead which is involved in obtaining many local locks.

These schemes are only briefly sketched here; a detailed analysis and comparison will be performed in Chapter 9.

1. *Write-locks-all, read-locks-one.* In this scheme exclusive locks are acquired on all copies, while shared locks are acquired only on one arbitrary copy. A conflict is always detected, because a shared-exclusive conflict is detected at

the site where the shared lock is required and exclusive-exclusive conflicts are detected at all sites.

2. *Majority locking.* Both shared and exclusive locks are requested at a majority of the copies of the data item (i.e., the number of copies which are locked is strictly greater than the number of copies which are not locked); in this way if two transactions are required to lock the same item, there is at least one copy of it where the conflict is discovered.

3. *Primary copy locking.* One copy of each data item is privileged (called the **primary copy**); all locks must be required at this copy so that conflicts are discovered at the site where the primary copy resides.

Deadlock detection   The second problem which is faced by the DTM is deadlock detection. A deadlock is a circular waiting situation which can involve many transactions, not just two. The basic characteristic of a deadlock is the existence of a set of transactions such that each transaction waits for another one. This situation can be conveniently represented with a **wait-for graph**. A wait-for graph is a directed graph having transactions as nodes; an edge from transaction T1 to transaction T2 represents the fact that T1 waits for T2. The existence of a deadlock situation corresponds to the existence of a cycle in the wait-for graph. Therefore, a system can discover deadlocks by constructing the wait-for graph and analyzing whether there are cycles in it.

Clearly, if the arcs of the wait-for graph are discovered at different sites, the deadlock detection problem becomes intrinsically a problem of distributed transaction management and cannot be dealt with by local transaction management. In this case, a *global* wait-for graph should be build by the DTM. The construction of a global wait-for graph requires the execution of rather complex algorithms, which are discussed in Chapter 8. However, most systems do not determine deadlocks in this way, and they simply use timeouts for deadlock detection.

With the timeout method a transaction is aborted after a given time interval has passed since the transaction entered a wait state. This method does not discover a deadlock; it simply observes a "long waiting" which could possibly be caused by a deadlock. The main problem with this method is to determine a good timeout interval. As the timeout interval is made shorter, more transactions which are not in deadlock will be unnecessarily aborted. As the timeout interval is made longer, more time will be wasted by transactions in deadlock before being aborted. In a distributed system it is even more difficult to determine a workable timeout interval than in a centralized system, because of the less predictable behavior of the communication network and of remote sites.

A very dangerous effect when short timeouts are used is the cascading effect due to system overload. This happens when a transaction is aborted after a timeout not because it was in deadlock, but because the system was overloaded and therefore slow. In this case, the abort operation itself causes additional messages to be exchanged and additional work to be done by the local systems, thus increasing the overload. This causes additional delay, thus causing other transactions to be aborted, and so on. Therefore, in general the timeout method is acceptable for lightly loaded systems but not convenient for congested systems.

7.3.3 Some Comments on Distributed 2-Phase-Locking

Two-phase-locking and availability   The concurrency control mechanism is related to the availability of the system in two ways: first, the fact that the concurrency control mechanism requires locking either all copies, or a majority of them, or a particular copy of a data item can possibly block the execution of a transaction in case of a failure. Notice that this can happen even if enough data is available for executing the transaction in the absence of concurrency requirements. For example, if the concurrency control mechanism locks all copies of a data item, then the failure of a site with one copy of the item blocks the transaction. Note that in this case the redundancy of the data item reduces the system's availability for the transaction.

Second, a subtransaction which is blocked (as described in Section 7.2.5) after having locked data items ties up resources which cannot be used by other transactions. In fact, for this reason it is often convenient to abort blocked subtransactions which have not yet declared to be ready to commit, instead of keeping them in wait.

Two-phase-locking and recovery   The relationship between 2-phase-locking and the recovery mechanism is characterized by two facts:

1. All locking mechanisms sometimes require aborting a transaction because a deadlock is detected. The recovery mechanism must make this abort possible. As we have seen, if a 2PC protocol is used for transaction recovery, the transaction's abort is possible only until the end of the first phase of commitment. Therefore, *the growing phase of a 2-phase-locked transaction and deadlock detection must be terminated before a participant has declared to be ready to commit.*

2. As we have seen already, if a failure blocks the execution of the 2-phase-commitment and some participant has already answered to be ready to commit, then *the participant must hold all the locks for the transaction until it is informed of the decision.*

7.4 ARCHITECTURAL ASPECTS OF DISTRIBUTED TRANSACTIONS

In this section we examine some aspects which characterize the structure of the computation and of the communication of a distributed transaction. These aspects are related on one hand to the features of the local operating systems, especially process management and interprocess communication, and on the other hand to the features of the communication network. Because of the number of different problems which are faced in these fields, in this section we can only present some of the principal alternatives for organizing the computation and communication of transactions and discuss their trade-offs; a precise evaluation or a suggestion of how a distributed transaction manager should be built is beyond the scope of this section.

7.4.1 Processes and Servers

In a centralized database the simplest way to organize transaction processing is probably to have one operating system process for each (concurrent) transaction. Of course, it is necessary that these processes share some common data structure, for example, lock tables. The main advantage of this organization is that there is a strong correspondence between the entities of the transaction manager (transactions) and the entities of the operating system (processes), so that it is relatively easy to take advantage of the features of the operating system. We will call this organization the **process model**.

A limitation of this approach is that every time a transaction issues an I/O request that cannot be satisfied by data which is already in the main memory buffers, a process switch is required. This switch is expensive in terms of CPU time in most operating systems. Moreover, process creation, which is also expensive, is required for each transaction, and the number of processes which exist in a system with high concurrency can be so high that main memory can represent a bottleneck.

Note that in order to reduce the above penalties, many transaction managers of centralized databases do their own scheduling; in other words, they are small monitors which run above the real operating system. These monitors are specialized for dealing with database transactions instead of general-purpose processes; taking advantage of this fact, they implement more convenient scheduling strategies, they perform a more efficient process switching, and reduce the overhead of process creation and the amount of memory which is tied up by each process.

An alternative organization is the **server model**. In this model "server processes" exist independent of transactions; transactions require services from the server process through request messages. A transaction is bound to a server dynamically by passing to it the transaction identifier; a server may service a transaction, then a different one, and then the first transaction again. Notice that when a server executes a recoverable action for a particular transaction, the log records are tagged with the transaction identifier, and not with the server identifier.

This organization reduces the overhead for process creation and for process switching; the number of existing processes is no longer dependent on the number of existing transactions, because when a server has finished its task on behalf of a transaction, it can begin servicing a different one.

A detailed discussion of the advantages and disadvantages of the above models in a centralized database is not within the scope of this book. The above considerations are sufficient for understanding the main features of these models with distribution.

Let us discuss distributed transactions with the process model. We consider an operating system process as a strictly local process (we do not consider the existence of a distributed operating system, implementing distributed processes, since distributed operating systems are not available today and their implementation requires solving the same problems which are discussed here anyway). Clearly, a distributed transaction involves the execution of several processes at different sites. We can consider each agent of the distributed transaction as being a separate local process. The state of the distributed transaction is constituted by the states of all processes which constitute it.

There are several possible variations on the above scheme. The most important one regards the number of processes which have to be created at the same site for performing multiple requests by the same transaction. The two extreme alternatives are to create a process for servicing each incoming request or to create only one process for the first request and retain that process for the whole transaction execution.

Creating a process for each request incurs in a penalty for the process creation that is larger than for retainig one process. However, presumably the processes which are created for each request are smaller than a unique process; moreover they can be eliminated after having executed their function, thus freeing resources.

In the server model, a distributed transaction requests the execution of a remote function by sending a request message to a server at the remote site. Note that the request message is tagged with the transaction identifier. We can identify the server with an agent of the transaction only for the time during which it executes on behalf of this transaction. Clearly, the state of a transaction is not represented by the state of the server processes which have been executed; the state of the transaction is a completely independent data structure which is modified by the execution of servers.

7.4.2 Sessions and Datagrams

The communication between processes or servers can be performed through sessions and/or datagrams, as defined in Chapter 2. In fact, this choice is not independent of whether a process or a server model has been adopted. Datagrams and sessions can be used with all the above approaches. With a process approach, sessions seem more convenient if one process per site is retained instead of creating a new process for each request. The reason for this fact is that sessions have a basic advantage: the authentication and identification functions need to be performed only once and then messages can be exchanged without repeating these operations. Clearly, this advantage is meaningful if many messages are exchanged between two processes; this happens if a single process is created and retained for each transaction at each site.

The use of sessions coupled with a retained process approach creates a sort of stable distributed computation structure which is maintained as long as required. In this case it is meaningful to establish the session when the remote process is created and to maintain it until the remote process is deleted.

7.4.3 Computational Structure of Distributed Transactions

The computational structure of distributed database transactions is organized in two basic ways: the centralized structure and the hierarchical structure. In the centralized structure one agent (the root agent) activates and controls all other agents. In a strictly centralized structure the other agents should not communicate between themselves. In fact, in order to reduce the transmission overhead which is incurred if all data is transmitted to the root agent, even in systems which have a centralized structure for control and synchronization some degree of direct data communication between nonroot agents is allowed. The centralized structure is, for instance, adopted by the SDD-1 system.

With a hierarchical structure, each agent can activate other agents, thus creating a tree of agents having the root agent as root. Clearly, this model is more general and can represent the previous one as a special case. Direct communication between agents is intrinsic to this model. Distributed systems which use the tree structure are R* and ENCOMPASS of Tandem.

The centralized approach restricts the possible computational structures in order to ensure that one agent knows the complete invocation structure of all the processes. In some system architectures, this fact can simplify the protocols which are used for concurrency control and for recovery (in Chapter 8, some concurrency control schemata are presented which take advantage of a centralized computational structure).

Another distinguishing aspect of the computational structure of transactions is whether parallelism is allowed or not. Clearly, in a distributed system it is more important than in a centralized system to allow parallelism. In most systems, therefore, several agents of the same transaction are allowed to execute in parallel. In order to obtain this result the activation of a new agent must be a nonblocking (asynchronous) primitive.

7.4.4 Communication Structure for Commit Protocols

We have considered so far the communication and computation structure for the agents of the transaction without considering the commit protocol; we analyze here the different communication structures which can be implemented for the DTM-agents in order to implement commit protocols.

The 2PC commit protocol which was described in Section 7.2 clearly requires a **centralized** communication structure (Figure 7.7a). The communication is always performed between the coordinator DTM-agent and the participants, but not between the participants directly.

It is easy to modify the above protocol so that a **hierarchical** communication structure is obtained (Figure 7.7b). The coordinator is the DTM-agent at the root of the tree. The communication between the coordinator and the participants is performed not by a direct broadcast, but by propagating the messages up and down the tree. Each DTM-agent which is an internal node of the communication tree collects messages from its sons or broadcasts messages to them.

Another class of communication protocol is the **linear protocol** (Figure 7.7c). In a linear protocol an ordering of sites is defined, so that each site except the first and the last one has a predecessor and a successor. Instead of broadcasting a message from the coordinator to all other participants, the message is passed from each participant to its successor.

A linear protocol works in the following way. Let the ordering of DTM-agents be represented by agent numbers from 1 to N.

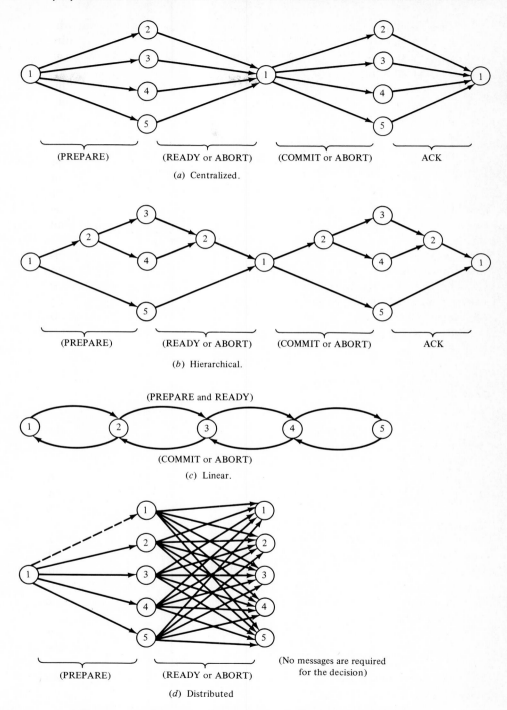

(a) Centralized.

(b) Hierarchical.

(c) Linear.

(d) Distributed

Figure 7.7 Communication structures for commit protocols.

1. The root agent of the transaction requires a (global) commit to the DTM-agent 1.

2. DTM-agent 1 decides whether it wants to abort or commit the transaction; if it decides to abort, it sends this information back to the root agent; otherwise it sends the commit decision to DTM-agent 2; DTM-agent 2 acts in the same way, sending an abort decision back to DTM-agent 1 or a commit decision forward to DTM-agent 3; this process continues until either an abort is propagated back to the root agent or a commit reaches the last DTM-agent.

3. DTM-agent N sends a commit or abort message back to DTM-agent $N - 1$; this message propagates back to the root agent; all participants receive this information and take the correct action.

Note that the linear protocol reduces the number of messages which are required with respect to the centralized protocol. This gain is important if the communication network is such that the cost of a broadcast is the same as the cost of sending N messages; however, in networks which have a convenient broadcast, the linear protocol does not represent a gain.

The linear protocol pays for the reduced number of required messages with a loss in parallelism in processing; in a linear protocol all participants decide in sequence, while in a centralized protocol all participants decide whether to abort or commit at the same time. This causes a serious difference in response time for the transaction.

A different class of communication protocol is the **distributed protocol** (Figure 7.7d). A distributed protocol for commitment requires that each DTM-agent communicate with each other participant. The number of messages which are needed by a distributed protocol is much greater than the number of messages which is required by a centralized or hierarchical protocol. Therefore, these protocols are suited only for networks where messages are very cheap, typically local networks. On the other hand, the delay required by this commitment protocol is less than the delay required by the centralized commitment.

The transformation of the centralized 2PC protocol into a distributed commit protocol is not difficult:

1. The root agent starts the commit phase by asking the DTM-agent at its site to begin the commitment procedure.

2. The DTM-agent broadcasts the PREPARE message.

3. Each agent sends its answer to all other agents.

4. Each agent receives answers from all the other agents and decides from this information whether to commit locally or abort locally.

Distributed protocols are very difficult to analyze with respect to their resiliency to different types of failure, because the decision process is distributed.

We can therefore summarize the above discussion by saying that

1. The above four protocols require a number of messages which depends on the number N of participants.

    a. The centralized and hierarchical protocol require $4N$ messages

    b. The linear protcol requires $2N$ messages

c. The distributed protocol requires $N(N+1)$ messages

Note that the final ACK message is not required by the linear protocol and is meaningless with the distributed protocol.

2. The delay required by the commitment depends on the end-to-end delay T of one transmission.

a. The centralized protocol has a delay $4T$

b. The linear protocol has a delay $2NT$

c. The hierarchical protocol has a delay contained between that of the centralized protocol and that of the linear protocol

d. The distributed protocol has a delay $2T$

It is not necessary that the communication structure for the commit protocol coincide with the communication structure which exists between the transaction's agents. For example, it is possible to have a hierarchical communication and computation structure for the transaction and use a centralized or a distributed commit protocol. This fact can be easily modeled in our reference model, because we have separated the agents of a transaction from the DTM-agents. However, in a real system where this separation is not clear, it can be difficult to have different communication structures coexisting.

CONCLUSIONS

Distributed transaction managers must ensure that all transactions have the atomicity, durability, seriability, and isolation properties. In most systems this is obtained by implementing on top of existing local transaction managers the 2-phase-commitment protocol for reliability, 2-phase-locking for concurrency control, and timeouts for deadlock detection.

The 2-phase-commitment protocol ensures that the subtransactions of the same transaction will either all commit or all abort, in spite of the possible failures; 2-phase-commitment is resilient to any failure in which no log information is lost. The 2-phase-locking mechanism requires that all subtransactions acquire locks in the growing phase and release locks in the shrinking phase. Timeout mechanisms for deadlock detection simply abort those transactions which are in wait, possibly for a deadlock.

Several computation and communication structures are possible for distributed transaction managers. The computation can use processes permanently assigned to transactions, or servers dynamically bound to them; processes can have a centralized structure, in which one agent activates all other agents, or a hierarchical structure, in which each agent can in turn activate other agents. The communication can use sessions or datagrams; the communication structure of the commitment protocol can be centralized, hierarchical, linear, or distributed.

EXERCISES

7.1 Define the strucure of a log record as a variant record in Pascal. Use the type of log record (begin_transaction, undo_redo, commit, abort, global_commit, global_abort, prepare, ready, complete, and checkpoint) as the tag field of the Pascal record. For the definition of the undo_redo log record, assume that all database tuples have the same length and that they have an unique identifier of the type integer.

7.2 Rewrite the FUND_TRANSFER application of Example 7.2, represented in Figure 7.2b, using low-level instructions. The transaction must use 2-phase-commitment for reliability, the write-ahead protocol for writing into the local logs, 2-phase-locking for concurrency control, and deadlock detection based on timeouts. Assume that each log record has the structure defined in Exercise 7.1. Use the following additional primitives for locking and for sending and receiving messages:

> **Lock** (trans_id, tuple_id, mode, timeout, ok)
> **Unlock** (trans_id, tuple_id)
> **Send** (trans_id, site, message)
> **Receive** (trans_id, site, message, timeout, ok)

Assign an arbitrary transaction identifier to the transaction and identify agents of transactions with the pair ⟨trans_id,site⟩. Use $FROM_ACC and $TO_ACC as tuple identifiers. In the Lock primitive, mode can be shared or exclusive, and ok indicates the success or failure of the primitive. If the timeout expires and the lock cannot be granted, ok is returned false; otherwise, ok is returned true. The Send primitive is used for sending messages and continuing the computation. The Receive primitive is used for receiving a message from a given transaction agent within a given time interval. If the timeout expires, then ok is returned false.

7.3 Write a restart procedure for transactions which follow the basic 2-phase-commitment protocol. Assume that the log file has been produced by the algorithm of Exercise 7.2 and that each log record has the structure defined in Exercise 7.1. Assume also that, at the beginning of the restart procedure, the file is positioned on the last checkpoint record. Use the primitive

> **Write** (tuple_id, tuple_value)

for performing the undo and redo operations. This primitive simply writes the provided tuple_value in the database tuple identified by tuple_id.

Annotated Bibliography

The papers which are referenced here contain an introduction to the basic aspects which have been considered in this chapter. Specific papers on distributed transaction recovery and concurrency control are found in the annotated bibliography of Chapters 8 and 9. The architectural aspects of existing systems are referred to in Part II. Introductory books on transaction management in a centralized database system have already been referenced in Chapter 2.

[7.1]   J. N. Gray, "Notes on Database Operating Systems," *Operating Systems: An Advanced Course*, Springer-Verlag, 1979.

This paper contains an introduction to most of the problems of transaction management in a centralized database, with particular emphasis on the aspects which relate to the operating system. Also some aspects of distributed transactions are marginally considered.

[7.2]   M. Stonebraker, "Operating System Support for Database Management," *Communications of the ACM*, **24**:7, 1981.

This paper contains an evaluation of the features which are provided by a typical operating system to the designer of a database management system. It deals only with centralized systems and databases.

[7.3]   K. Eswaran et al., "On the Notions of Consistency and Predicate Locks in a Relational Database System," *Communications of the ACM*, **19**:11, 1976.

This paper contains the definition of the 2-phase-locking mechanism and its proof of correctness, and a set of other aspects of consistency in centralized databases which have not been considered in this chapter.

[7.4]   J. N. Gray, "The Transaction Concept: Virtues and Limitations," *Seventh VLDB*, Cannes, 1981.

[7.5]   I. L. Traiger et al., "Transactions and Consistency in Distributed Database Management Systems," *ACM-TODS*, **7**:3, 1982.

[7.6]   A. Z. Spector and P. M. Schwarz, "Transactions: A Construct for Reliable Distributed Computing," *ACM Operating System Review*, **17**:2, 1983.

The above three papers contain an introduction to the problems of implementing the transaction concept in a distributed database and an evaluation of this concept.

[7.7]   P. A. Bernstein and N. Goodman, "Concurrency Control in Distributed Database Systems," *ACM Computing Surveys*, **13**:2, 1981.

[7.8]   P. A. Bernstein and N. Goodman, "A Sophisticate's Introduction to Distributed Database Concurrency Control," *Eighth VLDB*, Mexico City, 1982.

[7.9]   W. H. Kohler, "A Survey of Techniques for Synchronization and Recovery in Decentralized Computer Systems," *ACM Computing Surveys*, **13**:2, 1981.

The above three papers are tutorials and surveys on the problems of concurrency control and recovery for distributed transactions.

[7.10] B. G. Lindsay et al., "Computation and Communication in R*: A Distributed Database Manager," *Proc. 9th ACM Symp. on Operating Systems Principles*, 1983, to appear also in *ACM Transactions on Computer Systems*.

[7.11] J. B. Rothnie et al., "Introduction to a System for Distributed Databases (SDD-1)," *ACM-TODS*, **5**:1, 1980.

The computational structure of distributed transactions in the systems R* and SDD-1 are described in the above two papers; additional papers on the same and other systems are referenced in Part II.

[7.12] P. M. Merlin, "A Methodology for the Design and Implementation of Communication Protocols," *IEEE-Transactions on Communications*, COM-24, 1976.

[7.13] P. M. Merlin, "Specification and Validation of Protocols," *IEEE-Transactions on Communications*, COM-27, 1979.

An introduction to the general problem of describing and analyzing a communication protocol can be found in the above two papers.

[7.14]   Arvind and K. P. Gostelow, "A Computer Capable of Exchanging Processing Elements for Time," *Proc. IFIP Congress*, 1977.

[7.15]   P. C. Treleaven, D. R. Brownbridge, and R. P. Hopkins, "Data-Driven and Demand-Driven Computer Architecture," *ACM Computer Surveys*, **14**:1, 1982.

[7.16]   J. B. Dennis, "The Varieties of Data Flow Computers," *First Int. Conf. on Data Flow Computers*, IEEE, 1979.

The above three papers are an introduction and a survey of the **data flow model**. The basic idea of the data flow model of computation is that the computational structure is determined by the flow of data from one processing element to another. Each processing element performs its function as soon as its required data inputs are available and sends its results to the processing elements which need them. In this way no explicit control structure is needed; the control structure is implicitly represented by the producer-consumer relationship which exists between processing elements.

In a distributed transaction environment, the basic processing element can be considered to be a server at a site. Each server is permanently active and waits for operands to be processed. The system passes these operands between servers at the same or at different sites. The notion of a transaction's state is lost in this model. It seems that implementing reliable transactions would be difficult using this approach; however, for applications which are read-only and do not require possessing the transaction properties, this model could allow a very simple and efficient implementation.

Further research is required in order to exploit the application of the data flow idea to the processing of distributed transactions.

[7.17]   Report on the Workshop on Fundamental Issues in Distributed Computing, Fallbrook, CA, 1980.

[7.18]   B. Liskov and R. Scheifler, "Guardians and Actions: Linguistic Support for Robust, Distributed Programs," *Proc. Ninth ACM SIGACT-SIGPLAN Symp. on the Principles of Programming Languages*, 1982.

The above two papers deal with the problems of implementing distibuted systems in general; operating systems and linguistic issues are discussed together with reliability and concurrency issues.

Report [7.17] is a summary of the discussions which took place at a meeting on the most relevant aspects of distributed computing. Topics discussed included: real systems, atomicity, protection, applications, naming, communications, what is needed from theory, and what are important practical problems. Unfortunately the report is not very well edited, because it is not based on prewritten papers. However, it is of great interest because researchers in different areas relating to the general problem of distributed systems have spoken freely, and very different viewpoints have emerged.

Reference [7.18] describes an integrated system and programming language which supports the creation of distributed programs; the language is intended especially to support applications which use distributed data and have high concurrency and reliability requirements. An interesting aspect of this paper is that it addresses these problems from the viewpoint of the designer of general-purpose programming languages; this approach can be compared with the approaches which are typically proposed by the community of database researchers.

Chapter 8

Concurrency Control

In the previous chapter, we have presented 2-phase-locking as the most widely used technique for concurrency control. In this chapter, we complete the presentation of concurrency control in distributed databases. Section 8.1 presents the theory of serializability and the proof of correctness of 2-phase-locking. This section presents also the notion of time, timestamps, and the ordering of events in a distributed system. Section 8.2 deals with deadlock detection and prevention. In Chapter 7 we have already presented deadlock detection using timeouts; in this section we discuss more complex techniques. Section 8.3 presents timestamp-based concurrency control algorithms. Timestamp-based concurrency control uses unique transaction identifiers for determining the order of execution of transactions. Two algorithms, the basic and the conservative timestamp algorithm, are described. Section 8.4 deals with optimistic methods for concurrency control. Optimistic methods assume that transactions do not interfere most of the time; therefore, transactions are executed freely but their correctness is verified at the end, before making their effect visible to other transactions. Timestamp-based and optimistic concurrency control are seldom used in building systems but are of theoretical interest.

A classification and comparison of the concurrency control methods presented in this chapter is done in the conclusion. One aspect of concurrency control is not considered in this chapter but is deferred to the next one: the reliability of concurrency control algorithms.

8.1 FOUNDATIONS OF DISTRIBUTED CONCURRENCY CONTROL

In order to analyse the correctness of a distributed concurrency control method we need a formal model. Therefore, this section presents a formal model for analyzing the serializability of transactions which are executed concurrently. This model is applied to the proof of correctness of 2-phase-locking. To complete the theoretical foundations of distributed concurrency control, a model of time in a distributed system is also presented.

8.1.1 Serializability in a Centralized Database

A transaction accesses the database by issuing read and write primitives. Let $R_i(x)$ and $W_i(x)$ denote a read and write operation issued by a transaction T_i for data item x. The granularity of x does not concern us here; x can be a single tuple or a whole fragment. The set of data items read by T_i is called its **read-set** and the set of data items written by T_i is called its **write-set**. The read-set and write-set of a transaction are not disjoint; i.e., a data item can belong to both.

A **schedule** (also called a history or log) is a sequence of operations performed by transactions. For example, the following is a schedule:

$$S1 : R_i(x)\, R_j(x)\, W_i(y)\, R_k(y)\, W_j(x)$$

Two transactions T_i and T_j execute **serially** in a schedule S if the last operation of T_i precedes the first operation of T_j in S (or vice versa); otherwise they execute **concurrently**.

A schedule is **serial** if no transactions execute concurrently in it. For example, the following schedule S2 is serial:

$$S2 : R_i(x)\, W_i(x)\, R_i(y)\, R_j(x)\, W_j(y)\, R_k(y)\, W_k(x)$$

In a serial schedule the sequence of operations defines also a sequence of transactions, and we are sometimes interested only in the latter sequence. The notation Serial(S) is used for representing the sequence of transactions of a serial schedule S. For example, for the above schedule S2:

$$\text{Serial(S2)} : T_i\, T_j\, T_k$$

Given a schedule S, operation O_i *precedes* operation O_j, indicated by $O_i < O_j$, if O_i appears to the left of O_j in S. For instance, in schedule S1, $R_i(x)$ precedes $R_k(y)$. If a schedule S is serial, transaction T_i precedes transaction T_j in S, indicated by $T_i < T_j$, if T_i appears to the left of T_j in Serial(S). For example, in S2, $T_i < T_k$.

If a schedule S is not serial, Serial(S) is not defined, and therefore the precedence relationship between transactions is also not defined.

The serial execution of transactions which is described by a serial schedule is by definition correct. However, we do not want to force transactions to execute serially; we do want transactions to execute as concurrently as possible, provided that their execution is correct. We need therefore a definition of correctness which can be applied to a nonserial schedule in order to determine whether it is correct or not. The most widely accepted definition of correctness of a schedule is based on serializability:

> A schedule is correct if it is **serializable**; i.e., it is computationally equivalent to a serial schedule.

Having introduced serializability, we can further say that a concurrency control mechanism is correct if it allows transactions to execute operations in such a sequence that only serializable schedules are produced. A concurrency control mechanism restricts the possible sequences of operations performed by transactions by forcing some transactions to wait before they can perform some operations or by aborting and restarting transactions. For example, the locking mechanism forces a transaction to wait when it wants to operate on a data item which is already locked by another transaction.

In order to analyze the serializability of a schedule and the correctness of a concurrency control mechanism, we need conditions which can be checked for determining whether two schedules are equivalent. The following two conditions are *sufficient* to ensure that two schedules are equivalent:

Condition 1. Each read operation reads data item values which are produced by the same write operations in both schedules.

Condition 2. The final write operation on each data item is the same in both schedules.

These two conditions are sufficient, because each transaction reads the same values in both schedules and therefore performs the same computations; moreover, the final write operation on each data item is performed by the same transaction in both schedules; therefore, all data items have the same values after both executions.

In order to apply these two conditions in the analysis of concurrency control mechanisms, it is useful to introduce the notion of conflict between operations:

> Two operations are in **conflict** if they operate on the same data item, one of them is a write operation, and they are issued by different transactions.

For example $\langle R_i(x), W_j(x) \rangle$ and $\langle W_i(x), W_j(x) \rangle$ are pairs of conflicting operations, while $\langle R_i(x), R_j(x) \rangle$, $\langle W_i(x), W_j(y) \rangle$, and $\langle W_i(x), R_j(y) \rangle$ are pairs of nonconflicting operations.

By using the notion of conflict it is possible to state the sufficient condition for the equivalence of schedules in a different way:

> Two schedules S1 and S2 are equivalent if for each pair of conflicting operations O_i and O_j such that O_i precedes O_j in S1, then also O_i precedes O_j in S2.

This condition is the most convenient for checking whether a schedule is serializable. For example, consider the schedule

$$S3 : R_i(x) R_j(x) W_j(y) W_i(x)$$

This schedule is equivalent to the serial schedule

$$S4 : R_j(x) W_j(y) R_i(x) W_i(x)$$

because the unique pair of conflicting operations $\langle R_j(x), W_i(x) \rangle$ appears in the same order in both schedules. Note that T_j precedes T_i in Serial(S4); this ordering of transactions is forced by the pair of conflicting operations. The example shows that precedence of transactions in the serialization order does not depend on the order of execution of the first operation of the transactions, but on the order of conflicting operations only.

Notice that a serializable schedule could be equivalent to several serial schedules; for instance, the serial schedules

$$S5 : R_i(x) W_i(y) R_j(x) W_j(x) R_k(y)$$
$$S6 : R_i(x) W_i(y) R_k(y) R_j(x) W_j(x)$$

are both equivalent to schedule S1.

8.1.2 Serializability in a Distributed Database

In a distributed database, each transaction performs operations at several sites. The sequence of operations performed by transactions at a site is a *local schedule*. An **execution** of n distributed transactions $T_1, T_2, \ldots, T_n$ at m sites is modeled by a set of local schedules S1, S2, ..., Sm.

If we apply at each node a local concurrency control mechanism, we can ensure that all local schedules are serializable. However, the serializability of local schedules is not sufficient to ensure the correctness of the execution of a set of distributed transactions. Consider, for example, the following two schedules

$$S1(\text{site } 1) : R_i(x) W_i(x) R_j(x) W_j(x)$$
$$S2(\text{site } 2) : R_j(y) W_j(y) R_i(y) W_i(y)$$

Both local schedules are serial; however, there is no global serial sequence of execution of both transactions because $T_i < T_j$ in Serial(S1) and $T_j < T_i$ in Serial(S2). In order to guarantee the serializability of distributed transactions, a stronger condition than the serializability of local schedules is required

The execution of transactions $T_1, \ldots, T_n$ is correct if:

1. Each local schedule Sk is serializable
2. There exists a **total ordering** of $T_1, \ldots, T_n$ such that, if $T_i < T_j$ in the total ordering, then there is a serial schedule Sk' such that Sk is equivalent to Sk' and $T_i < T_j$ in Serial(Sk'), for each site k where both transactions have executed some action

The above condition can be expressed using the notion of conflicts (see references [8.1] and [8.2]):

Proposition 8.1
Let $T_1, \ldots, T_n$ be a set of transactions, and let E be an execution of these transactions modeled by schedules $S1, \ldots, Sm$. E is correct (serializable) if there exists a total ordering of the transactions such that for each pair of conflicting operations O_i and O_j from transactions T_i and T_j, respectively, O_i precedes O_j in any schedule $S1, \ldots, Sm$ if and only if T_i precedes T_j in the total ordering.

We will use proposition 8.1 in order to determine whether an execution of distributed transactions is correct. A distributed concurrency control mechanism is correct if it allows only correct executions of distributed transactions.

8.1.3 2-Phase-Locking as a Distributed Concurrency Control Method

First, let us show that if all distributed transactions are 2-phase-locked, then all local schedules are serializable. Consider a site where a distributed transaction executes some operations; clearly these operations, which are only a part of the whole set of operations performed by the distributed transaction, observe the rules of 2-phase-locking. In other words, if a distributed transaction is 2-phase-locked, then all its subtransactions at different sites, taken separately, are 2-phase-locked. Since 2-phase-locking is a correct concurrency control method for a centralized database, at each site the execution of subtransactions is serializable.

We prove now that 2-phase-locking is a correct distributed concurrency control method. Assume that for a given execution E the total ordering required by proposition 8.1 does not exist. In this case there must exist n pairs of conflicting operations such that

$$O_1(x) < O_2(x)$$
$$O_2(y) < O_3(y)$$
$$\ldots$$
$$O_{n-1}(v) < O_n(v)$$
$$O_n(z) < O_1(z)$$

in some schedules of E, otherwise it would be possible to determine a total ordering of transactions which satisfies proposition 8.1.

We now show that, if the transactions $T_1, T_2, \ldots, T_n$ are 2-phase-locked, this situation cannot occur. Consider the intermediate stage at which T_1 has locked x, T_2 has locked $y, \ldots, T_{n-1}$ has locked v, and T_n has locked z. Each one of these transactions is now required to lock a data item which is already locked by another transaction; therefore, each one of them will wait until that other transaction releases the lock. However, since the transactions are all 2-phase-locked, none of them releases any locks before having obtained all its locks, therefore the n transactions have reached a deadlock situation and will wait forever. Hopefully, one of the transactions will be aborted by a deadlock resolution algorithm. In any case, execution E cannot occur.

Let us finally observe that the above reasoning is independent of the number of transactions, n, and of the sequence of their activation, but depends only on the ordering of the pairs of conflicting operations. Note that deadlock detection and resolution are necessary with a 2-phase-locking mechanism.

Two-phase-locking ensures that all executions of transactions are serializable, but it does not allow all serializable executions to be produced. In other words, the 2-phase-locking mechanism is more restrictive than would be required by the serializability condition, and some transaction is forced to wait unnecessarily. This fact is shown by the following example.

Example 8.1
Consider two transactions T_i and T_j which both transfer funds from an account x located at site 1 to an account y located at site 2. As we are interested only in the read and write operations, the two transactions can be described by the following sequence of operations:

$$T_i : R_i(x) \, W_i(x) \, R_i(y) \, W_i(y)$$
$$T_j : R_j(x) \, W_j(x) \, R_j(y) \, W_j(y)$$

assuming that each transaction reads x, decrements its value, writes the new value, reads y, increments its value, and writes the new value.

Suppose that both transactions are activated almost simultaneously. As 2-phase-locking ensures serializability of their execution, there is a total ordering such that either $T_i < T_j$ or $T_j < T_i$; this means either that $W_i(x) < R_j(x)$ and $W_i(y) < R_j(y)$ or that $W_j(x) < R_i(x)$ and $W_j(y) < R_i(y)$. Because of the symmetry of the two cases, let us consider only the first one ($T_i < T_j$).

In order to analyze the degree of concurrency which is allowed by a concurrency control algorithm, we must also include in the model of an execution the notion of "concurrent operations" at different sites. Let us represent concurrency by assuming that two operations which appear one over the other in the execution are concurrent. Consider, for example, the following execution E:

$$
\begin{aligned}
S1 : \quad & R_i(x) \, W_i(x) \, R_j(x) \, W_j(x) \\
S2 : \quad & R_i(y) \, W_i(y) \, R_j(y) \, W_j(y)
\end{aligned}
$$

In this representation of the execution, the fact that operation $R_i(y)$ appears below $R_j(x)$ means that these two operations start at the same time. Therefore, T_j begins reading x immediately after T_i has written x, although T_i is not yet terminated. Execution E is serializable and allows the maximum degree of concurrency.

Execution E of Example 8.1 is not allowed by the 2-phase-locking mechanism, because T_i does not release the lock on x until it has obtained the lock also on y. Moreover, if we also take care of 2-phase-commitment, both write locks on x and y will be maintained until the end of the transaction, and released only at that time. T_j is forced to wait more than it would be required by the pure serializability condition. In practice, with 2-phase-locking, T_i and T_j are forced to execute in a strictly serial order, and no concurrency is allowed between them.

The reason why the 2-phase-locking mechanism must force transaction T_j to wait unnecessarily is that it resolves each conflict by itself and does not have a "complete view" of T_i's and T_j's execution. We are able to say that execution E is serializable because we consider the execution as a whole. Instead, when the 2-phase-locking mechanism resolves a conflict, it does not know which conflicts will arise in future.

Note that 2-phasedness is the condition which makes execution E impossible and that this condition cannot be simply eliminated from the concurrency control mechanism in order to obtain a higher degree of concurrency, because by eliminating it the mechanism would accept not only execution E but also nonserializable executions. For example, suppose that we eliminate the 2-phasedness condition, and a third transaction T_k is run which performs the opposite operation from T_i; i.e., it transfers funds from y to x operating as follows:

$$T_k : R_k(y)\,W_k(y)\,R_k(x)\,W_k(x)$$

The following *nonserializable* execution *NE* would be possible:

$$S1 : R_i(x)\,W_i(x)\,R_k(x)\,W_k(x)$$
$$S2 : R_k(y)\,W_k(y)\,R_i(y)\,W_i(y)$$

8.1.4 A Comment on Serializability

The last nonserializable execution *NE* allows us to exemplify a general aspect of correctness of concurrency control mechanisms.

Example 8.2
Assume that T_i transfers \$10 from x to y and T_k transfers \$20 from y to x; assume further that x and y are both initially at \$100. After the execution of both transactions we want x and y to have the following values: $x = \$110$ and $y = \$90$.
Consider the above nonserializable execution *NE*:
At site 1 T_i reads $x = 100$, decrements it by 10, and writes $x = 90$; then T_k reads $x = 90$, increments it by 20, and writes $x = 110$.
At site 2 T_k reads $y = 100$, decrements it by 20, and writes $y = 80$; then T_i reads $y = 80$, increments it by 10, and writes $y = 90$.

The result of the nonserializable execution of Example 8.2 is surprisingly correct. The reason of this fact is that both transactions do not transfer information from x to y or vice versa; the operations which are performed by each transaction on x are independent of the value of y, and vice versa. This fact depends on the **semantics** of the transactions, and cannot be derived from their form (i.e., the sequence of read and write operations). For example, this fact would not hold for a transaction which copies the value of x into y, although the form of the transaction could be the same as the form of T_i.

We can now state a general proposition on the validity of serializability as a correctness criterion [8.4]: Serializability is the weakest (i.e., the least restrictive) criterion for preserving consistency of concurrent transactions if no semantic knowledge about them is available; however, if semantic knowledge is available, then other approaches may be more attractive.

It is not easy to design a concurrency control mechanism which takes advantage of semantic knowledge, because the semantics of transactions is embedded in the application programs. However, an approach which can be useful is to define high-level operations which have different synchronization properties than simple read and write operations have. In a distributed database this approach can have the additional advantage that these high-level operations can be the same operations which are shipped to remote sites for performing remote database access. For example, consider the two following operations, where x is a data item of the database and w is a parameter:

$$\text{Increment} \quad I(x,w) : x + w \to x$$
$$\text{Decrement} \quad D(x,w) : x - w \to x$$

These operations are implemented, of course, by reading x, incrementing (or decrementing) its value, and writing the new value. By using these operations, the two funds transfer transactions T_i and T_k of Example 8.2 are modeled as follows, with $w = 10$ and $u = 20$:

$$T_i : D_i(x,w)\, I_i(x,w)$$
$$T_k : D_k(y,u)\, I_k(y,u)$$

The basic advantage of these two operations is that they commute; i.e., the two sequences $D(x,w)\, I(x,u)$ and $I(x,u)\, D(x,w)$ give the same result (namely, $x - w + u$). Therefore, D and I can be considered as nonconflicting operations, and their order is not relevant for determining a serialization order. If a concurrency control mechanism incorporates this knowledge about the I and D operations, it accepts the following concurrent execution of T_i and T_k:

$$\text{S1: } D_i(x,w)\, I_k(x,u)$$
$$\text{S2: } D_k(y,u)\, I_i(y,w)$$

Note that by substituting the read and write operations which implement D and I, we obtain exactly the nonserializable execution NE.

8.1.5 Time and Timestamps in a Distributed Database

In a distributed system, it is sometimes necessary to know if an event A at some site happened before or after an event B at a different site. Determining the order of events is simple in a centralized system, since it is possible to use the same clock to determine the time at which each event occurs. In a distributed system, instead, it is not realistic to assume that perfectly synchronized clocks are available at all sites.

Several distributed concurrency control and deadlock prevention algorithms need the determination of an ordering of events. The determination of an ordering of events consists in assigning to each event A which occurs in the distributed system a **timestamp** $TS(A)$ having the following properties:

1. $TS(A)$ uniquely identifies A (i.e., different events have different timestamps)
2. For any two events A and B, if A occurred before B, then $TS(A) < TS(B)$

The main inconvenience of the above definition is that the meaning of the relationship "occurred before" is not precisely defined if the two events A and B occurred at two different sites, since we do not possess a "global clock" for measuring the exact time of occurrence of all events in the distributed system. Therefore, in this section we first define precisely the meaning of the occur before relationship in a distributed system, and then present an algorithm which produces timestamps having the above two properties.

A precise definition of the **occur before** relationship in a distributed system is the following. Assume that we know the meaning of the statement "Event A occurred before event B at site i," i.e., that we know the meaning of time ordering at a single site. The relation occurred before, denoted $\rightarrow$, can be generalized to a distributed environment by the following rules:

1. If A and B are two events at the same site and A occurred before B, then $A \rightarrow B$.
2. If the event A consists in sending a message and event B consists in receiving the same message, then $A \rightarrow B$.
3. If $A \rightarrow B$ and $B \rightarrow C$, then $A \rightarrow C$.

The relation $\rightarrow$ is a partial ordering. We call two events A and B **pseudo-simultaneous** if neither $A \rightarrow B$ nor $B \rightarrow A$ (sometimes the word "concurrent" is used for A and B, but we avoid the use of this term because it could be misleading). Consider, for example, Figure 8.1. Events A and D, B and E, B and F, C and E, and C and F are pseudosimultaneous. The exact temporal relationship of two pseudosimultaneous events cannot be determined and is not relevant.

The second property of the definition of timestamps can therefore be restated more precisely as follows:

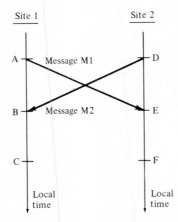

Figure 8.1 The "occurred before" relationship in a two-site system.

2. For any two events A and B, if $A \to B$, then $TS(A) < TS(B)$

Notice that, if A and B are pseudosimultaneous, it is possible that $TS(A) < TS(B)$ or that $TS(B) < TS(A)$. However, after we have assigned timestamps to events, a total ordering is defined between them, even if some are pseudosimultaneous. Therefore, the assignment of timestamps consists of the determination of a total order which is consistent with the partial order defined by the $\to$ relation. We say that an event A is younger (older) of an event B if $TS(A) > TS(B)$ ($TS(A) < TS(B)$).

We consider now the generation of timestamps. The first requirement of timestamps, uniqueness, can be easily satisfied in a distributed system. It is sufficient that each site add to a locally unique timestamp its site identifier in the *least* significant position. Clearly, using the least significant position instead of the most significant one avoids the possibility that all timestamps which are generated by one site are greater than all timestamps which are generated by another site, thus making any attempt to reflect the time ordering in the timestamp ordering impossible.

The second requirement is more complex to satisfy. First, we will use at each site a counter which is steadily incremented, so that the transactions which receive the timestamp at the same site are correctly ordered between themselves. The counter might be simply incremented each time that a new timestamp is generated; however, the synchronization between counters at different sites would be difficult with this approach. It is possible that the counter at a site, say site 1, is used to generate more timestamps than the counter at a different site, say site 2, and hence advances faster.

Fortunately, the counters of the two sites can be kept approximately aligned by simply including in each message the value of the counter of the sending site. If a site receives a message with a timestamp value TS which is greater than its current counter, it increments its counter to be $TS + 1$. In this way, the counters of cooperating sites are kept approximately synchronized; if two sites are not cooperating, it is not very important if their counters drift away.

Consider the example of Figure 8.1 and assume that the counter at site 1 is initially 0 while the local counter at site 2 is initially 10. Let $\langle x, y \rangle$ represent the timestamp generated at site y when the local counter has value x. Therefore, initially $TS(A) = \langle 0, 1 \rangle$ and $TS(D) = \langle 10, 2 \rangle$. A and D are pseudosimultaneous; hence their ordering is arbitrary. When message M2 arrives at site 1, it bears the timestamp of D; hence the local counter at site 1 is bumped and $TS(B) = \langle 11, 1 \rangle$. When message M1 arrives at site 2, since it bears a smaller timestamp than the current counter of site 2, the counter is simply incremented and $TS(E) = \langle 11, 2 \rangle$. Note that $TS(E)$ differs from $TS(B)$ only in the site identifier. The two pseudosimultaneous events have obtained "close" timestamps.

Finally, note that we have always used counters, not clocks, in the implementation of timestamps. However, in some applications it may be convenient to use clocks instead of counters. In this way timestamps reflect more closely the real time at which events occur. This is done, for instance, in the SDD-1 system (see Chapter 12).

8.2 DISTRIBUTED DEADLOCKS

The detection and resolution of deadlocks constitute important activities of a database management system. We recall from Section 7.3 that the detection of a deadlock corresponds to the determination of a cycle in a wait-for graph. The problem of deadlock detection is more difficult in a distributed database than in a centralized one, because the circular waiting situation which determines a deadlock can involve several sites and not just one.

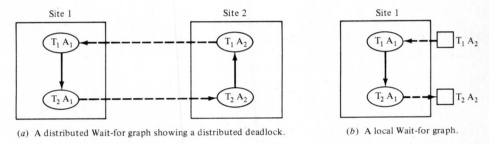

(*a*) A distributed Wait-for graph showing a distributed deadlock.   (*b*) A local Wait-for graph.

Figure 8.2   Distributed and local wait-for graphs.

Figure 8.2a shows a **distributed wait-for graph (DWFG)** which contains a cycle and thus corresponds to a deadlock situation. The notation T_iA_j refers to agent A_j of transaction T_i. In Figure 8.2a there are two sites and two transactions T_1 and T_2, each one consisting of two agents. For simplicity, we assume that each transaction has only one agent at each site where it is executed. A directed edge from an agent T_iA_j to an agent T_rA_s means that T_iA_j is blocked and waiting for T_rA_s. There are two reasons why an agent can be waiting for another one:

1.   Agent T_iA_j waits for agent T_rA_j to release a resource which it needs; in this case, T_i is a different transaction from T_r, and the two agents are at the same site, because agents request only local resources (recall that agents represent transactions at each site). This type of wait is represented by continuous edges in Figure 8.2a; for instance T_1A_1 is waiting for T_2A_1 to release a resource at site 1.

2.   Agent T_iA_j waits for agent T_iA_s to perform some required function; in this case, the two agents belong to the same transaction, and agent T_iA_j has requested that agent T_iA_s perform some function at a different site. This type of waiting is represented by the dashed edges in Figure 8.2a.

We call the **local wait-for graph (LWFG)** the portion of the DWFG consisting only of nodes and edges which are completely contained at a single site, extended with an indication of the nodes which represent remote agents having an edge connecting them to nodes of the local graph. An example of an LWFG is shown in Figure 8.2b and refers to site 1 of Figure 8.2a. The square nodes are called **input ports** if they have an edge entering the LWFG and **output ports** if they receive an edge exiting the LWFG.

A deadlock is local if it is caused by a cycle in an LWFG. The determination of local deadlocks is a local task which is not considered here. A deadlock is distributed if it is caused by a cycle in the DWFG which is not contained in any LWFG. The detection of a distributed deadlock is a distributed task, which obviously requires the exchange of information between different sites. In the rest of this section we will consider the detection and resolution only of global deadlocks.

Deadlock resolution involves the selection of one or more transactions to be aborted and restarted. When a transaction is aborted, it releases its resources, so that other transactions can proceed. The criteria which are used for the selection of the transaction to be aborted should try to minimize the cost of this operation. Possible criteria are the following: abort the youngest transaction; abort the transaction which owns less resources; abort the transaction with the smallest abort cost (recall that the abort of a transaction requires that all its previous operations be undone); abort the transaction with the longest expected time to complete.

The redundancy which is often present in a distributed database increases the probability of deadlocks. Consider for example two transactions T_1 and T_2, both of which must lock exclusively the same data item x and nothing else. If x is not replicated, then one transaction will obtain the lock and execute and the other one will wait. No deadlock can arise in this situation. However, if x is replicated, for instance two copies $x1$ and $x2$ of x exist at sites 1 and 2 and both transactions use the write-locks-all strategy defined in Chapter 7, then the following sequence of events at sites 1 and 2 determines a deadlock:

$$\text{At site 1: } T_1 \text{ locks } x1; T_2 \text{ waits}$$
$$\text{At site 2: } T_2 \text{ locks } x2; T_1 \text{ waits}$$

At this point the DWFG contains a cycle as in Figure 8.2a.

In the previous chapter we have seen the timeout method for deadlock detection; in the following we will consider several other methods for dealing with deadlocks in a distributed system:

1. Deadlock detection using centralized or hierarchical control
2. Distributed deadlock detection
3. Deadlock prevention

Methods 1 and 2 are based on the idea of transmitting the information of the DWFG between sites to detect deadlocks; method 3 consists in avoiding the occurrence of deadlocks by discovering "dangerous" situations a priori.

8.2.1 Deadlock Detection Using Centralized or Hierarchical Controllers

With the **centralized controller** method, described in reference [8.7], a selected site is chosen at which a centralized deadlock detector is run. The centralized deadlock detector has the responsibility of building the DWFG and of discovering cycles in it. Of course, in order to perform this task, the deadlock detector receives information from all other sites.

At each site there is a local deadlock detector. The responsibility of each local deadlock detector is to determine all **potential** global deadlocks at its site (and to discover also local deadlocks, of course). The idea of a potential global deadlock cycle can be understood by considering again the example of Figure 8.2. Consider the deadlock detector at site 1. The LWFG of site 1 (Figure 8.2b) contains the local edges and edges to remote sites. Since the local deadlock detector cannot know whether at a remote site there is a sequence of edges connecting T_2A_2 to T_1A_2, the sequence of connected nodes

$$T_1A_2 \rightarrow T_1A_1 \rightarrow T_2A_1 \rightarrow T_2A_2$$

constitutes a potential deadlock cycle. In this case the potential deadlock cycle coincides with the whole LWFG; however, this does not occur in general.

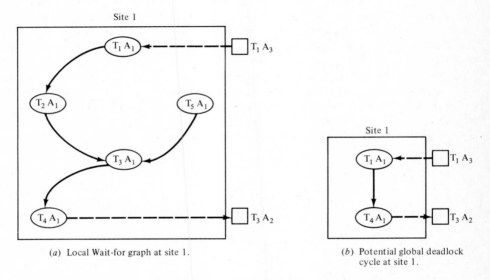

(a) Local Wait-for graph at site 1.   (b) Potential global deadlock cycle at site 1.

Figure 8.3   Derivation of a potential global deadlock cycle from a LWFG.

Consider now the more complex LWFG shown in Figure 8.3a. In order to determine potential deadlock cycles, the local deadlock detector starts from an input port and searches backward along the local graph until it reaches an output port. This part of the local graph constitutes a potential deadlock cycle. Only the initial and final agents of each potential cycle must be transmitted as it is shown in Figure 8.3b.

The global deadlock detector collects these messages, connects the partial information to build a simplified DWFG, determines cycles, and selects transactions to be aborted. This operation can be performed either periodically or every time there is a change in the situation of the potential deadlock cycles. The actual choice of a period for global deadlock detection is a trade-off between the cost of the detection process and the cost of determining deadlocks late.

Centralized deadlock detection is simple, but it has two main drawbacks. First, it is vulnerable to failures of the site where the centralized detector runs. Second, it may require large communications costs, because the centralized detector may be located very far from some other site in the network. A deadlock which is not local does not necessarily involve all other sites of the network. It is possible (and in fact very likely in many applications) that a deadlock involves only a few sites which are all close to one another. In this case, they could discover the deadlock without communicating with a distant central site. The **hierarchical controllers** method aims at exploiting this latter opportunity for reducing communication costs.

With the hierarchical controllers method, described in reference [8.8], a whole tree of deadlock detectors is built, instead of having a set of local deadlock detectors and a single centralized global deadlock detector. At the leaves of the tree we still have the local deadlock detectors (LDDs), while at nonleaf levels we have nonlocal deadlock detectors (NLDDs). Figure 8.4 shows an example of a hierarchy of deadlock detectors for a network consisting of five sites. Each local deadlock detector (denoted in the figure as LDD1,..., LDD5) behaves essentially like the local deadlock detectors of the centralized method: it determines local deadlocks and transmits information about potential global cycles to the NLDD at the immediately higher level in the hierarchy. Each nonlocal deadlock detector performs the detection of those deadlocks which involve only the deadlock detectors which are below it in the hierarchy and transmits a reduced potential deadlock graph to higher levels in the hierarchy. For example, referring to Figure 8.4, deadlocks involving LDD3, LDD4, and LDD5 are discovered by NLDD2, while a deadlock involving LDD2 and LDD3 is detected only by NLDD0 (the highest level detector).

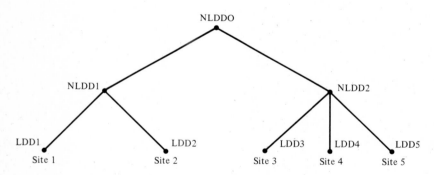

Figure 8.4 A tree of deadlock detectors.

The performance of a hierarchical deadlock detection mechanism depends on the choice of the hierarchy. This choice should reflect the network topology and the pattern of access requests to the different sites of the network. For example, assume that a group of sites is determined such that a high percentage of database access requests is within that group and only few requests are to sites outside the group. Such a group is a good candidate for building a subtree under the control of a common nonlocal detector. This problem is similar to the general problem of maximizing the locality of transactions in distributed database design (Chapter 4), with the additional aspect of considering not only locality at one single site but also "group locality," i.e., locality within a group of sites.

8.2.2 Distributed Deadlock Detection

In a distributed deadlock detection mechanism, there is no distinction between local and nonlocal deadlock detectors. Each site has the same responsibility. Sites exchange information about waiting transactions in order to determine global deadlocks.

Many algorithms have been proposed for distributed deadlock detection in distributed databases (see references [8.10] to [8.13]). We present a simplified version of the algorithm described in reference [8.10].

This algorithm is based on transmitting the information about potential deadlock cycles, like in the centralized algorithm. Potential deadlock cycles are detected by each site on their LWFGs. However, this algorithm uses a slightly different model of an LWFG: all output and input ports are collected into a single node, called external (EX). Moreover, since the indication of agents is irrelevant for the algorithm, only transaction identifiers are used. For example, Figure 8.5a and b represent the same distributed and local wait-for graphs of Figure 8.2a and b. Notice that, with this representation, a potential deadlock cycle is a cycle in the LWFG which contains the node EX.

The main difference between distributed and centralized deadlock detection is that in centralized deadlock detection all potential deadlock cycles are sent to one disignated site, while in distributed deadlock detection there is no such site. Therefore, in distributed deadlock detection, the local deadlock detectors need a rule for determining to which site potential deadlock cycles are transmitted. This rule must assure that global deadlocks are eventually detected and must attempt to minimize the amount of transmitted information.

The rule which is used by this distributed deadlock detection algorithm consists in transmitting the potential deadlock information "along" the deadlock cycle itself. For example, consider site 1 of Figure 8.5b. The local deadlock detector has detected a potential deadlock cycle involving T_1, T_2, and EX. Site 1 can choose to send this potential deadlock cycle to the following sites:

1.   The site where there is an agent of T_1 waiting for T_1 at site 1; this choice corresponds to transmitting potential deadlock information backward along the cycle.
2.   The site where there is an agent of T_2 for which T_2 at site 1 is waiting; this choice corresponds to sending the potential deadlock information forward along the cycle.

Clearly, it is not necessary to transmit in both directions. This algorithm transmits only in the forward direction.

If *all* sites transmit their potential deadlock cycles forward along the cycle, more information is transmitted than necessary. For example, consider the two sites of Figure 8.5b. Since the two situations at sites 1 and 2 are symmetric, both sites would send information about the same global deadlock to each other. This would cause that the same deadlock be discovered twice, which is not necessary. To avoid this unnecessary transmission, the algorithm uses the following rule: the potential deadlock cycle is transmitted only if the transaction identifier of the transaction for which EX waits is greater than the transaction identifier of the transaction waiting for EX. By applying this rule to the situation of Figure 8.5b, we obtain that only site 2 transmits the potential deadlock cycle, because at site 2 EX is waiting for T_2 and T_1 is waiting for EX in the potential cycle. At site 1 we have the opposite situation, therefore site 1 does not transmit the potential deadlock cycle. Figure 8.5b shows also how the potential deadlock cycle is transformed into a message to be transmitted: a string is built containing EX followed by the transaction identifiers of the transactions, in the order in which they appear in the cycle.

This algorithm works by successive iterations. At each iteration each site receives potential deadlock information which was produced by other sites during the previous iteration, then it performs deadlock detection, and finally it sends potential deadlock information to other sites. Therefore, the communication between local deadlock detectors occurs between different iterations of the algorithm.

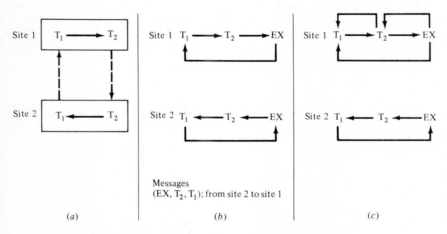

Figure 8.5 Distributed deadlock detection algorithm.

At each iteration, the local deadlock detectors at each site perform the following actions:

1. Build the LWFG using local information. The LWFG includes the node EX.
2. For each message which has been received, perform the following modification of the LWFG:
    a. For each transaction in the message, add it to the LWFG if it does not already exist.
    b. For each transaction in the message, starting with EX, create an edge to the next transaction in the message.

This step has included all potential deadlock information received from other sites into the local LWFG. Note that, by effect of action 2b, the modified LWFG contain edges corresponding to wait conditions at remote sites.

3. Find cycles not involving EX in the LWFG. Each such cycle indicates the existence of a deadlock. Deadlock resolution is invoked to eliminate these deadlocks.

4. Find cycles involving EX. These cycles are potential deadlock cycles. The rule described above is used to determine whether a potential deadlock cycle must be transmitted to a different site. If the transmission is required, the message is prepared and transmitted. The transmission of potential deadlock cycles terminates the current iteration of the deadlock detection process.

Example 8.3
Consider the LWFGs of Figure 8.5b. We have seen already that only site 2 sends a message to site 1. The message is shown in the figure.

Figure 8.5c shows the wait-for graph which is obtained by applying the above rules after the message from site 2 has arrived at site 1. The deadlock detector at site 1 searches for cycles not containing EX. In Figure 8.5c there is such a cycle between T_2 and T_1. A victim is choosen, for example T_1, and an abort message is sent to all sites where the victim was active (site 2 in our example).

8.2.3 False Deadlocks

The delay which is associated with the transmission of messages which transfer information for deadlock detection can cause the detection of "false" deadlocks. Suppose for example that the deadlock detector receives the information that a transaction T_i is waiting for a transaction T_j at a given time. Assume that after some time, T_j releases the resource which was requested by T_i and requests a resource held by T_i. If the deadlock detector receives the information that T_j requests a resource held by T_i before receiving the information that T_i is not blocked by T_j any more, a false cycle of length 2 is detected.

Another case of false deadlock occurs when a transaction T_j, which blocks a transaction T_i, aborts autonomously for some reason which is independent of deadlock detection and at almost the same time T_i requires a resource which was held by T_j. Also in this case it is possible that the message informing the deadlock detector of the latter request arrives earlier than the message informing it of the abort; thus the deadlock detector would determine a false deadlock.

There are two approaches to the problem of false deadlocks: either treating false deadlocks as real ones or validating the detected cycle. The first approach is acceptable if the number of false deadlocks is low. The second approach requires collecting again the information on the presumed cycle: if the deadlock was a real one, it will be still present and therefore detected again, otherwise not.

In general, distributed protocols are more vulnerable to the occurrence of false deadlocks than centralized or hierarchical ones.

8.2.4 Distributed Deadlock Prevention

With a deadlock prevention approach, a transaction is aborted and restarted if there is a risk that deadlock might occur. Since deadlocks can never occur in this way, deadlock prevention eliminates the need for deadlock detection and resolution.

Deadlock prevention is done in the following way: if a transaction T_1 requests a resource which is held by another transaction T_2, then a "prevention test" is applied; if the test indicates that there is a risk of deadlock, then T_1 is not allowed to enter a wait state. Instead, either T_1 is aborted and restarted (nonpreemptive method), or T_2 is aborted and restarted (preemptive method).

The prevention test must ensure that if T_1 is allowed to wait for T_2, then deadlock can never occur. This is typically obtained by ordering transactions, using for instance the lexicographical ordering of their identifiers. T_i is allowed to wait for T_j only if $i < j$. The reason why this method works is that it is impossible to build a closed chain

$$i_1 \to i_2 \to \cdots \to i_n \to i_1$$

such that if $i_j \to i_k$, then $i_j < i_k$ for all j, k.

In order to generate unique identifiers for transactions in a distributed system, it is sufficient that each site generate locally unique identifiers and append the site identifier to them. However, for the performance of the algorithm, it is better that identifiers reflect the "time" of transaction initiation. Therefore, timestamps are used for this purpose (recall the definition of timestamps in Section 8.1.5).

A **nonpreemptive method** for deadlock prevention based on timestamps is the following: If T_i requests a lock on a data item which is already locked by T_j, then T_i is permitted to wait only if T_i is older than T_j. If T_i is younger than T_j, then T_i is aborted and restarted with the same timestamp. The rationale of this method is the following: It is better always to restart the younger transaction. Therefore, in order to obtain a nonpreemptive method we must allow older transactions to wait for younger transactions which already hold a resource, and not allow younger transactions to wait for older ones.

A **preemptive method** works with the opposite rule: if T_i requests a lock on a data item which is already locked by T_j, then T_i is permitted to wait only if it is younger than T_j; otherwise, T_j is aborted and the lock is granted to T_i. The rationale of this method is the following: Since we still want to abort the younger transaction, with a preemptive method we must allow older transactions to preempt younger ones, and therefore only younger transactions wait for older ones.

The preemptive method can cause the following problem: suppose that T_j needs to be preempted while it is in the second phase of 2-phase-commitment; in this case, T_j cannot be aborted. There is, however, a simple solution to this problem, which consists of not preempting T_j. A deadlock situation cannot arise anyway, because a transaction which is in its second commit phase cannot be waiting for resources.

Both the above methods are correct in the sense that deadlock cannot arise and both methods restart the younger transaction. However, there are several differences between these methods; these differences, which also determine the tradeoffs in the selection of one of the two methods, are the following:

1. In the nonpreemptive method a transaction can only be restarted when it requests access to a new data item for the first time. Thus, a transaction which has accessed all the required data items will not be aborted by the concurrency control for any reason. This can be a very important characteristic for transactions which have to perform some nonreversible actions in the external world, like dispensing cash or controlling a process. With the preemptive method it is instead possible that a transaction which holds a lock on a data item is aborted because another, older transaction requests the same data item.

    In order to avoid this possibility, the preemptive method can be modified as follows. Let T_j be the transaction which holds the resource and must be aborted. T_j is immediately aborted only if it is already waiting for some other resource. Moreover, T_j must not wait anymore; therefore, either T_j commits without having to wait for any other resource, or it is aborted as soon as it tries to enter a wait state. By using this more complex mechanism, it ensures that transactions which obtain all the data items required for terminating will never be preempted.

2. In the nonpreemptive method, older transactions wait for younger ones, so that in some sense transactions lose priority by getting older; in the preemptive method, transactions increase their priority by getting older.

3. In the nonpreemptive method, let a transaction T_i be younger than a transaction T_j which has already locked a resource. When T_i attempts to lock that resource, T_i is aborted and restarted. Presumably, T_i will attempt to lock the same resource again; if T_j holds the resource for a long time, then T_i will be restarted several times. In the preemptive method, instead, if T_i holds a resource and is restarted because an older transaction T_j requires the same resource, then the new instance of T_i will have to wait until T_j has finished. Hence only one restart is required in this case.

In this subsection we have seen how deadlock prevention can be added to a 2-phase-locking scheme; in the next sections we will discuss several concurrency control algorithms which are not based on locking and are **deadlock-free**. Deadlock freedom of a concurrency control mechanism is based essentially on the same ordering concept which we have presented in this section for deadlock prevention.

8.3 CONCURRENCY CONTROL BASED ON TIMESTAMPS

With this method, a unique timestamp is assigned to each transaction; transactions are processed so that their execution is *equivalent* to a serial execution in timestamp order. Recalling proposition 8.1 of Section 8.1, this means that conflicting operations are processed in timestamp order.

This concurrency control mechanism allows a transaction to read or write a data item x only if x had been last written by an older transaction; otherwise it rejects the operation and restarts the transaction.

If the timestamps do not reflect with enough accuracy the younger-older relationship of transactions, then the following might happen. Suppose that a transaction T_i obtains a timestamp which is smaller than the timestamp of another, already completed, transaction T_j, which has written data items that are needed by T_i. T_i is aborted and restarted with a new timestamp until it obtains a timestamp which is greater than the timestamp of T_j. Note that even in this case the concurrency control mechanism produces correct executions, at the expense of needlessly restarting the same transaction several times.

8.3.1 The Basic Timestamp Mechanism

The basic timestamp mechanism applies the following rules:

1. Each transaction receives a timestamp when it is initiated at its site of origin.
2. Each read or write operation which is required by a transaction has the timestamp of the transaction.
3. For each data item x, the largest timestamp of a read operation and the largest timestamp of a write operation are recorded; they will be indicated as $RTM(x)$ and $WTM(x)$.
4. Let TS be the timestamp of a read operation on data item x.
   If $TS < WTM(x)$, the read operation is rejected and the issuing transaction restarted with a new timestamp; otherwise, the read is executed, and $RTM(x)$ is set to $\max(RTM(x), TS)$.
5. Let TS be the timestamp of a write operation on data item x. If $TS < RTM(x)$ or $TS < WTM(x)$, then the operation is rejected and the issuing transaction is restarted; otherwise, the write is executed, and $WTM(x)$ is set to TS.

Rules 4 and 5 ensure that conflicting operations are executed in timestamp order at all sites; hence the timestamp order is a total order satisfying the condition of proposition 8.1, and the executions produced by this mechanisms are correct.

Example 8.4

Consider the concurrent execution E of Example 8.1, which is repeated here for convenience:

$$S1: \quad R_i(x)\, W_i(x)\, R_j(x)\, W_j(x)$$
$$S2: \qquad\qquad\qquad R_i(y)\, W_i(y)\, R_j(y)\, W_j(y)$$

Recall that in this representation, the fact that two operations appear one below the other means that they start at the same time. This execution cannot be produced by the 2-phase-locking mechanism. With the basic timestamp mechanism this execution is accepted if $TS(T_i) < TS(T_j)$, because at site 1 after the execution of $W_i(x)$, $RTM(x) = WTM(x) = TS(T_i)$ and therefore $R_j(x)$ and $W_j(x)$ are not rejected. Similar considerations apply also to site 2. This appears to be an advantage of the timestamp mechanism.

However, if $R_j(x)$ were processed at site 1 before $W_i(x)$, then $W_i(x)$ would be rejected by rule 5 and T_i would be aborted and restarted. The same would happen if $R_j(y)$ were processed at site 2 before $W_i(y)$. Moreover, T_j would be restarted if the transactions had required operations in the order shown by execution E but with $TS(T_j) < TS(T_i)$. Other conditions which could lead to restart are possible. In fact, the high number of restarts is the main weakness of this mechanism.

An interesting feature of the basic timestamp mechanism is that it is deadlock-free, because transactions are never blocked: if a transaction cannot execute an operation, it is restarted. Waiting would be meaningless in this approach anyway. If an operation cannot be granted, this does not depend on the fact that another transaction is momentarily operating on the same data item, but instead depends on a permanent situation, since data items never decrease their timestamps. However, deadlock freedom is obtained at the cost of restarting transactions, rather than making them wait.

The basic rules which have been described above are sufficient to ensure the serializability of transactions; however, they need to be integrated with 2-phase-commitment to ensure atomicity. Two-phase-commitment requires that there be a time interval during which all the agents of a transaction are capable of aborting or committing. With a locking mechanism this is possible, because all exclusive locks are held by a transaction until the end of commitment (and no transaction can read the data which has been written by a not yet committed transaction). With the timestamp mechanism we need a different solution: instead of exclusive locks, we use **prewrites**. Prewrites are issued by transactions instead of write operations; they are buffered and not applied directly to the database. Only when the transaction is committed, are the corresponding write operations applied to the database. In this way, if the prewrites of a transaction have been accepted (buffered), at transaction commit the corresponding writes will not be rejected. Buffering of an operation means that the operation is neither executed, nor rejected; instead, it is recorded together with its timestamp for subsequent execution, and it is ensured that this execution will be possible at a later time.

In order to integrate the basic timestamp method and 2-phase-commitment, the above rules 4 and 5 are substituted by the following rules 4, 5, and 6.

4. Let TS be the timestamp of a prewrite operation P_i on data item x. If $TS < RTM(x)$ or $TS < WTM(x)$, then the operation is rejected and the issuing transaction is restarted; otherwise, the prewrite P_i and its timestamp TS are buffered.

5. Let TS be the timestamp of a read operation R_i on data item x. If $TS < WTM(x)$, the operation is rejected. However, if $TS > WTM(x)$, then R_i is executed only if there is no prewrite operation $P(x)$ pending on data item x having a timestamp $TS(P) < TS$. If there is one (or more) prewrite operation $P(x)$ with $TS(P) < TS$, R_i is buffered until the transaction which has issued $P(x)$ commits. The reason why R_i is buffered is that the write operation $W(x)$ corresponding to the prewrite $P(x)$ cannot be rejected; therefore, we must avoid $TS(W) < RTM(x)$. But $TS(W) = TS(P)$, because they are issued by the same transaction; we must avoid applying R_i since the value of $RTM(x)$ would be set equal to the value of TS, thus making $W(x)$ impossible. The read operation R_i will be executed and eliminated from the buffer when no more prewrites with a smaller timestamp than R_i are pending on x.

6. Let TS be the timestamp of a write operation W_i on data item x. This operation is never rejected; however, it is possibly buffered if there is a prewrite operation $P(x)$ with a timestamp $TS(P) < TS$, for the same reason

which has been stated for buffering read operations. W_i will be executed and eliminated from the buffer when all prewrites with smaller timestamps have been eliminated from the buffer.

Note that the use of prewrites is equivalent to applying exclusive locks on data items for the time interval between the prewrite and the commitment (write) or abort of the issuing transaction.

The "ignore obsolete write" rule Rule 5 of the basic timestamp mechanism can be modified in the following way: if the timestamp of a write operation $W_i(x)$ is smaller than the write timestamp $WTM(x)$ of the data item x, it is possible to ignore the operation, instead of rejecting the operation and restarting the transaction. The reason why this simplified rule works correctly is that if W_i and W_j are two write operations such that $TS(W_i) < TS(W_j)$, the execution of W_i followed by W_j is equivalent to the execution of W_j alone. If therefore W_i is issued after W_j, by ignoring it we obtain the same result as if it were executed before W_j.

Note that this situation can occur only if transaction T_j did not read data item x; otherwise, W_i would be rejected, because $TS(W_i) < RTM(x)$. This fact confirms an intuitive argument: if a transaction T_j writes a data item x *without reading it previously*, then the value of x after $W_j(x)$ is independent of the previous history (previous writes) of x. For example, if we have a transaction which changes the address of a person, the new address is not a function of the previous one; if there was a correction on the previous address pending, we can simply ignore this correction after the new address has been written. However, in general, transactions which write a data item do also read it.

8.3.2 The Conservative Timestamp Method

The main disadvantage of the basic timestamp method is the great number of restarts which it causes; conservative timestamping is a method which eliminates restarts by buffering younger operations until all older conflicting operations have been executed, so that operations are never rejected and transactions are never restarted. In order to execute a buffered operation it is necessary to know when there are no more older conflicting operations.

The conservative timestamp method, described in reference [8.18], is based on the following requirements and rules.

1. Each transaction is executed at one site only and does not activate remote programs. It can only issue read or write requests to remote sites.

2. A site i must receive all the read requests from a different site j in timestamp order. Similarly, a site i must receive all the write requests from a different site j in timestamp order.

    These requirements are not very simple to satisfy. First, let us assume that the communication network does not change the order of messages between two sites. Second, each site must be capable of sending request messages in timestamp order. This can be achieved in two ways. It is possible to process transactions serially at each site; this, however, is not very satisfying for a concurrency control mechanism. A more attractive solution is to execute transactions by issuing all read requests before their main execution and all write requests after their main execution. In this way, if $TS(T_i) < TS(T_j)$, it is sufficient to wait to send the R_j operations until all R_i operations have been sent and to wait to send the W_j operations until all W_i operations have been sent. The above requirement is thus satisfied, even if the two transactions run concurrently.

3. Assume that a site i has at least one buffered read and one buffered write operation from each other site of the network. Because of requirement 2, site i knows that there are no older requests which can arrive from any site. The concurrency controller at site i behaves therefore in the following way:

   a. For a read operation R that arrives at site i:
       If there is some write operation W buffered at site i such that $TS(R) > TS(W)$, then R is buffered until these writes are executed, else R is executed.

   b. For a write operation W that arrives at site i:
       If there is some read operation R buffered at site i such that $TS(W) > TS(R)$ or there is some write operation W' buffered at site i such that $TS(W) > TS(W')$, then W is buffered until these operations are executed, else W is executed.

It is easy to see that the buffering rules are similar to those which we have used to allow 2-phase-commitment with the basic timestamp method. With conservative timestamping, 2-phase-commitment is not a problem, because write operations are never rejected.

Conservative timestamping suffers from the following problem: if one site never sends an operation to some other site, then the assumption stated at the beginning of point 3 does not hold. This problem can be eliminated by requiring that each site periodically send timestamped "null" operations to each other site, so that timestamp information is transmitted instead of real operations. A different solution to the same problem is that timestamped "null" operations are requested explicitly by blocked sites.

Caution must be taken in the implementation of conservative timestamping in order to avoid deadlocks. While in the basic timestamp method transactions never wait, in the conservative timestamp method a wait condition exists, because when a read operation is buffered, then the corresponding transaction is forced to wait. Therefore, the waits must not cause deadlocks if deadlock freedom is desired.

Consider as an example of a possible deadlock the situation of Figure 8.6. Data items x and y are stored at sites 1 and 2, respectively. At site 1 transaction T_i is running, and consists of operations: $R_i(x)$, execute, $W_i(y)$. At site 2 transaction T_j is running, and consists of operations $R_j(y)$, execute, $W_j(x)$. Figure 8.6 shows the situation that exists after both read operations have been issued: both sites have buffered these reads, because they are waiting for a write operation from the other site.

Let us assume an apparently reasonable mechanism in which no null operation is sent when there are still transactions pending, because it is expected that these transactions will issue some useful operation. Both transactions are blocked in this

$$T_i, \text{ executed at site } 1: \quad R_i(x), \text{ execute, } W_i(y)$$
$$T_j, \text{ executed at site } 2: \quad R_j(y), \text{ execute, } W_j(x)$$

(a) Operations requested by transactions T_i and T_j

Site 1 (*stores item x*)	Site 2 (*stores item y*)
$R_i(x)$ buffered, waiting	$R_j(y)$ buffered, waiting
for a write from site 2	for a write from site 1

(b) A possible deadlock situation

Figure 8.6   Deadlock with conservative timestamping.

case and will never issue their writes. With this mechanism a deadlock has been created. This example is presented in reference [8.20].

In fact, the only way to avoid deadlocks is to send a null operation anyway after a timeout; however, this seems equivalent to performing deadlock detection by timeout.

The above example shows that care must also be taken with timestamp methods in order to avoid deadlocks, if it is possible that a transaction waits not only for older but also for younger transactions. The fact that T_i waits for a write from T_j and T_j waits for a write from T_i is not due to an explicit rule of the mechanism but seems more to be an undesired side effect. Note that this situation has occurred independently of any assumption on the timestamps of the two transactions. Clearly one is older, and the other one is younger; therefore one of the two is waiting for a younger transaction. As we know from the analysis of deadlock prevention mechanisms, this fact violates the basic requirement of deadlock prevention.

8.4 OPTIMISTIC METHODS FOR DISTRIBUTED CONCURRENCY CONTROL

The basic idea of optimistic methods is the following: instead of suspending or rejecting conflicting operations, like in 2-phase-locking and timestamping, always execute a transaction to completion. However, the write operations issued by transactions are performed on local copies of the data. Only at the end of the transaction, if a validation test is passed by the transaction, are the writes applied to the database. If the validation test is not passed, the transaction is restarted. The validation test verifies if the execution of the transaction is serializable. In order to perform the test, some information about the execution of the transaction must be retained until the validation is performed.

The optimistic approach is based on the assumption that conflicts are rare and therefore most transactions will pass the test. By processing operations without concurrency control overhead, a transaction is not delayed during its execution.

In the rest of this section each transaction is considered to consist of three phases:

1.   The read phase.   During this phase a transaction reads data items from the database, performs computations, and determines new values for the

data items of its write-set; however, these values are not written in the database. Note that the read phase contains almost the whole execution of the transaction.

2.   The validation phase. During this phase a test is performed to see whether the application of the updates to the database which have been computed by the transaction would cause a loss of consistency or not.

3.   The write phase. During this phase the updates are applied to the database if the validation phase has returned a positive result; otherwise the transaction is restarted.

In this section we are mainly interested in the criteria which can be used for performing the validation phase. We present two algorithms. The algorithm of Section 8.4.1 uses timestamps on data items and on transactions for performing the validation. This algorithm was one of the first algorithms proposed for optimistic concurrency control in distributed databases. The algorithm of Section 8.4.2 uses only timestamps on transactions and does not need timestamps on data items. These algorithm are mainly of theoretical interest and have not been used in the implementation of any real distributed system. Therefore, the next sections are more oriented to explaining the basic ideas than to describing the details of the algorithms.

Notice that the optimistic approach is used in some centralized DBMSs. For instance, in IMS-FASTPATH databases it is possible to implement a locking scheme which is in fact optimistic by using the "verify" and "change" primitives instead of the usual locking primitives. With the "verify" and "change" primitives it is possible to inspect the content of a record and to require its modification; however, no locks are acquired and the requested updates are not performed on the database. This is equivalent to performing the read phase of the optimistic approach. When the transaction commits, a validation phase is executed consisting in acquiring all locks at once and inspecting the content of the records again to see whether some other transaction has changed it. If the validation phase is successful, the updates are executed (write phase). We do not describe IMS-FASTPATH in further detail, since it is a centralized and not a distributed DBMS. Notice that the terminology which we have used is not the standard IMS terminology. In particular, the terms "optimistic," "validation," and "commit" are not IMS terms.

8.4.1 Validation Using Timestamps on Data Items and Transactions

This algorithm assumes a fully redundant database, where a copy of each data item is stored at each site. Since the database is fully redundant, each transaction is executed completely at its site of origin. During the execution of the transaction (read phase) the updates are written into an update list. The validation phase consists of checking that the updates can be applied at all sites.

Each transaction receives a unique timestamp when it starts execution, and each copy of each data item in the database carries the timestamp of the last transaction which has written into it.

A restrictive assumption of this algorithm is that the read-set contains the write-set; i.e., there are no data items which are written but not read.

At the end of the read phase, the transaction produces an **update list** containing the following elements:

1. The data items of the read-set with their timestamps
2. The new values of the data items of its write-set
3. The timestamp of the transaction itself

During the validation phase, the update list is sent to every site. Each site votes on the update list and communicates its vote to the site of origin of the transaction. The vote expresses whether the site considers the update list valid or not. If the site of origin receives a majority of yes votes, it decides to commit the transaction and communicates this decision to all other sites. If the majority voted no, all sites are told that the update list can be discarded, and the transaction is restarted. This algorithm therefore implements a majority approach to the update of multiple copies. We will not consider this aspect further in this section. The reason for the majority approach is essentially reliability; in the next chapter we will consider the reliability aspects of the majority approach in detail.

The key element for understanding the validation is in the **voting rule** which is followed by each site: Each site compares the timestamp of each data item of the read-set of the update list to be validated with the corresponding timestamp of the data items which are stored in its local database. If they are all equal, then the site votes yes; otherwise, it votes no, because the premises of the updates are no longer valid and some conflicting updates have been accepted. Between the time a site has voted on an update list and the time it receives the final command from the site of origin, the update list is said to be pending at this site.

The above basic voting rule must be extended in order to accomodate the fact that update lists are processed concurrently; therefore when a site takes a decision on an update list U, another update list U' can be pending at the same site. Since U' could contain conflicting updates with U, the data items of the read-set of U are likely to change their timestamps in the database because of the effect of executing U'.

The following voting rule is complete and takes care of pending update lists:

1. Compare the timestamps of the read-set of U with the corresponding timestamps in the database.
2. If they are not equal, vote no.
3. If they are equal but there is a pending update list U' that has conflicting updates and a higher timestamp than U, vote no.
4. If they are equal and there is a pending update list that has conflicting updates and a smaller timestamp, defer the decision;
5. otherwise, vote yes.

The reason why a no vote is given in rule 3, while the decision is deferred in rule 4, is that deferring the decision in both cases could lead to deadlocks, since a transaction could wait for a younger and for an older transaction. In this way, instead, the algorithm is deadlock-free.

The validation rule used by this algorithm exploits the following ideas:

1. The timestamps on data items record the effect of already committed transactions.
2. Pending (i.e., concurrent) transactions are explicitly analyzed for conflicts.

8.4.2 Validation Using Only Transaction Timestamps

Let us first consider this method in a centralized database. Each transaction receives a timestamp during its execution, however, not at its initiation, because we need timestamps only during the validation phase. Let TNC (for transaction number counter) denote a global counter which is used for assigning timestamps.

The validation procedure of a transaction T_j is based on checking that the schedule produced by already committed transactions, transactions which are in their validation phase when T_j is being validated, and T_j itself is equivalent to a serial schedule in timestamp order.

The validation condition for a transaction T_j with timestamp $TS(T_j)$ requires that, for all transactions T_i with $TS(T_i) < TS(T_j)$, one of the following three conditions hold:

Condition 1. T_i completes its write phase before T_j starts its read phase.

Condition 2. The write-set of T_i does not intersect the read-set of T_j, and T_i completes its write phase before T_j starts its write phase.

Condition 3. The write-set of T_i does not intersect the read-set or the write-set of T_j, and T_i completes its read phase before T_j completes its read phase.

In order to transform the above rules into an algorithm, during the execution of T_j the following information is recorded:

1. The read- and write-sets of T_j.
2. The value of TNC when T_j started: this is called START(T_j).
3. The value of TNC when T_j finished its read phase: this is called FINISH(T_j).

START(T_j) and FINISH(T_j) are therefore two local variables of T_j containing timestamp values that are needed for performing validation and that will be discarded after T_j is terminated completely; the definitive, unique timestamp $TS(T_j)$ is assigned to T_j only after the write phase if the validation succeeds. TNC is incremented only when the definitive timestamp is assigned, so that subsequent transactions will receive a greater timestamp. Figure 8.7a shows the meaning of START(T_j), FINISH(T_j), and $TS(T_j)$.

We can now derive an algorithm for the validation of a transaction T_j by considering each one of the above conditions separately as shown in Figure 8.7b, c, and d.

1. Figure 8.7b: For all transactions T_i such that $TS(T_i)<$START(T_j), nothing has to be checked. Therefore the validation algorithm has to consider only transactions T_i such that $TS(T_i)>$START(T_j).

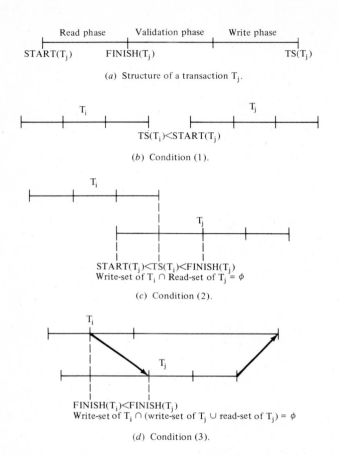

(a) Structure of a transaction T_j.

(b) Condition (1).

(c) Condition (2).

(d) Condition (3).

Figure 8.7   Validation conditions for optimistic concurrency control.

2.   Figure 8.7c: The transactions T_i which have terminated their write phase during the read phase of T_j are identified by the validation algorithm by checking whether $\text{START}(T_j) < TS(T_i) < \text{FINISH}(T_j)$. For all these transactions the above condition 2 is checked.

3.   Figure 8.7d: The transactions T_i such that $\text{FINISH}(T_i) < \text{FINISH}(T_j)$ are identified by keeping track of all transactions which have not yet terminated execution, and are called **active** transactions. For all these transactions the above condition 3 is checked.

Consider now a distributed database. Each distributed transaction is constituted by subtransactions. Let T_{ij} denote the subtransaction which executes at site j for transaction T_i. The validation method can be extended to the distributed environment in the following way:

1.   Each subtransaction of the same transaction receives the same global, unique transaction identifier.

2. Each site performs a local validation of each local subtransaction.

3. For each subtransaction T_{ij} the happened before set $HB(T_{ij})$ is built, which contains the identifiers of those global transactions which precede T_{ij} in the serialization order at site j. The information which is necessary for building the HB set is collected during the local validation phase.

4. Then, the real global validation phase is performed. Global validation is based on a simple (but pessimistic) idea: a subtransaction is considered valid only if all global transactions which belong to its HB-set have either committed or aborted. If it is not yet known for some of these transactions whether they have committed or aborted, the validation of T_{ij} is suspended. This waiting can cause a deadlock; hence, after a timeout, if the subtransaction cannot be validated, it is aborted. Therefore, this method is effective only if most transactions do not require waiting during global validation.

5. Write phase: 2-phase-commitment can be used. When a subtransaction has finished its global validation (positively or negatively), the corresponding message is sent to the transaction's master site. If all validations are positive, the transaction is committed, otherwise it is aborted.

The fundamental rule of global validation is rule 4. In order to understand it, let us assume that a nonserializable execution is produced: two transactions T_i and T_j have executed subtransactions at two sites h and k in such a way that the schedule at site h is equivalent to the serial schedule T_i,T_j and the schedule at site k is equivalent to the serial schedule T_j,T_i. This means that at both sites the following situation exists:

$$\text{Site } h\text{: } T_{ih} \text{ validated; } T_{jh} \text{ waiting with } HB(T_{jh}) = \{T_i\}$$
$$\text{Site } k\text{: } T_{jk} \text{ validated; } T_{ik} \text{ waiting with } HB(T_{ik}) = \{T_j\}$$

This is a typical deadlock situation. The timeout mechanism will cause at least one transaction to be aborted, so that the inconsistent execution cannot be produced.

Optimistic methods are assumed to be convenient for systems where transactions have only few conflicts. This is especially true in applications where most transactions are read-only. A read-only transaction has no write phase and no write-set, so that its validation consists only in checking condition 2: for all transactions T_i such that $\text{START}(T_j) < TS(T_i) < \text{FINISH}(T_j)$, check that the write-set of T_i has a void intersection with the read-set of T_j.

CONCLUSIONS

We have analyzed in this chapter three classes of concurrency control algorithms: 2-phase-locking, timestamps, and optimistic methods. Their basic features can be classified as follows.

1. There are two basic ways to avoid nonserializable executions: **waiting** or **restarting** transactions. Two-phase-locking uses waiting; timestamping and optimistic methods use restarting.

2. The conflicts of a transaction with other transactions can be determined in two different ways: **one by one**, i.e., each time that a transaction performs an operation, or **globally**, when all the operations of a transaction are known. Two-phase-locking and timestamp methods discover conflicts one by one, while optimistic methods discover them globally.

3. The serialization order of transactions is determined in two different ways: by *the order of access to data items* or by *transaction timestamp assignment*. Two-phase-locking produces schedules where transaction T_i precedes transaction T_j if T_i accesses a data item before T_j with a conflicting lock mode; with timestamping T_i precedes T_j if it has a smaller timestamp.

4. For all methods which cause waiting of transactions a solution must be given to the problem of deadlocks; this solution can be either **detection** or **prevention**. Note that dealing with deadlocks will always require a restart of some transactions; therefore, no pure waiting method exists which never needs a restart.

We have seen that a method which uses only restarts is by its nature deadlock-free. This seems to be an attractive feature of nonwaiting methods. However, this is not true since restarts are more expensive than waits. In fact, most methods which were originally pure restart methods have been extended with some waiting feature in order to reduce the number of restarts. For example, the conservative timestamp approach introduces waiting into the basic timestamp approach. Whenever waiting is introduced into a concurrency control method, the risk of deadlock must be taken into acount. We have seen that determining whether an algorithm is really deadlock-free can require a complex analysis.

In the absence of a general analysis which determines with a reasonable precision the areas where one method is better than another one, it is not surprising that commercial systems and real life applications are mainly based on the most experienced method: 2-phase-locking with timeout-based deadlock detection.

EXERCISES

8.1 Let objects x and y be stored at site 1, and objects z and w be stored at site 2. Determine, for each of the following executions, whether the execution is serializable or not. If the answer is affirmative, determine all possible total orders of transactions. If the answer is negative, prove that there is no total order possible.

Execution 1:
S1: $R_i(x) R_j(x) W_j(y) W_i(x)$
S2: $R_i(w) R_j(z) W_j(w) W_i(w)$

Execution 2:
S1: $R_i(x) R_j(x) W_j(y) W_i(y)$
S2: $W_i(z)$

Execution 3:
S1: $R_i(x) R_j(x) W_i(x) W_j(y)$
S2: $R_i(z) R_j(z) W_j(z) W_i(w)$

Execution 4:

S1: $R_i(y) \, R_j(x) \, W_j(x)$

S2: $W_i(z) \, R_i(w) \, R_j(w) \, W_i(w)$

8.2   Consider the two FUND_TRANSFER transactions T_i and T_j of Example 8.1 in Section 8.1.3. Show all possible executions of the two transactions if 2-phase-locking is used for concurrency control (use the "time-oriented" interpretation of execution described in Section 8.1.3, showing the possible overlapping of actions).

8.3   Consider the DWFG in the figure

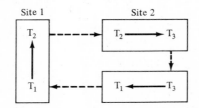

Detect the deadlock using the algorithms described in Section 8.2.

8.4   Assume that the same transactions of Exercise 8.3 are executed with a deadlock prevention method. Show that the deadlock is prevented using both the non-preemptive and the preemptive method. Assign arbitrarily transaction timestamps and determine which transactions are restarted in both cases.

8.5   Consider the two FUND_TRANSFER transactions T_i and T_j of Example 8.1 in Section 8.1.3. Assume that initially $RTM(x) = 25$, $WTM(x) = 25$, $RTM(y) = 30$, and $WTM(y) = 30$. Determine possible executions and transaction restarts in the following cases:

(a) $TS(T_i) = 35$; $TS(T_j) = 40$

(b) $TS(T_i) = 20$; $TS(T_j) = 40$

(c) $TS(T_i) = 40$; $TS(T_j) = 35$

8.6   Consider a data item x. Let $RTM(x) = 25$ and $WTM(x) = 20$. Let the pair $\langle R_i(x), TS \rangle$ $(\langle W_i(x), TS \rangle)$ denote a read (write) request of transaction T_i on the item x with timestamp TS. Indicate the behavior of the basic timestamp method with the following sequence of requests:

$$\langle R_1(x), 19 \rangle, \langle R_2(x), 22 \rangle, \langle W_3(x), 21 \rangle,$$
$$\langle W_4(x), 23 \rangle, \langle R_5(x), 28 \rangle, \langle W_6(x), 27 \rangle$$

8.7   Consider a data item x. Let $RTM(x) = 21$ and $WTM(x) = 20$. Let the pair $\langle P_i(x), TS \rangle$ denote a prewrite request of transaction T_i on the item x with timestamp TS. Indicate the behavior of the timestamp method with 2-phase-commitment if the following sequence of requests is received:

$$\langle P_1(x), 22 \rangle, \langle P_2(x), 26 \rangle, \langle R_3(x), 19 \rangle,$$
$$\langle R_4(x), 23 \rangle, \langle W_1(x), 30 \rangle, \langle R_5(x), 24 \rangle,$$
$$\langle P_6(x), 18 \rangle, \langle R_7(x), 27 \rangle, \langle W_2(x), 31 \rangle$$

8.8 Consider a data item x stored at site 1 in a distributed database with 2 sites. Let the triple $\langle R_i, j, TS \rangle$ ($\langle W_i, j, TS \rangle$) denote a read (write) request of transaction T_i on the item x generated at site j with timestamp TS. Assume that initially the following operations are buffered:

$$\langle R_1, 2, 12 \rangle, \langle W_2, 1, 8 \rangle, \langle W_3, 2, 9 \rangle$$

Indicate the behavior of the conservative timestamp method with the following sequence of requests:

$$\langle R_4, 1, 10 \rangle, \langle R_5, 1, 11 \rangle, \langle W_6, 1, 13 \rangle,$$
$$\langle W_7, 2, 14 \rangle, \langle R_8, 1, 14 \rangle, \langle R_9, 2, 17 \rangle,$$
$$\langle R_{10}, 1, 16 \rangle, \langle W_{11}, 1, 20 \rangle, \langle W_{12}, 2, 22 \rangle$$

Annotated Bibliography

References [8.1] to [8.4] deal with the foundations of the concurrency control problem. Other references of this kind have been given in Chapter 7 and are not repeated here. References [8.5] and [8.6] deal with two rather specific aspects of distributed concurrency control which have not been treated in this chapter: considering the user operations in the analysis of concurrency control mechanisms ([8.5]) and considering read-only transactions ([8.6]). References [8.7] to [8.15] are on distributed deadlock detection and prevention. References [8.16] to [8.20] are on timestamp-based concurrency control. References [8.21] to [8.24] present some optimistic algorithms. References [8.25] to [8.29] deal with the comparison, classification, and performance of concurrency control mechanisms.

[8.1] C. H. Papadimitriou, P. A. Bernstein, and J. B. Rothnie, "Some Computational Problems Related to Database Concurrency Control," *Proc. Conf. on Theoretical Computer Science*, Waterloo, 1977.

[8.2] C. H. Papadimitriou, "Serializability of Concurrent Updates," *Journal of the ACM*, **26**:4, 1979.

[8.3] P. A. Bernstein, D. W. Shipman, and W. S. Wong, "Formal Aspects of Serializability in Database Concurrency Control," *IEEE-TSE*, **SE-5**:3, 1979.

[8.4] H. T. Kung and C. H. Papadimitriou, "An Optimality Theory of Concurrency Control for Databases," *ACM-SIGMOD*, 1979.

[8.5] P. A. Bernstein, N. Goodman, and Ming-Yee Lai, "On Analysing Concurrency Control Algorithms When User and System Operations Differ," *IEEE-TSE*, **SE-9**:3, 1983.

This paper extends the problem of concurrency control from the level of the elementary read and write operations to the level of more complex user operations which are required by transactions. The paper suggests that traditional concurrency control methods, like locking, can be extended to take advantage of the properties of high level operations. This aspect has been considered in Section 8.1.4.

The paper analyzes formally concurrency control at the two levels (user and system) and proposes a method for proving the correctness of a concurrency control algorithm which takes care of the existence of both levels, called the 2-part proof scheme.

The idea presented in this paper is valid for both centralized and distributed database systems. However, it seems particularly appealing in a distributed system, because the high-level operations which are considered by the concurrency control mechanism can in this case be the remote operations needed by transactions (see Section 8.1.3). In this paper, the 2-part proof scheme is applied to an airline reservation system, consisting of several intelligent terminals which are capable of performing high-level operations.

[8.6]   H. Garcia-Molina and G. Wiederhold, "Read-only Transactions in a Distributed Database," *ACM-TODS*, **7**:2, 1982.

This paper discusses the various consistency and currency requirements for read-only transactions. Most concurrency control mechanisms do not account for the existence of read-only transactions; this paper suggests that a concurrency control mechanism can realize a great advantage from knowing in advance that a transaction is read-only.

The paper is based on the following assumptions: (1) that it is possible to distinguish a priori a read-only transaction from other transactions; (2) that no failures occur in the system; and (3) that the consistency and currency requirements for each read-only transaction are known when it is initiated.

The consistency requirements of a read-only transaction are classified as: (1) No consistency at all; in this case, the read-only transaction can read inconsistent data. As the read-only transaction does not modify the database, the correctness of the database cannot be invalidated by these transactions. (2) Weak consistency; the read-only transaction must read consistent data. (3) Strong consistency; the execution of the read-only transaction with update transactions and other strong consistency transactions must be serializable.

The currency requirements specify which updates should be reflected by the data which is read.

The most important concept of this paper is R-insularity. A read-only transaction is said to be insular if all the items referenced by it are stored at its site of origin. A read-only transaction processing algorithm is said to be R-insular if it can process an insular read-only transaction completely at its site of origin.

This concept is very useful in distributed databases. Recall that data replication is often introduced in a distributed database in order to allow locality of read-only transactions (Chapter 4). However, in order to take full advantage of this fact the concurrency control mechanism must provide the R-insularity property.

[8.7]   J. N. Gray, "Notes on Database Operating Systems," *Operating Systems—an Advanced Course*, Springer Verlag, Section 5.7.7.4 on deadlock detection, 1978.

This paper has given the first definition of a distributed wait-for graph and proposed a centralized deadlock detection algorithm (see Section 8.2.2).

[8.8]   D. A. Menasce and R. R. Muntz, "Locking and Deadlock Detection in Distributed Databases," *IEEE-TSE*, **SE-5**:3, 1979.

[8.9]   V. D. Gligor and S. H. Shattuck, "On Deadlock Detection in Distributed Systems," *IEEE-TSE*, **SE-6**:5, 1980.

These two papers are the basis for hierarchical deadlock detection of section 8.2.2. Reference [8.8] also presents a distributed deadlock detection algorithm which is refined and corrected in reference [8.9].

[8.10]   R. Obermarck, "Distributed Deadlock Detection Algorithm," *ACM-TODS*, **7**:2, 1982.

This paper is the basis of the algorithm of Section 8.2.4.

[8.11]   L. M. Haas and C. Mohan, "A Distributed Deadlock Detection Algorithm for a Resource-Based System," IBM Res. Rep. RJ3765, San Jose, CA, 1982.

[8.12]   K. M. Chandy, L. M. Haas, and J. Misra, "Distributed Deadlock Detection," *ACM Transactions on Computer Systems*, **1**:2, 1983.

[8.13]   K. M. Chandy and J. Misra, "A Distributed Algorithm for Detecting Resource Deadlocks in Distributed Systems," *Proc. ACM SIGACT-SIGOPS Symp. on Principles of Distributed Computing*, ACM 1982.

References [8.11] to [8.13] deal with a deadlock detection algorithm. The basic idea of this algorithm is that each blocked process can start a deadlock detection computation in order to determine whether it is involved in some deadlocks. There are no specialized deadlock detectors which build a wait-for graph. It is required that a process P_i knows the set of processes to which it has made a request which is still unsatisfied, called the set of **debtors** of P_i, and the set of processes from which P_i has received requests which it has not yet granted, called the set of **dependents** of P_i. This very general model can be adapted to the distributed database environment by considering transaction agents and local resource controllers as processes; however, this algorithm requires just the notion of process.

[8.14]   J. N. Gray, P. Homan, R. Obermarck, and H. Korth, "A Straw Man Analysis of Probability of Waiting and Deadlocks," *Fifth Int. Conf. on Distributed Data Management and Computer Networks*, 1981.

[8.15]   D. J. Rosenkrantz, R. E. Stearns, and P. M. Lewis, "System Level Concurrency Control for Distributed Database Systems," *ACM-TODS*, **3**:2, 1978.

The preemptive and nonpreemptive methods of Section 8.2.5 are the "wait-die" and "wound-wait" algorithms of [8.15].

[8.16]   L. Lamport, "Time, Clocks and the Ordering of Events in a Distributed System," *Communications of the ACM*, **21**:7, 1978.

This is a fundamental paper on the time aspect in distributed systems. Section 8.1.5 is based on this paper.

[8.17]   P. A. Bernstein, J. B. Rothnie, N. Goodman, and C. A. Papadimitriou, "The Concurrency Control Mechanism of SDD-1: A System for Distributed Databases (the Fully Redundant Case)," *IEEE-TSE*, **SE-4**:3, 1978.

[8.18]   P. A. Bernstein, D. W. Shipman, and J. B. Rothnie, "Concurrency Control in a System for Distributed Databases (SDD-1)," *ACM-TODS*, **5**:1, 1980.

[8.19]   P. A. Bernstein and D. W. Shipman, "The Correctness of Concurrency Control Mechanism in a System for Distributed Databases (SDD-1)," *ACM-TODS*, **5**:1, 1980.

[8.20]   G. McLean, "Comments on SDD-1 Concurrency Control Mechanism," *ACM-TODS*, **6**:2, 1981.

Timestamp-based concurrency control mechanisms have been studied mainly by the designers of the SDD-1 system, which is described in Part II of this book. Papers [8.17] to [8.19] describe the concurrency control mechanism of SDD-1, which is based on a conservative timestamp approach enhanced by several additional characteristics. Section 8.3 is largely based on these papers and other papers by the same authors. The discussion of the risk of deadlock in conservative timestamping was suggested by the fact that paper [8.20] has shown that deadlocks can occur with the concurrency control mechanism of SDD-1.

[8.21]   R. W. Thomas, "A Majority Consensus Approach to Concurrency Control for Multiple Copy Databases," *ACM-TODS*, **4**:2, 1979.

This paper was one of the first in the field of distributed concurrency control. It presented a complete algorithm that has many features which have been only partially considered in this chapter. The optimistic concurrency control algorithm of Section 8.4.1 is based on this paper, although the term "optimistic" was not used. Also the "ignore obsolete write" rule of Section 8.3.1 and the majority approach to concurrency control for multiple copies, that will be described in the next chapter, were presented by this paper first.

[8.22]   H. T. Kung and J. T. Robinson, "On Optimistic Methods for Concurrency Control," *ACM-TODS*, **6**:2, 1981.

[8.23]   S. Ceri and S. Owicki, "On the Use of Optimistic Methods for Concurrency Control in Distributed Databases," *Sixth Int. Conf. on Distributed Data Management and Computer Networks*, 1983.

Papers [8.22] and [8.23] proposed the optimistic approach which has been presented in Section 8.4.2.

[8.24]   R. Bayer, K. Elhardt, H. Heller, and A. Reiser, "Distributed Concurrency Control in Database Systems," *Sixth VLDB*, 1980.

[8.25]   E. Gelembe and R. Sevcik, "Analysis of Update Synchronization for Multiple Copy Databases," *Third Int. Conf. on Distributed Data Management and Computer Networks*, 1978.

[8.26]   H. Garcia-Molina, "Performance Comparison of Two Update Algorithms for Distributed Databases," *Third Int. Conf. on Distributed Data Management and Computer Networks*, 1978.

[8.27]   D. R. Ries, "The Effect of Concurrency Control on the Performance of a Distributed Database Management System," *Fourth Int. Conf. on Distributed Data Management and Computer Networks*, 1979.

[8.28]   D. Z. Badal, "Concurrency Control Overhead or Closer Look at Blocking vs. Nonblocking Concurrency Control Mechanisms," *Fifth Int. Conf. on Distributed Data Management and Computer Networks,* 1981.

[8.29]   D. Z. Badal, "The Analysis of the Effects of Concurrency Control on Distributed Database System Performance," *Sixth VLDB,* 1980.

Chapter 9

Reliability

In this chapter we study the techniques which are used for building a reliable distributed database. In reference [9.1] **reliability** is defined as "a measure of the success with which the system conforms to some authoritative specification of its behavior.... When the behavior deviates from that which is specified for it, this is called a **failure**." The reliability of the system is inversely related to the frequency of failures.

The reliability of a system can be measured in several ways, which are based on the incidence of failures. Measures include mean time between failures (MTBF), mean time to repair (MTTR), and **availability**, defined as the fraction of the time that the system meets its specification.

There are many interrelated aspects in the field of distributed reliability, and it is not easy to understand how they affect each other. Therefore, before we present the structure of this chapter, which is based on a decomposition of the overall reliability problem into subproblems, we explain some basic concepts.

9.1 BASIC CONCEPTS

In order to apply the definition of reliability to a distributed database, we need to discuss the specification of the desired behavior of the database. In a database system application, the highest-level specifications are application-dependent and include the so-called consistency constraints, that we have described in Section 3.6. It is convenient to split the reliability problem into two separate parts, an application-dependent part and an application-independent part. This result is obtained through the concept of transaction which was defined in Chapter 7. The application-independent specification of reliability consists in requiring that transactions maintain their atomicity, durability, serializability, and isolation properties.

The application-dependent part consists of requiring that transactions fulfill the general system's specifications, including the consistency constraints.

We are interested here in the techniques which can be applied for ensuring application-independent reliability, and assume therefore that transactions will preserve the consistency of the database as long as the system is capable of maintaining their atomicity, durability, serializability, and isolation properties. As a consequence, we are not interested here in the techniques which deal with the specification, proof, and testing of application programs, nor with techniques for run-time checking to ensure that transactions do not violate consistency constraints, although these techniques are also relevant for ensuring the overall reliability of the system.

We emphasize two related aspects of reliability: correctness and availability. It is important not only that a system behave correctly, i.e., in accordance with the specifications, but also that it be available when necessary. In some cases there is a trade-off between the correctness and availability aspects of reliability, because we can increase the availability of the system by agreeing to continue the processing under circumstances which increase the risk of obtaining wrong results. On the other hand, a very cautious strategy, consisting of halting the system whenever there are anomalies which increase the risk of incorrect results, reduces availability.

In some applications, like banking applications, correctness is an absolute requirement, and errors which may corrupt the consistency of the database cannot be tolerated; other applications may tolerate the risk of inconsistencies in order to achieve a greater availability. It is the designer of the database and of the information system who has to evaluate this trade-off.

Let us consider an example which illustrates this trade-off in the context of a distributed database.

Example 9.1

Consider a distributed database consisting of two sites 1 and 2. Let $x1$ and $x2$ be two copies of the same data item x, stored at sites 1 and 2, respectively. Consider a transaction T which updates x. Assuming that 2-phase-locking is used to ensure serializability and 2-phase-commitment is used to ensure atomicity, T will perform as follows in its final phase: lock $x1$, lock $x2$, prepare updates, and perform 2-phase-commitment. Suppose that site 1 acts as the site of origin of the transaction and as coordinator of commitment.

Now assume that the communication network fails after both sites have decided that they are ready to commit; however, the failure occurs before the commit command is sent from site 1, the coordinator, to site 2. How should the system behave at this point? At site 1 the coordinator can commit the transaction; however, at site 2 it is not known what is done by the coordinator. There are two possible strategies. The first one, which considers correctness an absolute requirement, consists of keeping $x2$ locked until the failure is repaired; when the communication will be reestablished, the transaction will be correctly terminated. Availability is sacrificed by this solution, because copy $x2$ of data item x is not available for transactions executing at site 2. A second strategy, which maximizes availability at the risk of introducing inconsistencies in the database, consists of unlocking $x2$ and letting other transactions use its value. Assuming that commits are more frequent than aborts, it might be convenient to apply the update before unlocking $x2$, as if the commit command had arrived. If this second strategy is adopted, then it is convenient to check, after the communication is reestablished between the two sites, whether inconsistencies have occurred, and try to correct them.

Although the above example is very simple, it allows us to illustrate most of the problems which arise when trying to design a reliable distributed database system.

Commitment of transactions   The first problem in the above example is caused by the commitment of transactions. The 2-phase-commitment protocol described in Chapter 7 implements the first strategy of Example 9.1, therefore it sacrifices availability. If we want to obtain better availability, we have to go in the direction of the second strategy. However, we can try to do something better than simply assume that the transaction has committed; we can try to design protocols which allow a transaction to *correctly terminate* even in the presence of failures. These protocols are called **termination protocols**. The termination protocol is invoked to correctly terminate the transaction at all operational (i.e., nonfailed) sites when the normal commitment procedure is interrupted by a failure.   The possibility of termination depends on the state in which the commitment protocol leaves the transaction when it is interrupted by a failure. Termination protocols exist only for some types of failures, not for all of them. Termination protocols are treated in Section 9.2.

Multiple copies of data and robustness of concurrency control   Consider again Example 9.1.   Assume now that we have used a commitment and termination protocol such that, after the failure, all pending transactions have been terminated; for the present discussion it does not matter whether they were committed or aborted, provided that they have released their locks upon resources. From the viewpoint of availability, if we want to execute new transactions which access data item x three very different alternatives are possible:

1.   To use the available local copy at each site
2.   To consider only one copy of x available (in this case we should also have a rule for determining which one)
3.   To consider data item x not available at all

Clearly, the availability of the database is very different for each one of the above approaches.

The type of solution which can be given to the above problem depends essentially on the concurrency control mechanism which is used. This can be shown by the following reasoning: suppose that we know that only one transaction T which operates on data item x will be executed before the failure is repaired; in this case T can be executed at site 1 or at site 2 without any problem. If T updates the available copy of x, say $x1$, it is sufficient that the recovery procedure updates also $x2$ before resuming normal processing. However, if two transactions which update x are allowed to execute at sites 1 and 2, respectively, then the serializability of their execution cannot be ensured (recall from Section 8.1.5 that the two transactions are pseudosimultaneous in this case, because no messages can be exchanged between the two sites).

It seems reasonable from the above discussion to let transactions execute at only one site during the failure. However, the choice of the site is not a trivial task. It is important to choose the "best" site at which to make data item x available.

The above discussion is only a hint to the problems which have to be solved in order to allow the system to continue to accept and process new transactions after a failure has occurred, without waiting for it to be repaired. These problems are discussed in Section 9.3.

Determining the state of the network   Several reliability algorithms rely on the assumption that all operational sites have a consistent view of the state of all sites of the network (including themselves), i.e., of whether each site is **up** (operational) or **down** (failed). In fact, it is not simple to obtain such a consistent view, and specialized algorithms are required.

In order to understand the reason why it is important to have a consistent view of the network, consider the following example. Suppose that we want to make the 2-phase-commitment protocol more reliable by nominating backup coordinators, i.e., sites which take over the function of coordinator if the original coordinator crashes. Clearly, it is of fundamental importance that at each time only one coordinator exist, and that all participants agree in considering it the coordinator. Therefore, we order the backup coordinators so that the first backup takes over only if the original coordinator fails, the second backup takes over if the first backup fails, and so on.

It is evident that the whole mechanism is based on a consistent view of the network state; for example, if the original coordinator considers itself up but the first backup coordinator considers it down, then both will try to perform the coordinator function.

Protocols for achieving a consistent view of the network are considered in Section 9.4. An important by-product of these protocols is that they monitor the network state and signal its changes to processes which have required this facility, thus eliminating the need for timeouts from higher-level protocols.

Detection and resolution of inconsistencies   We have seen in Example 9.1 that a strategy for dealing with failures can sacrifice correctness to availability, thus accepting the risk of inconsistencies. In this case, techniques are useful for detecting these inconsistencies and resolving them if possible. This is the subject of Section 9.5.

Checkpoints and cold restart   The problem of checkpoints and cold restart is not directly related to the above problems. In fact, cold restart should be extremely rare in a database system and is due to catastrophic failures which cannot be solved by the algorithms of Sections 9.2 to 9.5. Typically, cold restart is required if the log information is lost at a site of the network. In this case, the affected site is not capable of reconstructing its most recent state, thus a previous state is reconstructed, and the effect of some local subtransaction is lost.

In a distributed database, cold restart is more difficult than in a centralized one, because the whole distributed database must be reset to a **globally consistent** previous state. It is therefore not correct to make the cold restart only at the site where the failure has occurred using its local checkpoints. This problem is treated in Section 9.6.

Commission errors   In the above examples, we have always considered failures which occurred because a component did not perform some required action; for example, a site did not answer to a message. These errors are called **omission**

errors, and most reliability mechanisms for distributed databases deal only with this type of error. However, failed components can sometimes also perform some wrong actions instead of simply ceasing their activity. These errors are called **commission** errors and are more difficult to resolve.

We can easily show that commission errors are more difficult to deal with than omission errors using the following example. The 2-phase-commitment protocol is resilient to omission errors provided that under some circumstances we agree to wait until the failure is repaired to terminate the transaction. However, this protocol is not resilient to commission errors, for example, the coordinator sending wrong commands to some participants.

Recognizing wrong messages sent by a failed site is analogous to solving a very general problem, the so called **byzantine agreement**. In byzantine agreement, n processors which are capable of exchanging messages must agree on the value of a message which is sent by one of them to all the others; processes or communication links can fail to deliver a message or can even **lie** about its content.

Byzantine agreement has been extensively studied, many algorithms for reaching byzantine agreement under different assumptions have been proposed, and several general results on the possibility of reaching byzantine agreement under given circumstances and with a given cost have been stated. Dealing with this problem is outside the scope of this book; a survey of the literature on byzantine agreement can be found in reference [9.29] and an application of the byzantine agreement to reliability protocols in distributed databases can be found in reference [9.31].

9.2 NONBLOCKING COMMITMENT PROTOCOLS

A commitment protocol is called **blocking** if the occurrence of some kinds of failures forces some of the participating sites to wait until the failure is repaired before terminating the transaction. A transaction which cannot be terminated at a site is called **pending** at this site. In Chapter 7 we have seen that the 2-phase-commitment protocol is blocking if the coordinator fails and some participant has at the same time declared itself ready to commit. In this case, the participant must wait for the recovery of the coordinator. We have also seen that pending transactions reduce the availability of the system, because the locks which are held by them cannot be released.

For simplicity, in the rest of this section we do not consider the final ACK message in the commitment protocols, because it is not required for understanding the problem of blocking.

Before considering how a commitment protocol can be made nonblocking, let us introduce a useful tool for describing the evolution of the coordinator and participants during the execution of a protocol: **state diagrams**. Figure 9.1 shows the two state diagrams for the 2-phase-commitment protocol without the ACK messages. For each transition, an input message and an output message are indicated. A transition occurs when an input message arrives and causes the output message to be sent. State information must be recorded into stable storage

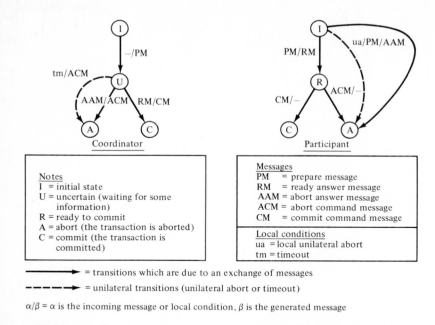

Figure 9.1   State diagrams for the 2-phase-commitment protocol.

for recovery purposes; this corresponds to writing appropriate records in the logs.

If a state diagram of this kind is used for analyzing reliability aspects of a protocol, care must be taken in assuming that transitions from one state to another are atomic. Consider for example a transition from state X to state Y with input I and output O. The following behavior is assumed:

1. The input message I is received.
2. The new state Y is recorded on stable storage.
3. The output message O is sent.

If the site fails between the first and the second event, the state remains X, and the input message is, in fact, lost. If the site fails between the second and the third event, then the site reaches state Y, but the output message is not sent. On restart, the site will not be able to tell whether O was sent or not, because only the state information is available. In general, a site which recovers from a failure cannot know whether the last message was sent or not. Note that this problem is independent of the ordering of the second and third events, and exchanging their order does not eliminate it.

9.2.1 Nonblocking Commitment Protocols with Site Failures

Assume that site failures are possible but network partitions cannot occur. We want to design a termination protocol for the 2-phase-commitment protocol which allows the transaction to be terminated at all operational sites, when a failure of the coordinator site occurs. However, this is possible just in the following two cases:

1.   At least one of the participants has received the command. In this case, the other participants can be told by this participant of the outcome of the transaction and can terminate it.

2.   None of the participants has received the command, and only the coordinator site has crashed, so that all participants are operational. In this case, the participants can elect a new coordinator and resume the protocol.

In both the above cases, the transaction can be correctly terminated at all operational sites. Termination is instead impossible when no operational participant has received the command and at least one participant failed, because the operational participants cannot know what the failed participant has done and cannot take an independent decision. Note that in many cases the coordinator site acts also as a participant in the commitment (because updates are performed at the site of origin of the transaction). Thus, if the coordinator's site fails, we have exactly the situation in which termination is impossible.

In order to eliminate the above case of blocking, we can observe (Figure 9.1) that the operational participants are blocked because, during the second phase of commitment, the participants go directly from the R state, where they are ready either to abort or to commit the transaction, to the abort state A or the commit state C. For this reason, even if all the operational participants have not received a command, the failed participant might have already performed a definitive action (abort or commit), which cannot be undone. This problem can be eliminated by modifying the 2-phase-commitment protocol in the 3-phase-commitment protocol.

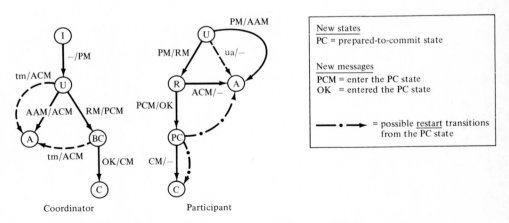

Figure 9.2   State diagrams for the 3-phase-commitment protocol.

9.2.1.1 The 3-phase-commitment protocol   In this protocol, the participants do not directly commit the transaction during the second phase of commitment; instead, they reach in this phase a new prepared-to-commit (PC) state, as shown in Figure 9.2. An additional third phase is then required for actually committing the transaction. In this case, the command which is issued by the coordinator during the second phase is either the normal ABORT command (ACM message in Figure 9.2) or a new ENTER-PREPARED-STATE command (PCM message in Figure 9.2). Once PCM messages are sent, the coordinator enters a new before-commitment (BC) state. Each participant must send an OK message when it has executed this command; i.e., it has entered a new prepared-to-commit state and recorded this state in stable storage. Finally, when the coordinator has received all OK messages, it enters the final commit state (C) and sends the final commit command (CM). This new protocol eliminates the blocking problem of the 2-phase-commitment protocol, because:

1. If one of the operational participants has received the command and the command was ABORT, then the operational participants can abort the transaction; the failed participant will abort the transaction at restart if it has not done it already. This is therefore the same as in 2-phase-commitment.
2. If one of the operational participants has received the command and the command was ENTER-PREPARED-STATE, then all the operational participants can commit the transaction, terminating the second phase if necessary and performing the third phase. The failed participant will commit the transaction at restart. The failed participant has surely not unilaterally aborted the transaction, because it had answered READY; otherwise, the coordinator would not have issued the ENTER-PREPARED-STATE command. Also this case was dealt with correctly by 2-phase-commitment.
3. If none of the operational participants has received the ENTER-PREPARED-STATE command, we have the case which cannot be terminated for a 2-phase-commitment protocol. With this new protocol, instead, the operational participants can *abort* the transaction, because the failed participant has surely not yet committed it. At most, if it has received the ENTER-PREPARED-STATE command, it has reached this new state. The failed participant will therefore abort the transaction at restart. Note that the restart procedure can abort a transaction even if the participant has reached the prepared-to-commit state, because the actual commitment has not yet been executed. This fact is indicated by the two possible restart transitions in Figure 9.2.

The new protocol allows termination for all failures during the second phase which blocked the standard 2-phase protocol; however, we must show that blocking cannot occur because of a failure during the third additional phase which has been added. This is simple, because all participants are in the prepared-to-commit state when this phase begins. Hence the termination protocol will elect a new coordinator and commit the transaction in case of failure of the original coordinator.

The new protocol requires three phases for committing a transaction and two phases for aborting it. Several termination protocols for operational participants and restart protocols for failed participants can be designed to operate correctly with the 3-phase-commitment protocol.

9.2.1.2 Termination protocols for 3-phase-commitment   The design of termination protocols is based on the following property:

If at least one operational participant has not entered the prepared-to-commit state, then the transaction can be safely aborted; if at least one operational participant has entered the prepared-to-commit state, then the transaction can be safely committed.

Since the above two conditions are not mutually exclusive, in several cases the termination protocol can decide whether to commit or abort the transaction. A protocol which always commits the transaction when both cases are possible is called **progressive**. Termination protocols can be centralized, i.e., based on the election of a new coordinator which directs termination, or decentralized. They can be progressive or not.

The simplest termination protocol is the centralized, nonprogressive protocol. First, a new coordinator is elected by the operational participants. Then the new coordinator behaves as follows:

1. If the new coordinator is in the prepared-to-commit state, it issues to all operational participants the command to enter also in this state; when it has received all the OK messages, it issues the COMMIT command.
2. If the new coordinator is in the commit state, i.e., it has committed the transaction, it issues the COMMIT command to all participants.
3. If the new coordinator is in the abort state, it issues the ABORT command to all participants.
4. Otherwise, the new coordinator orders all participants to go back to a state previous to the prepared-to-commit (i.e., the ready state in Figure 9.2), and after it has received all the acknowledgments, it issues the ABORT command.

Note that this protocol is very similar to the original 3-phase-commitment protocol. In this way, in case of a failure of the new coordinator, the same termination protocol can be reentered by the remaining operational sites by electing a new coordinator. This is a general requirement for termination protocols: they must be **reenterable**.

The disadvantage of this termination protocol is that it is not progressive, because in case 4 the new coordinator decides to abort even if some other participant has reached the prepared-to-commit state. However, making this protocol progressive is simple. It is sufficient to add an initial phase during which the new coordinator sends inquiries to the other operational participants about their state. If at least one of them reports that it is in the prepared-to-commit state, then the new coordinator behaves as in point 1 above instead of as in point 4.

There are several ways in which a new coordinator can be elected. As an example, let us consider the way in which this is done by the reliability mechanism of the SDD-1 system. A total order is assigned to the sites, and the protocol chooses the operational site which is first in this order. Clearly, the original coordinator is the first in this order; moreover, the current coordinator is the first operational site in the order, because the fact that it is currently coordinator means that all higher-order sites have failed. The protocol consists simply of the following: when a participant discovers the failure of the current coordinator, it controls whether all the higher-order sites are up; if none of them is up, then it decides to become the new coordinator. This algorithm requires that a consistent view of the network be ensured (recall the example in Section 9.1).

9.2.1.3 Restart protocols for 3-phase-commitment

A restart protocol is executed by a site when it recovers from a failure. In the case of 2-phase-commitment, the restart protocol requires accessing remote recovery information, if the participant failed while it was in the ready state. With 3-phase-commitment and termination protocols, the restart procedure will have to access remote recovery information if the participant has already completed the first phase, independently of whether it has reached the prepared-to-commit state or not, because at restart it is not known how the transaction has been terminated. The probability of having to access remote recovery information is therefore higher with 3-phase-commitment protocols.

9.2.2 Commitment Protocols and Network Partitions

We have seen that the 2-phase-commitment protocol blocks the participants which belong to a participant-group in case of network partitions. If we consider termination protocols for 2-phase-commitment and we allow partition failures, we know already that a transaction can be terminated only if at least one site of each participant-group has received the command message. In this case, the termination protocol can operate in a similar way as for the failure of the coordinator site. It elects as a new coordinator a site of the participant-group. This site asks all participants of its group which command they have received. By assumption, at least one participant knows the command. The new coordinator sends the command to all participants of its group.

Clearly, the above termination protocol works only in some cases. We are therefore interested in knowing whether there exist commitment protocols which always allow termination at all operational sites.

9.2.2.1 Existence of nonblocking protocols for partitions

The problem of the existence of nonblocking protocols in case of partitions can be addressed by considering a different problem: the existence of protocols which allow **independent recovery** in case of site failures. By independent recovery, we mean that a failed site determines the outcome of the transaction at restart without having to access remote recovery information. Note that the protocols which we have considered in the previous section were not independent recovery protocols.

The relevance of independent recovery protocols to the problem of nonblocking protocols in case of partitions can be understood by considering Example 9.1. Suppose that we can build a protocol such that if one site, say site 2, fails, then

1.   The other site, site 1, terminates the transaction (this is the normal nonblocking condition).
2.   Site 2 at restart terminates the transaction correctly without requiring any additional information from site 1.

If we could design such a protocol, then we could use it also as a nonblocking protocol for partition failures. Suppose that a partition occurs instead of the failure of site 2. We could design a termination protocol which behaves at site 1 as the termination protocol for independent recovery, and at site 2 as the restart protocol of the independent recovery case. In both cases (independent recovery and partitions), both sites should have the same information. Termination of a transaction in a participant-group is therefore a specular problem to independent recovery from a site failure.

The above equivalence is also not surprising because a site cannot distinguish a site crash of another site from a partition. In the 3-phase protocol of the previous section, the operational sites assumed that the other sites were down simply because partitioning was not considered a possible failure. In fact, the 3-phase-commitment protocol is not resilient to partitions. For example, if a partition has occurred instead of a coordinator crash, both the coordinator-group and the participant-group would terminate the transaction assuming that the other sites are down, but there is no guarantee that they would terminate the transaction in the same way. Hence, *the 3-phase-commitment protocol has achieved the nonblocking property at the risk of catastrophic failures in case of partitions.*

The following propositions on the existence of independent recovery protocols and nonblocking protocols are mainly negative. They state the very limited conditions under which protocols of this type exist.

Proposition 9.1
Independent recovery protocols exist only for single-site failures; however, there exists no independent recovery protocol which is resilient to multiple-site failures.

A formal proof of this proposition can be found in reference [9.16]. In this reference, an independent recovery protocol which is resilient to single-site failures is described. This protocol is obtained by modifying the standard 2-phase-commitment protocol. The modified protocol is based on the following assumptions:

1. A site discovers that another site is down by not receiving a required message within a given timeout.
2. A message can be lost only because of a site failure.
3. Each site receives a message, changes state, and sends the required answer as an atomic transition.

These are rather optimistic assumptions, which make the negative part of proposition 9.1 even more restrictive. Therefore, we stress the negative part of proposition 9.1 and we do not present the proposed protocol. If no resilient protocol exists under these assumptions, then no protocol exists in real conditions.

Other propositions on the existence of nonblocking protocols in case of partitions are derived from the results on independent recovery in reference [9.16].

Proposition 9.2
There exists no nonblocking protocol that is resilient to a network partition if messages are lost when the partition occurs.

A message is lost if the sender does not know whether it has been delivered or not; if the message has not been delivered but the sender knows this fact, then the message is not lost and the following two propositions hold.

Proposition 9.3

There exist nonblocking protocols which are resilient to a single network partition if all undeliverable messages are returned to the sender.

Proposition 9.4

There exists no nonblocking protocol which is resilient to a multiple partition.

9.2.2.2 Protocols which can deal with partitions

The above results show that in general we cannot find protocols which are nonblocking in case of partitions. Hence alternative strategies must be chosen. It is convenient to allow the termination of the transaction by at least one group of sites, possibly the largest group, so that blocking is minimized. However, it is impossible for a group to determine whether it is the largest one, because it cannot know the sizes of the other groups, except for the case in which it comprises a majority of sites.

There are two approaches to this problem, the primary site approach and the majority approach. In the primary site approach, a site is designated as the primary site, and the group which contains it is allowed to terminate the transaction. In the majority approach, only the group which contains a majority of sites can terminate the transaction. In the latter approach, it is possible that no single group reaches a majority; in this case, all groups are blocked.

Primary site approach   If the 2-phase-commitment protocol is used together with a primary site approach, then it is possible to terminate all the transactions of the group of the primary site (the primary group), if and only if the coordinators of all pending transactions belong to this group. This can be achieved by assigning to the primary site the coordinator function for all transactions. This approach is inefficient in most types of networks; moreover, it is very vulnerable to primary site failures. A primary site failure is more likely to occur than a partition in many subnetworks, so that this approach can result in an increase of blocking, instead of a reduction of it.

If we avoid the above condition (i.e., having all coordinators at the primary site) and nevertheless we desire to terminate transactions in the primary group, then a 3-phase-commitment protocol should be used. In this case, the transaction is terminated by the sites of the primary group as if the other sites were down. In fact, the sites of a group cannot distinguish a partition from a multiple failure of the other sites. When the partition is repaired, the sites of the secondary groups have to behave exactly as if they were restarting from a crash with respect to all pending transactions. Of course, they must not have released their locks during the partition.

Majority approach and quorum-based protocols   The majority approach avoids the above disadvantages of the primary site approach. Its basic idea is that a majority of sites must agree on the abort or commit of a transaction before the transaction is aborted or committed. A majority approach requires a specialized commitment protocol; it cannot be applied with the standard 2-phase-commitment protocol.

A straightforward generalization of the basic majority approach consists of assigning different weights to the sites. The protocols which use a weighted majority are called **quorum-based protocols**. The weights which are assigned to the sites are usually called **votes**, since they are used when a site "votes" on the commit or abort of a transaction.

The basic rules of a quorum-based protocol are:

1. Each site i has associated with it a number of votes V_i, V_i being a positive integer.
2. Let V indicate the sum of the votes of all sites of the network.
3. A transaction must collect a commit quorum V_c before committing.
4. A transaction must collect an abort quorum V_a before aborting.
5. $V_a + V_c > V$.

Rule 5 ensures that a transaction is either committed or aborted; hence it implements the basic majority idea. In practice, the choice $V_a + V_c = V + 1$ is the most convenient one.

A commitment protocol which implements the above rules must guarantee that at some time a number of sites such that the sum of their votes is greater than V_c agree to commit; this means that these sites have entered a prepared-to-commit state. Therefore a quorum-based commitment protocol can be obtained from the 3-phase-commitment protocol simply by including the quorum requirement (rule 3) to the third phase, as shown in Figure 9.3a. A protocol with this structure obeys rule 3, because the transaction is committed only if a commit quorum is reached by the sites which are in the prepared-to-commit state. This protocol also obeys rule 4 without having to check explicitly for the existence of an abort quorum V_a, because all sites which are in the ready state agree to possibly abort the transaction. They participate therefore implicitly in building an abort quorum. Hence when all sites are in the ready state at the end of phase 1, an abort quorum exists. The same holds also for the uncertain state, so that unilateral aborts are allowed also by this protocol before the ready state is reached.

Termination and **restart** are more complex in this case than in the case of the nonblocking protocols of the previous section. With this protocol, restarting

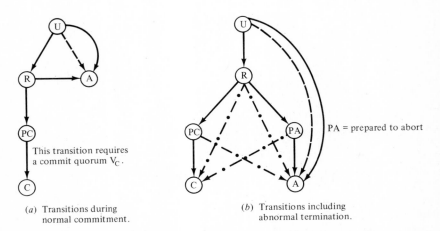

This transition requires a commit quorum V_C.

PA = prepared to abort

(*a*) Transitions during normal commitment.

(*b*) Transitions including abnormal termination.

Figure 9.3 Quorum-based 3-phase-commitment protocol.

sites must participate in the formation of quorums; otherwise, there is the risk that a quorum will never be reached. Moreover, if the site which coordinates the voting fails, there can be uncertainty on whether the quorum was reached or not. Hence it is dangerous to let sites which have voted for commit or for abort to "change their mind"; *once a site has participated in building a commit (abort) quorum, it cannot participate in an abort (commit) quorum.* Since a site can fail after having participated in building a quorum, its participation must be recorded in stable storage. Therefore a new prepared-to-abort state is introduced. A site, after having participated in building a quorum, is either in a prepared-to-commit or in a prepared-to-abort state, and it will never be allowed to change from one state to the other. However, a site which is in the prepared-to-commit (prepared-to-abort) state can abort (commit) the transaction if it turns out that the weighted majority of sites has voted differently. In conclusion: A site in the ready state has declared that it agrees to go in any direction. A site in a prepared state can still go in any direction; however, it has already expressed its unchangeable opinion. The possible state transitions of this termination protocol are shown in Figure 9.3b; the dotted transitions are performed by sites which did not participate in building the quorum.

A centralized termination protocol for the quorum-based 3-phase-commitment has the following structure:

1. A new coordinator is elected.

2. The coordinator collects state information and acts according to the following rules:

    a. If at least one site has committed (aborted), send a COMMIT (ABORT) command to the other sites.

    b. If the number of votes of sites which have reached the prepared-to-commit state is greater than or equal to V_c, send a COMMIT command.

    c. If the number of votes of sites in the prepare to abort state reaches the abort quorum, send an ABORT command.

    d. If the number of votes of sites which have reached the prepare-to-commit state plus the number of votes of uncertain sites is greater than or equal to V_c, send a PREPARE-TO-COMMIT command to uncertain sites, and wait for condition 2b to occur.

    e. If the number of votes of sites which have reached the prepare-to-abort state plus the number of votes of uncertain sites is greater than or equal to V_a, send a PREPARE-TO-ABORT command to uncertain sites, and wait for condition 2c to occur.

    f. Otherwise, wait for the repair of some failure.

9.3 RELIABILITY AND CONCURRENCY CONTROL

The problem which we consider in this section is the following: Suppose that there is a failure. How can we maximize the number of transactions which are executed during this failure by the operational part of the system?

Consider a transaction T having read-set $RS(T)$ and write-set $WS(T)$ and suppose that we want to run T alone, so that no concurrency control is needed. In order to run T it is necessary that at least one copy of each data item x belonging to $RS(T)$ be available. If this elementary necessary condition is not satisfied, T cannot be executed, because it lacks input data. The availability of the data items of the write-set of T is not strictly required if we run T alone during a failure, because a list of **deferred updates** can be produced which will be applied to the database when the failure is repaired. Deferred updates can be implemented using the "spooler" method which was presented in Chapter 7 for solving the remote recovery information problem in the 2-phase-commitment.

The availability of a system which allows only one transaction to be run during failures is not satisfactory; therefore, concurrency control must be taken in account. In fact, *the strongest limitations on the execution of transactions in the presence of failures is due to the need for concurrency control.*

9.3.1 Nonredundant Databases

If the database is nonredundant, then it is very simple to determine which transactions can be executed. Suppose that 2-phase-locking is used for concurrency control. A transaction tries to lock all data items of its read- and write-sets before commitment. As there is only one copy of each data item, this copy is either available or not. If the unique copy of some data item of the read- or write-set is not available, the transaction cannot commit and must therefore be aborted.

If we assume that only site crashes occur but no partitions, then the availability of the items which belong only to the write-set is not required, and it is possible to spool the update messages for these items. All transactions which have their read-set available execute completely, including commitment; however, the updates affecting sites which are down are stored at spooler sites. Upon recovery, the restart procedures of the failed sites will receive this list of deferred updates and execute them. In practice, we consider a crashed site as if it were exclusively locked for the transaction; in fact, no other transaction can read the values of data items which are stored there. However, in the case of partitions the deferred update rule will cause inconsistent results to be produced: the failure is catastrophic.

In conclusion, if the database is nonredundant, there is not very much to do in order to increase its availability in the presence of failures. Therefore, most reliability techniques consider the case of redundant databases.

9.3.2 Redundant Databases

The reasons why redundancy is introduced in a distributed database are twofold:

1. To increase the locality of reads, especially in those applications where the number of reads is much larger than the number of writes
2. To increase the availability and reliability of the system

We deal here essentially with the second aspect; however, in designing reliable concurrency control methods for replicated data the first goal also should be kept in mind.

In Chapter 7 we have already seen that there are three main approaches to concurrency control based on 2-phase-locking in a redundant database: write-locks-all, majority locking, and primary copy locking. Let us review the basic tradeoffs of these approaches with an example.

Example 9.2

A distributed database consists of three sites and three data items X, Y, and Z, which are duplicated and stored as shown in Figure 9.4a. All possible ways in which the network can be partitioned are shown in Figure 9.4b. There are three simple partitions and one double partition. In Figure 9.4c, the read- and write-sets of several transactions are shown. These transactions do not contain all possible combinations of read- and write-sets, but a significant subset of them. The first nine transactions are update transactions, and the last three are read-only transactions. We will now analyze the availability of the system for these 12 transactions in the four partition cases if each one of the three approaches to concurrency control is used.

Sites

		1	2	3
	X	x_1	x_2	
Data items	Y	y_1		y_3
	Z		z_2	z_3

(a) Allocation of copies of data items at sites

	Group 1	Group 2	Group 3
A)	1	2,3	–
B)	2	1,3	–
C)	3	1,2	–
D)	1	2	3

(b) Possible Partitions

Trans.	Read Set	Write Set
1	xyz	xyz
2	xy	xyz
3	x	xyz
4	xyz	xy
5	xy	xy
6	x	xy
7	xyz	x
8	xy	x
9	x	x
10	xyz	–
11	xy	–
12	x	–

(c) Read- and Write-Sets of Transactions

Figure 9.4 Data for Example 9.2.

9.3.2.1 Write-locks-all Figure 9.5a shows, for each transaction and for each type of partition, the group, if any, in which the transaction can be executed. The read-only transactions 10′, 11′, and 12′ are the same as 10, 11, and 12, except that consistency is not required for them; hence, no locks are used. The values of Figure 9.5a confirm the intuition: For transactions with a small write-set and especially for read-only transactions, the system is much more available than for transactions with a large write-set. For read-only transactions it makes no difference whether consistency is required or not, because the copy which is locked is required anyway for reading. Note that read-only transactions sometimes can run in more than one group, because if a data item has two copies in two different groups, then no update transaction can write on it and read-only transactions can use each copy consistently.

If we make the assumption that no partitions occur, but only site crashes, then the same approach can be used as with a nonredundant database; i.e., the updates of nonavailable copies of data items can be spooled. In this case, the availability of the database for update transactions increases very much. In fact, since only the read-set matters in this case, transactions 1, 4, and 7 have the same availability as transaction 10; transactions 2, 5, and 8 as transaction 11; and transactions 3, 6, and 9 as transaction 12. Obviously, the example must be carefully interpreted. The fact that a transaction can run in a given group means now that it can be run if all other sites are down, instead of building separate groups. The high increase in availability is obtained at the risk of catastrophic partitions.

Let us now consider the locality aspect, which is the other motivation for redundancy. For this purpose we distinguish between the transmission cost of control messages and the transmission cost of data. Requests to lock or unlock a data item and the messages of the 2-phase-commitment protocol are required for

		Transactions													
		1	2	3	4	5	6	7	8	9	10	11	12	10′	11′	12′
Partitions	A	-	-	-	-	-	-	-	-	-	2	(1,2)	(1,2)	2	(1,2)	(1,2)
	B	-	-	-	-	-	-	-	-	-	2	2	(1,2)	2	2	(1,2)
	C	-	-	-	-	-	-	2	2	2	2	2	2	2	2	2
	D	-	-	-	-	-	-	-	-	-	-	1	(1,2)	-	1	(1,2)

(a) Write-locks-all, read-locks-one

		Transactions													
		1	2	3	4	5	6	7	8	9	10	11	12	10′	11′	12′
Partitions	A	-	-	-	-	1	1	-	1	1	-	1	1	2	(1,2)	(1,2)
	B	-	-	-	-	2	2	-	2	2	-	2	2	2	2	(1,2)
	C	2	2	2	2	2	2	2	2	2	2	2	2	2	2	2
	D	-	-	-	-	1	1	-	1	1	-	1	1	-	1	(1,2)

(b) Weighted majority, with
$V(x_1) = V(y_1) = V(z_2) = 2$ and
$V(x_2) = V(y_3) = V(z_3) = 1$

Figure 9.5 Availability of transactions of Example 9.2.

the control of transactions. Control messages carry control information and are short. Data messages contain database information and can be long.

As already stated in Chapter 4, when evaluating the opportunity of adding an additional copy of a data item at a site i, the designer has to evaluate the benefit which is obtained by transactions which can read the item locally and the additional cost for updating this copy by all other transactions. With the write-locks-all approach, we have:

1. *Benefit.* For each transaction executed at site i having x in its read-set, one lock message and one data message are saved.
2. *Cost.* For each transaction which is not executed at site i and has x in its write-set, one lock message and one data message are required, plus the messages required by the commitment protocol.

In Chapter 4, we have made essentially the same assumptions, however, without considering the control messages. In fact, it depends on the relative size of the data versus control messages whether control messages are important or not.

9.3.2.2 Weighted majority locking The pure majority locking approach is not very suitable for our example, because two copies of each data item exist; hence to lock a majority we must lock both. We will therefore consider a weighted majority approach, or quorum approach, which adopts the same rules which have been used for quorum-based commitment and termination protocols.

These rules, applied to the locking problem, consist of assigning to each data item x a total number of votes $V(x)$, and assigning votes $V(x_i)$ to each copy x_i in such a way that $V(x)$ is the sum of all $V(x_i)$. A read quorum $V_r(x)$ and a write quorum $V_w(x)$ are then determined, such that:

$$V_r(x) + V_w(x) > V(x)$$
$$V_w(x) > V(x)/2$$

A transaction can read (write) x if it obtains read (write) locks on so many copies of x that the sum of their votes is greater than or equal to $V_r(x)(V_w(x))$. Due to the first condition, all conflicts between read and write operations are determined, because two transactions which perform a read and a write operation on x cannot reach the read and write quorum using two disjoint subsets of copies. Likewise, because of the second condition, all conflicts between write operations are determined. Notice that the second condition can be omitted if transactions read all data items which are written.

Let us assign votes for the copies of data items of Example 9.2 in the following way:

$$V(x) = V(y) = V(z) = 3$$
$$V(x1) = V(y1) = V(z2) = 2$$
$$V(x2) = V(y3) = V(z3) = 1$$

With this assignment we can now consider the availability of the system in the case of partitions. We choose the read and write quorums to be 2 for all data items. The availability for the 12 transactions is shown in Figure 9.5b. The following can be observed:

1. Transactions 1, 2, 3, 4, 7, and 10 have all the same availability. They are characterized by the fact that they access all three data items either for reading or for writing or for both. Since the read quorum is equal to the write quorum, it makes no difference whether the data item is read or written from the viewpoint of availability. For the same reason, transactions 5, 6, 8, and 11, which access only data items x and y, have the same availability. Also, transactions 9 and 12 have the same availability of the latter group, because the copy with highest weight for data item x resides at the same site as the copy with highest weight for y.

2. The availability for update transactions is greater with the weighted majority approach than with write-locks-all, while the availability for read-only transactions is smaller.

3. With this method, read-only transactions increase their availability if they can read an inconsistent database, i.e., if they do not need to lock items; in fact, columns 10′, 11′, and 12′ are the same for the majority approach as for the write-locks-all approach.

With the majority approach it is not reasonable to consider the assumption that partitions do not occur. Notice that if we assume the absence of partitions, then the majority approach is dominated by the write-locks-all approach (an approach is dominated by another one if it is worse under all circumstances). In fact, we have seen that the majority and quorum ideas have been developed essentially for dealing with partitions.

Consider now the locality aspect. A transaction reads a data item x at its site of origin, if a copy is locally available. Hence, also in this case a data message is saved if a local copy is available. However, read locks must be obtained at a number of copies corresponding to the read quorum. Therefore, the addition of a copy of x can also force transactions which read x to request more read locks at remote sites. This additional cost depends on the number of copies and on the distribution of votes. The same additional cost is incurred by transactions which have x in their write-set, which must obtain write locks at a number of sites corresponding to the write quorum. Moreover, they have to send a data message to all the sites where there are copies of x.

It is clear that, considering only data messages, the same advantages and disadvantages exist for the majority and the write-locks-all method. When control messages are also considered, then the situation is more complex; however, some of the locality motivations for read-only transactions are lost.

9.3.2.3 Primary copy locking   In the primary copy locking approach, all locks for a data item x are requested at the site of the primary copy. We will assume first that also all the read and write operations are performed on this copy; however, writes are then propagated to all other copies. Considering the database of Example 9.2, if we choose $x1$, $y1$, and $z2$ as primary copies, then the availability of the database for the 12 transactions is the same as in the majority approach (Figure 9.5b), because the assignment of votes which we had applied determined a primary copy situation. This will always happen if we apply weighted voting to items having only two copies. However, this is a particular case; if many copies exist, so that different majorities can be built, then the two approaches are different. The weighted majority mechanism is more general and can simulate the primary copy approach by a particular assignment of votes.

Several enhancements of the primary copy approach exist which make it more attractive. The principal ones are:

1. Allowing consistent reads at different copies than the primary, even if read locks are requested only at the primary; this enhances the locality of reads.
2. Allowing the migration of the primary copy if a site crash makes it unavailable; this enhances availability.
3. Allowing the migration of the primary copy depending on its usage pattern. This also enhances the locality aspect.

The first point deserves a comment. In order to obtain consistent reads at different copies from the primary one, we should use the primary copy method for synchronization, but perform the write and read operations according to the "write all/read one" method. In this approach, the locks are all requested at the primary copy; however, at commitment all copies are updated before releasing the write lock. A read can be performed in this way at any copy, obtaining consistent data.

This method is very similar to write-locks-all, except that it spends less control messages for write locks but in general more messages for read locks, since a read lock must be requested at the primary copy and not at the local copy. The availability of this method is inferior to the write-locks-all method, since for each data item of the write-set all copies must be available, and for each item of the read-set the primary copy must be available.

9.4 DETERMINING A CONSISTENT VIEW OF THE NETWORK

There are two aspects of this problem: monitoring the state of the network, so that state transitions of a site are discovered as soon as possible, and propagating a new state information to all sites consistently. In previous sections we have used timeouts in the algorithms in order to discover if a site was down. The use of timeouts, however, can lead to an inconsistent view of the network. Consider the following example in a 3-site network: Site 1 sends a message to site 2 requesting an answer; if no answer arrives before a given timeout, site 1 assumes that site 2 is down. If site 2 was just slow, then site 1 has a wrong view of the state of site 2, which is inconsistent with the view of site 2 about itself. Moreover, a third site 3 could try the same operation at the same time as site 1, obtain an answer within the timeout, and assume that site 2 is up, thus having a different view than site 1.

In this section, we assume that a generalized networkwide mechanism is built such that all higher-level programs are provided with the following facilities:

1. There is at each site a **state table** containing an entry for each site. The entry can be **up** or **down**. A program can send an inquiry to the state table for state information.

2.   Any program can set a "watch" on any site, so that it receives an interrupt when the site changes state.

The meaning of the state table and of a consistent view in the presence of partition failures is defined as follows: A site considers up only those sites with which it can communicate; therefore all crashed sites and all sites which belong to a different group in case of partitions are considered down. A consistent view can be achieved only between sites of the same group; thus in case of a partition there are as many consistent views as there are isolated groups of sites. The consistency requirement is therefore that a site has the same state table as all other sites which are up in its state table.

We will now consider separately the problem of monitoring and propagating state information. The approach which is described here follows the algorithm of reference [9.12].

9.4.1 Monitoring the State of the Network

We have seen that the basic mechanism for deciding whether a site is up or down is to request a message from it and to wait for a timeout. Let us call the requesting site the **controller** and the other site the **controlled** site. In a generalized monitoring algorithm, instead of having the controller request messages from the controlled site, it is more convenient to have the controlled site send I-AM-UP messages periodically to the controller. This avoids one message at the expense of having timers in both the controller and the controlled site.

Note that if only site crashes are considered, the monitoring function essentially has to detect transitions from up to down states, because the opposite transition is detected by the site which performs recovery and restart; this site will inform all the others. If, however, partitions also are considered, then the monitoring function has also to determine transitions from down to up states: when a partition is repaired, sites of one group must detect that sites of the other group become available.

Using this basic mechanism for detecting whether a site is up or down, the problem consists of assigning controllers to each site so that the overall message overhead is minimized and the algorithm survives correctly the failure of a controller. The latter requirement is of extreme importance, since in a distributed approach each site is controlled and at the same time performs the function of controller of some other site.

A possible solution is to assign circular ordering to the sites and to assign to each site the function of controller of its predecessor. In the absence of failures, each site periodically sends an I-AM-UP message to its successor and controls that the I-AM-UP message from its predecessor arrives in time. If the I-AM-UP message from the predecessor does not arrive in time, then the controller assumes that the controlled site has failed, updates the state table and broadcasts the updated state table to all other sites (see the next section).

If the predecessor of a site is down, then the site also has to control its predecessor, and if this one is also down, the predecessor of the predecessor, and so on backward in the ordering until an up site is found (if none is found, then the site is isolated or all other sites have crashed; this does not invalidate the algorithm). In this way, each operational site always has a controller. For example, in Figure 9.6 site k controls site $k-3$; i.e., it checks the arrival of I-AM-UP messages from site $k-3$. Moreover, site k is responsible for discovering that sites $k-1$ and $k-2$ recover from down to up. Symmetrically, if the successor of a site is down, then this site has as a controller the first operational site following it in the ordering. For example, site $k-3$ has site k as controller. Note that in Figure 9.6 sites $k-1$ and $k-2$ are not necessarily crashed; they could belong to a different group after a partition. Figure 9.6 reflects, therefore, the view of the network of sites k and $k-3$, not necessarily the "real" state.

Figure 9.6   State of sites.

9.4.2 Broadcasting a New State

Each time that the monitor function detects a state change, this function is activated. The purpose of this function is to broadcast the new state table so that all sites of the same group have the same state table. Since this function could be activated by several sites in parallel, some mechanism is needed to control interference. A possible mechanism is to attach a globally unique timestamp to each new version of a state table. By including the version number of the current state table in the I-AM-UP messages all sites in the same group can check that they have a consistent view.

The site which starts the propagation of a new state table first performs a synchronization step in order to obtain a timestamp and then sends the state table to all sites which have answered.

9.5 DETECTION AND RESOLUTION OF INCONSISTENCY

When a partition of the network occurs, transactions should be run at most in one group of sites if we want to preserve strictly the consistency of the database. Sections 9.2 and 9.3 have dealt with partitions under this requirement of absolute correctness. However, in some applications it is acceptable to lose consistency in order to achieve more availability. In these cases, transactions are allowed to run in all partitions where there is at least one copy of the necessary data. Later, when the failure is repaired, one can try to eliminate the inconsistencies which have been introduced into the database. For this purpose it is necessary first to discover which portions of the data have become inconsistent, and then to assign to these portions a value which is the most *reasonable* in consideration of what has happened. The first problem is called the **detection** of inconsistencies; the second is called the **resolution** of inconsistencies. While exact solutions can be found for the detection problem, the resolution problem has no general solution, because transactions have been executed in the different groups of sites during the partition in a nonglobally serializable way. Therefore the word "reasonable" and not the word "correct" is used for the value which is assigned by the resolution procedure.

9.5.1 Detection of Inconsistencies

Let us assume that, during a partition, transactions have been executed in two or more groups of sites, and that independent updates may have been performed on different copies of the same fragment. Let us first observe that the most naive solution, consisting of comparing the contents of the copies to check that they are identical, is not only inefficient, but also not correct in general. For example, consider an airline reservation system. If, during the partition, we allow taking reservations for the same flight independently on different copies until the maximum number is reached, then all copies might have the same value for the number of reservations; however, the flight would be overbooked in this case.

A correct approach to the detection of inconsistencies can be based on version numbers. Assume that one of the approaches of Section 9.3 is used for determining, for each data item, the one group of sites which is allowed to operate on it. The copies of the data item which are stored at the sites of this group are called **master** copies; the others are called **isolated** copies.

During normal operation all copies are master copies and are mutually consistent. For each copy an **original version number** and a **current version number** are maintained. Initially the original version number is set to 0, and the current version number is set to 1; only the current version number is incremented each time that an update is performed on the copy. When a partition occurs, the original version number of each isolated copy is set to the value of its current version number. In this way, the original version number records the current version number of the isolated copies before any "partitioned updates" are performed on it. The original version number is not altered until the partition is repaired. At this time, the comparison of the current and original version numbers of all copies reveals inconsistencies.

Let us consider an example of this method. Assume that copies $x1$, $x2$, and $x3$ of data item x are stored at three different sites. Let $V1$, $V2$, and $V3$ be the version numbers of $x1$, $x2$, and $x3$. Each Vi is in fact a pair with the original and current version number. Initially all three copies are consistently updated. Suppose that one update has been performed, so that the situation is

$$V1 = (0, 2), \quad V2 = (0, 2), \quad V3 = (0, 2)$$

Now a partition occurs separating $x3$ from the other two copies. A majority algorithm is used which chooses $x1$ and $x2$ as master copies. The version numbers become now

$$V1 = (0, 2), \quad V2 = (0, 2), \quad V3 = (2, 2)$$

Suppose now that only the master copies are updated during the partition. The version numbers become

$$V1 = (0, 3), \quad V2 = (0, 3), \quad V3 = (2, 2)$$

and after the repair it is possible to see that $x3$ has not been modified, since its current and original version numbers are equal. In this case, no inconsistency has occurred, and it is sufficient to perform the updates on $x3$.

Suppose now that only $x3$ is updated during the partition. We have

$$V1 = (0, 2), \quad V2 = (0, 2), \quad V3 = (2, 3)$$

Since the original version number of $x3$ is equal to the current version numbers of $x1$ and $x2$, the master copies have not been updated. If there are no other copies, then we can simply apply to the master copies the updates of $x3$, since the situation is exactly symmetrical to the previous one. If there are other isolated copies, for example $x4$ with $V4 = (2, 3)$, we cannot tell whether $x4$ was updated consistently with $x3$ even if version numbers are the same; hence we have to assume inconsistency.

Finally, if both the master and the isolated copies have been updated, which also reveals an inconsistency, then the original and the current version number of the isolated copy are different, and the original version number of the isolated copy is also different from the current version number of the master copies; for example:

$$V1 = (0, 3), \quad V2 = (0, 3), \quad V3 = (2, 3)$$

9.5.2 Resolution of Inconsistencies

After a partition has been repaired and an inconsistency has been detected, a common value must be assigned to all copies of a same data item. The problem of resolution of inconsistency is the determination of this value.

Since in the different groups transactions have been executed without mutual synchronization, it seems correct to assign as a common value the one which would be produced by some serializable execution of these same transactions. However, besides the difficulty of obtaining this new value, this is not a satisfactory solution, because the transactions which have been executed have produced effects outside of the system which cannot be undone and cannot be simply ignored.

Note that the transactions requiring the high degree of availability which motivates the acceptance of inconsistencies are exactly those which perform effects outside of the system. For example, take the airline reservation example considered before. The reason for running transactions while the system is partitioned is to tell the customers that flights are available; otherwise, it would be simpler to collect the customers' requests and to apply them to the database after the failure has been repaired.

However, if overbooking has occurred during the partition, then forcing the system to a serializable execution would force the system to perform arbitrary cancellations. From the viewpoint of the application, it might be better to keep the overbookings and let normal user cancellations reduce the number of reservations. A possible way of reducing or eliminating overbooking due to partitions is to assign to each site a number of reservations which is smaller than the total number. This number could be proportional to the size of each group or to some other application-dependent value.

The above example shows that the resolution of inconsistencies is, in general, application-dependent, and hence not within the scope of this book, which deals with generalized mechanisms. Reference [9.36] proposes some general principles for designing databases and transactions so that reasonable resolution strategies can be applied.

9.6 CHECKPOINTS AND COLD RESTART

Cold restart is required after some catastrophic failure which has caused the loss of log information on stable storage, so that the current consistent state of the database cannot be reconstructed and a previous consistent state must be restored. A previous consistent state is marked by a checkpoint.

In a distributed database, the problem of cold restart is worse than in a centralized one; this is because if one site has to establish an earlier state, then all other sites also have to establish earlier states which are consistent with the one of that site, so that the global state of the distributed database as a whole is consistent. This means that the recovery process is intrinsically global, affecting all sites of the database, although the failure which caused the cold restart is typically local.

A consistent global state C is characterized by the following two properties:

1. For each transaction T, C contains the updates performed by all subtransactions of T at any site, or it does not contain any of them; in the former case we say that T is contained in C.
2. If a transaction T is contained in C, then all conflicting transactions which have preceded T in the serialization order are also contained in C.

Property 1 is related to the atomicity of transactions: either all effects of T or none of them can appear in a consistent state. Property 2 is related to the serializability of transactions: if a conflicting transaction T' has preceded T, then the updates performed by T' have affected the execution of T; hence, if we keep the effects of T, we must keep also all the effects of T'. Note that durability of transactions cannot be ensured if we are forced to a cold restart; the effect of some transactions is lost.

The simplest way to reconstruct a global consistent state in a distributed database is to use local dumps, local logs, and **global checkpoints**. A global checkpoint is a set of local checkpoints which are performed at all sites of the network and are synchronized by the following condition: if a subtransaction of a transaction T is contained in the local checkpoint at some site, then all other

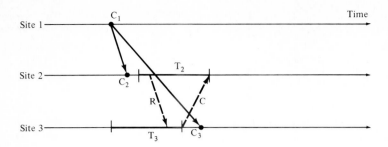

T_2 and T_3 are subtransactions of transaction T; T_3 is coordinator for 2-phase-commitment. C_1, C_2, C_3 are local checkpoints (started from site 1).

→ "Write checkpoint" messages.

⇢ Messages of 2-phase-commitment protocol (R = READY, C = COMMIT).

Figure 9.7 Synchronization problem for global checkpoints.

subtransactions of T must be contained in the corresponding local checkpoints at other sites.

If global checkpoints are available, then the reconstruction problem is relatively easy. First, at the failed site the latest local checkpoint which can be considered safe is determined; this determines which earlier global state has to be reconstructed. Then all other sites are requested to reestablish the local states of the corresponding local checkpoints.

The main problem with the above approach consists in recording global checkpoints. It is not sufficient for one site to broadcast a "write checkpoint" message to all other sites, because it is possible that the situation of Figure 9.7 arises; in this situation, T_2 and T_3 are subtransactions of the same transaction T, and the local checkpoint C_2 does not contain subtransaction T_2, while the local checkpoint C_3 contains subtransaction T_3, thus violating the basic requirement for global checkpoints. Figure 9.7 shows also that the fact that T performs a 2-phase-commitment does not eliminate this problem, because the synchronization of subtransactions during 2-phase-commitment and of sites during recording of the global checkpoint are independent.

The simplest way to avoid the above problem is to require that all sites become inactive *before* each one records its local checkpoint. Note that all sites must remain inactive simultaneously, and therefore coordination is required. A protocol which is very similar to 2-phase-commitment can be used for this purpose: a coordinator broadcasts "prepare for checkpoint" to all sites, each site terminates the execution of subtransactions and then answers READY, and then the coordinator broadcasts "perform checkpoint." This type of method is unacceptable in practice because of the inactivity which is required at all sites. A site has to remain inactive not only for the time required to record its checkpoints, but until all other sites have finished their active transactions. Three more efficient solutions are possible:

1. To find less expensive ways to record global checkpoints, so called **loosely synchronized checkpoints**. All sites are asked by a coordinator to record

a global checkpoint; however, they are free to perform it within a large time interval. The responsibility of guaranteeing that all subtransactions of the same transaction are contained in the local checkpoints corresponding to the same global checkpoint is left to transaction management. If the root agent of transaction T starts after checkpoint C_i and before checkpoint C_{i+1}, then each other subtransaction at a different site can be started only after C_i has been recorded at its site and before C_{i+1} has been recorded. Observing the first condition may force a subtransaction to wait; observing the second condition can cause transaction aborts and restarts. These are the main disadvantages of this method, described in reference [9.38].

2. To avoid building global checkpoints at all, let the recovery procedure take the responsibility of reconstructing a consistent global state at cold restart. With this approach, the notion of global checkpoint is abandoned. Each site records its local checkpoints independently from other sites, and the whole effort of building a consistent global state is therefore performed by the cold restart procedure. This method is described in reference [9.39].

3. To use the 2-phase-commitment protocol for guaranteeing that the local checkpoints created by each site are ordered in a globally uniform way. The basic idea is to modify the 2-phase-commitment protocol so that the checkpoints of all subtransactions which belong to two distributed transactions T and T' are recorded in the same order at all sites where both transactions are executed. Let T_i and T_j be subtransactions of T, and let T'_i and T'_j be subtransactions of T'. If at site i the checkpoint of subtransaction T_i precedes the checkpoint of subtransaction T'_i, then at a different site j the checkpoint of subtransaction T_j should precede the checkpoint of subtransaction T'_j. This method is described in reference [9.37].

CONCLUSIONS

Several problems must be considered in the design of a reliable distributed database. The basic 2-phase-commitment protocol assures that transactions are correctly committed or aborted at all sites even in presence of failures. However, in some cases transactions are blocked until the failure is repaired, thus blocking resources and reducing the system's availability. The 3-phase-commitment protocol can be used to eliminate this inconvenience. This protocol allows terminating transactions in case of site failures, but is not correct with network partitions. No termination protocol exists which allows terminating transactions at all sites after a network partition.

After a network partition it is not possible to process transactions at all sites, because no concurrency control method exists which is capable of ensuring transactions' serializability in this case. Therefore, if transactions are processed at all sites in a partitioned database, it is possible that inconsistencies arise. Inconsistencies can be detected after the repair of the failure, although their resolution is a difficult problem, without a general, application-independent solution. With network partitions, however, it is possible to process transactions within partitions which include a majority of copies or the primary copy of all required data items.

Cold restart is a very hard problem in distributed databases. Therefore, it should be made very uncommon by storing the local logs on stable storage. Several techniques have been proposed for performing cold restart in a distributed database, although all of them produce a high overhead for the system.

EXERCISES

9.1   Consider a system which uses 3-phase-commitment. Define the log records which are required by the local recovery managers in this case, using the same approach of Exercise 7.1.

9.2   Rewrite the FUND_TRANSFER application of Example 7.2 using the 3-phase-commitment protocol. Use the log records defined in Exercise 9.1 and the primitives of Exercise 7.2 for locking and communication.

9.3   Write the local recovery procedure for 3-phase-commitment.

9.4   Write the termination algorithm for 3-phase-commitment assuming that the coordinator site has failed, that no network partition has occurred, and that the operational sites have a consistent view of the network.

9.5   Consider a data item x which is replicated at all sites of a 4-site network. Assign votes in three different ways to the sites and assign in each case a commit and an abort quorum. For each possible network partition and each one of the three vote assignments, build a table showing in which group of sites a transaction which reads and writes x can be terminated and whether the transaction is aborted or committed.

9.6   Consider the transactions and the distributed database of Example 9.2 in Section 9.3.2 and in Figure 9.4. Determine the "availability tables" of the same kind as those of Figure 9.5 for the following modified replications of data items:

(a)   The database is fully replicated (there is a copy of each data item at each site).

(b)   Copies y_3 and z_3 are eliminated with respect to the allocation of Figure 9.5a.

(c)   Copy x_1 is eliminated with respect to the allocation of Figure 9.5a.

Determine the availability tables for all the three approaches of Section 9.3.2: write-locks-all, majority locking, and primary copy locking.

Annotated Bibliography

References [9.1] to [9.9] deal with the foundations of the reliability problem in distributed systems in general and in distributed databases in particular. Other references of this kind have been given in Chapter 7 and are not repeated here. References [9.10] to [9.14] present the integrated solutions for the reliability problem which have been applied by some systems and which have been partially considered in this chapter. Other references of this kind will be found in Part II. References [9.15] to [9.19] deal with the reliability of commitment protocols. References [9.20] to [9.28] deal with the reliability of concurrency control methods. References [9.29] to [9.33] deal with commission error problems. References [9.34] to [9.36] deal with the detection and resolution of inconsistencies. References [9.37] to [9.39] deal with distributed checkpoints and cold restarts.

[9.1]   B. Randell, P. A. Lee, and P. C. Treleaven, "Reliability Issues in Computing Systems Design," *ACM-Computing Surveys*, **10**:2, 1978.

[9.2]   H. Garcia-Molina, "Reliability Issues for Fully Replicated Distributed Databases," *IEEE Computer*, September 1982.

[9.3]   H. Garcia-Molina and D. Barbara, "How to Assign Votes in a Distributed System," EECS Report 311, Princeton University, 1983.

[9.4]   L. Svobodova, "Reliability Issues in Distributed Information Processing Systems," *Ninth Symp. on Fault Tolerant Computing*, Madison, WI, 1979.

[9.5]   P. A. Alsberg and J. D. Day, "Principle for Resilient Sharing of Distributed Resources," *Second International Conf. on Software Engineering*, San Francisco, CA, 1976.

[9.6]   L. Lamport, "The Implementation of Reliable Distributed Multiprocessor Systems," *Computer Networks*, **2**, 1978.

[9.7]   H. Garcia-Molina, "Elections in Distributed Computing Systems," *IEEE-TC*, **C-31**:1, 1982.

[9.8]   B. Lampson and H. Sturgis, "Crash Recovery in a Distributed Data Storage System," Tech. Report, Xerox Palo Alto Res. Center, Palo Alto, 1979.

[9.9]   B. G. Lindsay, "Single and Multisite Recovery Facilities," in *Distributed Databases*, Draffan and Poole, eds., Cambridge University Press, 1980.

[9.10]   M. Hammer and D. Shipman, "Reliability Mechanism for SDD-1," *ACM-TODS*, **5**:4, 1980.

This paper was one of the first to present an integrated solution to all the reliability problems of a distributed database system. It deals with several problems which have been discussed in this chapter. Several mechanisms are defined to provide a very reliable network. The main disadvantage of this system is that it is not resilient to network partitions, since it is designed for operating on the ARPA network, where partitions should be very rare. See also the chapter on SDD-1 in Part II of this book.

[9.11]   M. Stonebraker, "Concurrency Control and Consistency of Multiple Copies of Data in Distributed INGRES," *IEEE-TSE*, **SE-5**:3, 1979.

This paper describes the concurrency control and reliability mechanisms of Distributed INGRES. The basic approach is a "primary copy" method.

[9.12]   B. Walter, "A Robust and Efficient Protocol for Checking the Availability of Remote Sites," *Sixth Int. Workshop on Distributed Data Management and Computer Networks*, 1982.

[9.13]   B. Walter, "Strategies for Handling Transactions in Distributed Database Systems During Recovery," *Sixth VLDB*, 1980.

[9.14]   B. Walter, "Global Recovery in a Distributed Database System," *Second Int. Symp. on Distributed Data Sharing Systems*, North-Holland, 1982.

Papers [9.12] to [9.14] describe transaction management in the distributed database system POREL. The method for obtaining a consistent view of the network described in Section 9.4 is based on the reliability algorithms of POREL. The detailed description of the protocol for obtaining a consistent view of the network in POREL is given in reference [9.12].

[9.15]   D. Skeen, "Non-blocking Commit Protocols," *ACM-SIGMOD*, 1981.

See Section 9.2.1.

[9.16]   D. Skeen and M. Stonebraker, "A Formal Model of Crash Recovery in a Distributed System," *Fifth Int. Workshop on Distributed Data Management and Computer Networks*, 1981.

[9.17]   D. Skeen, "A Quorum-based Commit Protocol," *Sixth Int. Workshop on Distributed Data Management and Computer Networks*, 1982.

Section 9.2.2 is based on these two papers.

[9.18]   E. C. Cooper, "Analysis of Distributed Commit Protocols," *ACM-SIGMOD*, 1982.

[9.19]   C. Mohan and B. G. Lindsay, "Efficient Commit Protocols for the Tree of Processes Model of Distributed Transactions," *Proc. 2nd ACM SIGACT-SIGOPS Symposium on Principles of Distributed Computing*, Montreal, 1983.

[9.20]   C. A. Ellis, "A Robust Algorithm for Updating Duplicate Databases," *Second Int. Workshop on Distributed Data Management and Computer Networks*, 1977.

[9.21]   D. Gifford, "Weighted Voting for Replicated Data," *Operating System Review*, **13**:5, 1979.

Section 9.3.2.2 is based on this paper.

[9.22]   D. L. Eager and K. C. Sevcik, "Achieving Robustness in Distributed Database Systems," *ACM-TODS*, **8**:3, 1983.

[9.23]   D. A. Menasce, G. J. Popek, and R. R. Muntz, "A Locking Protocol for Resource Coordination in Distributed Databases," *ACM-TODS*, **5**:2, 1980.

[9.24]   T. Minoura and G. Wiederhold, "Resilient Extended True-copy Token Scheme for a Distributed Database System," *IEEE-TSE*, **SE-8**:3, 1982.

[9.25]   T. Minoura, "A New Concurrency Control Algorithm for Distributed Database Systems," *Fourth Int. Workshop on Distributed Data Management and Computer Networks*, 1979.

[9.26]   G. Gardarin and W. W. Chu, "A Reliable Distributed Control Algorithm for Updating Replicated Data," *Proc. Sixth Data Communication Symposium*, IEEE, 1979.

[9.27]   H. Garcia-Molina, "A Concurrency Control Mechanism for Distributed Databases which Uses Centralized Locking Controllers," *Fourth Int. Workshop on Distributed Data Management and Computer Networks,* 1979.

[9.28]   R. H. Thomas, "A Majority Consensus Approach to Concurrency Control for Multiple Copy Databases," *ACM-TODS,* **4**:2, 1979.

[9.29]   H. R. Strong and D. Dolev, "Byzantine Agreement," *Proc. IEEE Compcon,* 1983.

[9.30]   M. Pease, R. Shostak, and L. Lamport, "Reaching Agreement in the Presence of Faults," *Journal of the ACM,* **27**:2, 1980.

Reference [9.29] surveys the literature and summarizes existing results on byzantine agreement. The problem of byzantine agreement was introduced formally in reference [9.30].

[9.31]   C. Mohan, H. R. Strong, and S. Finkelstein, "Method for Distributed Transaction Commit and Recovery Using Byzantine Agreement with Clusters of Processors," *Proc. 2nd ACM SIGACT-SIGOPS Symposium on Principles of Distributed Computing,* Montreal, 1983.

[9.32]   H. Aghili et al., "A Highly Available Database System," *Proc. IEEE Compcon,* 1983.

[9.33]   W. Kim, "AUDITOR: A Framework for High Availability of DB/DC Systems," IBM Res. Rep. RJ3512, 1982.

References [9.31] to [9.33] deal with several aspects of the Highly Available System project, developed at the IBM Research Center of San Jose. This project consists in the design of a very reliable DB/DC system. Reference [9.31] describes the application of byzantine agreement to the 2-phase-commitment protocol. Reference [9.33] describes the fundamental AUDITOR subsystem, which has to keep the whole distributed system under control and to detect failures.

[9.34]   D. S. Parker et al., "Detection of Mutual Inconsistency in Distributed Systems," *IEEE-TSE,* **SE-9**:3, 1983.

[9.35]   P. Brereton, "Detection and Resolution of Inconsistencies among Distributed Replications of Files," *Operating Systems Review,* 1983.

[9.36]   H. Garcia-Molina et al., "Data Patch: Integrating Inconsistent Copies of a Database after a Partition," EECS Report 304, Princeton University, 1983.

The method for the detection of inconsistencies described in Section 9.5 is based on the algorithm proposed in [9.35]. A more complex method, which requires whole histories to be maintained instead of a single version number, is presented in reference [9.34]. Reference [9.36] deals with the resolution of inconsistencies. It defines principles for the design of transactions and databases which should be followed in order to make the resolution problem easier and presents a tool for aiding in the resolution problem.

[9.37]   H. Kuss, "On Totally Ordering Checkpoints in Distributed Databases," *ACM-SIGMOD,* 1982.

[9.38]   P. Dadam and G. Schlageter, "Recovery in Distributed Databases Based on Non-synchronized Local Checkpoints," *Information Processing 80*, North-Holland, 1980.

[9.39]   G. Schlageter and P. Dadam, "Reconstruction of Consistent Global States in Distributed Databases," *Proc. Int. Symp. on Distributed Databases*, North-Holland, 1980.

Reference [9.38] presents the loosely synchronized approach to global checkpoints, reference [9.39] the reconstruction without global checkpoints, and reference [9.37] the use of transaction commit for synchronizing transaction checkpoints.

Chapter 10

Distributed Database Administration

Database administration typically refers to a variety of activities for the development, control, maintenance, and testing of the software of the database application. Database administration is not only a technical problem, since it involves the statement of policies under which users can access the database, which is clearly also an organization problem.

In this chapter, we concentrate on the technical aspects of database administration in a distributed environment. We focus on the following problems:

1. The content and management of the **catalogs**; with this name, we designate the information which is required by the system for accessing the database. In distributed systems, catalogs include the description of fragmentation and allocation of data and the mapping to local names; catalogs themselves become a distributed database, which must be distributed and managed efficiently.

2. The extension of **protection** and **authorization** mechanisms to distributed systems; we briefly describe the problems which arise in a distributed environment compared with those which arise in a centralized one.

This chapter does not deal with decentralized authorization; i.e., the possibility of one user granting to a different user the access rights which he or she owns on a database object. This problem is not typical of a distributed environment, since decentralization of authorization can also occur in a centralized system. Decentralized authorization is described in references [10.14] to [10.16].

The most important issue in database administration is the degree of **site autonomy** given to each site. There are two extreme solutions, the absence of any local autonomy and complete local autonomy.

In the first case, the functions of a global database administrator are not different from those of the administrator of a centralized database; however, performing these functions is much harder due to the distribution of the system. A system with no local autonomy can differ very much in the "degree of distribution" of the algorithms which implement the administration functions.

In the second case, the functions of a global database administrator are very limited, since every site is independently administrated. Sharing of data betweeen two sites is the result of an agreement between them; two sites are "introduced" to each other, and then decide, on an autonomous basis, which portion of data of one site will be available to the other site, and which rules will be followed by remote users.

10.1 CATALOG MANAGEMENT IN DISTRIBUTED DATABASES

Catalogs of distributed databases store all the information which is useful to the system for accessing data correctly and efficiently and for verifying that users have the appropriate access rights to them. Catalogs are used for:

1. *Translating applications.* Data referenced by applications at different levels of transparency are mapped to physical data (physical images in our reference architecture).
2. *Optimizing applications.* Data allocation, access methods available at each site, and statistical information (recorded in the catalogs) are required for producing an access plan.
3. *Executing applications.* Catalog information is used to verify that access plans are valid and that the users have the appropriate access rights.

Catalogs are usually updated when the users modify the **data definition**; this happens, for instance, when global relations, fragments, or images are created or moved, local access structures are modified, or authorization rules are changed.

10.1.1 Content of Catalogs

Several classifications of the information which is typically stored in distributed database catalogs are possible. Following our reference architecture, we have:

1. *Global schema description.* It includes the name of global relations and of attributes.
2. *Fragmentation description.* In horizontal fragmentation, it includes the qualification of fragments; in vertical fragmentation, it includes the attributes which belong to each fragment; in mixed fragmentation, it includes both the fragmentation tree and the description of the fragmentation corresponding to each nonleaf node of the tree.
3. *Allocation description.* It gives the mapping between fragments and physical images.

4. *Mappings to local names.* It is used for binding the names of physical images to the names of local data stored at each site.

5. *Access method description.* It describes the access methods which are locally available at each site. For instance, in the case of a relational system, it includes the number and types of indexes available.

6. *Statistics on the database.* They include the profiles of the database, as defined in Chapter 6.

7. *Consistency information (protection and integrity constraints).* It includes information about the users' authorization to access the database, or integrity constraints on the allowed values of data.

   Examples of authorization rules are:

   a. Assessing the rights of users to perform specific actions on data. The typical actions considered are: read, insert, delete, update, move.

   b. Giving to users the possibility of granting to other users the above rights.

Some references in the literature also include in the catalog content state information (such as locking or recovery information); it seems more appropriate to consider this information as part of a system's data structure and not of the catalog's content.

10.1.2 The Distribution of Catalogs

Catalogs constitute a distributed database, whose fragmentation and allocation can be carefully designed following the guidelines of Chapter 4. When catalogs are used for the translation, optimization, and execution of applications, their information is only retrieved; when they are used in conjunction with a change in data definitions, they are updated. In a few systems, statistics are updated after each execution, but typically updates to statistics are batched. In general, retrieval usage is quantitatively the most important, and therefore the ratio between updates and queries is small.

The allocation and management of catalogs are strictly connected with the degree of local autonomy of each site. In fact, one of the distinguishing features of site autonomy is that each site must be capable of managing its own data regardless of the other sites. Consider, for instance, the creation of a new named object. In order to preserve site autonomy, the naming mechanism must ensure that the new name will be unique within the distributed system without accessing all the catalogs, and the catalog information about the new object need not be immediately available to the other sites. Whenever site autonomy is not required, the creation of a new object can involve the access to catalogs at all sites.

Solutions given to catalog management with and without site autonomy are thus very different; we initially disregard the issue of site autonomy in designing catalogs, and we examine catalog management with site autonomy separately in Section 10.1.3.

Catalogs can be allocated in the distributed database in many different ways; the three basic alternatives are:

Centralized catalogs The complete catalog is stored at one site; this solution has obvious limitations, such as the loss of locality of applications which are not at the central site and the loss of availability of the system, which depends on this single central site.

Fully replicated catalogs Catalogs are replicated at each site; this solution makes the read-only use of the catalog local to each site, but increases the complexity of modifying catalogs, since this requires updating catalogs at all sites.

Local catalogs Catalogs are fragmented and allocated in such a way that they are stored at the same site as the data to which they refer.

Several intermediate alternatives are possible; for instance, it is possible to have both centralized catalogs at one site and local catalogs at all other sites. This is typical of distributed database systems with a central site and a star network which connects the central site to the remote sites; either the catalog information is found locally, and in this case the application is processed locally, or catalog information is accessed at the central site.

Moreover, it is possible to distribute the different parts of the catalog in different ways; for instance, items 1 to 3 of the catalog content could be fully replicated, while item 4 could be locally stored. A mathematical model for determining the allocation of catalogs is described in reference [10.17].

A practical solution which is used in several systems consists of periodically **caching** catalog information which is not locally stored. This solution differs from having totally replicated catalogs, because cached information is not kept up-to-date; in this case, a version number qualifies the cached catalog information. If an application is translated and optimized with a different catalog version than the up-to-date one, this is revealed by the difference in the version numbers. This difference can be observed either at the end of compilation, when the access plan is transmitted to remote sites, or at execution time. In this case, the translation and optimization are repeated.

We examine here the catalog management of Distributed-INGRES [10.2] and SDD-1 [10.3], which do not have site autonomy.

In the design of catalogs for Distributed-INGRES, five alternatives were considered

1. The centralized approach
2. The full replication of items 1, 2, and 3 and the local allocation of remaining items
3. The full replication of items 1, 2, 3, 4, and 5 and the local allocation of remaining items
4. The full replication of all items
5. The local allocation of all items with remote "caching"

The trade-off between solutions is influenced by the fact that in Distributed INGRES statistics are updated after each execution. Solution (2) allows directing the catalog information request to the site which stores catalog information, solution (3) allows translating applications locally, solution (4) allows translating and optimizing applications locally. Solutions (2) and (5) were ultimately preferred; full replication of items 1, 2, and 3 allows each site to know which data exist in the network. Caching is a practical way for saving remote references in many cases.

SDD-1 considers catalog information as ordinary user data; therefore an arbitrary level of redundancy is supported. Security, concurrency, and recovery mechanisms of the system are also used for catalog management. In many cases, the most convenient solution for SDD-1 is the same as in Distributed-INGRES: the information for locating catalog entries (i.e., items 1, 2, and 3) is fully replicated and caching of remote catalog information is performed.

10.1.3 Object Naming and Catalog Management with Site Autonomy

We now turn our attention to the different problems which arise when site autonomy is required. The major requirement is to allow each local user to create and name his or her local data independently from any global control, at the same time allowing several users to share data. Therefore:

1. Data definition should be performed locally.
2. Different users should be able, independently, to give the same name to different data.
3. Different users at different sites should be able to reference the same data.

In the following, we describe the solution given to these problems in R* [10.11]. In the R* prototype, two types of names are used:

1. **Systemwide names** are unique names given to each object in the system. They have four components:

    a. The identifier of the user who creates the object
    b. The site of that user
    c. The object name
    d. The birth site of the object, i.e., the site at which the object was created

    An example of a systemwide name is

$$\text{User}\_1 \text{ @San\_Jose}.EMP@\text{Zurich}$$

    where the symbol @ is a separator which precedes site names. In this case, User_1 from San Jose has created a global relation *EMP* at Zurich. Notice that the same user name at different sites corresponds to different users (i.e., John@SF is not the same as John@LA); this allows creating user names independently.

2. **Print names** are shorthand names for systemwide names, since the above items *a*, *b*, and *d* can be omitted; in this case, name resolution is made by context, where a context is defined as the current user at the local site. Therefore:

    a. A missing user identifier is replaced by the identifier of the current user.
    b. A missing user site or object site is replaced by the current site.

It is also possible for each user to define synonyms, which map simple names to systemwide names. Synonyms are created for a specific user at a specific site; synonym mapping of a simple name to a systemwide name is attempted before name resolution.

The above schema for systemwide names allows different users to reference different objects with the same name (because of the inclusion of the user identifier and site), and also allows different users to reference the same object with different object names in different contexts, which are mapped to the same systemwide name (for instance, *EMP*@Zurich in the context of User_1 at San_Jose references the same relation as User_1@San_Jose.*EMP* at Zurich).

Catalog management in R* satisfies the following requirements:

1. Global replication of a catalog is unacceptable, since this would violate the possibility of autonomous data definition.
2. No site should be required to maintain catalog information of objects which are not stored or created there.
3. The name resolution should not require a random search of catalog entries in the network.
4. Migration of objects should be supported without requiring any change in programs.

The above requirements are met by storing catalog entries of each object as follows:

1. One entry is stored at the birth site of the object, until the object is destroyed. If the object is still stored at its birth site, the catalog contains all the information; otherwise, it indicates the sites at which there are copies of the object.
2. One entry is stored at every site where there is a copy of the object.

Thus, local references to data can be locally performed; on the other hand, if a remote reference is required, the systemwide name allows knowing the birth site of the object, and requesting catalog information from there. If, in the meanwhile, the object has migrated to a different site, this information is returned to the requester, and one additional remote catalog request will be required.

The catalog content in R* includes relation names, column names and types, authorization rules, low-level objects' names, available access paths, and profiles. R* supports the "caching" of catalogs, using version numbers to verify the validity of cached information.

10.2 AUTHORIZATION AND PROTECTION

In this section, we briefly indicate which problems in authorization and protection are due to distribution, and suggest some solutions for them; a general treatment of authorization and protection in a centralized environment can be found in [10.18].

10.2.1 Site-to-Site Protection

The first security problem which arises in a distributed database is initiating and protecting intersite communication. When two database sites communicate, it is important to make sure that:

1. At the other side of the communication line is the intended site (and not an intruder).
2. No intruder can either read or manipulate the messages which are exchanged between the sites.

The first requirement can be accomplished by establishing an identification protocol between remote sites. When two remote databases communicate with each other, on the first request they also send each other a password, similar to what happens at the login of users. When two sites decide to share some data, then the two sites are "introduced," by exchanging passwords. This mechanism is used in R*.

The second requirement is to protect the content of transmitted messages once the two identified sites start to communicate. Messages in a computer network are typically routed along paths which involve several intermediate nodes and transmissions, with intermediate buffering. Requiring that all these intermediate steps be performed after identification and under secure mechanisms seems inappropriate and inefficient (because of the large number of nodes involved, which might dynamically change).

The best solution to this problem consists of using cryptography, a standard technique commonly used in distributed information systems, for instance for protecting communications between terminals and processing units. Messages ("plaintext") are initially encoded into cipher messages ("ciphertext") at the sender site, then transmitted in the network, and finally decoded at the receiver site. Encoding involves not only transformations of groups of bits into groups of bits, but also transposition, "confusions," and logical operations (see references [10.8] and [10.9]); these operations need, of course, to be reversible. The rules used for encoding and decoding are called the key of the cryptographic system. Site-to-site cryptography requires the sender and the receiver of the transmission to agree on the key.

10.2.2 User Identification

When a user connects to the database system, he or she must be identified by the system; the identification is a crucial aspect of preserving security, because if an intruder could pretend to be a valid user, then security would be violated. Assuming a password mechanism, identification requires the password provided by the user to match with the password available to the system. In a distributed database, users could, in principle, identify themselves at any site of the distributed database. However, this feature can be implemented in two ways which both show negative aspects.

1. Passwords could be replicated at all the sites of the distributed database. This would allow user identification to be performed locally at each site, but would also compromise the security of passwords, since it would be easier for an intruder to access them (for example, going to the "less protected" site).

2. Users could each have a "home" site where their identification is performed; in this scenario, a user connecting to a different site would be identified by sending a request to the home site and letting this site perform the identification. The disadvantage of this solution is that sites would "trust" the identifications made by other sites. This is not compatible with the preservation of site autonomy.

A reasonable solution is to restrict each user to identifying him(her)self at the home site. This solution is consistent with the idea that users seem to be more "static" than, for instance, data or programs. A "pass-through" facility could be used to allow users at remote sites to connect their terminals to their "home" sites in order to identify themselves.

10.2.3 Enforcing Authorization Rules

Once users are properly identified, database systems can use authorization rules to regulate the actions performed upon database objects by them. In a distributed environment, additional problems include the allocation of these rules, which are part of the catalog, and the distribution of the mechanisms used for enforcing them. Two alternative, possible solutions are:

1. Full replication of authorization rules. This solution is consistent with having fully replicated catalogs, and requires mechanisms for distributing online updates to them. However, this solution allows authorization to be checked either at the beginning of compilation or at the beginning of execution. Thus, the fact that the user does not have the required access rights can be discovered locally and early, increasing the possibility of quickly invalidating compilation or execution.

2. Allocation of authorization rules at the same sites as the objects to which they refer. This solution is consistent with local catalogs and does not incur the update overhead as in the first case; however, invalidation of users who have no right to access remote data can be done only by accessing these data at some intermediate stage of compilation or execution. Invalidation in this case requires undoing the already performed actions.

The second solution is consistent with site autonomy, while the first is consistent with considering a distributed database as a single system; in this case, full replication of authorization rules is appropriate if it is also cost-effective.

The authorizations that can be given to users of a centralized database include the abilities of reading, inserting, creating, and deleting object instances (tuples) and of creating and deleting objects (relations or fragments). In a distributed database, the additional privilege of "moving" an object from a site to another is added to the previous ones. Having the privilege of moving an object is less than having both insertion and deletion privileges; though moving an object involves the deletion of the object at one site and the creation of the same object at a different site, no information of the original object is lost, and no new information is created. Therefore, this privilege must be considered as a new one.

10.2.4 Classes of Users

For simplifying the mechanisms which deal with authorization and the amount of stored information, individual users are typically grouped into classes, which are all granted the same privileges. For instance, all employees of the administration department constitute a class, and all employees of the manufacturing department constitute a different class. Users of the first class can access information about employee salaries, while those of the second class can access information about project management.

In distributed databases, the following considerations apply to classes of users:

1. A "natural" classification of users is the one which is induced by the distribution of the database to different sites; it is likely that "all users at site x" have some common properties from the viewpoint of authorization. An explicit naming mechanism for this class should be provided (R* uses the term Public@Site_X to denote all users of site X; see reference [10.13]).

2. Several interesting problems arise when groups of users include users from multiple sites; for instance, where should the information about a group's access rights be stored, and which rules should be used for manipulating them? Problems are particularly complex when multiple-site user groups are considered in the context of site autonomy. It appears that any decision concerning the group (revoking privileges or adding and deleting members) cannot really be done on an autonomous basis; thus, mechanisms involve the consensus of the majority or of the totality of involved sites, or a decision made by a higher-level administrator. In conclusion, multiple-site user groups contrast with "pure" site autonomy.

CONCLUSIONS

Distributed administration depends on the degree of site autonomy of the system: in absence of site autonomy, all the features of centralized database administration should be provided, however with different "degrees of distribution" of the algorithms which implement them. Catalogs are a small, distributed database, whose distribution and allocation is not constrained.

With site autonomy, instead, catalog design and naming schemes must allow each site to independently name and manage its local portion of data; two sites decide to share some data as the result of an agreement between them.

The degree of site autonomy influences also the mechanisms for the identification of sites, users, and groups of users and the enforcement of authorization rules.

Annotated Bibliography

[10.1]   F. W. Allen, M. E. S. Loomis, and M. V. Mannino, "The Integrated Dictionary—Directory System," *ACM-Computing Surveys,* **14**:2, 1982.

This paper describes the existing data dictionary-directory (DD) systems. A data dictionary-directory stores, in some cases, the catalogs, i.e., the information required by the DBMS; it also stores information for the users of the database, such as high-level descriptions of data objects, processes, and events which characterize the database application.

The DD and DBMS communicate in several ways; in the paper, the following approaches are described:

1.   The "independent" approach, in which the two systems are autonomous, with few and simple interfaces between them.
2.   The "DBMS-application" approach, in which the DD appears to the DBMS as just another database, but the DBMS maintains its own catalogs.
3.   The "embedded" approach, in which the DD is a component of the DBMS.

The three approaches can be used also in the context of distributed databases.

[10.2]   E. Neuhold and M. Stonebraker, "A Distributed Version of INGRES," *Proc. 2nd Berkeley Workshop on Distr. Data Manag. and Computer Networks,* 1977.

[10.3]   J. B. Rothnie and N. Goodman, "An Overview of the Preliminary Design of SDD-1: A System for Distributed Databases," *Proc. 2nd Berkeley Workshop on Distr. Data Manag. and Computer Networks,* 1977.

These introductory papers to Distributed INGRES and SDD-1 include the description of catalog management, summarized in Section 10.1.2.

[10.4]   F. A. Schreiber and G. Martella, "A Data Dictionary for Distributed Databases," *Conf. on Distributed Databases,* C. Delobel and W. Litwin, eds., North-Holland, 1980.

[10.5]   F. A. Schreiber and G. Martella, "Creating a Conceptual Model of a Data Dictionary for Distributed Databases," *Data Base,* **11**:1, 1979.

These two papers describe the features of data dictionaries (DD) in distributed databases. They identify the items of information that should be included in the data dictionary, describe the levels at which administration of distributed data can be performed, and consequently develop a very general layered architecture for DDs, stressing in particular their conceptual organization.

[10.6]   J. M. Gross, P. E. Jackson, J. Joyce, and F. A. McGuire, "Distributed Database Design and Administration," *Distributed Databases: An Advanced Course,* Draffan and Poole, eds., Cambridge University Press, 1981.

[10.7]   H. Walker, "Administering a Distributed Database Management System," *ACM-SIGMOD Record,* **12**:3, 1982.

The above two references deal with the administration function in a distributed database. In particular, reference [10.7] gives an analytic definition of these functions, indicating which of them should be under the responsibility of a global administrator and which should be instead delegated to the local administrators. However, this paper does not stress the importance of site autonomy in defining the administration functions.

[10.8] D. H. Hsiao and D. S. Kerr, "Privacy and Security of Data Communications and Data Bases," *Fourth VLDB*, 1978.

[10.9] V. L. Voydock and S. T. Kent, "Security Mechanisms in High-Level Network Protocols," *ACM-Computing Surveys*, **15**:2, 1983.

The above papers deal with several aspects of privacy and security in the communications; they both describe the mechanisms which can be used for encryption.

[10.10] U. Bussolati and G. Martella, "Data Security Management in Distributed Data Bases," *Information Systems*, **7**:3, 1982.

This paper presents a scheme for describing security data which uses a binary data model, and a layered architecture for supporting security in distributed databases. Mapping rules between different representations of security are developed.

[10.11] B. G. Lindsay, "Object Naming and Catalog Management for a Distributed Database Manager," *Proc. 2nd Int. Conf. on Distr. Computing Systems*, Paris, 1981.

[10.12] B. G. Lindsay and P. Selinger, "Site Autonomy Issues in R*: A Distributed Database Management System," Res. Report RJ2927 (36822), IBM Res. Lab., San Jose, CA, 1980.

[10.13] P. F. Wilms and B. G. Lindsay, "A Database Authorization Mechanism supporting Individual and Group Authorization," Res. Report RJ3137 (38514), IBM Res. Lab., San Jose, CA, 1981.

The above three papers describe the catalog management and site autonomy requirements for the R* system, which have been summarized in Section 10.1.3; reference [10.13] deals with authorization mechanisms in both centralized and distributed environments, and explains the major differences between them.

[10.14] P. Selinger and B. W. Wade, "An Authorization Mechanism for a Relational Database System," *ACM-TODS*, **1**:3, 1976.

[10.15] C. Wood and E. Fernandez, "Decentralized Authorization in a Database System," *Fifth VLDB*, 1979.

[10.16] J. Arditi and E. Zukovsky, "An Authorization Mechanism for a Database," in *Databases: Improving Usability and Responsiveness*, B. Schneidermann, ed., Academic Press, 1978.

The above three papers describe mechanisms for decentralized authorization. The term "decentralized authorization" denotes the distribution of the authorization functions from a single database administrator to the users of the system.

[10.17] W. W. Chu, "Performance of File Directory Systems for Data Bases in Star and Distributed Networks," *National Computer Conference*, 1976.

This paper analyzes the trade-off between alternative placement methods of the directory information (catalogs) in distributed file systems or distributed databases. The considered alternatives are:

Centralized directory (C) at a single site, where all requests are routed. This solution seems reasonable only in star networks.

Extended centralized directory (EC), in which every application program which requires a given part of the directory brings to its site the required information and keeps it during its execution; thus, future references to the directory are likely to be local. The copies of the directory information are kept up-to-date by propagating updates to them.

Local directory (L), in which each site has the directory of its own data.

Distributed directory (D), in which the directory is totally replicated.

A mathematical model is developed for comparing these alternatives; the ratio between updates and queries to the directory turns out to be the relevant parameter. If the ratio is below 10 percent, then solution D is preferred; if this ratio is between 10 percent and 50 percent, then solution EC is preferred; finally, if the ratio is over 50 percent, solution L is preferred.

[10.18] E. B. Fernandez, R. C. Summers, and C. Wood, "Database Security and Integrity," Addison-Wesley, Reading, MA, 1981.

This book describes security and integrity problems in database systems; in particular, a brief chapter deals with distributed databases. By integrity of distributed databases, the authors really mean the preservation of transaction integrity; therefore, they briefly present some of the problems in concurrency control, commitment, and recovery management. The chapter also includes decentralized authorization as one of its topics; therefore, very little space is left for the description of distributed database administration problems.

Distributed Database Systems

Part II describes distributed database management systems and shows how the techniques which have been presented in Part I are used for their design and implementation.

Chapter 11 discusses how and to what extent distributed databases are built with today's commercially available systems; the Tandem system ENCOMPASS and the IBM system CICS/ISC are extensively described, and the features of other systems are summarized and compared.

Chapter 12 describes SDD-1, the first prototype of a distributed database management system, developed at Computer Corporation of America.

Chapter 13 describes R*, developed at IBM San Jose Research Laboratory. R* is the most important ongoing research effort in distributed database management.

Chapter 14 contains an overview of other homogeneous distributed database system prototypes: DDM, developed at Computer Corporation of America, Distributed-INGRES, developed at the University of California at Berkeley, POREL, developed at the University of Stuttgart, and SIRIUS-DELTA, developed at INRIA. The features of the homogenous distributed database management system prototypes presented in Chapters 12 to 14 are then summarized and compared.

Chapter 15 describes two major research prototypes in the field of heterogeneous distributed database systems: MULTIBASE, developed at Computer Corporation of America, and DDTS, developed at Honeywell Corporate Computer Science Center.

Chapter 11

Commercial Systems

The field of distributed databases is experiencing a rapid evolution not only at the level of research and prototype development but also at the level of industrial products and real-life applications. As is always the case with a new technology, there is some confusion about the characteristics which a commercial system should possess in order to be called a distributed database management system. We will therefore in this chapter not attempt to give a survey of existing systems which could be considered distributed database management systems; instead we focus on a few systems which illustrate the directions in which the industrial world is moving in order to create distributed databases.

In Section 11.1 we describe Tandem's ENCOMPASS distributed database management system. The reasons for this choice are twofold: first, ENCOMPASS is an advanced system, and second, the whole architecture of Tandem's computer system, operating system, communication network, and database management is highly integrated and homogeneous, making the system's features relatively simple to understand. Other transaction processing systems have been developed that have an approach similar to Tandem's; see, for example, reference [11.7].

In Section 11.2 we review the main aspects of IBM's Inter System Communication facility. This product represents a completely different situation from ENCOMPASS, because it was developed to connect several preexisting software components in a much more complex environment, comprising several database management systems.

The two systems considered in Sections 11.1 and 11.2 illustrate, therefore, two rather extreme situations, and many other products lie in between. In the conclusions of this chapter we consider several other systems and derive from these examples some considerations about the state of the art of distributed database management systems.

11.1 TANDEM'S ENCOMPASS DISTRIBUTED DATABASE SYSTEM

ENCOMPASS is a homogeneous distributed database management system. It is built upon Tandem's NonStop computer architecture and the GUARDIAN operating system. Both the computer architecture and the operating system have characteristics which are very useful for the implementation of a distributed database management system; we will therefore briefly review these characteristics.

11.1.1 Overview of the System's Architecture

The most relevant characteristic of a Tandem computer is that it is composed of several (at least two) independent CPUs, which are connected by a high-throughput bus and share access to common disk drives. The distinguishing feature of a Tandem computer with respect to a classical multiprocessor is that each CPU has independent memory and that two CPUs are much more similar to two communicating independent computers than to two processors of the same multiprocessor. We will therefore call the structure of a Tandem computer a **multicomputer** structure to distinguish it from a classical multiprocessor.

In a Tandem computer not only the CPUs are replicated but also all other components, in particular disk drives and buses. One of the objectives which is achieved by this replication of independent resources is a high availability in cases of single module failures. We will not discuss this aspect, since it is not directly related to distributed database management.

Since the basic architecture of a Tandem computer is distributed, the GUARDIAN operating system provides easy communication between processes which are executed by different CPUs. *All communication between processes is via messages.* The message system makes the distribution of hardware components transparent to processes. Through its message and file systems, the GUARDIAN operating system makes the multicomputer structure appear as a single computer to higher levels of software.

Several Tandem computers can be connected to build a local or a geographic network. The extension of the operating system to support a network is based on the generalization of message destinations to include also processes which reside at different computers. It is important to understand that the basic communication between two processes is the same whether they reside in the same CPU, in two different CPUs of the same multicomputer system, at two different sites of a local network, or at two different sites of a geographic network. Of course, since the performance of the communication is very different for each of the above cases, critical functions have to distinguish between these cases; for example, 2-phase-commitment is implemented in two slightly different ways within a single multi-computer site and within a multisite network. However, the application programmer is relieved from using different mechanisms, depending on the distribution of processes to computers; in fact, the basic system organization provides distribution transparency.

Based on this computer architecture and operating system, the distributed database management system provides data distribution, query processing, and distributed transaction management.

11.1.2 Data Distribution

ENCOMPASS supports fragmentation transparency for horizontal fragmentation. A global relation can be horizontally partitioned into limited number of fragments. The approach is, however, less general than the one presented in Chapter 3. A global relation can be fragmented only by different values of the primary key. For this reason, the fragmentation attribute (or at least part of it) must be incorporated into the primary key. For example, if we consider the *SUPPLIER* relation of EXAMPLE_DDB of Chapter 3, it is not possible to define the horizontal fragmentation by different values of *CITY*, as was done in Figure 3.4. In order to obtain the same fragmentation, we must add the prefix "SF" or "LA" to the values of the primary key *SNUM*. Fragmentation predicates on the primary key must be simple: the set of key values can be decomposed into disjoint intervals, and all the tuples which have a primary key value in the same interval belong to the same fragment. For instance, fragment *SUPPLIER*$_1$ of Figure 3.4 would be defined as consisting of all tuples having a primary key value beginning with "SF".

This approach to horizontal fragmentation has the advantage that it is possible to control the uniqueness of the primary key with a local procedure at the site where a tuple must be inserted; if the new key value is locally unique, it is also globally unique, since it incorporates the fragmentation attribute. However, this approach has the disadvantage of forcing the global schema to take care of fragmentation aspects; the logical model of the data is affected by the need to define the fragmentation.

All files (corresponding to global relations in our reference model) have a unique name which includes a sitename. When the file is fragmented, the filename of a file refers to the first fragment of the file. For example, the filename SanFrancisco.SUPPLY refers to the whole file *SUPPLY*. The programmer who accesses the file SanFrancisco.SUPPLY can be unaware of fragmentation. The primary key of the record to be accessed enables the system to correctly direct the requests to the appropriate site. However, this scheme requires a user to have initial access to site SanFrancisco even if the data is at site LosAngeles.

ENCOMPASS does not currently support vertical fragmentation and data replication. A user has to explicitly update different copies of the same file, because they are considered different files by the system. Transaction management, which is described below, facilitates this task, because it supports distributed atomic transactions and a "guaranteed delivery" mechanism for posting updates to sites which are currently unavailable.

The definition of the data fragmentation and allocation is not incorporated into the main catalog (data dictionary) of the system. A separate utility is used for dealing with these aspects.

11.1.3 Query Processing

Tandem provides a relational query language, called **ENFORM**, which has also
a record-at-a-time interface (so that ENFORM queries can be embedded in a host
language). ENFORM does not have a knowledge of data distribution. It relies
on the main catalog for accessing the database. It is just as unaware of the
fragmentation of a file as a programmer would be.

A user who knows data location can influence where the processing is done in
the following way. ENFORM is composed of two parts. A frontend that parses
queries and formats reports and a backend that does the actual database accesses
(selections and projections). The user can allocate the backend to the site where
most of the required data resides, independently of where the frontend runs. This
corresponds to performing selections and projections at the site where the data
is accessed and is consistent with the query optimization criterion 2 stated in
Chapter 5.

ENFORM does not currently perform distributed query processing in the sense
of Chapters 5 and 6. However, it provides several features which will facilitate
extending it in this direction.

11.1.4 Distributed Transaction Management

In the Tandem system the computational structure of a transaction is based on
a requester-server approach. Figure 11.1 shows an example of this structure.
In Figure 11.1 two requester processes control several terminals and call server
processes for performing database access. The requester and server processes communicate via messages and can reside at different sites of a network.

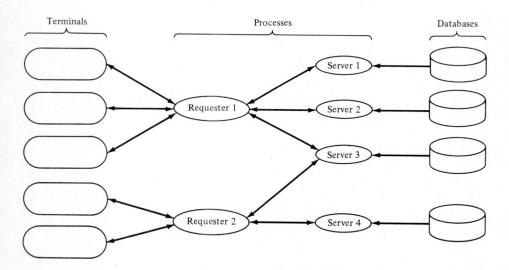

Figure 11.1 Requesters and servers in the Tandem system.

The requester process performs the following functions: terminal interface, field validation, data mapping, and transaction control. The terminal interface deals with the protocols which are used by various terminals. Field validation is used for the control of the input data (type checking of fields, existence of required fields, etc.). The data mapping function deals with the conversion of data from external to internal form and vice versa. Transaction control includes the high-level application logic: interpretation of the input, request of execution of server processes for database manipulation, and interaction with the terminal.

The server processes are responsible for database access and for performing computations. They implement the detailed application logic as required by the requester. For example, consider the same FUND_TRANSFER transaction described in Chapter 7 (Figure 7.2). In the Tandem system this transaction would be reasonably implemented by one requester process and two server processes. The two server processes would be responsible for updating the TO_ACCOUNT and the FROM_ACCOUNT, respectively. The requester process would be responsible for:

1. Receiving the transaction activation and the input parameters from the terminal
2. Checking the input parameters (checking the validity of account numbers, the numeric amount, and checking that no parameters are missing)
3. Calling the two servers for performing the database update
4. Displaying the answer at the terminal

Referring to the general model of a distributed transaction presented in Chapter 7, the requester is the root agent and the servers are the other agents of the transaction. Since a server can request the execution of another server, the computational structure of applications is hierarchic. Tandem's requester-server structure precisely defines the features of requester and server processes. The following aspects characterize Tandem's requester-server structure:

1. A requester process should be multithreaded (i.e., capable of dealing with more than one request at the time).
2. A server is always single-threaded. It performs a single function completely before initiating a new one.
3. A server process should be context-free: it should not be required to remember past requests. All the information which is needed by a server process for executing a single request is received when it is requested.
4. Server and requester processes can reside at different sites of the network.
5. The same server process can perform its function on behalf of different requesters.
6. The communication between requester and server is by means of messages.

Notice that the allocation of the requester and server processes should try to minimize the cost of data communication. Figure 11.1 shows that there are three levels at which data communication occurs: between the terminal and the requester process, between the requester and the server processes, and between the server and the database. In most applications, it is convenient to allocate the requester at the terminal's site and the server at the database site, because communication between requester and servers is generally minimum.

Since the development of multithreaded requester processes would impose a very difficult burden on the application programmer, Tandem provides a transaction processing system (**PATHWAY**) which simplifies the development and maintenance of requester-server transactions. PATHWAY includes a standard terminal control process (**TCP**), and the programmer has to define the specific high-level transaction logic without worrying about system dependent aspects and multithreading. In fact, the main task of the application programmer is to define the interaction between TCP and the terminal. This is done using a high-level language called **screen-COBOL**.

The atomicity and serializability aspects of a distributed transaction are supported by Tandem's transaction monitoring facility (**TMF**). TMF uses 2-phase-locking for concurrency control. Locks can be obtained either at a single record level or at the file level. Only exclusive locks are used.

No deadlock detection is provided by TMF. Application programmers are expected to use timeouts to detect their deadlocks. Timeouts can be inserted at two different levels: the requester and the server. In the first case, a timeout parameter is set when a request message is sent by the TCP to a server. The TCP will abort the transaction when the timeout expires if it has not received an answer from the server. In the second case, the timeout is set when a disk *READ* is issued by the server.

TMF implements a 2-phase-commitment protocol, but uses two different mechanisms for implementing it within a single multicomputer site or within a multisite network. Within a single site, TMF assumes that communication is very cheap. Therefore a broadcast is performed to all processors, independently of whether they are participants of the transaction or not. For a multisite transaction, instead, TMF performs a 2-phase-commitment involving only the actual participants of the transaction.

TMF can handle site crashes and network partitions. If a site is disconnected from the coordinator and is waiting for the outcome of a transaction, a manual override is provided for terminating the transaction. In all other cases TMF automatically resolves the transaction. If phase 2 of commitment has not been reached, the transaction is aborted.

11.1.5 A Distributed Database Application Using ENCOMPASS

ENCOMPASS has been used for building the manufacturing information control system EMPACT, which is used by Tandem's manufacturing division. EMPACT implements a distributed database approach, storing manufacturing data at the different plants of the network. Currently, the data is distributed at eight sites, located as follows:

Austin, Texas
Chicago, Illinois
Cupertino, California (two sites)
Neufahrn, Germany
Reston, Virginia

Sunnyvale, California
Watsonville, California

A growth rate of one new plant every nine months is predicted. EMPACT implements, therefore, a geographically distributed and widely dispersed distributed database.

The functions which are controlled by EMPACT are all the typical functions of manufacturing control, including parts master, bill of material, inventory control, purchasing/receiving, work in process, scheduling, material requirement planning, and interplant material transfer.

The data which is used by these applications has been divided into two major classes, **global data** and **local data**. Global data is common to all sites; for example, the item master file, containing Tandem's parts catalog, and the bill of material file, which describes the structure of each product, are global data. Local data is instead relevant only for the site storing it. Typical examples of local data are the inventory, scheduling, purchasing/receiving, and work in process files.

The database has been distributed in the following way: each global file is completely replicated at each site, while each file storing local data is horizontally fragmented so that each site stores only the relevant portion of it. For example, Texas inventory information is stored only at the Austin site. Notice that with this approach all local files at different sites have the same structure, although they store different data.

This data distribution has been designed to satisfy two main objectives: **continuous availability** and **site autonomy**. A user at any site has all the relevant data available for inquiries, since he or she has a copy of each global file and the locally relevant portion of each local file. The main difficulty in the design of EMPACT, however, was to also obtain the continuous availability and site autonomy objectives for update transactions on global data, since ENCOMPASS does not support replicated data. The designers of EMPACT have discarded the most straightforward solution, consisting in broadcasting an update request to servers at each site where a global file copy resides, because this solution has three drawbacks:

1. Servers which perform updates on a global file have to know where the replicas of the file reside in order to request the remote updates; location transaparency would be lost in this way.
2. The response time of a global update transaction would be too long.
3. Availability of all sites and of the communication network is required for performing each global update; this may cause a loss of site autonomy.

The first problem has been solved by using a "replication file," which describes the location of all replicas of each global file; in this way it was possible to avoid incorporating distribution information into the application programs.

The solution of the other two problems has been obtained at the expense of accepting temporary inconsistencies of the replicated global files. An update is immediately applied to the local copy, independently of the availability of the other sites, obtaining in this way both a short response time and site autonomy. The update is also recorded in a special "suspense file," and an asynchronous process performs the remote updates as soon as possible by requesting the activation of the corresponding remote servers. Each update is treated as a separate TMF transaction. The database is therefore completely consistent only when the suspense files at all sites are empty.

There is a major problem with the above approach: concurrent updates may occur at two different sites on two inconsistent copies of the same data; the update transactions would read, in this case, inconsistent data and would produce inconsistent updates. To prevent this problem, the following restrictions on update transactions have been established: each global record can be "owned" by only one site, and only the owner site can initiate the updating of the record. Notice that this solution works only for update transactions, so that read-only transactions may, in fact, read inconsistent data.

In terms of the general classification of reliable multiple-copy concurrency control approaches which has been presented in Chapter 9, the approach of EMPACT can be classified as a primary copy approach with deferred updates to replicas and without strict consistency for read transactions. In fact, because of the limitations of the data distribution in ENCOMPASS, some of the data distribution aspects of EMPACT are incorporated in the application logic.

We can describe global files by applying the reference model of Chapter 3: global files are horizontally fragmented, and each fragment is fully replicated at all sites of the distributed database. One copy of each fragment is used as a primary copy for update transactions.

The experience with the EMPACT application has shown that by using the ENCOMPASS distributed database management system, it is possible to build a distributed database that has most of the features described in Part I. The EMPACT application has also shown that it is possible to bypass the limitations of ENCOMPASS through suitable solutions at the application level.

An area where many difficulties have been encountered is operational control. Operations like the addition of a new site to the system, the quiescing of all global transactions, and the control of the status of distributed transactions are very difficult and specialized tools are needed for this purpose.

11.2 IBM'S INTER SYSTEM COMMUNICATION

The variety of software products which are available on IBM's computers, including database management systems and transaction handlers, constitutes a much more complex environment for the designer of a distributed database than the strictly homogeneous environment offered by a network of Tandem's computers with the ENCOMPASS database system. IBM has developed and is developing tools which facilitate building distributed databases on top of homogeneous and heterogeneous local systems. The most important of these tools are the System Network Architecture (SNA) and the Inter System Communication (ISC).

SNA includes communication software for building a network of IBM computers and terminals and for dealing with their specific characteristics. The features which are interesting from the viewpoint of distributed databases are the support of logical sessions between processes at different sites and the communication protocol between programs. We will not discuss the features of SNA, because SNA defines essentially the architecture of the communication network but not the features for distributed transaction processing and distributed databases.

ISC is a set of protocols allowing any systems following them to communicate with each other. ISC protocols have been implemented for the CICS transaction handler and for the IMS database management system. In the sequel we will refer to CICS/ISC, since currently CICS is the system which implements most of the ISC protocols.

11.2.1 CICS/ISC

Before considering the intersystem communication feature of CICS, let us review a few aspects of the basic CICS system. CICS is a so-called TP-monitor or transaction handler. Its main function is to control the execution of online applications which are requested by the end-users at the terminals. When the user types an application code, CICS activates the corresponding application program. CICS performs, therefore, the same function as the scheduler of an operating system. The reasons for using CICS instead of the basic operating system are the following:

1. CICS allows defining the terminal configuration, the codes of applications which can be requested from the terminals, the corresponding application programs which have to be executed, the access rights of applications, and similar configuration parameters.

2. CICS is capable of controlling the execution of transactions more efficiently than a general-purpose operating system. Typical online applications are very different from other types of functions which can be performed by the computer: they require a very short computation, are strongly I/O-bound, and must have a short response time. CICS uses its knowledge of the characteristics of these applications for more efficient scheduling and more efficient resource allocation, so that many more applications can be run concurrently on the same system than it would be possible if they were controlled by the general-purpose operating system.

A CICS application can consist of one or several transactions. When the application is invoked, a begin-transaction is implicitly executed. The application program can specify a synchronization point which corresponds to the execution of a commit primitive immediately followed by a new begin-transaction primitive. CICS mantains a log for supporting the atomicity of transactions.

The above description shows that CICS is *not* a database management system. Its function is simply to execute application programs at the request of the users at the terminals and to manage system resources. However, the application programs which are controlled by CICS are, in general, database accessing programs. Application programs can call therefore a database mangement system like IMS. For this reason there is a strong integration between the transaction handler and the database management system. It is also possible that CICS/ISC transmits a IMS primitive from one site to a target site; in this case, we assume that at the target site an IMS database manager interprets it, since CICS does not directly interpret any database access primitive.

Because CICS manages applications which access databases under the control of different database management systems, CICS/ISC can be used to build a heterogeneous distributed database. Currently, the two IBM database managers which can execute with CICS are IMS and SQL/DS. CICS applications can also call other database management systems which run on IBM computers but are not IBM products, such as Cullinane's IDMS and DATACOM/DB of Applied Data Research. However, building a heterogeneous database using also these products is more difficult than using only IMS and SQL.

IMS is a navigational, essentially one-record-at-a-time database management system. In addition, it has components which perform transaction handling (the data communication component IMS/DC) and even a multiple IMS coupling feature (MSC). However, when running with CICS, only the database management component of IMS (IMS/DB or IMS/DL1) is used.

SQL/DS is a relational database management system which uses the SQL language, which we have partially described in this book. SQL/DS can be used not only by the end-user as a query language, but also by the programmer for writing online applications. In the latter case, the application programs which contain calls to SQL/DS can be run under the CICS monitor.

The above description shows that CICS/ISC is not simply a tool for allowing the communication of two systems; it is a step in the direction of developing an integrated data management environment comprising several different software components.

A distributed transaction can be implemented using the CICS/ISC facility in three different ways, which are called **function shipping, asynchronous transaction processing**, and **distributed transaction processing**.

11.2.1.1 Function shipping

Function shipping consists of sending a single data access primitive to a remote site. If a transaction at site 1 requires data from a file at site 2, this can be obtained by function shipping. If the existence of the file at site 2 has been specified to CICS/ISC, this operation is performed transparently to the program. The program issues a request for the file, and it is the responsibility of CICS/ISC to recognize that the file is located at site 2, to send the request to site 2, to control its execution, to receive the result back, and to deliver it to the program as if the request had been executed locally. CICS/ISC implements, therefore, complete location transparency for data access primitives which are issued by a program. Assuming that the database management system IMS/DL1 is used for database access, then CICS/ISC implements the execution of DL1 primitives at remote sites.

The implementation of a DL1 primitive issued by transaction A at site 1 and requiring access to an IMS database at site 2 is shown in Figure 11.2. The following sequence of steps is performed by CICS/ISC:

1. A session is obtained from the communication network software VTAM (an SNA component), establishing the communication with CICS at site 2.
2. The DL1 primitive is sent to the CICS system at site 2.
3. The CICS system at site 2 creates a specialized transaction for handling the

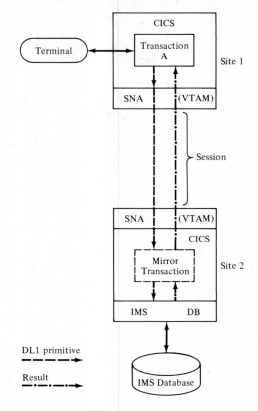

Figure 11.2 Function shipping in CICS/ISC.

request (these transactions, which are created by CICS for performing remote requests, are called **mirror transactions**).

4. The mirror transaction is executed by the system at site 2 like any other transaction of site 2. Obviously, the body of the mirror transaction consists of the execution of a DL1 primitive on the local IMS system.

5. The result is sent back. If the mirror transaction has not performed any updates, it is canceled and the session is terminated. However, if the mirror transaction has performed updates, then the session must be maintained until a commit point (called a **synchronization point** in CICS terminology) is reached, in order to allow recovery and preserve file integrity.

Function shipping is quite inefficient in terms of both resource usage and response time of the individual transactions. This is because the establishment of a session and a mirror transaction is required for a relatively small operation like a single file access. Experience has shown that while a local file access requires a time of the order of a tenth of a millisecond, a remote file access through function shipping can require a time of the order of hundreds of milliseconds or even seconds.

Therefore function shipping should be limited to a few cases. If many remote file accesses are required, then one of the two approaches which are described in the next sections should be used. However, function shipping has one advantage over these approaches which warrants its use in some cases: no application programs are required at the remote site and so location transparency is provided by this mode of operation.

11.2.1.2 Asynchronous transaction processing   With asynchronous transaction processing, a local transaction starts a named transaction at a remote site, which proceeds asynchronously with respect to its initiator. A session is required for transmitting the request; however, once the specified transaction is started, the session is dropped. Both transactions then proceed independently.

The remote transaction can, in turn, activate other transactions. Very often it will activate a third transaction at the initiating site for displaying the final result. For example, Figure 11.3 shows that transaction A at site 1 activates transaction B at site 2, which, in turn, activates transaction C at site 1. The terminal which has invoked transaction A receives the result back from transaction C.

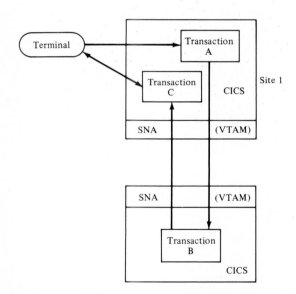

Figure 11.3 Asynchronous transaction processing in CICS/ISC.

Asynchronous transaction processing is convenient if several functions have to be performed independently at the remote site, and integrity is not critical. This mode of operation is more efficient than function shipping, because it requires approximately the same resources as for shipping one request (i.e., the establishment of a session for a rather short time), but the cost of these resources is compensated by the execution of the whole remote transaction, which typically involves more than just a single file access.

The main problem with this approach is that the atomicity of the distributed transaction is not guaranteed by the system, and therefore the required recovery procedures must be included in the application programs. For example, the system does not provide recovery if transaction B of Figure 11.3 fails before starting transaction C. If the atomicity of distributed transactions is required, then distributed transaction processing should be used instead of asynchronous transaction processing.

11.2.1.3 Distributed transaction processing   With distributed transaction processing (Figure 11.4), a local transaction can start a remote transaction, as with asynchronous transaction processing.   However, the initiating transaction waits until the initiated transaction has performed the required function.   The two transactions proceed synchronously, and the session is held for the whole cooperation time. Several messages can be exchanged across the session while the two transactions cooperate.

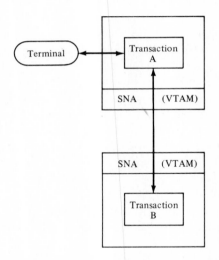

Figure 11.4   Distributed transaction processing in CICS/ISC.

This mode of operation ensures the atomicity of the distributed transaction. The major cost with respect to asynchronous transaction processing is the cost of the session, which is held for the whole time of transaction execution.

The main disadvantage of distributed transaction processing is that it does not provide location transparency, because an application program must specify the site at which the remote transaction resides when requesting its activation.

11.2.1.4 Comparison   We have seen that each one of the three approaches has its own advantages and disadvantages. These are summarized in Table 11.1, which ranks the three approaches with respect to the following aspects: location transparency, transaction atomicity, response time, and resource consumption.

Table 11.1 Comparison of operation modes of CICS/ISC

	Location transparency	Transaction atomicity	Response time	Resource consumption
Function shipping	1	1	3	3
Asynchronous transaction processing	2	3	2	1
Distributed transaction processing	3	1	1	2

1. Location transparency is best with function shipping, because an application program simply issues a database access primitive, without knowing where the data are located. File migration can be easily managed in this case by simply changing the definition of file locations, without affecting application programs. Asynchronous transaction processing permits an application program to invoke the execution of another program without knowing its location and is therefore ranked higher than distributed transaction processing, which does not provide location transparency at all.

2. Both function shipping and distributed transaction processing support transaction atomicity and are therefore ranked higher for this aspect than asynchronous transaction processing, which does not provide atomicity.

3. The response time of a transaction which requires several remote database accesses is best with distributed transaction processing and worst with function shipping; the reasons for this fact have been discussed already. Asynchronous transaction processing has worse response times than distributed transaction processing if a distributed transaction requires several exchanges of messages between the two sites, since with distributed transaction processing the same session is used for this purpose.

4. Resource consumption is minimum with asynchronous transaction processing and maximum with function shipping, as already discussed in the presentation of the approaches.

The above comparison shows that no one of the three approaches dominates or is dominated by another one under all respects and in all applicative environments; therefore, all three have their right to exist. Although some of the characteristics of these approaches depend on the peculiarity of a specific system, the considerations which are reflected in Table 11.1 are consistent with the general considerations of Part I of this book.

CONCLUSIONS

Currently, no single, commercially available, distributed database management system possesses all the features which we have described in Part I of this book. However, the industrial world is moving very fast in this direction. We analyze now the main areas in which this effort is directed.

The following considerations are based not only on Tandem's ENCOMPASS and IBM's CICS/ISC, but also on the following systems:

1. **D-NET** by Applied Data Research (ADR)
2. **IDMS-DDS** by Cullinane Corporation
3. **IDMS-DDB50** by International Computers Limited (ICL)
4. **VDN** by Nixdorf Computer AG
5. **UDS-D** by Siemens AG
6. **NET-WORK** by Software AG

Some of these products are still in development and not yet released. All of them are changing rapidly. Therefore, we do not compare their features; we simply use them as a sample of the existing commercial distributed database management systems. From this sample we can deduce which features are considered important and feasible by the designers of these systems.

All these systems, except VDN, have been developed as extensions of a preexisting centralized DBMS, used as the local DBMS. In some cases the preexisting DBMS had to be modified extensively. In the case of VDN both the local and the distributed system were designed together. The local systems of IDMS-DDS, IDMS-DDB50, and UDS-D are the Codasyl systems IDMS and UDS. The local systems of D-NET and NET-WORK are DATACOM/DB and ADABAS, which belong to the class of relational systems with inverted lists. The local system of VDN is a compromise between a Codasyl and a relational system.

Distribution transparency   Although no system is currently commercially available which possesses the general distribution transparency features defined in Chapter 3, the importance of this aspect is recognized, and all the considered systems provide some degree of distribution transparency. We have seen that Tandem's ENCOMPASS provides transparent horizontal fragmentation of files and that IBM's CICS/ISC provides location transparency for remote file access.

The above two systems do not use the data dictionary for obtaining location transparency. Other systems, like IDMS-DDS and D-NET, are instead centered on the data dictionary. In these systems, location transparency is obtained by including all the information which is needed for describing the database distribution in the data dictionary.

Units of distribution   The basic unit of distribution of most systems is the file; only VDN and ENCOMPASS allow the partitioning of files into smaller units. The Codasyl systems have additional restrictions on the mapping of logical units to sites. For example, in IDMS-DDB50 each Codasyl set must be stored entirely at one site. In UDS-D each Codasyl realm must be stored entirely at one site.

Data replication   Only three systems (D-NET, VDN, and NET-WORK) provide support for data replication. In D-NET a file can be replicated, however, only the master file is consistently updated; the other copies can be used for performing "dirty" reads by transactions without consistency requirements. In NET-WORK the copies of a file can either be used as in D-NET or they can be forced to be consistent. VDN allows the replication of fragments, which can also be overlapping.

Remote database access   The possibility of accessing a remote file is provided by many computer networks, independently on the existence of a database management system. We have seen that with CICS/ISC it is possible to execute a remote IMS/DL1 primitive (function shipping). The main disadvantage of this approach is that most file and database access primitives access too few data to compensate for the cost of establishing the interprocess communication. One way to ameliorate this situation is to build more powerful primitives which can be interpreted by the remote database manager. For example, IDMS-DDS, which is based on the navigational Codasyl database management system IDMS, suffers from the fact that a single record request is too small for efficient remote database access. The efficiency of site-to-site communication can be increased through the use of the **logical record facility** (LRF) of IDMS. LRF allows defining several database records (or portions of them) as a single logical record. Since each request of an application program can retrieve a logical record, a single remote call is able of retrieving several physical records.

Remote process-to-process communication This type of facility is fundamental for developing a distributed database system; it is provided by most homogeneous computer networks. For heterogeneous networks the situation is more critical, but process-to-process communication between different DBMSs can be supported. For example, both SNA and ISC support remote process-to-process communication.

Distributed transaction recovery Several systems already support 2-phase-commitment, and it is easy to foresee that a distributed transaction recovery protocol will be incorporated in all the systems which claim to manage a distributed database. The situation appears much more critical with respect to the problem of replication and of robustness of concurrency control.

Annotated Bibliography

The description of the systems in this chapter can be found in the manuals and other documentation supplied by the vendors. We do not reference this type of documentation, since it is continuously changing. References [11.1] to [11.3] are on the Tandem system. Reference [11.4] is on ISC, and references [11.5] and [11.6] are on SNA. Reference [11.7] contains several papers on recently developed systems which are oriented to high availability and efficient transaction processing using modular multicomputer structures. Reference [11.8] describes VDN.

[11.1]   A. J. Borr, "Transaction Monitoring in ENCOMPASS: Reliable Distributed Transaction Processing," *Seventh VLDB*, Cannes, 1981.

[11.2]   A. Norman and M. Anderton, "EMPACT: A Distributed Database Application," *Proc. National Computer Conference*, 1983.

[11.3]   J. F. Bartlett, "A 'NonStop' Operating System," *Proc. Eleventh Hawaii Int. Conf. on System Sciences*, 1978.

[11.4]   R. D. Acker and P. H. Seaman, "Modelling Distributed Processing across Multiple CICS/VS Sites," *IBM Systems Journal*, **21**:4, 1982.

[11.5]   J. H. McFayden, "System Network Architecture: An Overview," *IBM Systems Journal*, **15**:1, 1976.

[11.6]   J. P. Gray P. Homan P. J. Hansen M. A. Lerner and M. Pozefsky "SNA's Advanced Program-to-Program Communication " *IBM Systems Journal* to be published.

[11.7]   Special Issue on Highly Available Systems *Database Engineering* **6**:2 1983.

[11.8]   R. Munz "Gross Architecture of the Distributed Database System VDN " *IFIP Working Conference on Database Architecture·* G. Bracchi and G. M. Nijssen eds. Venice 1979.

Chapter 12

SDD-1: A System for Distributed Databases

The SDD-1 project, developed at the Computer Corporation of America, was the first prototype of a distributed database management system; it was designed between 1976 and 1978, and implemented by 1979 on DEC-10 and DEC-20 computers. Sites were connected by the ARPANET, and used an existing DBMS, called **Datacomputer**. This project made a significant contribution to the understanding of the important problems of distributed databases, and to the solution of some of them.

This chapter describes the overall architecture of SDD-1, and then discusses how query processing, concurrency control, and reliability mechanisms fit in this architecture. In particular, we focus on the description of the reliability mechanisms specifically designed for SDD-1. Several features of SDD-1 have already been presented in Part I: query processing in Section 6.2.2, concurrency control using timestamps in Section 8.3, several reliability problems in Chapter 9, and catalog management in Section 10.1.2.

12.1 ARCHITECTURE

SDD-1 supports the relational data model. Global relations can be fragmented in two steps, first horizontally and then vertically; fragments can be stored redundantly. SDD-1 provides fragmentation transparency (i.e., the user is unaware of fragments and their allocation). The manipulation of relations is done using **Datalanguage**, a high-level procedural language available on Datacomputers.

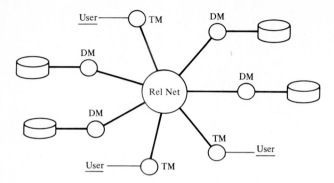

Figure 12.1   The architecture of SDD-1.

The architecture of SDD-1 is based on three rather independent virtual machines: data modules, transaction modules, and a reliable network. This architecture, represented in Figure 12.1, allows separating the problems of distributed database management into three subsystems, with limited interaction.

Data modules (DMs) manage local data; they provide to the transaction modules the following features:

1.   Reading data from the local database into local workspaces assigned to each transaction
2.   Moving data between workspaces at different sites
3.   Manipulating data in the workspaces
4.   Writing data from the workspaces into the local databases

Transaction modules (TMs) plan and control the execution of transactions; each Datalanguage command is considered as a separate transaction. TMs are responsible for:

1.   Query translation and access planning
2.   Concurrency control
3.   Control of distributed query executions

The **reliable network (RelNet)** interconnects TMs and DMs, providing the following features:

1.   Guaranteed delivery, consisting in guaranteeing that a message will be delivered even when the sender and receiver are never up simultaneously
2.   Transaction control, ensuring atomicity of transactions
3.   Site monitoring, to indicate sites which are up or down at a given time
4.   A global network clock, which is roughly synchronized at all sites

Also the execution of transactions in SDD-1 is based on the principle of keeping problems of transaction management distinct, and solving them in different phases. Transaction execution is divided into three phases: read, execute, and write. Each phase deals with an individual problem: the **read phase** deals with concurrency control, the **execute phase** deals with distributed query execution, and the **write phase** deals with the execution of updates at all copies of modified data.

During the read phase of a transaction the fragments to be read by the transaction, called the **read-set**, are determined by the TM at the site of origin, which acts as supervisor, and a nonredundant set of physical copies of the fragments of the read-set, called a **materialization**, is selected. Then, a command is sent to all DMs storing some portion of the materialization, in order to put the required data into workspaces assigned to the transaction. In this phase, all concurrency control requirements of transactions are managed. The workspace is implemented using a *differential file mechanism*, and thus data are not immediately copied from the disks into the workspace. Rather, a **page map** indicating the physical location of required pages is associated with the transaction; these pages cannot be modified by other transactions, because if another transaction wants to update them, it has to allocate new physical storage and to write the updated page into it.

During the execute phase, Datalanguage programs are compiled, generating an access plan, and then immediately executed, with a compile-and-go approach. Execution is supervised by the TM at the site of origin. Thus, SDD-1 has a centralized computation involving one master TM and several DMs at the different sites (recall Section 7.4.3). All actions are performed in the local workspaces of the transaction during this phase.

During the write phase, updates produced at one DM for each modified fragment are distributed to all the DMs where there are copies of the fragment, and then write commands are issued to all involved DMs (thus, copies are written with a write-all approach); atomicity of transactions is preserved by a specialized 4-phase-commitment protocol which allows the commitment of transactions even when the involved sites have failed. This protocol uses the guaranteed delivery mechanism of RelNet.

In the following, we examine concurrency control, execution of queries, and reliability aspects in the order in which they are dealt with by an SDD-1 transaction.

12.2 CONCURRENCY CONTROL (READ PHASE)

Concurrency control in SDD-1 uses the conservative timestamp method with the "ignore obsolete write" rule, described in Sections 8.3.1 and 8.3.2. This combination of methods allows write commands to be processed as soon as they are received, and puts all the concurrency control overhead in the read phase. In order to fulfill the requirements for a correct execution of the conservative timestamp method, described in Section 8.3.2, DMs perform all read (write) actions on behalf of the same transaction atomically (i.e., all reads are performed at the beginning of the transaction and all writes are performed at the end of the transaction). Two messages from the TM to the DMs involved in a transaction specify the data to be retrieved (in the read phase) and, after the execution of the transaction, the updates to be performed (in the write phase). Moreover, TMs send read requests of the transactions controlled by them in timestamp order.

We recall that the advantage of this method with respect to basic timestamping consists of requiring a lower number of restarts, at the price of waiting (conservatively) until potentially conflicting operations are executed. Clearly, this waiting is not useful most of the time: if we consider a particular read operation, in most cases the mechanism will keep it waiting for operations which are not in conflict (because, for instance, they use different data items). However, conflicts are only known a posteriori (in fact, for the correctness of the method, they need not to be known at all). In SDD-1, special techniques have been developed for recognizing a priori that transactions do not conflict and for taking advantage of this knowledge.

When transactions are designed, a static set of **transaction classes** is established. Transaction classes are defined by assigning to them a read-set and a write-set (read-sets and write-sets have been introduced in Section 8.1.1); for instance:

Class C1 has read-set $\{x, y, z\}$, write-set $\{x, t\}$.
Class C2 has read-set $\{x, z, w\}$, write-set $\{w, t\}$.

As this example shows, read- and write-sets of different classes can overlap. Two classes are said to conflict when the write-set of any of the two has a nonempty intersection with either the read- or the write-set of the other; in practice, two nonconflicting classes are allowed to have some intersection only in their read-sets.

A transaction is said to **fit** in a given class C if its read-set is contained within the read-set of C and its write-set is contained within the write-set of C. Thus, the same transaction can fit in more than one class; for instance, a transaction with read-set $\{x, z\}$ and write-set $\{t\}$ fits in both C1 and C2. A rather obvious application of classes is that two transactions cannot conflict if their classes are not conflicting; thus, a built-in knowledge of classes in the concurrency control mechanism is useful for avoiding waits.

In order to do so, each class is assigned to one particular TM and each TM is located at only one site. When a transaction is submitted to a given TM, its read- and write-sets are analyzed, and one class in which it fits is determined. If this class is not managed by the local TM, then the transaction is forwarded to the site with the TM which manages the appropriate class; each transaction must fit in at least one class.

Transactions within the same class are certainly conflicting and thus their execution is done in strict timestamp order; a "pipeline" rule, which disciplines the order in which read and write messages can be processed, is followed by the TM which supervises each class in issuing read and write requests. For the sake of simplicity, we can think that this rule imposes a strict serialization of transactions within the same class.

We have already noticed that nonconflicting classes need not be serialized; in particular, considering a transaction T which fits in a class C, if all classes of a remote site are not conflicting with C, then it is not required to wait for operations from that site before issuing operations of T. However, the notion of classes can be used with greater profit by performing a more sophisticated analysis, called a **conflict graph analysis**.

A **conflict graph** is a synthetic representation of conflicts between classes. Each class is modeled by two nodes, labeled r (for read) and w (for write), which

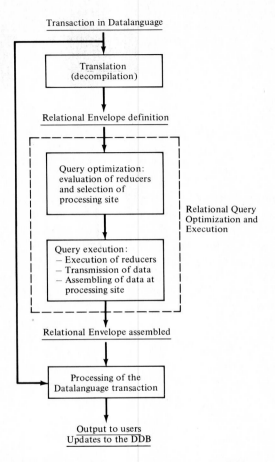

Figure 12.3 Distributed query execution in SDD-1.

2. The possibility of describing all sites of the network as "up" or "down," and of monitoring transitions between these states, called crashes and recoveries, which are instantaneous with respect to the global clock

The lowest level of RelNet is built upon the ARPANET message transmission layer, which should at least guarantee that:

1. If any two messages sent from site 1 to site 2 are received, they are received in the same order as they were sent.
2. If the receiver does not fail between any two message transmissions, then there is no other message from the sender between them.

If these features are not provided by the network, then a catastrophe occurs (see Chapter 7), and the behavior of the system is unpredictable. Moreover, SDD-1

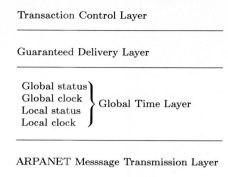

Figure 12.4 Layers of RelNet.

considers network partitions as catastrophes, which cannot be managed by RelNet. This limitation is justified by the fact that network partitions are rather unlikely in the ARPANET, which has several alternative connections between sites.

Clearly, RelNet cannot provide a 100 percent reliability; the approach taken in RelNet is to indicate, for each of its layers, the types of failure which lead to a catastrophe. Thus, catastrophic failures are delimited, and can be made arbitrarily unlikely by adding replication at the corresponding levels.

In describing the features of each RelNet layer, we proceed from the lowest level to the upper level.

12.4.1 Global Time Layer

The global time layer is divided into four sublayers, as shown in Figure 12.4. One of the major features provided by this level is a global clock, required for establishing an ordering of events according to the following rules:

1. Events within the same process are ordered by their execution.
2. If a process knows about event 1 of a different process before performing event 2, then 1 must precede 2.

12.4.1.1 Local clock sublayer The lowest level is the local clock sublayer. It maintains at each site a logical local clock, which is simply a monotonically increasing counter. This counter is used to generate timestamps, which are assigned to transactions and messages. The method of Section 8.1.5 is used for the generation and management of timestamps consistently with the "occurred before" relationship.

This layer also supports a real time clock, which is used by timeout mechanisms and also is used for keeping logical clocks "roughly" synchronized with real time. To obtain this synchronization, different granularities are used for time intervals of the two clocks, giving a coarser granularity to the real time clock. Logical clocks are "bumped" beyond real clocks when real clocks pass them.

12.4.1.2 Local status sublayer The major activity performed by this sublayer is to manipulate a local **status table**, which gives the status of all network sites as "down" or "up". This layer is responsible for marking states as "up" or "down" on the basis of instructions from higher-level layers. RelNet also provides the possibility of setting a **watch** on a given site; a process which waits for the recovery of that site sets the watch, and it will be informed, via an interrupt, when this event occurs. The local status layer is responsible for generating the interrupt.

Two special messages are exchanged between sites to inform about states and state changes:

1.   An "I am up" message is sent by a recovering site.
2.   A "you are down" message is sent from one site to another, to force a local recovery at that site.

The local status layer intercepts all incoming messages. The action which is performed depends on the status of the sender, marked in the status table, and on the type of message. Four cases are possible:

1.   *The sender is marked "up" and the message is not a "you are down."* In this case, the message is regularly processed by higher-level layers of RelNet.
2.   *The sender is marked "down" and the message is "I am up."* Also in this case, the message is passed to higher-level layers of RelNet, which will thus be informed that the receiver has completed a local recovery. This will eventually result in changing its status.
3.   *The sender is marked "down" and the message is not "I am up."* In this case, the sender was erroneously considered failed. However, since some actions might have been done based on this assumption, a local recovery of the sender is forced. This is accomplished by sending a "you are down" message to it. Note that it is possible that a site performs a recovery even if it is operational. This prevents the production of inconsistencies which are due to the disagreement on local status tables.
4.   *The message is "you are down."* In this case, for symmetrical reasons, the receiver must behave as if it were failed, and a local recovery is started.

Cases 3 and 4 are not mutually exclusive.

12.4.1.3 Global clock sublayer This sublayer is responsible for providing to higher levels a uniform global clock. We have seen that this global clock should monitor relative time rather than absolute time, and this function is "almost" provided by the local clock layer. However, there is one case in which one site is aware of an event at another site without receiving any message from it; this happens when one site observes the failure of another site. Special processes, called **guardians**, have been designed in order to be able to set the local clock at a greater value than that of the remote failed site.

Guardians are processes which watch other sites in order to reveal their failures. Several guardians are provided for each site. Periodically, guardians request the acknowledgment of a message sent to the controlled site. If the acknowledgment does not arrive within a given timeout, then the controlled site is deemed crashed.

A "you are down" message is sent to it in order to force a local recovery; this message has effect when the controlled site is actually operational.

When a guardian detects the failure of the controlled site, it "bumps" the local clock a sufficient interval to ensure that the new local time is greater than the time at which the remote site failed. In order to ensure this property, guardians should repeat controls within given time intervals.

The global time layer faces a catastrophe when all guardians of a given site are down and that site fails; the catastrophe consists of the inaccuracy of global time. This event can be made arbitrarily unlikely by increasing the number of guardians of each site.

12.4.1.4 Global status sublayer

The global status sublayer coordinates the various facilities provided by the sublayers beneath it and presents a view of the network to higher layers with the following features:

1.   All sites are marked "up" or "down" and the transitions between these two states occur instantaneously
2.   Global time is provided

This layer is responsible for marking site states, handling inquires about the site status, and providing to user processes a watch on a designated site. It is also responsible for bringing back sites which have completed their local recovery to fully operational status, by performing the following steps:

1.   Sending an "I am up" message to all other sites
2.   Receiving timestamped answers from them; this allows setting the local time and the status table appropriately
3.   Sending "you are down" messages to sites which do not respond
4.   At the end, setting the local status "up"

12.4.2 Guaranteed Delivery Layer

Messages in SDD-1 can be marked for "guaranteed delivery"; this ensures that they will eventually be received. The guaranteed delivery layer of RelNet provides this feature. Notice that all delivered messages arrive in the same order as they are sent, regardless of their marking; however, nonguaranteed delivery messages could be lost.

RelNet accomplishes this result by depositing the messages for failed sites into the so-called reliable buffers. There is one such buffer for each site. Reliable buffers are implemented through several physical buffers, called **spoolers**, distributed at several sites. When a message is marked "guaranteed delivery" and the receiver site is down, it is the responsibility of this layer to distribute the message to the spoolers of that site. When the message is safely stored at these spoolers, the transmission is acknowledged to the sending process, even if the message has not yet reached its destination. In fact, it is ensured that the destination site will examine the message upon its recovery, in the appropriate order with respect to all other "guaranteed delivery" messages.

We sketch the algorithms used by sender, receiver, and spooler sites for exchanging "guaranteed delivery" messages; however, we do not deal with the management of failures of spoolers and with possible message "gaps" (i.e., messages not received by spoolers because of their temporary failures); a detailed description can be found in reference [9.10]. Sender, receiver, and spooler sites can be in two states: spooling, during failures of the destination, and nonspooling, in the normal situation.

The sender in the nonspooling state sends messages normally; however, if one of the messages is not acknowledged within a given timeout, the sender requests the global clock layer to regard the receiver as crashed, sends a "start-spooling" message to spoolers, and enters the spooling state.

The sender in the spooling state sends its messages to all spoolers and waits for their acknowledgments. It enters the nonspooling state upon receipt of the "stop-spooling" message from the spoolers.

The receiver in the nonspooling state acknowledges received messages normally; it enters the spooling state after a crash or after having received a "you are down" message.

The receiver in the spooling state, during its restart, selects one of its spoolers and empties it by requesting the spooled messages. When all messages have been examined, the receiver receives a "stop-spooling" message from the spooler, and at this time the receiver switches to a different spooler. In order not to process the same message twice, a list of message timestamps is initially requested from each spooler.

The spooler in the nonspooling state replies "stop spooling" to all incoming messages, with the only exception of a "start spooling" message, which causes it to enter the other state.

The spooler in the spooling state can receive messages from the sender, which are normally acknowledged, and can receive a message request from the receiver; upon receipt of this message, the next message stored in the buffer is sent to the receiver. The message is deleted from the buffer when the transmission is acknowledged. When the buffer is empty, the spooler enters the nonspooling state.

A catastrophe at this level arises when a message marked "guaranteed delivery" gets lost. This can happen when the destination and all its spoolers are down at the same time; by having an adequate number of spoolers for each site, this catastrophe can be made arbitrarily unlikely.

12.4.3 Transaction Control Layer

This layer provides the higher-level features of RelNet:

1. The capability of obtaining a new transaction identifier, required at the beginning of the read phase of transaction execution.
2. The capability of creating participant processes (or agents) of a transaction; they are destroyed when the transaction is committed or aborted.
3. The capability of ensuring transaction atomicity. This entails the capability of either committing the transaction at all sites or aborting it at all sites.

In order to provide the third feature, 2-phase-commitment has been adapted to the SDD-1 environment. The simple use of 2-phase-commitment would lead to the following protocol for the coordinator:

Phase 1*a*   The coordinator sends to participants update messages marked "guaranteed delivery."

Phase 1*b*   The coordinator waits for acknowledgments of guaranteed delivery messages.

Phase 2*a*   The coordinator sends its decision marked "guaranteed delivery."

Phase 2*b*   The coordinator waits for acknowledgments of guaranteed delivery messages.

Notice that the guaranteed delivery feature allows committing a transaction even if some of the participants are not "up" at commitment time: it is only required that update messages be safely stored in the spoolers. Thus, the above mechanism is insensitive to crashes of participants during 2-phase-commitment; however, it is very sensitive to the failure of the coordinator.

In order to deal with failures of the coordinator, **backup processes** are used. These processes are created by the coordinator before initiating the commitment protocol, and can substitute for the coordinator in case of its failure. In order to ensure that only one process will substitute for the coordinator, backups are linearly ordered, so that the first one "looks" at the coordinator, the second looks at the first one, and so on. If one backup fails (say, backup k), backup $k + 1$ starts looking at backup $k - 1$; backup k will never again be involved in the transaction. "Looking" in this case means periodically sending control messages (similar to guardians).

The commitment protocol including backups consists of four phases:

Phase 1*a*   The coordinator establishes n linearly ordered backups. Each backup is informed of the participants' identity.

Phase 1*b*   The coordinator receives the confirmation of the existence of backups.

Phase 2*a*   The coordinator sends to participants update messages marked "guaranteed delivery."

Phase 2*b*   The coordinator waits for acknowledgments of guaranteed delivery messages.

Phase 3*a*   The coordinator communicates its decision to backups.

Phase 3*b*   The coordinator waits for the acknowledgment from backups, and considers as failed those sites which do not respond within a given timeout.

Phase 4*a*   The coordinator sends to participants its decision marked "guaranteed delivery."

Phase 4*b*   The coordinator waits for acknowledgments of guaranteed delivery messages. Then it destroys the backups.

When a backup substitutes for the coordinator or for another backup acting as the coordinator, either it has received the decision or it takes the abort decision. It first performs phase 3 of the protocol by communicating the decision to the other backups and waiting for an acknowledgment. This is required even if the new coordinator confirms the decision of the previous coordinator, because the new coordinator does not know whether the decision had been already communicated to the backups by the previous coordinator. Then the new coordinator performs phase 4 of the above protocol.

With this protocol a catastrophe is represented by the unavailability of any backup for the transaction when the coordinator fails. As in the other cases, it can be made arbitrarily unlikely.

CONCLUSIONS

SDD-1 has been the first large project in distributed database management and has experienced many new techniques. Many of the ideas which have been presented in Part I of this book have been proposed and used for the first time in the SDD-1 project, such as fragmentation, semi-joins, timestamps for concurrency control, spoolers, and backup coordinators. The overall architecture of SDD-1 has a clear decomposition in modules and layers. However, the performance of the SDD-1 system is poor, and some of its features appear now rather weak:

1. Concurrency control is conservative and is not deadlock-free. The usefulness of conflict graph analysis in a real-life environment has not been demonstrated.
2. The use of Datamodule and Datalanguage as the local DBMS and DML introduces some limitations in query processing which would not be required by a fully relational system.
3. The reliability system does not survive network partitions.

Annotated Bibliography

The papers describing SDD-1 have already been referenced in other chapters. References [3.1] and [10.3] contain an overview of SDD-1, reference [6.5] describes query processing, references [8.18] and [8.19] describe concurrency control, and reference [9.10] describes the reliable network.

Chapter 13

The R* Project

The R* system is developed at the IBM San Jose Research Laboratory in California. The goal of the R* project is to build a distributed database made of cooperating but autonomous sites, each one supporting a relational database system. R* is the natural extension toward distributed environments of System R, a relational database management system prototype, which is now commercially available as the IBM product SQL/DS. The star in R* comes from the Kleene Star operator (R* = R, RR, RRR, ...), denoting an arbitrary number of R's.

Data in R* is stored in relations; presently, R* does not support fragmentation and replication. In R*, sites need not be geographically distant: different sites can be on the same computer. This is considered important not only for the development and testing of the database applications, but also for operational systems, in which different R* modules can be placed on the same computer for security, accounting, or performance reasons.

The most important objective of R* is to provide site autonomy. Site autonomy is achieved when each site is able both to control accesses from other sites to its own data and to manipulate its data without being conditioned by any other site. While the first goal is completely achieved by R*, we will see that the second goal is only partially achieved, since a loss of site autonomy cannot be avoided during the 2-phase-commitment of transactions.

Site autonomy also requires that the system be able to grow incrementally and to operate continuously, with new sites joining to existing ones, without requiring existing sites to agree with joining sites on global data structures or definitions.

Another important issue in R* is location transparency (the user is not aware of the actual location of data); thus, from the programmer's viewpoint, the use of R* is essentially equivalent to the use of a centralized system. The relevant extensions to the SQL language due to distribution are:

1. Naming, which is extended according to the mechanisms described in Section 10.1.3. An R* "systemwide" name includes for each object the specification of

$$\langle creator \rangle @ \langle creator\text{-}site \rangle . \langle object \rangle @ \langle birth\text{-}site \rangle$$

   Notice that this naming scheme includes the birth site of each object, which is a static property, but does not include the actual location of the object, which can change from time to time. Synonyms and defaults are used for simplifying this naming scheme.

2. The possibility of moving objects between sites (object "migration").

While few additional language features have been introduced in R*, the major achievement of the R* system is to provide most of the functionalities of SQL/DS in a distributed environment.

This chapter describes the most relevant features of R*; we first outline the architecture of the system and the structure of computation and communication. Section 13.2 describes the compilation, recompilation, and execution of queries; we show that the compilation of a query is a distributed transaction which requires the agreement of all sites at which the compiled query will be executed. Section 13.3 presents the management of a particular kind of view, called a **shorthand view**. Section 13.4 describes protocols for data definition, which are based upon interpretation instead of compilation. Section 13.5 describes transaction management, in particular the presumed commit and presumed abort protocols for commitment, which are optimized variations of the standard 2-phase-commitment protocol. Finally, Section 13.6 describes a distributed terminal management facility developed in the context of the R* project.

Some features of R* have been already described in Part I of this book; access path selection (query optimization) was described in Section 6.2.4; object naming and catalog management were described in Section 10.1.3. R* uses the algorithm for distributed deadlock detection developed by Obermarck, a simplified version of which has been presented in Section 8.2.2.

13.1 ARCHITECTURE OF R*

R* is composed of three major components: a local database management system, a data communication component which provides message transmission, and a transaction manager which coordinates the implementation of multisite transactions. The local database management system is further divided into two components: a storage system, concerned with the storage and retrieval of data, and a database language processor, which translates high-level SQL statements into operations on the storage system. The storage system used in the R* project, called **RSS***, is based on the research storage system of System R, which is described in reference [13.1]. These components are shown in Figure 13.1.

R* sites communicate via the Inter System Communication (ISC) facility of CICS, described in Chapter 11. Each R* site runs in a CICS address space, and CICS handles terminal I/O and message communication. The communication is

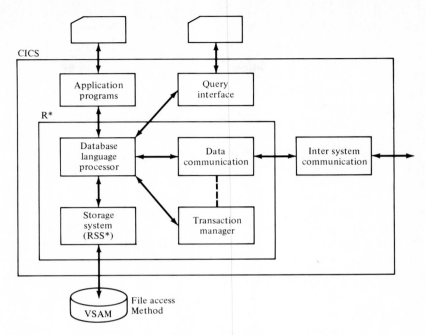

Figure 13.1 Architecture of the R* system.

assumed to be unreliable (i.e., there is no guarantee that a transmitted message will be eventually delivered), but it is assumed that delivered messages are correct, not replicated, and received in the same order as they were sent.

An application program makes all database access requests to the R* system at its local site. All intersite communications are between R* systems at different sites, since R*, rather than an application program, is responsible for locating distributed data. Thus, in the R* environment there is no need for remote application programs.

The transaction manager at the site of the application considers the first SQL statement which is not within an explicitly defined transaction as the start of a transaction, and implicitly performs a begin_transaction. When the user completes a session, an implicit end_transaction is assumed, and all the work done is committed.

Explicit commit and abort instructions can enclose several SQL statements when the application programmer wants them to be considered as an atomic unit by the transaction manager; after any explicit commit or abort instruction, R* will assume that the next statement begins a new unit of work, and will implicitly issue a begin_transaction.

R* can also be invoked using a "user-friendly-interface" (UFI); in this case, SQL statements are individually submitted from UFI to R*, and each statement is treated as an individual transaction.

To each transaction, the transaction manager assigns a unique transaction identifier, made with a local transaction counter and the identifier of the site.

The computation model of R*, described in reference [7.10], has been developed with the objective of supporting the repeated execution of predefined applications. It is expected that many SQL statements will be issued by the same application program, and therefore that a user session with R* will last a long time. Thus, it is convenient to establish a computational structure that can be used for several database access requests, and to maintain information about the state of the distributed application at all involved sites.

R* uses the "process" model of computation (recall the discussion in Section 7.4.1). Instead of allocating a different process to each database access request, a process is created for a user on the first request at a remote site, and maintained until the end of the application. Thus, the number of processes assigned to an application is limited, and the cost of process creation is reduced. User identification is performed only once, at the creation of the process, and at that time all the access plans required by that particular application are loaded into the process memory.

A process activated at a remote site can, in turn, request the activation of a process at another site. In general, a computation in R* may require the generation of a tree of processes which all belong to the same application.

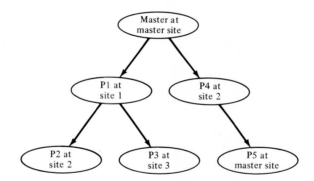

Figure 13.2   Tree of processes in a R* computation.

Figure 13.2 shows that multiple processes belonging to the same application can execute at the same time on the same site. This is not contradictory with the above statement that a process is created at a remote site at the first request and maintained until the end of the application; as shown in the figure, two processes are created for the same application at the same site only if they are requested by two different processess of the same application. The problems which are due to the concurrent execution of several processes on behalf of the same transaction at the same site are avoided by strictly serializing their accesses.

Processes communicate using sessions which are established when the remote process is created and are retained for the whole processing. Thus, processes and sessions constitute a stable computational structure for an application. Sessions of R* operate in half duplex, with one of the processes controlling the flow of messages. After having sent a request using a session, the requester can either wait for a response or proceed; in the latter case, it can issue another request to a different process using a different session, thus starting a parallel computation.

Sessions are particularly useful for the detection of processor and communication failures; communication failures are reported to the communicating processes, taking advantage of low-level protocols (acknowledgments and timeouts). When the session between two processes fails, the current transaction is aborted; processes which cannot communicate with parents also destroy the sessions for communicating with their children (as they have been "isolated" from the requesting application), while other sessions are retained for subsequent attempts to continue the application with a different access strategy.

Two additional types of communication are possible in R*. Signals can be passed, along a session, from the receiver to the sender in order to halt the transmission of data; this is useful when the receiver is no longer interested in receiving additional information.

Messages can be also sent using datagram protocols. A datagram generates a process at the receiver site which runs a program to handle it. Datagrams are used for deadlock detection and transaction recovery; in fact, these functions are continuously performed by R*, and therefore the loss of messages is solved by simply repeating message transmission at the next cycle.

13.2 COMPILATION, EXECUTION, AND RECOMPILATION OF QUERIES

In the R* system, SQL queries can be either statically compiled (once for several executions) or dynamically compiled (immediately before a single execution). The former case is used for repetitive queries, and the latter for unanticipated ones; in the R* project, more importance is given to repetitive queries than to unanticipated ones. In both cases, nonprocedural SQL statements are translated into access plans which specify the order in which relations are accessed, the site at which the access is made, the method used for performing each operation, and the access path used to retrieve or manipulate tuples in the RSS*.

Query compilation, described in reference [6.11], corresponds to the generation and distribution of low-level programs for accessing the RSS* for every high-level SQL statement. These programs can be executed repeatedly, and recompilation is required only when definitions of data used by the SQL statement are changed. In order to be able to detect that a recompilation is required, it is necessary to store information about the dependencies of the compiled query on data definitions. If a query is interpreted, then the determination of an access plan is done for every execution of the query.

In the design of R*, several options have been considered about which site should be responsible for doing the compilation of a query. The centralized solution, with one site in charge of all compilations, was clearly unacceptable, since this contrasts with the basic concept of site autonomy. Likewise, doing the compilation only at the site on which the query is presented was considered not acceptable, because of the need for preserving the autonomy of the other sites, which must be able to reject the plans regarding their own data.

The "recursive" compilation approach, in which each site performs part of query compilation and then asks some other site to compile the remainder subquery, has the drawback that it requires negotiations among the sites which perform the compilation. Different sites could generate different plans for the execution of the same query because they do not have consistent catalog information. For example, consider a query that can be answered using two different access plans and assume that each site is convinced that the best access plan is the one which involves the other site. Most likely, in this situation each site would transmit the query to the other site for compilation, thus determining an endless loop.

The solution which has been selected for R* is to give to the site at which the query is presented, called the **master**, the responsibility for the "global" compilation of the query. The global plan specifies the order of the operations and the method that should be used in order to perform them. The other sites which participate in the compilation are called **apprentices**; they receive the portion of the global plan which pertains to them, and select the best plan of access to their local data consistent with the global plan.

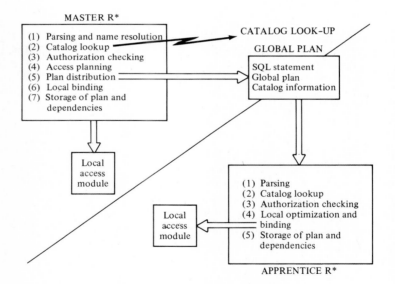

Figure 13.3 Query compilation in R*.

The query compilation process at the master and apprentice sites is shown in Figure 13.3. Query compilation at the master site involves the following steps:

1. *Parsing of the query*. This step involves syntax verification of the SQL statement and the resolution of names, which corresponds to the transformation from print names to systemwide names, done in the context of the user at the master site (recall Section 10.1.3); the parser generates a tree representation of the query.

2.   *Access to catalog information.* If the data used by the query are stored locally, catalog information is also local. Otherwise, catalog information can be retrieved either from local caches of remote data or from remote catalogs at the sites which store the data. The identity of these sites is known by looking at the catalog at the birth site of the data (see Section 10.1.3).

   Catalogs contain the profiles of relations (i.e., relation name and synonyms, attribute names and types, the number of distinct values of attributes, etc.) and information on available access paths. The master distributes to the apprentices, together with the plan produced at step 4, the version numbers of the catalog entries used in the compilation, and apprentices check the version number of the catalog entries at their sites in order to ensure that the catalog information upon which the global plan is built is consistent with the local catalog information.

3.   *Authorization checking.* Authorization checking is performed on local relations (initially at the master, later at the apprentice sites). It consists in determining whether the user compiling the query has the appropriate access rights.

4.   *Access planning (query optimization).* The methods presented in Section 6.2.4 are used for determining a global access plan. The R* optimizer considers the amount of I/O, CPU, and messages required by the query for producing the global plan, instead of just minimizing the number of messages required for data transmission.

5.   *Plan distribution.* The full global plan is distributed to all apprentices. It specifies the order of operations and the method used for them, together with some suggestions for local operations, which might or might not be followed by apprentices. It also includes the original SQL statement (with resolved systemwide names), catalog information, and the specification of parameters to be exchanged between sites when the query is executed.

6.   *Local binding.* The names used in the part of the plan which is executed at the master's site are bound to internal names of objects at that site.

7.   *Storage of plan and dependencies.* The local plan at the master site is translated into a "local access module," which will be executed at the local instance of the RSS*. This plan is stored together with the related "dependencies," which indicate the relations and access methods used by the plan. When these data become unavailable (for instance, because a relation used by the access module is deleted), then dependencies are violated, and execution is suspended.

   Apprentices receive their portions of the plan, which consist of the following information:

1.   The original SQL statement
2.   The global plan prepared for them by the master, from which they isolate the portion which pertains to them
3.   The catalog information used by the master

   Notice that the master assembles a high-level SQL statement describing the subquery to the apprentice, rather than sending to it some internal representation produced by the parser. The rationale for this choice is that, in the future, each apprentice could store a different local version of the optimizer; therefore, passing a high-level language statement gives more independence and portability.

Each apprentice performs the following steps: parsing, catalog look-up (at its site), authorization checking, and local access optimization. Local optimization is useful for modifying some erroneous decision of the master about operations involving the apprentice, based on incomplete information about available access paths. Thus, different access methods (e.g., different indexes) could be used, or different join methods for local joins. Finally, local names are bound, and plans and dependencies are stored.

When all SQL statements of the same application program have been compiled by all apprentices, the master requests the transaction manager to commit the compilation, considered as an atomic unit; the 2-phase-commitment protocol is used to ensure that either the compilation is successful at all sites, or it fails at all sites.

Execution   At execution time, plans previously sent to apprentices are retrieved and executed. The master site sends "execute" requests to apprentices, which in turn send "execute" requests to their subordinates; thus, a tree of processes is activated. Each intermediate-level process receives result data, packed in blocks, from subordinates, and as soon as the first results are received, it can begin its own execution; results, also packed in blocks, are immediately sent to the higher-level processes; thus, pipelining is achieved. A signal can be used by superiors in the tree to stop the transmission of results from subordinates.

Recompilation   At execution time, a flag in the catalogs is tested to determine if the access module is valid. This flag is set to valid after the successful completion of a compilation, and becomes invalid when data definitions it depends on are changed. In fact, any change in data definition causes a search through the catalogs which record dependencies, to find the access methods (or the views; see the next section) which depend on the object.

If the flag is found to be invalid, recompilation is required. First a **local recompilation** is attempted; i.e., the site at which the data definition has changed tries to recompile its local portion of the query using the data structures which are locally available. Even if this new version could not be "optimal" in a global sense, local recompilation seems to be less expensive than repeating the global compilation of the entire application.

In some cases, however, **global recompilation** is necessary (for instance, when data has been moved to a different site). If no local recompilation is possible, then the entire statement is recompiled, with the site where the application was presented acting as the master site.

13.3 VIEW MANAGEMENT

In SQL/DS, views are defined as the result of a SQL select statement, producing a result relation from one or more operand relations. The result relation gives to the user a new "view" of the database (or external schema in the ANSI-SPARC terminology), which is built through the standard query language. Views are objects of authorization, and in fact views are typically used for granting to users the capability of accessing selected information, instead of complete relations. An example of a view is shown in Figure 13.4.

Create view *TOYSUPPLIER@SF* as
    Select *SNUM, NAME, QTY, DEPT*
    from *SUPPLY@SF, SUPPLIER@SF*
    where *SUPPLY@SF.SNUM=SUPPLIER@SF.SNUM*
    and *SUPPLY@SF.PNUM=*"P1".

Figure 13.4   View definition in R*.

Views are dependent on the existence of the objects used in the SQL statement which define them; clearly, if a view references data which are deleted, the view must be invalidated. Therefore, dependencies of views from actual relations must also be stored. Views are typically used for read-only accesses, since determining the effect of updates of views on the underlying relations is not always possible.

In R*, views can be defined using relations which are not local to the view definition site; therefore, view management is also distributed. In R* terminology, views without associated authorization properties are called **shorthand views**, their use being mainly to provide an easier interface to users; those views which are used for providing authorization are called **protection views**. The management of shorthand views is described in [13.7].

Distribution introduces the additional problems of determining where and how view definitions and dependencies should be stored, and how queries referencing views should be compiled. In R*, view definitions are stored at the site where they are declared; view dependencies are stored at the sites where actual data used in the view definition are stored, also called view's **glue sites**. The latter choice is consistent with site autonomy, since validity of views can be verified by local operations, and is also efficient, since programs using the view require access to the glue sites anyhow. As a consequence of both choices, view definition and deletion are distributed operations.

View definition involves a master site (the site at which the view is presented) and several apprentices (the view glue sites). The master site performs the usual steps in query compilation: parsing, name resolution, and catalog look-up. When a view references another view in its definition, a recursive view composition is performed, producing a compound definition in which only real relations appear (and not views). Then, view definition requests are propagated to all the glue sites of the view; here, the consistency with catalog information of the master site is checked, and then dependencies are stored.

Since the definition of a view is a SQL statement, at the commitment either all glue sites agree with the master, and then the definition is committed, or some of them disagree with the master, and the definition is rejected. In the current implementation of views, no validation is done of the authorizations of the user presenting a view definition, but authorization checking is performed on actual relations at glue sites when the view is used, i.e., when a query which references a view is compiled.

A SQL statement can use a view as if it were an existing relation; the SQL statement is compounded, at the query master site, with the view definition statement, generating a single SQL query which operates on actual data. Notice that this transformation is similar to the "canonic" transformation of Chapter 5, in that an expression operating on virtual objects is translated into an expression operating on physical objects. An example of the composition of a SQL query with the view definition of Figure 13.4 is shown in Figure 13.5.

> Select *DEPTNUM, SNUM*
> from *TOYSUPPLIER@SF, DEPT@SJ*
> where *TOYSUPPLIER@SF.DEPTNUM=DEPT@SJ.DEPTNUM*

(a) User query

> Select *DEPTNUM, SNUM*
> from *SUPPLY@SF, SUPPLIER@SF, DEPT@SJ*
> where *SUPPLY@SF.SNUM=SUPPLIER@SF.SNUM*
> and *SUPPLY@SF.DEPTNUM=DEPT@SJ.DEPTNUM*
> and *SUPPLY@SF.PNUM=*"P1".

(b) Composition

Figure 13.5 Composition of an SQL query with the view definition of Figure 13.4.

Deleting a relation upon which the view was defined has the effect of invalidating the programs operating on the view, as well as the view definition itself; this, however, will be discovered by the first application which uses the view. Global recompilation of the view is attempted at the view definition site. If the recompilation fails, then the view is deleted, by notifying all the glue sites.

13.4 PROTOCOLS FOR DATA DEFINITION AND AUTHORIZATION IN R*

In R*, queries are compiled because it is expected that they will be repeatedly executed. The same assumption, however, cannot be made for data definition, configuration, and authorization statements of SQL. Therefore, these statements are interpreted. These statements can operate on objects which are allocated at remote sites. Moreover, objects could move from one site to another, requiring more than one remote access for executing each statement. In order to facilitate the interpretation of these statements, special protocols have been designed, with a common basic structure; the description of these protocols is taken from reference [13.6].

Interpreted statements are classified into two categories:

1. **Statically oriented processing statements (SOPS)** include statements which reference only static entities, i.e., entities whose location does not change (users, programs, sites). With SOPS, the site of execution can be deduced from the statement itself.
2. **Dynamically oriented processing statements (DOPS)** include statements which reference dynamic entities, i.e., entities whose location can change (such as relations and views). With DOPS, the site(s) upon which the statement will be executed is not known beforehand.

The protocols for dealing with both types of statements have the same basic structure. The migration of execution from one site to another is made using a remote procedure call mechanism. Each statement is programmed as an individual procedure which can either execute its function at the local site or ask to be executed at a different site. When a procedure says: "I wish I were executed at site x," a distributed recursive procedure call is made to that site, by passing the user identification and the statement itself. In this way, the remote execution of the statement at site x is initiated. During this execution, the same mechanism can be used, in turn, for requesting the execution at a different site y. Clearly, a procedure asks to be executed at site x because it requires to access data which is at site x; the possibility of determining dynamically the "next" site x to visit allows translating DOPS statements efficiently.

This method gives several advantages:

1. Procedures are specified on the basis of the function to be performed, and not on the basis of data distribution.
2. Site autonomy is preserved, because each request is distributed in the form of a high-level statement and each site can independently make a decision about the request.

The scheme of a distributed recursive procedure is the following:

1. Parsing of the statement and local user identification are performed.
2. The sites at which some work has to be done are determined.
3. For a site x at which work must be done, either x is the current site, and the work is performed locally, or x is a remote site, and the work is performed by issuing recursively a remote procedure call at that site.

Step 3 of the method is performed sequentially, with only one process executing at a given time; the remote procedure call is made synchronously, with the calling process suspending itself at the call and resuming its execution only when the remote process is completed. The possibility of broadcasting the same request to several remote sites with an asynchronous procedure call, thus having remote sites working in parallel, was considered but not implemented. In fact, efficiency in executing these nonrepetitive statements is not considered very important.

Example 13.1

This example of execution of a distributed recursive call for a DOPS statement is a simplified version of an example presented in reference [13.6]. Consider a catalog modification operation (for instance, the creation of a new index on a relation). This operation can be requested by calling the recursive procedure

$$\text{CATMOD(user\_id, site\_id, presumed, found)}$$

where user_id is the user identifier, site_id indicates the site at which the procedure wants to be executed, presumed is a boolean parameter indicating if the site is supposed, according to cached catalog information, to store the catalog entry, and found is a boolean parameter indicating whether the catalog modification has been performed.

procedure CATMOD (USER_ID, SITE_ID, PRESUMED, FOUND)

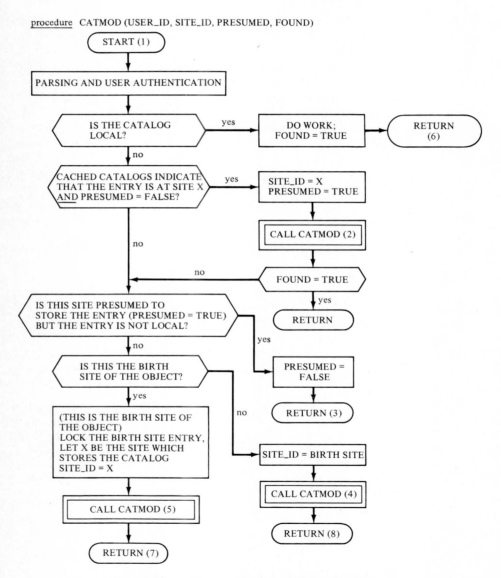

Figure 13.6 Flowchart of procedure CATMOD.

Since R* does not presently provide replication, this statement will ultimately be executed at one site only (the site which stores the entry together with the relation; recall Section 10.1.3 on catalog management in R*). Unfortunately, this site is not known before executing the statement. Thus, if the entry is not at the user site, the simplest way to determine its allocation is to access the birth site, and to find the allocation information there. The CATMOD procedure uses a more sophisticated method, by trying to determine the allocation of the entry using cached catalog information, if available. As we have seen, this information could be wrong, since updates are not propagated to cached catalog entries. Thus, only one attempt is performed; if the cached information is wrong, then the birth site is accessed.

The CATMOD procedure is written according to the following schema (see the flowchart of Figure 13.6):

1. Parsing of the statement and identification of the user
2. If this site has the catalog entry, then do local work and return to caller
3. If the cached catalogs at this site indicate that a remote site x stores the catalog entry, then site_id is set to x, presumed is set to true, and a recursive remote procedure call is issued
4. It this site is supposed to store the catalog entry (presumed is true), but this assumption is wrong, then return to the caller
5. If this site is not the birth site of the object, then site_id is set to the birth site and a recursive remote procedure call is issued
6. If this site is the birth site of the object, then the identity of the current storage site of the object is read in the local catalog. Recall from Section 10.1.3 that the birth site of an object has always a catalog entry for it, which contains the indication of the current storage site of the object. The local catalog entry is locked to prevent object migration, then site_id is set to the storage site of the object and a recursive remote procedure call is issued
7. Return to caller

The execution of CATMOD is requested by the call of the CATMOD procedure with the user_id of the current user, site_id of the current site, presumed and found set to false.

The maximum number of remote procedure calls is three. A first remote procedure call might be done on the basis of the cached catalog entries at the site where the statement is presented; this is attempted only once. This attempt should be successful most of the time. If it fails, however, a second remote procedure call is required at the birth site of the object. Finally, if the birth site does not store a copy of the object, then the catalog entry at the birth site gives the identity of the remote site storing the object, which is accessed with a third remote procedure call. Figure 13.7 shows the sequence of remote procedure calls and returns which are required in this last case. The numbers in Figure 13.7 refer to the statement numbers of the flowchart of Figure 13.6.

13.5 TRANSACTION MANAGEMENT

A transaction in the R* system is an atomic and durable unit of execution. It is constituted by one or more SQL statements enclosed within a begin_transaction and

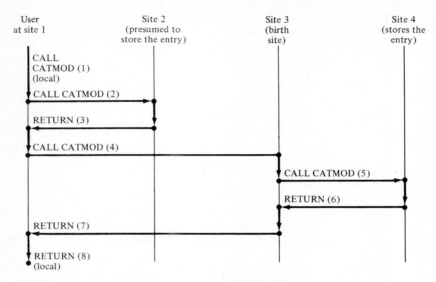

Figure 13.7 Remote procedure calls required by procedure CATMOD.

an end_transaction. Transactions are given unique transaction identifiers, made up of a sequence number and the identifier of the site at which the transaction is requested. Concurrency control is provided by the 2-phase-locking mechanism, with transactions holding their locks until the commit or abort to provide isolation. Distributed deadlock detection is performed as we have described in Section 8.2.2. When a deadlock is detected, its resolution consists of aborting one of the transactions in the wait-for cycle (the one which has performed less work is typically aborted).

In the R* system, transactions are committed using two variations of the standard 2-phase-commitment protocol described in Chapter 7. These variations, described in reference [9.19], have been designed with the purpose of improving the performances of protocols, in terms of both messages exchanged and operations required on logs. In the description of these protocols we will use the term "force a log" for the operation of copying a log record into stable storage, and the term "write a log" for the operation of writing a log record into virtual memory which will eventually be taken to stable storage. When a record is forced in the log, the local recovery mechanism will certainly be aware of the record. When the record is only written, a system crash before copying it into stable storage could cause log information to be lost (see the discussion of this problem in Section 7.2.1).

Before discussing the variations to standard 2-phase-commitment, we stress that this protocol causes a loss of site autonomy that cannot be eliminated. In fact, before entering the ready state, any site can abort a transaction at any time, thus maintaining its autonomy from the coordinator. However, when a participant enters the ready state, it is no longer allowed to abort the transaction; therefore, the transaction's resources are "sequestered" by the coordinator and are not available to the participant until the coordinator sends a message containing its decision. This loss of site autonomy cannot be eliminated, since it is required for providing atomicity of transactions.

13.5.1 Presumed Abort Protocol

In the "presumed abort" algorithm, when the recovery mechanism has no information about a transaction, it presumes that the transaction has been aborted. If this deduction is made consistently by the recovery mechanism, it is possible to design a 2-phase-commitment algorithm in which the coordinator can forget an aborted transaction earlier than in the standard 2-phase-commitment schema. In fact, when the coordinator receives a negative answer and makes the decision of aborting the transaction, it can broadcast the abort messages to all participants, write a global abort record in the log without the need to force it, and then forget the transaction.

The recovery mechanism will then be able to deduce the abort from the log at the coordinator's site which either contains the global abort record, or has no information available at all. Notice that this approach allows writing the global abort records, instead of forcing them. Also the participants force in the log only the commit records, and can write abort records in their logs.

Another feature of the presumed abort protocol is related to the possibility of discovering that some participants of the commitment are in fact read-only subtransactions. When a participant does not make any write, it does not need to log records, and can release the locks and forget the transaction immediately after having sent its positive decision. In fact, it does not need to know whether the transaction will eventually commit or abort.

If all the participants are read-only, then the coordinator need not enter the second phase of the commit; it forces a commit record, releases its locks, and forgets about the transaction. When part of the participants are read-only and part require an update, then the only participants which enter in the ready state are those which require an update.

13.5.2 Presumed Commit Protocol

The presumed commit protocol is dual to the presumed abort protocol, because it is developed in such a way that "no information" available to the recovery process at the master site is equivalent to a commit. The duality leads to the development of an approach in which aborts have to be acknowledged, while commits do not. This approach, however, is not immediately correct: a crash of the coordinator after having sent the prepare messages but before having written the global commit record would lead to the scenario in which coordinator recovery would undo the transaction and abort, while the participants would find no information and commit. This is avoided by forcing in the log of the coordinator the prepare record, which was not required by the presumed abort protocol. We recall from Section 7.2.4 that the prepare record stores the identity of participants. Thus, when the recovery mechanism at the coordinator site discovers the above crash situation, it can notify the participants of the abort. This notification must be acknowledged, and the global abort record is forced by the recovery mechanism only after all acknowledgment messages are received. In this commitment protocol, the commit records are written, and only the abort records are forced in the log.

Notice that the coordinator needs to force a record in the log with the identities of all participants even if the transaction will turn out to be read-only.

13.5.3 Comparison of Presumed Abort and Presumed Commit

The presumed commit protocol is more efficient than the presumed abort protocol with participants which perform update transactions successfully, since it does not require acknowledgments and forcing of commit records. On the other hand, the presumed abort protocol is more efficient with participants which perform read-only transactions successfully, because the additional record with the participant information need not be forced in the log of the coordinator. In R*, it is possible to select the protocol for each individual transaction; presumed abort is suggested for transactions which are supposed to be read-only, presumed commit for all other transactions.

13.6 TERMINAL MANAGEMENT

In the context of the R* project, a distributed terminal management (DTM) facility has been developed for allowing users at a single terminal to interact with multiple computations, possibly executed at different sites. Using this facility, a user can see the outputs produced by multiple processes, or produce inputs for them. Terminal management systems are typically developed either by partitioning the display of the terminal and assigning a partition to each computation or by multiplexing the display and switching between different computations. DTM belongs to the latter category.

The description of the DTM developed for the R* project is in reference [13.8]. For the sake of simplicity, the interaction between the terminal operator and the computation is regarded simply as a sequential stream of data; in fact, DTM can use more sophisticated display features. DTM commands are prefixed with a special character "%" which distinguishes them from other inputs.

Each process is connected to a logical terminal for receiving input from a user and producing output for a user. Possibly, several processes share the same logical terminal. The command %CONNECT ⟨computation⟩ is used for assigning a physical terminal to the logical terminal of an existing computation or for initiating a new computation.

Output lines from multiple processes associated with the same logical terminal go into an output stream buffer (OSB); lines from different processes are labeled by the process identifier (or, more simply, are in different colors). Output lines from the same computation are produced in the appropriate sequence; output lines from different computations can be interleaved.

When processes assigned to the same logical terminal require input, this input must be time-multiplexed. The command %SWITCH is available to the user for cycling through the processes which are competing. The use of %SWITCH is not required when a single process at a time is requesting input (for instance, when the computation consists of synchronous procedure calls).

Finally, it is possible to logically attach a physical terminal to a remote site and to start a computation on that site, using the command %PASSTHRU ⟨system⟩. For example, this facility allows a user of site y connected to a physical terminal at site x to pass through to the home site, where the log-in and identification can be performed. Several levels of pass-throughs are permitted. Pass-throughs are terminated using a %QUIT command.

CONCLUSIONS

All the features of the R* prototype presented in this chapter are operational, including data definition and manipulation statements of SQL, transaction management, deadlock detection, and recovery mechanisms. Experiments on the performance of the system are now ongoing, as well as the initial demonstrations. Though R* is a research prototype, it has been developed in a systematic and sound way, using the most experienced techniques for transaction management (i.e., 2-phase-locking and 2-phase-commitment). This prototype can be therefore considered a reasonable basis for the development of advanced systems.

In the context of the R* project, several other research problems are being investigated.

Snapshots   Snapshots, as described in Section 3.5, are temporary relations produced as the result of a SQL statement. They present a view of the database which was consistently retrieved at some past time, and which is periodically "refreshed" but not updated online. Snapshots are used in centralized databases to avoid repeated executions of the same query for those read-only applications which do not really require the latest version of data. In a distributed environment, snapshots can be used for replicating data from a remote site without incurring the high overhead that is caused by replicated updates.

Protection views   As we briefly mentioned in Section 13.3, protection views are objects for which it is possible to grant and revoke access authorizations. In managing protection views, several problems arise as a result of the fact that protection views need to be composed with user's queries at the view definition site; it is not acceptable to let some other site compose the definitions of protection views, since this site could violate the authorization constraints imposed on the view.

Fragmentation and replication   Fragmentation and replication are not presently supported by the R* system. Views can simulate fragmentation. In fact, a global relation of our reference architecture can be defined as a view built on top of several relations at different sites, which represent fragments. However, a more sophisticated view management is necessary in order to perform most of the transformations discussed in Chapter 5 for efficiently translating a global query into a fragment query.

Annotated Bibliography

The R* project is described in detail in several papers and technical reports from the IBM San Jose Research Laboratory in California; this chapter is primarily a synthesis of their content. References [13.1] to [13.3] describe System R, the earlier project developed at San Jose from which System R* originated. Many papers on the R* project have been referenced already in other chapters. They are: references [10.11] and [10.12] on naming and site autonomy issues, references [6.10] to [6.13] on query processing, reference [7.10] on transaction management, and reference [9.19] on the presumed abort and presumed commit protocols. The other aspects described in this chapter are derived from references [13.4] to [13.8].

[13.1]   M. M. Astrahan et al., "System R: A Relational Approach to Database Management," *ACM-TODS*, **1**:3, 1976.

[13.2]   D. Chamberlin et al., "Support for Repetitive Transactions and Ad-hoc Queries in System R," *ACM-TODS*, **6**:1, 1981.

[13.3]   D. Chamberlin et al., "SEQUEL 2: A Unified Approach to Data Definition, Manipulation, and Control," *IBM Journal of Research and Development*, **20**:6, 1976.

[13.4]   R. Williams et al., "R*: An Overview of the Architecture," *Proc. Int. Conf. on Database Systems*, Jerusalem, 1982.

[13.5]   L. M. Haas et al., "R*: A Research Project on Distributed Relational DBMS," *Data Base Engineering*, **5**:4, 1982.

[13.6]   P. F. Wilms, B. G. Lindsay, and P. Selinger, "I wish I were over there: Distributed Execution Protocols for Data Definition in R*," *ACM-SIGMOD*, San Jose, CA, 1983.

[13.7]   E. Bertino, L. M. Haas, and B. G. Lindsay, "View Management in Distributed Database Systems," *Ninth VLDB*, Florence, 1983.

[13.8]   R. A. Yost and B. G. Lindsay, "A Distributed Terminal Management Facility," IBM Report RJ3752, IBM Res. Laboratory, San Jose, CA, 1983.

Chapter 14

Other Homogeneous
Distributed Database Systems

In this chapter, other prototypes of homogeneous distributed database systems are described. They include:

1. DDM, developed at the Computer Corporation of America
2. Distributed-INGRES, developed at the University of California at Berkeley
3. POREL, developed at the University of Stuttgart (Germany)
4. SIRIUS-DELTA, developed at INRIA (France)

Each system is presented in a different section. Finally, a comparison of the features of homogeneous research prototypes, including SDD-1, R*, and these systems, is presented in the conclusions.

14.1 DDM: A DISTRIBUTED DATABASE MANAGER BASED ON THE LANGUAGE ADAPLEX

Adaplex is a language developed at the Computer Corporation of America in Boston by embedding Daplex, a language for accessing and manipulating databases (described in reference [14.1]), into ADA, a new programming language sponsored by the U. S. Department of Defense (described in reference [14.2]).

Two systems supporting the Adaplex language are currently being developed for a centralized and a distributed database, respectively. The former, a local database manager (LDM), is a single-site database system. The latter, a distributed database manager (DDM), will interconnect multiple LDMs, and will allow the development of distributed database applications. Since DDM is being developed at the same research center where SDD-1 was developed, it has inherited several architectural features from that project, in particular the reliability features of the network and the commitment protocol. In this section, we outline the relevant features of DDM (references [14.5] and [14.6]); we also describe those features of LDM which are required for understanding the architecture of DDM (references [14.3] and [14.4]).

Some background information on the language Daplex is also required. Daplex supports the notion of entities, functions, and generalization hierarchies. Thus, it provides more modeling capabilities than the conventional hierarchical, Codasyl, or relational data models. Daplex belongs to the category of functional data models. An example of a Daplex schema is presented in Figure 14.1.

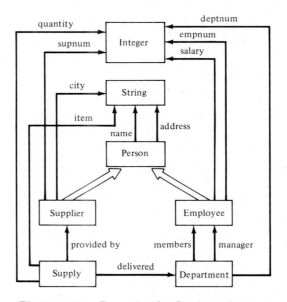

Figure 14.1   Example of a Daplex schema.

1. **Entities** represent conceptual objects. Entities with the same set of properties are grouped together into entity sets. Examples of entity sets are Department, Supplier, and Employee, represented as square boxes in Figure 14.1.

2. **Functions** correspond to the properties of conceptual objects; they are represented as simple arrows in Figure 14.1. Applying a function to an entity of a given entity set returns either a single value or a set of values. Values either are from a given domain (integers, strings, enumeration types, etc.) or refer to other entities. In the former case, functions are similar to attributes of relations (with the additional possibility of returning multiple values for the same tuple). In the latter case, a meaningful connection is provided between entity sets (for instance, for each department entity the member function returns the set of employees who are members of the department and the manager function returns the single employee who manages the department).

3.   **Generalization hierarchies** indicate special relations between entity sets, which are established when one entity set, called the **subtype**, has all the properties (functions) of the other entity set, called the **supertype**. For instance, Employee is a subtype of Person, since all employees have all the properties of persons, and likewise Supplier is a subtype of Person. Hierarchies are represented by double arrows in Figure 14.1.

14.1.1 Data Fragmentation and Distribution

DDM supports horizontal fragmentation of entity sets; i.e., entity sets can be partitioned into disjoint subsets. Horizontal fragmentation is defined using the following two methods.

Primary fragmentation   Entities of the same entity set can be fragmented according to a complete set of disjoint predicates based on properties of the entity set; predicates are the conjunction of conditions which specify subtype membership or a value for a single-valued function. In the presence of generalization hierarchies, all fragmentation conditions are given for the higher-level type in the hierarchy, called the **base type** of the hierarchy, while the partitioning of subtype entity sets is implicitly defined by these conditions. For instance, consider the entity set Person which is the base set of a generalization hierarchy including Employee and Supplier; the following is a valid set of predicates:

$$p_1: \quad \text{Is-supplier AND city} = \text{``LA''}$$
$$p_2: \quad \text{Is-supplier AND city} = \text{``SF''}$$
$$p_3: \quad \text{Is-employee AND } 1 \leq \text{empnum} \leq 100$$
$$p_4: \quad \text{Is-employee AND } 101 \leq \text{empnum} \leq 200$$
$$p_5: \quad \text{Is-employee AND } 201 \leq \text{empnum} \leq 300$$
$$p_6: \quad \text{NOT Is-supplier AND NOT Is-employee}$$

These predicates define the primary horizontal fragmentation of the entity set Person, with the relevant feature that predicates can be built also on subtype membership conditions. Notice that, because of this fragmentation, Supplier entities are partitioned into two subsets and Employee entities into three subsets.

Derived fragmentation   The fragmentation of an entity set can also be made using a single-valued function, which maps each entity of the entity set to an entity of a different entity set for which fragmentation has been already defined. For instance, assume that the Department entity set is fragmented according to different locations. Consider the inverse of the function member which associates each employee to his or her department. Using the inverse of the member function, the Employee entity set (now considered as a base set and not as part of a generalization hierarchy) can be fragmented in the same way as the Department entity set. This fragmentation is equivalent to the derived horizontal fragmentation defined in Chapter 3.

Fragments in DDM can include more than one entity set. **Fragment groups** have been introduced in DDM for collecting entities related by derived fragmentation. A fragment group is constituted of one or more subsets of entities from one or more entity sets, such that one of them has a primary fragmentation and the others have a fragmentation derived from it.

Entities of the same fragment group are stored at the same location. Thus, all references within a fragment group are local. Therefore, locality of reference is the relevant criterion for the design of fragment groups; the methods described in Chapter 4 can be used to this purpose.

In general, each fragment group is replicated at several sites. **Regular sites** for a fragment group are those which store copies to be used during normal activity, while **backup sites** store copies which are used to improve failure resiliency.

14.1.2 Query Compilation

The compilation of an Adaplex program is complicated by the tight coupling of Daplex with ADA, and also by the fact that Daplex is a procedural, one-record-at-a-time language. Thus, before query optimization, a preprocessor isolates the Daplex statements from the ADA program and transforms them into an internal non-procedural representation, called **envelope**; this process is called **decompilation** (recall Section 3.5). The internal representation is a set-oriented expression, because the one-record-at-a-time approach is not appropriate for building distributed access plans. The preprocessing includes in the ADA programs both procedure calls to DDM for building the envelope and calls to procedures for obtaining from the envelope the data required by the one-record-at-a-time processing of ADA.

Query optimization is applied to an envelope for determining the best access plan; the optimization criteria have been briefly described in Section 6.3.3. Compile time optimization consists of determining the partial order of operations (including the selection between nondistributed and distributed join execution) and the use of local access methods. However, a materialization is not selected at compile time (recall that a materialization is a nonredundant copy of the database for executing the query); access plans are built based on the pessimistic assumption that each fragment group is stored at a different site. At execution time, each fragment group is mapped to one of its copies, stored at available "regular" sites, i.e., sites which are operational and have copies available for processing. The assignment is such that intersite communications are minimized.

This approach differs from the "standard" approach to query processing presented in Section 6.1 in the following aspects:

1. The selection of a materialization in order to reduce transmission costs is performed; thus, replication is effectively taken into account in query optimization.
2. Access plan selection takes into account both local and transmission costs.
3. The possibility of dynamically determining the materialization results in a greater flexibility at runtime, since it is possible to select a materialization which requires all its data from sites which are operational.

The negative aspect of this approach is that by postulating the availability of access methods to fragment groups at all sites, a strict constraint is imposed on the applications; i.e., compiled plans should be stored at all "regular" sites. As a consequence, changes in data definition and the recompilation of applications are rather expensive, and site autonomy is not preserved.

14.1.3 Transaction Management and Concurrency Control

Transactions in DDM have a centralized computational structure (recall Chapter 7). At initiation, a transaction identifier is assigned to the root agent. This identifier includes the site of origin of the transaction. Only one agent is selected by the root agent for reading and writing on each particular **fragment group** (**FG**). Since DDM supports replication, the root agent can select this agent at any regular, operational site (only regular copies are available for access).

The commitment of a transaction is performed by a process called **transaction manager** (**TM**), which interacts with the other TMs at all regular sites of the FGs used by the transaction. The TM uses a modified version of the SDD-1 commitment protocol.

The agent which performs write actions on a given FG is also required to propagate the updates to all regular copies of the FG before committing the transaction; backup copies are instead updated in a background fashion. Write operations are broadcast to all regular copies before the commitment. The commitment protocol has a two-level, hierarchical communication structure (see Section 7.4.4).

Concurrency control uses a 2-phase-locking technique with multiversions. Locks are set incrementally, and held until the end of the transactions; thus, 2-phasedness and isolation are provided. Deadlocks are possible, and they are periodically detected and resolved.

The more interesting feature of concurrency control in DDM is the possibility of using old page versions; this feature was developed for the local database manager (LDM), and then extended to DDM.

Each LDM manages a single common pool of pages, called a **buffer pool**, which stores old pages which could be useful for transactions still in progress. Before updating a page, its current version is copied into the buffer pool. By storing an appropriate number of old pages, it is always possible to give to read-only transactions a consistent view ("snapshot" in [3.3]) of the database regardless of concurrent updates. In fact, it is necessary to present to the read-only transaction the version that it would have seen at the beginning of its processing. Thus, read-only transactions do not require synchronization, while update transactions use 2-phase-locking (and so, only one transaction at one time can write a given page). Another use of the buffer pool is for backing up transactions at abort; in this case, the old version is restored from the buffer pool, undoing the effects of the transaction.

In order to implement this idea in the LDM, it is necessary to solve the following problems:

1. To designate the copy of a page which should be read by each transaction
2. To manage the buffer pool (and in particular, to eliminate useless pages from it)

The first problem has been solved by maintaining lists of completed transactions; this information is associated with each new read-only application, while each page identifier contains, among other information, the transaction identifier of the transaction which has written it. By using these identifiers, it is possible to select the appropriate page for reading.

In LDM, the representation of the list of completed transactions is based on the fact that transaction numbers are incrementally assigned. Hence, it is sufficient to give a base transaction number (indicating that all previous transactions are completed) and a bit map (to indicate other completed transactions). Periodically, the base number is advanced.

In DDM, a similar technique is used. This representation, consisting of a base number and a bit map, is associated with each site of the distributed database. Thus, completed transactions can be represented by vectors of base numbers and by the corresponding bit maps. Complications arise in determining which transactions have effectively completed at a given time, and determining this requires the exchange of some information at commitment and at the initiation of read-only applications (see reference [14.5]).

For the second problem, pages in the buffer pool which have become useless must be identified so that they can be canceled. Pages can be in three possible states:

1. **Active**, when they have been written by an ongoing update transaction. Since an active page could be used for backup purposes if the transaction aborts, active pages cannot be deleted.
2. **Potentially active**, when there are ongoing read-only transactions that might read them. Deleting potentially active pages might result in the future need for aborting these read-only transactions.
3. **Free**, when there are no ongoing transactions which require them.

The page replacement algorithm considers the buffer pool as a ring buffer, and maintains several pointers to distinguish pages in these three sets. Pointers need to be updated at transaction initiation and termination. Clearly, if some space is always left in the buffer pool, no read-only transaction will ever incur the risk of being aborted.

14.1.4 Reliability

The reliability features of DDM resemble those of SDD-1. In particular, DDM relies on an **enhanced network** which has very similar properties to RelNet (described in Section 12.4). Features provided by the enhanced network are:

1. To maintain site status tables, which give a consistent view of which sites are up or down
2. To maintain a "watch," which can register remote events (such as recoveries or failures)
3. To have "spoolers" which collect update messages whose destinations are nonoperational sites

The protocols for maintaining global status in the network are similar to those described in Section 9.4 and in reference [9.12].

For each fragment group FG, an appropriate degree of redundancy is determined. Let us assume that, for a particular FG under normal operation, k regular copies are available. When one of them fails, a copy at one of the backup sites is brought online (by performing the missing updates) and becomes a regular copy. When one of the regular sites recovers, its copy is brought online, and if appropriate, one of the online copies of the backup sites goes offline. Managing fragment groups involves deciding, in a distributed fashion, whether each local copy should be kept online or offline and performing the required recoveries and state changes. A confederation of **fragment group managers** (**FGM**s) performs this function. FGMs also provide facilities for reading and writing FGs.

Recovery at each site is performed for each FG. As soon as an FG is backed up, it becomes available to other sites. This increases the availability of the system as compared with other cases (including SDD-1), in which a recovering site must complete the recovery before making any of its data available to other sites.

14.2 DISTRIBUTED-INGRES

Distributed-INGRES was developed at the University of California at Berkeley, as a distributed version of the relational database system INGRES. Distributed-INGRES is designed to operate on both a local (Ethernet-like) network and a geographical (ARPANET-like) network; some aspects of query processing are parametric with respect to the type of network. References to data are classified as either local, typically with 95 percent probability, or remote. In this latter case, it is not important whether the accessed site is close or distant: in Distributed-INGRES there is no notion of "closeness" between sites. This is consistent with our assumptions in Chapters 4 (design) and 6 (query optimization).

Distributed-INGRES provides to its users a relational global schema with fragmentation and allocation transparency. Horizontal fragmentation is supported, while vertical fragmentation is not. Fragments can be replicated; one of them is designated as primary, and this notion is used by transaction management, concurrency control, and reliability algorithms.

Either horizontal fragments are defined by a selection condition, or no selection condition is specified for them; in this case, tuples inserted by an application program running at a given site are stored in the fragment at that site (notice, however, that this last possibility does not allow an explicit control of replication).

14.2.1 Query Processing

Global query processing in Distributed-INGRES extends the decomposition strategy used for single-site INGRES, described in reference [14.8]. The basic idea of decomposition is to apply reductions (projections and selections) and then to decompose the query into irreducible components that overlap on one relation only (i.e., which are connected by a single join condition); components are progressively analyzed and solved by a tuple-substitution technique. In the distributed version of this algorithm, described in reference [6.19], the tuple-substitution technique was replaced by the selection and solution of "pieces" (i.e., subqueries) of irreducible components. The initial version of the algorithm used a heuristic choice of "pieces." Later versions have been developed in which all possible choices of "pieces" were exhaustively tested.

The optimizer of Distributed-INGRES has two very peculiar aspects:

1. Processing is distributed for exploiting parallelism; thus, the more sites involved, the greater the parallelism. This consideration leads to redistributing fragments of relations at the execution sites of operations, with the purpose of "equalizing" fragments (i.e., having fragments of about the same size and therefore requiring about the same processing time). Equalization is used especially with local networks, where communication is less expensive. Note that equalization and locality of processing are conflicting goals, since equalization requires distributing a relation even when processing would be local.

2. During execution, if intermediate results are unexpectedly large, the "backtracking" of a tactic can be done. In this case, it is possible to require an additional optimization in order to change the query processing strategy. The optimizer thus has some precise information from the portion of the already performed execution.

In Distributed-INGRES, the possibility of distributing aggregate functions to fragments, discussed in Chapter 5, is considered; aggregate functions are processed independently from the remainder of the query. Distributed processing is limited to aggregate functions which do not require removing duplicates.

14.2.2 Transaction Management

Distributed-INGRES uses 2-phase-locking for concurrency control. Deadlocks are detected and resolved with a centralized deadlock detector (recall Section 8.2.1). All wait-for information is sent to a single process, called **scoop**. This method has the disadvantage of heavy communications and requires solving the reliability problems of failures and recoveries of the site where the scoop is located.

Transactions in Distributed-INGRES amount to *one* statement in QUEL, the INGRES query language. This limitation is due to the single-site crash recovery mechanism of the version of centralized INGRES that was used for this project. Each QUEL statement is decomposed, by the query optimizer, into a sequence of interactions, which include retrieve and update commands, and transmissions of intermediate results between sites.

The algorithms for transaction commitment perform a protocol which is similar to the 2-phase-commitment protocol, with the additional capability of promoting a participant to coordinator after the coordinator's failure. Algorithms for reliability perform local recovery of a site after a failure and reconfigure dynamically a table of "up" sites on which all sites agree.

Distributed-INGRES uses two sets of algorithms:

1. **Performance algorithms**, which allow executing transactions efficiently, but can generate inconsistent databases
2. **Reliable algorithms**, which have worse performances but are resilient to an arbitrary number k of failures

The performance algorithms are based on the idea of deferring updates to nonprimary copies. In the commitment of transactions, each participant responds "ready to commit" to the coordinator after having updated the primary copy, and waits for the decision from the coordinator. In the case of successful commitment, each participant generates a process which coordinates several "copy" agents for applying the deferred updates to nonprimary copies. Clearly, this protocol is not resilient to a failure of participants which occurs after having performed the local commit but before having generated the "copy" agents; this protocol is also nonresilient to the following types of failures, discussed in reference [9.11]:

1. Mutual consistency of different fragments could be lost when the same update transaction operates on different fragments; then only part of them would be correctly updated
2. Messages to crashed sites could get lost and compromise local recovery

These limitations are very strong, and therefore performance algorithms appear too weak for practical applications. However, there are some cases in which inconsistencies can be limited:

1. When all update transactions affect just one fragment (problem 1 does not arise in this case)
2. When all updates are performed locally
3. When all updates can be executed in strict sequence

The reliable algorithms are simply obtained by incorporating nonprimary copies in the 2-phase-commitment and queuing messages for crashed sites to at least k other sites (for having k-resiliency). Notice that the primary copy method is substituted by a write-all method.

Local recovery and reconfiguration algorithms are common to the two approaches. Local recovery is based on reading the outstanding messages for the recovering site, and then either backing up or committing incomplete transactions. Reconfiguration uses a total ordering of sites. The site which receives a "reconfigure" message and is the lowest in the ordering sends the list of all operating sites to all sites, which must agree on the list. If there is agreement, the reconfiguration is completed; otherwise, it is attempted again. This algorithm is simpler than that of Section 9.4.1, but it is not clear what happens with multiple failures or if two different sites, having inconsistent information, both decide to lead the reconfiguration process.

14.3 POREL

POREL is a distributed database system developed at the University of Stuttgart in Germany on a network of minicomputers. Each minicomputer supports a relational DBMS called **relational base machine** (RBM) that was developed in the framework of this project. One of the major goals of POREL is portability on a large variety of machines, including very small ones. Thus:

1. A high-level programming language was used for developing the system; Fortran was initially chosen and later substituted by Pascal.
2. A very limited address space (64K) is sufficient for running POREL, which therefore was developed as a set of cooperating processes, some of them with overlays. This feature allows POREL to be used in any microcomputer with 16-bit addressing, but also reduces the efficiency of POREL on larger mainframes.

Another feature of POREL is the use of a slow communication system with point-to-point connections; thus data and message communication are considered the major overheads.

14.3.1 Architecture

POREL supports horizontal fragmentation, and fragments are nonoverlapping. The system provides fragmentation and allocation transparency; thus the user sees a global, nondistributed relational schema. The relevant features of the software architecture of POREL are shown in Figure 14.2. There are three possible ways to use the POREL system:

1. Dialoguing interactively using a relational database language (RDBL), similar to SQL. The user has the two statements begin_transaction and end_transaction available for explicitly indicating transactions; otherwise any RDBL statement is taken as an individual transaction.
2. Using RDBL embedded into Pascal (P_RDBL). If not otherwise stated in the programs, all RDBL statements which are requested by the same application program are considered part of one transaction.
3. Executing predefined applications, taken from an application library. It is possible to specify run time parameters for them.

In interactions 1 and 2, compilation directly precedes execution, while in interaction 3 compilation and execution take place at distinct times, and typically execution is repeated many times. However, from the system's viewpoint, case 3 is not different from cases 1 and 2, respectively. Thus, the interactions presented to the **source/sink** module of Figure 14.2 are in RDBL or in P_RDBL.

The **first precompiler** filters RDBL statements from P_RDBL and identifies Pascal variables. Then RDBL is translated into sequences of single-site subqueries for the relational base machines, written in relational machine language (RML). Optimization is done in two steps, **network-independent** and **network-oriented**, respectively. Finally, the notion of RML statements and of Pascal variables in RML

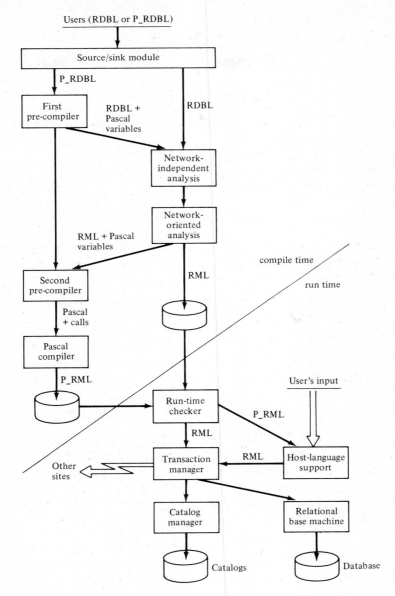

Figure 14.2 Software architecture of the POREL system.

statements allows Pascal code to be separated, in the **second precompiler**, from calls to RML. Pascal code is compiled, and Pascal object code and RML statements are stored in libraries; this completes the compile time part of the system.

The run time part of the system includes a **run time checker**, to test that assumptions upon which applications were precompiled still hold at run time; a

host language support, to coordinate communications between executing Pascal programs and POREL; the **transaction manager**, which interacts with other sites and retrieves and updates data from the local RBM and from the **catalog manager**.

Catalogs include data which are used for network-dependent compilation, replicated at each site, and nonreplicated data which refer to locally stored data. Access to catalogs can be obtained only by using special-purpose, precompiled transactions, which preserve catalog integrity; the catalog manager can be seen from the rest of the system as an abstract data type with its own data and procedures.

14.3.2 Query Optimization

RDBL is a SQL-like relational language; RDBL queries are parsed, generating an operator tree, similar to those presented in Chapter 5. The first optimization is network-independent, and consists of applying standard transformations (such as eliminating common subexpressions and pushing selection and projections down in the tree). The subsequent network-dependent analysis performs the following functions:

1. **Fragment substitution** (substituting global relations with their fragments). In doing this, a fixed transformation schema is followed (for instance, the join between fragmented relations is done always distributedly); then operations which generate empty relations are eliminated.
2. **Site selection**, which assigns to each "logical" fragment one of its "physical" copies. The optimizer does not analyze all possible assignments of sites to fragments (that would lead to a combinatorial complexity). Copies are assigned by a heuristic algorithm which performs a bottom-up traversal of the tree, creating intermediate results in a locally optimum way.
3. Finally, data transmission are determined and the required send-receive instructions are inserted into the plan.

14.3.3 Transaction Management, Concurrency Control, and Reliability

Transaction management in POREL uses a centralized computational structure, with one coordinator and several participants. The basic 2-phase-commitment is used, with reliability mechanisms which operate in case of failures of participants and of the coordinator. When one of the participants fails, the two alternatives of aborting the transaction or waiting for the recovery of the participant are compared, and the alternative which is assumed to be the cheapest one is selected. Reliability algorithms rely on the notion of which sites are operational; this global state table is built according to the algorithm described in Section 9.4.

Concurrency control is done by 2-phase-locking, and locks are kept until the end of transactions, for guaranteeing isolation. In order to avoid deadlocks, locks are preclaimed: there is a total ordering of sites, and lock requests cannot be granted at one site unless all locks at precedent sites have already been granted. In this way, no circular waiting conditions can arise.

An original feature of transaction control in POREL is its management of replication. One of the copies of fragments is designated as the primary copy. Update transactions need to lock exclusively the primary copy, thus operating in mutual exclusion. They perform updates to the primary copy and possibly to a local copy. However, they also perform the following operations, before declaring to be "ready to commit":

1. At the primary copy site, an "intention list," containing the updates to be sent to other copies, is stored on stable storage.
2. At all other sites, copies are marked invalid. Note that new locks are not required for this marking.

Copies are updated by a different transaction which is started either when workload conditions are favorable or when a read transaction must make a consistent read.

The following three types of read can be selected by an application:

1. *Without read repeatability.* This is done without requesting locks at all.
2. *With read repeatability, without mutual consistency.* Read locks are required on accessed local copies (which therefore cannot be changed by concurrent update transactions), but copies can be mutually inconsistent.
3. *Consistent read.* Read locks are required on the primary copy, and if copies required for reading are marked invalid, the update transactions pending for them must be executed before reading.

This overall strategy for managing copies is reasonable in some contexts and unreasonable in others. For instance, if all retrievals need to be consistent and typically at least one retrieval occurs between two consecutive updates, then this mechanism "transfers" overhead from updates to retrievals without real advantages. This method is motivated by the need for limiting the number of different sites at which locks are requested by an individual transaction, since preclaiming locks from different sites is a rather long process.

14.4 SIRIUS-DELTA

The SIRIUS project was initiated in 1977, with a number of small subprojects and contracts all over France. Since 1979, most of the work has been done at the main INRIA research center of Rocquencourt, close to Paris. Several prototypes have been developed under the common denominator of the SIRIUS project; in this section, we describe SIRIUS-DELTA, the major prototype developed in this framework. In the next chapter, we will describe the heterogeneity aspects of SIRIUS-DELTA.

The architecture of schemata of SIRIUS-DELTA is described in Figure 14.3a. This architecture seems very different from our reference architecture of Chapter 3. However, when we analyze the content of each schema, we find several common aspects with it.

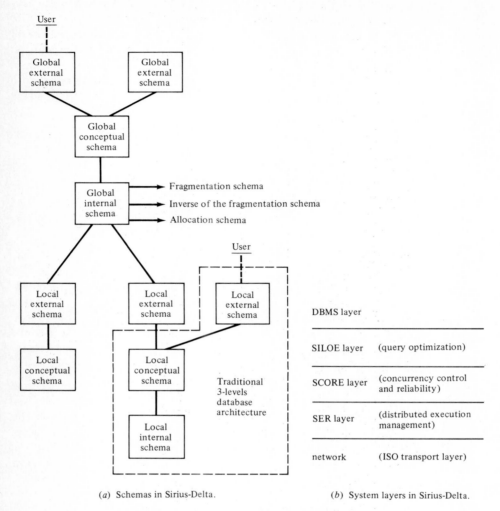

(a) Schemas in Sirius-Delta.   (b) System layers in Sirius-Delta.

Figure 14.3 Architecture of SIRIUS-DELTA.

The highest level in this architecture, the **global external schema**, provides different views to the users of the distributed database and has no counterpart in our reference architecture. The next level, the **global conceptual schema**, is a relational description of the database which provides fragmentation and allocation transparency; thus, it is equivalent to our global schema.

SIRIUS-DELTA uses the relational model for describing data. Relations can be fragmented horizontally and vertically. However, mixed fragmentation is limited to fragmentation trees of depth 2 in which horizontal fragmentation can be applied to vertical fragments.

Derived horizontal fragmentation can be defined by the "VIA" clause, which specifies that tuples of a given relation or vertical fragment are allocated at the same site as tuples or subtuples of another relation having the same primary key attributes. In practice, the latter relation has an autonomous fragmentation and allocation, and the former relation derives its fragmentation and allocation "VIA" a semi-join. Notice that this clause is less general than the definition given in Chapter 3, since it requires the use of a key attribute in the semi-join specification.

The information at the next level, **global internal schema**, is distributed in three sections:

1   A **definition section**, which defines the structure of horizontal or vertical fragments (but does not give their construction formulas from global relations)
2.   A **mapping section**, which specifies how global relations are reconstructed from fragments (similar to the inverse of the fragmentation schema)
3.   A **localization section**, which possibly makes a further horizontal partition of vertical fragments defined in the first section and then assigns each final fragment to one or more sites (similar to the allocation schema)

The overall information contained in the sections of the global internal schema is equivalent to the fragmentation and allocation schemata of Chapter 3.

The global schemata are interfaced to the local schemata by means of an **external view**; the purpose of this view is to mask a possible heterogeneity of the underlying DBMSs and to allow the definition of the portion of data which are part of the distributed database (while other data are managed only locally). Some users might have a local external view of the local database, without requiring any remote information.

The role of local external schemata is simple in the case of homogeneous systems (where it is similar to the role of local mapping schemata in our reference architecture). We will analyze heterogeneity aspects of SIRIUS-DELTA in the next chapter.

The conceptual and internal schemata of local DBMSs are used as in the ANSI-SPARC Architecture; notice that they are not fully developed in all DBMSs.

The software of SIRIUS-DELTA has a layered structure, shown in Figure 14.3b.

1.   At the highest level, we have the functionalities of the SIRIUS-DELTA DBMS.
2.   The **SILOE level** is responsible for global and local query optimization.
3.   The **SCORE level** is responsible for concurrency control and reliability.
4.   The **SER level** is responsible for managing the distributed execution of applications.

The SER level is built on top of a computer network which provides functionalities roughly equivalent to those of the transport layer of an ISO/OSI architecture.

Query optimization, the major task of the SILOE level, consists in tranforming a conceptual algebraic expression (equivalent to a global query) into an access plan. The query is mapped to a conceptual tree, whose leaves are global relations, and then this tree is transformed into an internal tree, whose leaves are fragments; since there is, in general, more than one way to build global relations from fragments, this mapping is not unique. A reduction phase is then performed, in which some simplifications similar to those of Chapter 5 are done, generating a reduced internal tree. This is the input to an optimizer, which produces the final access plan by minimizing communication costs.

The SCORE level is responsible for concurrency control and reliability of transactions. Concurrency control is provided by 2-phase-locking with a deadlock prevention strategy. A token-passing mechanism, described in reference [14.16], was initially used for concurrency control, but it is now used just for giving unique and progressive identifiers to transactions.

The commitment of transactions is controlled by a standard 2-phase-commitment protocol; an "inquiry protocol" is incorporated for determining how participants should terminate a transaction when the coordinator fails. The protocol requires participants to exchange messages in order to take a common decision. The transaction is committed if all participants are ready to commit or if at least one of them has already committed; the transaction is aborted in all other cases.

The SER level supplies applications with the services of activating remote programs, synchronizing them, evaluating condition variables, transferring data between programs, detecting normal and abnormal terminations of programs, and signaling failures to higher level mechanisms.

A prototype of SIRIUS-DELTA is operating, and some measures of its performances are given in [14.14] in terms of the number of executed instructions. The system appears CPU-bound, but this is mostly due to the use of very slow computers at each site.

CONCLUSIONS

In Chapters 12, 13, and 14, we have examined six prototypes of homogeneous distributed database management systems. Some of their features, summarized in Table 14.1, can be compared:

1. Fragmentation is supported in all systems, with the only exception of R*. All other systems allow primary horizontal fragmentation. Only two of them allow derived fragmentation; this is probably because the advantages of this type of fragmentation are just now being explored. Two of them allow vertical fragmentation, and in this case they also allow mixed fragmentation, but with just two levels and in a fixed order (SDD-1 requires horizontal fragmentation before vertical fragmentation, while SIRIUS-DELTA requires the inverse ordering).

2. All systems support the highest possible level of fragmentation, i.e. fragmentation transparency. R*, which does not have fragments, supports allocation transparency.

3. All systems support the relational model, with the only exception of DDM.

4. All systems have a query interface; all systems, except SIRIUS-DELTA and SDD-1, support embedding into a host programming language. Host programming languages are PL-1, ADA, C, and Pascal. Finally, all systems, except SDD-1, support precompiled applications. SDD-1 uses a compile-and-go approach.

5. DDM and POREL use a first step in query optimization which is network-independent, followed by a phase in which fragments are mapped to one

	SDD-1	R*	DDM	D-INGRES	POREL	SIRIUS-DELTA
1. Fragmentation supported?						
—Horizontal	–	N	–	–	Y	Y
—Primary	Y	–	Y	Y	Y	Y
—Derived	Y	–	Y	Y	N	Y
—Vertical	N	–	N	N	N	Y
—Mixed	Y	–	N	N	N	Y
2. Fragmentation transparency supported?	Y	N (allocation transparency)	Y	Y	Y	Y
3. Relational data model used?	Y	Y	N (Daplex)	Y	Y	Y
4. Interfaces provided						
—Query	Y	Y	Y	Y	Y	Y
—Host-programming language imbedding	N	Y (PL/I)	Y (Ada)	Y (C)	Y (Pascal)	N
—Precompiled applications	N	Y	Y	N	Y	Y
5. Query processing						
—With an initial allocation-independent analysis	N	N	Y	N	Y	N
—Separating global from local optimization?	Y	N	N	N	Y	Y
—Taking only transmission costs into account?	Y	N	N	N	Y	Y
—Using semi-joins?	Y	N	Y	N	N	N
6. 2-phase-commitment used?	N (4-phase)	Y	N (4-phase)	N	N	Y
7. 2-phase-locking used?	N (timestamps)	Y	Y	Y	Y	Y
8. Deadlocks are avoided (A) or detected (D)? How?	A timestamp-based c.c.	D distributed detection	D distributed detection	D centralized detection	A preclaiming of locks	A prevention
9. Replication supported? —update method for copies	Y write-all	N –	Y write-all (regular copies only)	Y deferred updates	Y deferred updates	Y write-all
10. Requires global status of network sites?	Y	N	Y	Y	Y	N
11. Centralized (C) or hierarchical (H) computational structure	C	H	H	C	C	C

of their physical copies. This optimization is done at run time in DDM and at compile time in POREL. Half of the systems separate global and local optimization completely, and they are also, clearly, the ones which assume communications as being the major overhead and do not take into account other costs. SDD-1 and Adaplex, both from Computer Corporation of America, use semi-joins, whereas other systems do not use them.

6. Two-phase-commitment is used by all systems, with the exception of SDD-1, which has a 4-phase-commitment, and DDM, which has derived its commitment protocol from SDD-1.

7. Two-phase-locking is used by all systems with the exception of SDD-1, which uses timestamps. Notice that DDM, which in several respects is consistent with SDD-1, has abandoned timestamps, and likewise SIRIUS-DELTA has abandoned the initial token-based technique for 2-phase-locking.

8. Deadlocks are avoided in three systems, by timestamping transactions, by preordering resources, and by preventing conflicts in the wait-for graph. Deadlocks are detected and solved in three other systems; two of them use distributed deadlock detection and one of them uses centralized deadlock detection.

9. Replication is supported by five systems; three of them use the write-all approach and two of them use the primary copy approach, with deferred updates.

10. A global status table, indicating which sites are up, is used in four systems.

11. The computational structure of transactions is centralized in four cases and hierarchical in two cases.

Annotated Bibliography

References [14.1] to [14.6] describe the DDM system, and the languages ADA and Daplex. References [14.7] to [14.10] describe INGRES and Distributed-INGRES (see also [6.19] and [9.11]). References [14.11] to [14.13] describe POREL (see also [9.12] to [9.14]). References [14.14] to [14.16] describe SIRIUS-DELTA (see also [15.19]).

[14.1]   U. S. Dept. of Defense, "Reference Manual for the ADA Programming Language," Proposed Standard Document, 1982.

[14.2]   D. Shipman, "The Functional Data Model and the Data Language Daplex," *ACM-TODS*, **6**:1, 1981.

[14.3]   A. Chan et al., "Storage Access Structures to Support a Semantic Data Model," *Eighth VLDB*, Mexico City, 1982.

[14.4]   A. Chan et al., "The Implementation of an Integrated Concurrency Control and Recovery Scheme," *ACM-SIGMOD*, Orlando, FL, 1982.

[14.5]   A. Chan et al., "Overview of an ADA Compatible Distributed Database Manager," *ACM-SIGMOD*, San Jose, CA, 1983.

[14.6] A. Chan et al., "Supporting a Semantic Data Model in a Distributed Database System," *Ninth VLDB*, Florence, 1983.

[14.7] M. Stonebraker, E. Wong, P. Kreps, and G. Held, "The Design and Implementation of INGRES," *ACM-TODS*, **2**:3, 1976.

[14.8] E. Wong and K. Youssefi, "Decomposition—A Strategy for Query Processing," *ACM-TODS*, **1**:3, 1976.

[14.9] M. Stonebraker and E. Neuhold, "A Distributed Data Base Version of INGRES," *Second Berkeley Work. on Distributed Data Management and Computer Networks*, 1977.

[14.10] M. Stonebraker, "Homogeneous Distributed Data Base Systems," *Distributed Databases*, I.W. Draffan and F. Poole, eds., Cambridge University Press, Cambridge, 1980.

[14.11] E. J. Neuhold and B. Walter, "An Overview of the Architecture of the Distributed Data Base System POREL," *Distributed Databases*, H. J. Schneider, ed., North-Holland, 1982.

[14.12] B. Walter, "Transaction Management in the Distributed Database System POREL," Universitat Stuttgart Report, 1983.

[14.13] E. J. Neuhold and G. Peter, "The Distribution of Data in the Distributed Data Base System POREL," *Fifth Symp. on Algorithms*, Vysoke Tatry, USSR, 1979.

[14.14] W. Litwin et al., "SIRIUS System for Distributed Data Management," *Distributed Databases*, H. J. Schneider, ed., North-Holland, 1982.

[14.15] J. Le Bihan et al., "SIRIUS-DELTA, Un prototype de systeme de gestion de bases de donnees reparties," *Distributed Databases*, C. Delobel and W. Litwin, eds., North-Holland, 1981.

[14.16] G. Le Lann, "A Distributed System for Real-Time Transaction Processing," *IEEE Computer*, **14**:2, 1981.

Chapter 15

Heterogeneous Distributed Database Systems

Though great importance is given to heterogeneous distributed databases, very few research prototypes of heterogeneous DDBMSs and very few commercial systems connecting heterogeneous DBMSs have been developed.

The most ambitious requirement of heterogeneous systems is the capability of providing a view of the system which is transparent not only to data distribution, but also to heterogeneity of DBMSs. This is a very difficult goal. Thus, some prototypes do not pursue this overall objective. For instance, the MULTIBASE system is developed for providing transparency to retrieval applications, while updates are performed by each individual DBMS, without coordination. In Chapter 11 we have shown that some commercial systems allow application programs to request services to multiple DBMSs; this is typically done without providing transparency.

A system might be considered heterogeneous when it has different computers at each site, or different operating systems, or different DBMSs. In Chapter 1 we anticipated that we would consider a system to be heterogeneous when it uses different DBMSs. This statement allows for very different "degrees" of heterogeneity, since we might have different releases of the same system, or different systems of the same type (e.g., different DBMSs of the Codasyl family), or finally systems of different types (e.g., a relational and a Codasyl system). It is also important to consider the differences in power, speed, and degree of sophistication of the DBMSs in the system.

This chapter first summarizes some of the problems of heterogeneous systems and then presents three research prototypes of heterogeneous DBMSs: MULTIBASE, DDTS, and heterogeneous SIRIUS-DELTA. A comparison of their features is done in the conclusions.

15.1 PROBLEMS OF HETEROGENEOUS DISTRIBUTED DATABASES

Selection of a common data model and data manipulation language

The most convenient way for allowing the communication of several heterogeneous DBMSs is by using a common data model and data manipulation language (DML); data representations and DML primitives of each DBMS are mapped to equivalent representations and primitives of the common data model and DML. One advantage of having a common data model is the possibility of using it to describe the global schema of our reference architecture. Thus, also in a heterogeneous environment, it becomes possible to have a global and consistent view of the database, as if the database were not distributed and as if all DBMSs were of the same type. Another relevant advantage is that mappings and translations need not be done between each pair of DBMSs, which would require a number of translators growing with the square of the number of DBMSs in the system. Instead, mappings and translations need to be done only between each DBMS and the common data model and DML, which requires a number of translators growing linearly with the number of DBMSs.

Thus, the first and more general problem in the development of a heterogeneous system is to select an appropriate common data model and DML. The selected data model and DML should have the following properties:

1. They should allow a simple translation from the data models and DMLs of the DBMSs constituting the heterogeneous system.

2. They should be suited to represent data and processing of distributed databases conveniently; in particular, the data model should be capable of representing the global, fragmentation, and allocation schemata, while the DML should possess "set-oriented" primitives.

The first property (i.e., the simplicity of translation) indicates that the common data model should be as simple as possible. In fact, simple elements can be arranged to build complex data structures, while it is not always possible to convert a complex data representation into a different, complex one. Thus, models representing "atomic" facts (such as binary or functional ones) are good candidates to constitute the common data model.

The second property (i.e., the possibility of representing layered schema architectures and set-oriented processing) excludes the use of complex database models and procedural, one-record-at-a-time DMLs, and points out that set-oriented models and languages, such as the relational model and algebra, are good candidates.

Translation to the common data model and DML   The translation between different DBMSs is not peculiar to distributed systems; translation problems arise whenever two DBMSs are interfaced within the same system, or whenever the DBMS is changed and applications written for the old DBMS are interfaced with the new DBMS (similar problems can also arise when a new version of the same DBMS is introduced!). Translation problems in a distributed database are classified as follows.

1. *Data conversion.*

    a. *At the schema level.* This problem requires generating a schema of the data model of each local DBMS that is equivalent to the schema of the common data model (or vice versa).

    b. *At the instance level.* This is the problem of converting automatically large amounts of data from one representation to another; two database states (i.e., two database schemata populated by database instances) are equivalent when they have equivalent schemata and the stored data represent the same facts.

2. *Program conversion.* This is the problem of converting between two different DMLs. We can say that two programs are equivalent if, for any initial equivalent database states and for any input provided to them, they produce the same output and leave the databases in two equivalent final states.

The above definitions of equivalence are only indicative; for a more formal treatment, see references [15.5] to [15.7].

Let us consider now the problem of determining whether the translation of programs should precede or follow their optimization. In a homogeneous system, no translation is required; we distinguish global optimization, in which the distribution of the execution among sites is determined, from local optimization, in which each site determines the best method for evaluating its portion of execution. In particular, if the application can be locally executed, then global optimization has no effect.

In heterogeneous systems with a common global data model and DML, it appears reasonable to perform global optimization after the translation of applications into the common DML. Thus, instead of building several versions of the global optimizer, we need just one version of it, which assumes as input the description of the application in the common DML. A disadvantage of this solution is that an application must be translated also when it can be completely executed at its site of origin.

A different solution consists of submitting the application to a local analyzer which is able to decompose it into local and remote portions. Only the remote portion is translated into the common DML. Thus, if no remote site is involved in the application, no translation is required.

A simpler solution consists of limiting the sophistication of the analysis by classifying applications into two sets: completely local applications (those which do not need any remote resource) and all other applications. The former should use the local DBMS directly; the latter should be translated and then optimized. In the absence of the analyzer, the user should make this selection, and request the service of either the local DBMS or of the heterogeneous DDBMS. This is the case of the MULTIBASE and DDTS systems, in which the user can write distributed applications only by directly using the common DML which operates on the global schema.

Integration of different schemata   Heterogeneous DDBMSs are typically built by aggregating preexisting systems, using a bottom-up approach (recall

Section 4.1.2). Thus, it is possible that the same facts are already described in the schemata of two different DBMSs, and it is possible that the two descriptions do not agree. Differences in data definition of the same facts are called conflicts (see references [4.6] to [4.8] and [15.9]). Let us consider the conflicts that can arise between two schemata which use the common data model. Conflicts are classified as follows:

1. **Name conflicts**, which typically involve homonyms (different facts denoted with the same name) and synonyms (different names used for the same fact).

2. **Scale conflicts**, which involve the use of different units of measure; for example, degrees of Fahrenheit in one schema and Celsius degrees in the other.

3. **Structural conflicts**, which arise when the same facts are described in two schemata using different elements of the data model. A typical structural conflict, with a common model including entities and attributes, consists of regarding the same fact as an autonomous entity in one schema and as the attribute of a different entity in the other schema.

4. **Different levels of abstraction**, when one schema contains more detailed information than the other one. For example, one schema contains office phone number and home phone number, and the other schema only contains phone number.

Performing the integration of two or more schemata requires discovering and resolving the conflicts. In heterogeneous systems, solving conflicts by forcing one interpretation is not always required or possible, since typically data definitions of component DBMSs should not be altered. Thus, the integration process could leave some conflicts unsolved but produce an **auxiliary database**, to be used during normal operation, typically for name or scale conversions, and sometimes also for mediating structural and abstraction conflicts.

Query processing problems Heterogeneous databases create some new query processing problems in addition to those discussed in Chapters 5 and 6. Note that most heterogeneous systems allow only distributed retrievals, while update applications must be done under the control of each local DBMS.

A precise evaluation of processing costs becomes more difficult, because of the presence of DBMSs with different features; the distribution of a query should now take into account the differences in performances of the various sites. Some of the functions requested by an application either might be more expensive or might not be available at all on remote DBMSs, and in this case it becomes necessary to transmit a superset of the data required by the application to the site of origin of the application, where those functions can be performed. Thus, query distribution should try to balance the amount of remote versus local processing very carefully.

When each DBMS is independently generated and updated, inconsistencies of replicated data are very likely. Several policies are possible for dealing with inconsistent data; for instance, taking their average value, or taking the maximum (minimum) value, or considering one arbitrary value as the right one. These problems have been studied in detail in the MULTIBASE system.

15.2 MULTIBASE

MULTIBASE is a software system developed at the Computer Corporation of America for retrieving data from a heterogeneous distributed database. The system provides users a uniform view of the database and a single DML language for writing read-only applications; the functional data model and the language Daplex, presented in Section 14.1, are used for this purpose.

MULTIBASE provides a very high level interface for read-only applications, which is transparent to data allocation and to heterogeneity of the DBMSs. MULTI-BASE does not manage fragments directly; however, it is possible to use derivation mechanisms for generating global data from local data. Thus, when several local databases autonomously store local data objects which can be regarded as portions of the same global data object, the global schema includes that global data object and does not make any reference to its components; in this sense, MULTIBASE provides a sort of fragmentation transparency.

MULTIBASE does not manage update applications, which are under the direct responsibility of local DBMSs and are not coordinated. Likewise, no facility is provided to synchronize read operations across several sites; in fact, the major objective of MULTIBASE is to interface preexisting systems without modifying their software. This goal contrasts with the need for interfering with concurrency control subsystems of local DBMSs, which presently do not provide clear interfaces. Since the updates to local databases are not controlled, it is not realistic to postulate the perfect alignment of data. Thus, particular attention has been given in MULTIBASE to the management of incomplete and inconsistent data.

The major design objectives of MULTIBASE are generality, compatibility, and extensibility. "Generality" means that MULTIBASE was not designed with a specific application in mind. "Compatibility" is required with respect to existing software, which need not to be modified. "Extensibility" is the ability to add new features to MULTIBASE.

15.2.1 Architecture of MULTIBASE

The software architecture of MULTIBASE is presented in Figure 15.1. MULTIBASE has two components:

1. The **global data manager (GDM)**, responsible for all global aspects of a query
2. The **local database interface (LDI)**, responsible for interfacing DBMSs at the various sites

The schemata architecture of MULTIBASE includes:

1. The **global schema**, which uses the functional data model and is defined in the data language Daplex. This schema offers an integrated view of the distributed database, which provides fragmentation, allocation, and heterogeneity transparency.

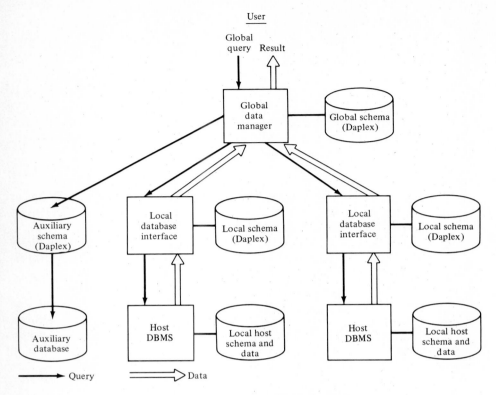

Figure 15.1 Architecture of MULTIBASE.

2. The **local schemata**, which describe the portion of data stored at each individual site. They are also defined in Daplex, and they perform the same function as the local mapping schemata in a homogeneous system.

3. The **auxiliary schema**, which describes data which are not stored in any of the participant DBMSs, but rather in an **auxiliary database** under the control of MULTIBASE. An auxiliary database is stored at each site where MULTIBASE can be accessed. Auxiliary databases are used for solving incompatibilities; they store conversion tables and information for schema mapping and integration.

4. The **local host schemata**, which describe the actual data stored at each DBMS. They are written using the data definition language (DDL) of each DBMS.

The GDM takes as input the user queries on the global schema, written in Daplex. Its function is to decompose a Daplex query about the global schema into several Daplex queries about the local schemata and the auxiliary database. GDM is also responsible for assembling the data received from the various sites, possibly performing some final processing on them, and returning the answer to the user.

The LDI is responsible for all specific aspects of each local system. It receives as input a single-site Daplex query, translates it into a query written in the DML of the local system, requests the execution of the query, and assembles an answer to be sent to the site of origin of the MULTIBASE application.

The optimization and translation of queries in MULTIBASE are shown in Figure 15.2. The GDM is composed of five modules: transformer, global optimizer, decomposer, filter, and monitor. The LDI is composed of four modules: network interface, local optimizer, translator, and host interface (there is also a data formatter module that we do not describe).

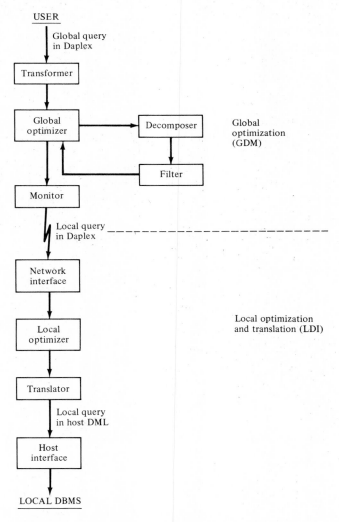

Figure 15.2 Optimization and translation of queries in MULTIBASE.

The **transformer** takes the global query in Daplex as input and produces as output a Daplex global query which references the local and auxiliary Daplex schemata. The transformation requires the expression of elements of the global schema in terms of elements of the local and auxiliary data schemata, and therefore is similar to the canonical transformation shown in Chapter 5.

The **global optimizer** uses the output of the transformer to produce an overall plan. Global optimization is followed by decomposition and filtering; these three steps can be repeated several times before producing an acceptable plan. The global optimizer uses an algorithm similar to that of SDD-1, described in Section 6.2.2; however, it has been extended to deal with some additional problems of heterogeneous environments. We will discuss some of the innovative features of global optimization in MULTIBASE in Section 15.2.4. The **decomposer** separates the global plan produced by the global optimizer into single-site Daplex queries, which reference local and auxiliary schemata, and data movements. The **filter** removes from each single-site query those operations which are not supported by the corresponding DBMS. These removed operations will be part of the processing required on the results which are collected separately from the different sites.

The **monitor** controls the execution of the query. It transmits single-site Daplex queries to the remote LDIs and to the auxiliary database, receives the results, and combines them into the answer. The **network interface** at each site receives Daplex single-site queries and is responsible for transmitting their results back.

The **local optimizer** determines an optimal query processing strategy for the single-site Daplex query and the specific DBMS operating at that site. The **translator** produces a DML program for the local DBMS which implements the above strategy.

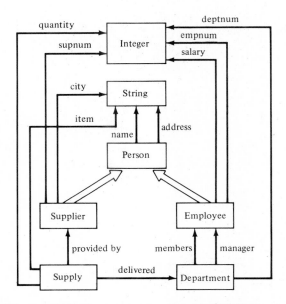

Figure 15.3 A global schema in MULTIBASE.

Finally, the **host interface** simulates a local application program which requests services from local DBMSs.

15.2.2 Schemas and Queries at Different Levels of the MULTIBASE Architecture

In this section, we present examples of global and local functional schemata and the corresponding DBMS schemata for a 2-site heterogeneous distributed database; we assume a Codasyl DBMS at site 1 and a SQL/DS DBMS at site 2.

Consider the global schema presented in Figure 15.3 (this is the same schema that was presented in Section 14.1). This global schema contains the entity sets Person, Employee, Department, Supplier, and Supply, and is very similar in content to the DDB_EXAMPLE of Part I of this book.

In Figure 15.4a and b, the two local functional schemata are shown. All the entity sets, functions, and generalization hierarchies of the global schema are found

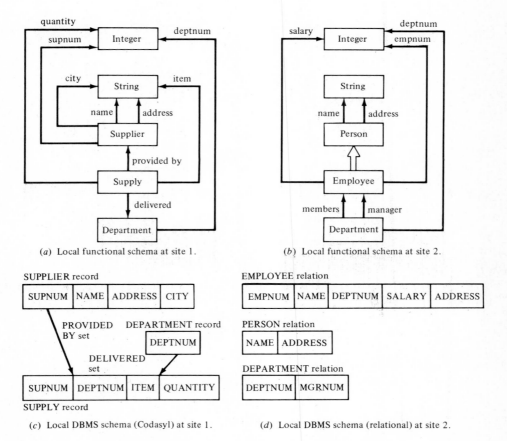

(a) Local functional schema at site 1.

(b) Local functional schema at site 2.

(c) Local DBMS schema (Codasyl) at site 1.

(d) Local DBMS schema (relational) at site 2.

Figure 15.4 Local schemata in MULTIBASE.

in either of the two schemata; the Department entity set and the function deptnum are replicated in both schemata. Notice that the mapping from the global schema to the local functional schemata is very simple in this example; the two schemata are linked by the fact that the entity set Department appears in both. However, the fact that the function's name and address are applied to the entity sets Person and Supplier indicates that they can be related by a generalization hierarchy; in fact, Supplier is a subtype of Person in the global schema.

In Figure 15.4c and d, the DBMS schemata corresponding to the local functional schemata are presented. The first DBMS is a standard Codasyl system; entity sets of the functional model are mapped to Codasyl record types, and each single-valued function from entity sets to strings or integers is considered a field of the record type. Functions between entity sets of the functional model are mapped to set types of Codasyl (some care must be given to multivalued functions, not present in our example).

for each E in Employee such that

    for some D in Department
    manager$(D) = E$ and   Subquery for site 2
    salary$(E) > \$50,000$ and

    for some S in Supply
    quantity$(S) > 3$ and   Subquery for site 1
    item$(S) = $ "printer" and
    $D = $ delivered(S)

(a) Global user query in Daplex

```
     OPEN DB1.
01   FIND FIRST DEPARTMENT RECORD OF DEPARTMENT_SYSTEM SET.
     GOTO 03.
02   FIND NEXT DEPARTMENT RECORD OF DEPARTMENT_SYSTEM SET.
     AT END GOTO 08.
03   FIND FIRST SUPPLY RECORD OF PROVIDED_BY SET.
     GOTO 05.
04   FIND NEXT SUPPLY RECORD OF PROVIDED_BY SET.
     AT END GOTO 02.
05   IF ITEM NE "PRINTER" OR QUANTITY LE 3 GOTO 04.
06   WRITE DEPTNUM INTO $DEPTNUMREL.
07   GOTO 04.
08   CLOSE DB1.
```

(b) Local query on the Codasyl DBMS at site 1

Select *DEPTNUM, NAME* into $MGRNAMEREL
from *EMPLOYEE, DEPARTMENT*
where *EMPLOYEE.EMPNUM = DEPARTMENT.MGRNUM*
and *SALARY* > $50,000

(c) Local query on the SQL/DS DBMS at site 2

Figure 15.5 Queries at different levels in MULTIBASE.

The second DBMS is relational. Entity sets of the functional model correspond to relations, and functions from entity sets to strings or integers correspond to attributes. However, functions between entity sets must be represented by adding appropriate attributes. Notice also that the generalization hierarchy between Person and Employee is modeled by introducing the two relations PERSON and EMPLOYEE. The former relation is used for all persons which are *not* employees.

Given this schema representation, let us consider a global user query and its decomposition and translation. The query asks for the name of those managers who:

1. Earn more than $50,000
2. Whose department has issued a single order for more than three "printers"

The Daplex formulation of this query is shown in Figure 15.5a. The Daplex language is rather self-explicative. The only difficulty of this example is in the statement which relates D, a variable over Department, to E, a variable over Employee, through the function manager. The meaning is that the function manager, applied to the entity D, should return the entity E, i.e., that E denotes the manager of department D. Likewise, the function delivered is used in such a way that S denotes a supply that was delivered at department D.

Since condition 1 operates on data at site 2 and condition 2 operates on data at site 1, the decomposition of the Daplex query into two components is rather straightforward, and is indicated directly in Figure 15.5a.

Figure 15.5b and c shows the local queries on the DBMSs at sites 1 and 2. The first one is written in Codasyl DML and requires one-record-at-a-time processing. In order to enumerate all department records, a system-owned set is used (which was not shown in Figure 15.4c for simplicity). The second query is written in SQL; the use of the manager function in the Daplex subquery is translated into a join between relations *EMPLOYEE* and *DEPARTMENT* on the attribute *DEPTNUM*. The translation from Daplex to the Codasyl DML query is complicated by the fact that the local DBMS requires a highly procedural specification. The translation from Daplex to SQL is simpler, although it converts a one-record-at-a-time language into a nonprocedural one.

Notice that the two queries have the effect of retrieving, respectively, the departments which satisfy condition 2 (i.e., which have one order for more than three printers) and pairs of department numbers and names of managers of the departments which satisfy condition 1 (i.e., which have a given salary). The two results have the following relation schemata:

$$\text{\$DEPTNUMREL}(DEPTNUM)$$
$$\text{\$MGRNAMEREL}(DEPTNUM,\ NAME)$$

They must be further joined on *DEPTNUM* and then projected on *NAME* to produce the answer to the user query, as follows:

$$RESULT = \mathbf{PJ}_{NAME}(\text{\$DEPTNUMREL}\ \mathbf{NJN}\ \text{\$MGRNAMEREL})$$

This processing is the responsibility of the monitor module in the GDM.

15.2.3 Integration of Local Schemata

In the example of the previous section, there was a clear, one-to-one mapping between the (few) common elements of the local schemata, and therefore their integration for constituting a global schema was a simple task. However, schemata might show conflicts in the definition of facts. In this section, we give examples of conflicts in schema definition and of their resolution.

Let us consider the two local Daplex schemata of Figure 15.6a and b. They describe information related to external workers of a company. The first one describes advisers, who have a yearly salary and have an office in the company. The second one describes consultants, who can have several consultancies at the same time, but have not an office. The same external worker can be both an adviser and a consultant.

To integrate these two schemata, several conflicts must be solved; for instance:

1. The salary function is used in both schemata but with a different meaning. In the first one, it relates advisers to just one salary, established for the current year. In the second case, it relates consultants to the separate payments for each current consultancy. Notice that in this example it is not at all clear how to define the salary of an external worker, especially for external workers who are both consultants and advisers.

2. The phone function is directly applied to the entity set Consultant, while the composition of the function member (giving the adviser's office) and the function phone (giving the office's phone number) should be used for the entity set Adviser.

The requirements for the global schema are to give an integrated view of external workers, in which Adviser and Consultant are seen as subtypes of generalization hierarchies having External_worker as the supertype. The External_worker entity set should have three single value functions: name, phone, and salary; the information about offices of advisers is not relevant. The global schema is shown in Figure 15.6c. The functions of the global schema must be derived from the functions of the local Daplex schemata. While the function name is trivially derived, problems arise for the functions phone and salary. In particular, for those external workers who are both advisers and consultants, it is assumed that:

1. The phone number is derived from local schema 1 (i.e., the phone number of advisers' offices is used).

2. The salary is computed by adding the salary as adviser to all salaries as consultant.

The salary of external workers who are consultants and not advisers is computed as the sum of all their salary values as from the local schema 2.

The derivation of the global schema from the local schemata by using Daplex data definitions is described in Figure 15.6d. The entity set External_worker is constituted by the union (+) of the entity sets Adviser and Consultant. A "case" statement introduces three different definitions, given for entities belonging to the intersection (×) between Adviser and Consultant, or to the two differences (−) between them. Consider, for example, the case of entities which belong to the intersection Adviser × Consultant.

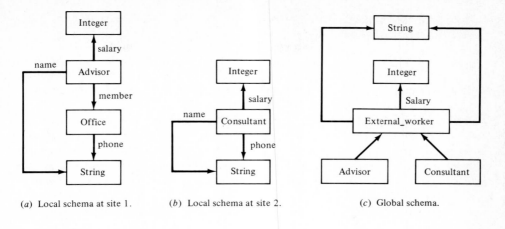

(a) Local schema at site 1.　　(b) Local schema at site 2.　　(c) Global schema.

Define External_worker from
　　for each I in Adviser + Consultant
　　　　case I is
　　　　　　when Adviser $\times$ Consultant $\rightarrow$
　　　　　　　　derive External_worker to be
　　　　　　　　　　(name $\rightarrow$ name(I),
　　　　　　　　　　phone $\rightarrow$ phone(the(O in Office where I = member(O))),
　　　　　　　　　　salary $\rightarrow$ salary(the(A in Adviser where name(A) = name(I)))
　　　　　　　　　　　　+ sum(salary(the(C in Consultant where name(C) =
　　　　　　　　　　　　name(I)))));

　　　　　　when Adviser $-$ Consultant $\rightarrow$
　　　　　　　　derive External_worker to be
　　　　　　　　　　(name $\rightarrow$ name(I),
　　　　　　　　　　phone $\rightarrow$ phone(the(O in Office where I = member(O))),
　　　　　　　　　　salary $\rightarrow$ salary(I));

　　　　　　when Consultant $-$ Adviser $\rightarrow$
　　　　　　　　derive External_worker to be
　　　　　　　　　　(name $\rightarrow$ name(I),
　　　　　　　　　　phone $\rightarrow$ phone(I),
　　　　　　　　　　salary $\rightarrow$ sum(salary(I)));

(d) Derivation of the global schema from the local schemata in Daplex

Figure 15.6　Schema integration in MULTIBASE.

1.　The function name is trivially mapped
2.　The function phone is generated by performing the composition of the functions member and phone in the first schema
3.　The function salary is generated by adding the (single) salary of the first schema with the (multiple) salaries of the second one

　　These derivation rules for the global schema solve all the conflicts presented by the two local schemata: they play a similar role as inverse transformations of the fragmentation schema. In fact, the role of the transformer module in GDM is exactly to transform a query over the global schema into the corresponding query over the local schemata, by using these derivation rules.

15.2.4 Special Query Optimization Problems in MULTIBASE

Query optimization in MULTIBASE must solve several problems which do not arise in homogeneous systems. Some of them derive from structural differences of the local DBMSs; some from the need for processing queries about inconsistent or incomplete information; and some from the fact that Daplex is a semantically richer model than the relational model, and thus its special features (such as generalization hierarchies) require a special treatment.

The structural difference of DBMSs in the distributed database is responsible for the following problems:

1. The cost of performing queries of the same complexity can be very different at different sites, with different DBMSs and different computing powers. Thus, the features of local systems must be taken into account in global optimization, which becomes more complex.
2. The ability of receiving and referencing transmitted data is also very different at each site. Some DBMSs might not support the creation and loading of temporary data.
3. Some sites might not be able to compute portions of the local queries which they receive, either because the features of local DBMSs are limited or because the power of the local optimizer and translator of the LDI is limited.

Given the above problems, a difficult compromise must be determined between:

1. Having efficient local subqueries, which restrict data locally to the maximum extent but have a difficult translation and optimization
2. Having less efficient but simpler local processing, which requires transmitting more data and performing additional processing on the partial results from the various sites

Several solutions are considered in MULTIBASE for dealing with inconsistencies of replicated data:

1. Considering the most recent value as the correct one. This solution postulates that the reason for inconsistency is a transient misalignment of updates, which sooner or later will disappear when updates are applied.
2. Triggering a control action. In this case, it is instead postulated that data should be consistent at each time, and therefore some action should be performed on them before answering the query.
3. Using the more credible data, for instance the data which are stored on a reliable site and DBMS.
4. Applying an aggregate function to inconsistent data in order to compute a single value for them. Examples of functions are average, minimum, and maximum.

Solution 4 is the one most often applied in MULTIBASE. In practice, the aggregate function that should be used in case of value inconsistency becomes part of the derivation rules. This gives rise to several interesting problems in the distribution of algebraic expressions. For instance, consider the selection on an attribute A whose value is computed as the average of two distinct values; clearly, it becomes difficult (or even impossible) to distribute the selection to local databases. If, on the other hand, the aggregate function considered is the minimum (maximum) of the two values, then the selection can be distributed, followed by some local processing of the collected results.

The distributivity of operations to sites when attribute values are defined by aggregate functions is described in reference [15.11], which also analyzes the extensions required for evaluating queries over generalization hierarchies.

15.3 DDTS: A DISTRIBUTED TESTBED SYSTEM

The Distributed Database Testbed System (DDTS) was developed at the Honeywell Corporate Computer Science Center as a heterogeneous DDBMS research prototype. The design of DDTS emphasizes modularity and flexibility in order to maximize its utility as a testbed for experimental studies. DDTS is composed of subsystems which provide the services of user interface, query translation, and distributed execution. Particular subsystems may easily be replaced in order to appropriately support an experiment. Like Multibase, DDTS is capable of integrating heterogeneous processors and DBMSs, providing allocation and machine transparency. However, DDTS provides additional functionalities: users can compile and store multiple queries and update requests which can be executed repeatedly; atomicity and reliability of transactions are supported by DDTS. Currently, DDTS is supporting research in automatic enforcement of semantic integrity constraints, query optimization, and concurrency control.

15.3.1 Architecture of DDTS

The system architecture of DDTS consists of a set of **application processors** (AP) and **data processors** (DP). The APs control the user interfaces and manage applications; the DPs manage data. The APs and DPs are allocated to physical processors (sites) during system configuration. A communication subsystem transfers messages between processes in the APs and DPs. Notice that APs, DPs, and communication subsystem play approximately the same roles as TMs, DMs, and RelNet in SDD-1 (recall Section 12.1).

Data definition in DDTS is based on a 5-level schema architecture. **External schemata** describe which portions of the database may be accessed by a user. The **conceptual schema** is a semantic description of the entire database, corresponding to the global schema of our reference architecture. It is specified using the Entity-Category-Relationship (ECR) semantic data model of reference [15.12], an extension of the Entity-Relationship data model of reference [15.13]. The DML language used is GORDAS, a high-level language for the ECR data model, defined in reference [15.14].

The **global representational schema** is a relational description of the entire database structurally equivalent to the conceptual schema (but without many of the constraints supported at the conceptual level). The **local representational schemata** are subsets of the global representational schema, identifying the data resident at each site. Finally, the **local internal schemata** describe the data at each site in terms of the local DBMS. Currently, DDTS is capable of integrating Codasyl-type DBMS. This schema architecture is very similar to the architecture of SIRIUS-DELTA that was represented in Figure 14.3 (without also including a local external schema).

The software modules of DDTS are shown in Figure 15.7. The application processors include four modules: the command interface, translator and integrity controller, materialization and acces planner, and distributed execution monitor. The data processors include two modules: the local execution monitor and local operation module.

The **command interface** provides the interactive user interface to DDTS; it provides functions for storing, editing, compiling, and executing applications.

The **translator and integrity controller** translates a GORDAS application to relational form. References to entity types, attributes, and relationships in the GORDAS application are mapped to references to relations and attributes in the relational representational schemata. This module should also automatically insert run time checks in applications to ensure that they do not violate the integrity constraints; the enforcement algorithm has been specified but not yet implemented.

The **materialization and access planner** derives a strategy for the efficient processing of distributed applications. Since control constructs (e.g., if-then-else) may appear in the application, **data flow techniques** (see references [7.14] to [7.16]) are used to group retrieval and update requests into operation blocks that serve as units of optimization, and to determine an order dependency of requests within each block. The blocks are formed based on the control constructs in the application (e.g., then-part and else-part of an if). The blocks are then optimized independently. The optimization algorithm currently implemented in DDTS determines first a materialization that minimizes transmission costs by selecting copies closest to the site of origin of the application. Then a minimum cost execution strategy is determined.

The **distributed** and the **local execution monitors** (DEM and LEMs) cooperate for the distributed execution of transactions. A DEM process creates a set of LEM processes dedicated to the transaction, at all the involved sites. Thus, the process model of computation is used rather than the server model (recall Section 7.4.1 and 7.4.3). The DEM sends compile and/or execute requests to initiate the processing of a transaction at the LEMs. Each DEM process is retained until the commit or abort of the transaction. If a transaction is to be compiled only, the DEM stores the execution strategy and operation blocks for later execution. During execution, the LEMs cooperate and synchronize their effective execution by dataflow, i.e., each LEM executes its portion of the execution strategy in parallel, and the synchronization occurs when an operation requires an intermediate result generated and sent from another site. Standard 2-phase-commitment and 2-phase-locking are used; deadlocks are prevented using both the preemptive and nonpreemptive algorithms of Section 8.2.4.

The **local operation modules** are responsible for local translation and optimization of subtransactions. Local optimization aims at the minimization of I/Os. These modules also store compiled applications for later execution.

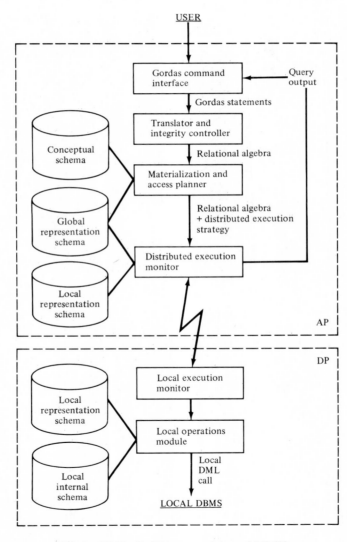

Figure 15.7 Software modules of DDTS.

15.3.2 Schemas and Queries at Different Levels of DDTS Architecture

We present an example based on the same global schema and query of Section 15.2.2. We again assume a Codasyl DBMS at site 1 and an SQL/DS DBMS at site 2.

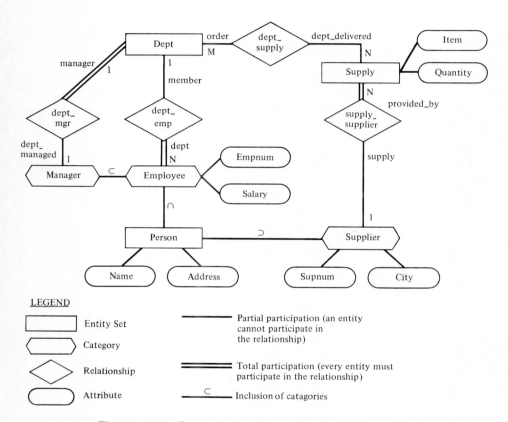

Figure 15.8 Conceptual schema using the ECR model.

Figure 15.8 represents the conceptual schema using the ECR model. The **entities** of this example, identified by rectangles in the figure, are Dept, Supply, and Person. **Categories**, identified by hexagons, define subsets of entities. In our example, we have the categories Supplier and Employee, which define subsets of the entity Person. The category Manager represents a narrower set of the category Employee. Relationships are represented by diamonds in the figure. Arcs connecting diamonds to the entities or categories which participate in a relationship are labeled with **connection names** (e.g., dept-managed, order) used in the GORDAS language. **Attributes** of entities, categories, and relationships are represented graphically by ovals. Note that categories inherit the attributes of the entities or categories from which they are derived, in the same way as with generalization hierarchies of the Daplex model. Several **semantic constraints** can be specified in the ECR model; for instance, the cardinality constraints of relationships (which can be $1 : 1$, $1 : N$ or $M : N$) and the type (total or partial) of participation of each entity or category in a relationship (total participation requires that each instance of an entity or category participate in the relationship).

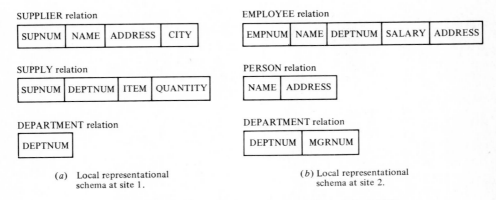

SUPPLIER relation

SUPNUM	NAME	ADDRESS	CITY

SUPPLY relation

SUPNUM	DEPTNUM	ITEM	QUANTITY

DEPARTMENT relation

DEPTNUM

(*a*) Local representational schema at site 1.

EMPLOYEE relation

EMPNUM	NAME	DEPTNUM	SALARY	ADDRESS

PERSON relation

NAME	ADDRESS

DEPARTMENT relation

DEPTNUM	MGRNUM

(*b*) Local representational schema at site 2.

Figure 15.9   Local representation schemata in DDTS.

The data distribution of this example is the same as in the example of Section 15.2.2. The local representation schemata are shown in Figure 15.9*a* and *b*. The global representation schema is constituted of all relations appearing in these two schemata. Finally, local internal schemata at sites 1 and 2 are the same as in Section 15.2.2; they were represented in Figure 15.4*c* and *d*.

The GORDAS formulation of the example query described in Section 15.2.2 is shown in Figure 15.10*a*. The query retrieves the managers who earn more than $50,000 and whose department has issued an order for more than three printers. Notice the use of connection names in the GORDAS query.

This request is translated into a relational algebra expression by the translator; the corresponding operator tree is shown in Figure 15.10*b*. Then, a materialization is selected, and an access plan is determined. This access plan incorporates explicit "send" instructions, while the "receive" instructions are implicitly generated when a nonlocal data object is needed in an operation. The access plan for this query is shown in Figure 15.10*c*. At execution time, the necessary portions of the plan are sent to the DPs for execution. Subgraphs are translated to the DML of the local DBMS, and optimized if possible. In this example, the Codasyl DML program to be executed at site 1 is the same as the program of Figure 15.5*c*. Figure 15.10*d* shows the SQL/DS program to be executed at site 2.

get name of Manager where
   salary > \$50,000 and
     ⟨item, quantity⟩ of order of dept_managed = ⟨"printer", 3⟩

(a) Global user query in GORDAS

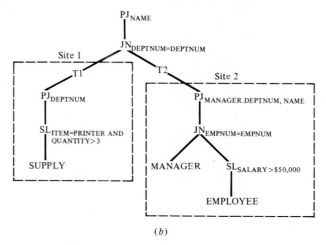

(b)

(b) Operator tree of the global query

Evaluate $T1$ at DP of site 1
send $T1$ to site 2
evaluate $\textbf{PJ}_{NAME}(T1 \textbf{ JN } T2)$ at DP of site 2
send the result to user's AP.

(c) Access plan for the user query

Receive $T1$ from site 1

Select $NAME$ into $RESULT$
from $EMPLOYEE$
where $SALARY > 50{,}000$
and $EMPNUM =$
   Select $EMPNUM$
   from $MANAGER, T1$
   where $MANAGER.DEPTNUM = T1.DEPTNUM$

Send $RESULT$ to user's AP

(d) Local query on the SQL/DS DBMS at site 2

Figure 15.10 Example of a query and of its translation in DDTS.

15.3.3 Research and Experiments Involving DDTS Subsystems

DDTS is supporting studies of several problems and subsystems, including the automatic enforcement of semantic integrity constraints, query optimization, and concurrency control. Each of these studies involves a prototype implementation and empirical evaluation of the subsystem under study.

Enforcement of semantic integrity constraints   DDTS is supporting research in automatic enforcement of semantic integrity constraints in a database described by the ECR data model. The traditional approach to dealing with semantic integrity constraints is by incorporating them in the application programs, thus leaving their enforcement under the responsability of the application programmer. In DDTS, the features of the ECR data model and of GORDAS are used for specifying several constraints in the conceptual model and for inserting constraint checks into each update transaction. The automatic modification of GORDAS transactions to incorporate constraints is under investigation.

Distributed query optimization   In DDTS, a version of the access planner based on the AHY algorithms, described in Section 6.2.3, has been implemented. Empirical studies comparing the efficiency of the execution plans generated by these algorithms under varying workloads, database designs, and communication costs are performed.

Deadlock prevention   DDTS uses the preemptive and the nonpreemptive algorithms of Section 8.2.4 in order to prevent deadlocks. We recall that a precise evaluation of the methods and a comparison between them is rather difficult; the evaluation and comparison under various workloads are being performed. Notice that these algorithms rely on purely local information at each site to decide when a transaction may wait or when it must be restarted; thus, these algorithms can be implemented rather easily using the local concurrency control mechanisms of centralized systems.

15.4 HETEROGENEOUS SIRIUS-DELTA

The SIRIUS-DELTA architecture was developed with the purpose of being easily interfaced to other DBMSs. Thus, experiments have been conducted to connect SIRIUS-DELTA to other systems, including MRDS, a relational DBMS on a large Honeywell computer, and PHLOX, a DBMS for microcomputers. In these experiments, described in references [14.14] and [15.19], the two DBMSs were used for the sole purpose of storing data, without having local users.

The multilevel architecture of SIRIUS-DELTA schemata and software, described in Figure 14.3, does not require modifications in order to introduce heterogeneity. The global conceptual schema plays the same role as the global schema of MULTIBASE, i.e., providing fragmentation, allocation, and heterogeneity transparency; we already noted in Chapter 14 that the global schema is a relational one and that the global query language is algebraic. Local external schemata interface local DBMSs directly, and subqueries operating on local external schemata are translated into the DML of the local DBMS at each site in a different way.

From the viewpoint of software architecture, a set of common functions is defined. These functions must be provided by each DBMS willing to participate in the heterogeneous system. They are defined using the various software levels of the SIRIUS-DELTA system (SILOE, SCORE, and SER), and constitute a subsystem called a **pivot system**. For instance, the ability of aborting and undoing an application is part of the pivot system. This function can be implemented in several ways by each individual DBMS, but each of them must offer the same high-level interface to their respective pivot systems. In particular, it is possible to perform update operations; the functions of the individual pivot systems on each participating DBMS support locking, commit, and recovery algorithms necessary for performing the updates.

Let us consider now how the system PHLOX is interfaced to the pivot system. PHLOX is a DBMS of the Codasyl family for minicomputers and microcomputers. The interface consists of two modules:

1.   An interface to the network, which is capable of passing the algebraic sub-queries to the lower level module and directly interpreting messages for the SER and SCORE levels in terms of instructions for the local system.
2.   A relational interface, which performs the interpretation of subqueries in the algebraic "pivot" language and their translation to PHLOX instructions. This module also performs some local optimization, consisting of clustering the operations that can be executed simultaneously and selecting the local access methods.

The lower module of this interface operates directly on the PHLOX DBMS.

CONCLUSIONS

In this chapter we have examined three prototypes of heterogeneous distributed database management systems: MULTIBASE, DDTS, and SIRIUS-DELTA. The features of MULTIBASE and DDTS are summarized in Table 15.1; the table does not include SIRIUS-DELTA, already summarized in Table 14.1 of Chapter 14, since heterogeneity aspects do not change the basic features of this system.

1.   Fragmentation is not supported by MULTIBASE and DDTS. This can be motivated recalling that these systems are developed for supporting preexisting local DBMSs, with a bottom-up design approach. In this case it is more difficult (and perhaps less convenient) to introduce fragments.

2.   Both systems support the highest possible transparency, i.e., allocation transparency. In fact, they also support machine and DBMS transparency, which are required for providing allocation transparency in a heterogeneous system.

3.   Both systems use for the global schema a model which is more elementary and at the same time richer than the relational model. MULTIBASE uses Daplex, and DDTS uses the Entity-Category-Relationship (ECR) model. This is justified by the need of mapping local DBMS models of different types.

4.   MULTIBASE provides a read-only query interface; DDTS provides also updates and pre-compiled applications.

5.   Query processing is performed both in MULTIBASE and in DDTS by separating global optimization from local optimization, by taking only transmission costs into account in global optimization, and by using semi-joins. Neither systems performs an initial network-independent analysis.

Table 15.1 Comparison of features of homogeneous research prototypes

	MULTIBASE	DDTS
1. Fragmentation supported?	N	N
2. Allocation transparency supported?	Y	Y
3. Global data model used	Daplex	ECR and Relational
4. Provided interfaces		
—Query	Y(read-only)	Y
—Host-programming language imbedded	N	N
—Precompiled applications	N	Y
5. Query processing		
—With an initial allocation-independent analysis	N	N
—Separating global from local optimization?	Y	Y
—Taking only transmission costs into account?	Y	Y
—Using semi-joins?	Y	Y
6. 2-phase-commitment used?	N (not required)	Y
7. 2-phase-locking used?	N (no concurrency control)	Y
8. Deadlocks are avoided (A) or detected (D)? How?	–	A prevention
9. Replication supported?	Y	Y
—Update method for copies	–	write-all

6. MULTIBASE does not support concurrency control and does not manage transactions; the rationale for this choice is that MULTIBASE is built on top of existing systems which need not to be modified. In fact, MULTIBASE is seen as an application by these systems. Thus, it is not possible for MULTIBASE to perform those functions which interfere with the concurrency control and reliability managers of local systems. DDTS instead supports transactions, with the standard 2-phase-commitment protocol.

7. DDTS uses 2-phase-locking.

8. DDTS uses deadlock prevention.

9. Both systems allow replication. MULTIBASE has developed specialized techniques for dealing with inconsistent data, since it is assumed that copies are updated autonomously by the local systems. DDTS does not consider the possibility of inconsistent data, since all copies are updated with a write-all method.

Despite the technical difficulties, there is a growing interest in heterogeneous distributed databases. Very different types of systems are being developed as heterogeneous distributed databases; for instance, workstations and personal computers with their own small database connected by local networks with several remote database servers, or international networks of computers which provide access to very large databases. Heterogeneity can also be interpreted with respect to the kinds of information that can be accessed, which will include unstructured information (such as text, image, and voice). These fields are too immature now to allow a systematic presentation; however, there is a clear trend towards the development of new integrated heterogeneous systems.

Annotated Bibliography

References in this chapter are partly on general problems of heterogeneous systems. References [15.2] to [15.5] are on data and program translation (see also reference [3.6]); reference [15.5] deals also with the equivalence of database schemata. The specification and correctness of mappings in database systems is dealt with in references [15.6] and [15.7]. References for the problem of integrating different schemata were given in Chapter 4 ([4.6] to [4.8]). References [15.8] to [15.11] describe MULTIBASE, references [15.12] to [15.18] are related to DDTS, and reference [15.19] describes the heterogeneity aspects in the SIRIUS project.

[15.1]   S. Spaccapietra, "Heterogeneous Data Base Distribution," in *Distributed Databases*, I. W. Draffan and F. Poole, eds., Cambridge University Press, Cambridge, 1980.

[15.2]   R. Taylor et al., "Database Program Conversion: A Framework for Research," *Fifth VLDB*, Rio de Janeiro, 1979.

[15.3]   J. A. Larson, "Bridging the Gap Between Network and Relational Database Management Systems," *IEEE-Computer*, **16**:11, 1983.

[15.4]   B. Demo, "Program Analysis for Conversion from a Navigational to a Specification Database Interface," *Ninth VLDB*, Florence, 1983.

[15.5]   H. Biller, "On the Equivalence of Data Base Schemas. A Semantic Approach to Data Translation," *Information Systems*, **4**:1, 1979.

[15.6]   G. Pelagatti, P. Paolini, and G. Bracchi, "Mappings in Database Systems," *Information Processing 77*, B. Gilchrist, ed., North-Holland, 1977.

[15.7]   A. C. Klug, "Theory of Database Mappings," Tech. Rep. CSRG-98, University of Toronto, 1978.

[15.8]   T. Landers and R. L. Rosenberg, "An Overview of MULTIBASE," *Distributed Databases*, H. J. Schneider, ed., North-Holland, 1982.

[15.9]   U. Dayal and H. Y. Hwang, "View Definition and Generalization for Database Integration in MULTIBASE: A System for Heterogeneous Distributed Databases," *Sixth Berkeley Conf. on Distributed Data Management and Computer Networks*, 1982.

[15.10] J. M. Smith et al., "MULTIBASE: Integrating Heterogeneous Distributed Database Systems," *Proc. National Computer Conference*, 1981.

[15.11] U. Dayal, "Processing Queries over Generalization Hierarchies in a Multidatabase System," *Ninth VLDB*, Florence, 1983.

[15.12] J. A. Weeldreyer, "Structural Aspects of the Entity-Category-Relationship Model of Data," *Honeywell Report HR-80-249*, Honeywell Corporate Computer Science Center, Bloomington, MN, 1980.

[15.13] P. P. S. Chen, "The Entity-Relationship Model: Towards a Unified View of Data," *ACM-TODS*, **1**:1, 1976.

[15.14] R. El-Masri and G. Wiederhold, "GORDAS: A Formal High-Level Query Language for the Entity-Relationship Model," *Proc. Second Int. Conf. on Entity-Relationship Approach*, 1981.

[15.15] R. El-Masri, "Semantic Integrity in DDTS (Distributed Database Testbed System)," *Honeywell Report HR-80-274*, Honeywell Corporate Computer Science Center, Bloomington, MN, 1980.

[15.16] C. Devor and J. Weeldreyer, "DDTS: A Testbed for Distributed Database Research," *Honeywell Report HR-80-268*, Honeywell Corporate Computer Science Center, Bloomington, MN, 1980.

[15.17] C. Devor, R. El-Masri, J. Larson, S. Rahimi, and J. Richardson, "Five-Schema Architecture Extends DBMS to Distributed Applications," *Electronic Design*, 1982.

[15.18] P. A. Dwyer and A. R. Hevner, "Transaction Optimization in a Distributed Database Testbed System," *Proc. IEEE-COMPSAC*, 1983.

[15.19] A. Ferrier and C. Stangret, "Heterogeneity in the Distributed Database Management System SIRIUS-DELTA," *Eighth VLDB*, Mexico City, 1983.

Index